Asia Inside Out: Changing Times

ASIA INSIDE OUT

CHANGING TIMES

Edited by

ERIC TAGLIACOZZO

HELEN F. SIU

PETER C. PERDUE

Harvard University Press
Cambridge, Massachusetts
London, England
2015

Printed in the United States of America

First printing

Library of Congress Cataloging-in-Publication Data.
Asia inside out : changing times / edited by
Eric Tagliacozzo, Helen F. Siu, and Peter C. Perdue.
pages cm
Includes bibliographical references and index.
ISBN 978-0-674-59850-8 (alk. paper)
1. Asia—History. 2. Asia—Civilization. I. Tagliacozzo, Eric. II. Siu, Helen F. III. Perdue, Peter C., 1949–
DS33.2.A85 2015
950'.3—dc23 2014016511

ISBN 978-0-674-59850-8

Contents

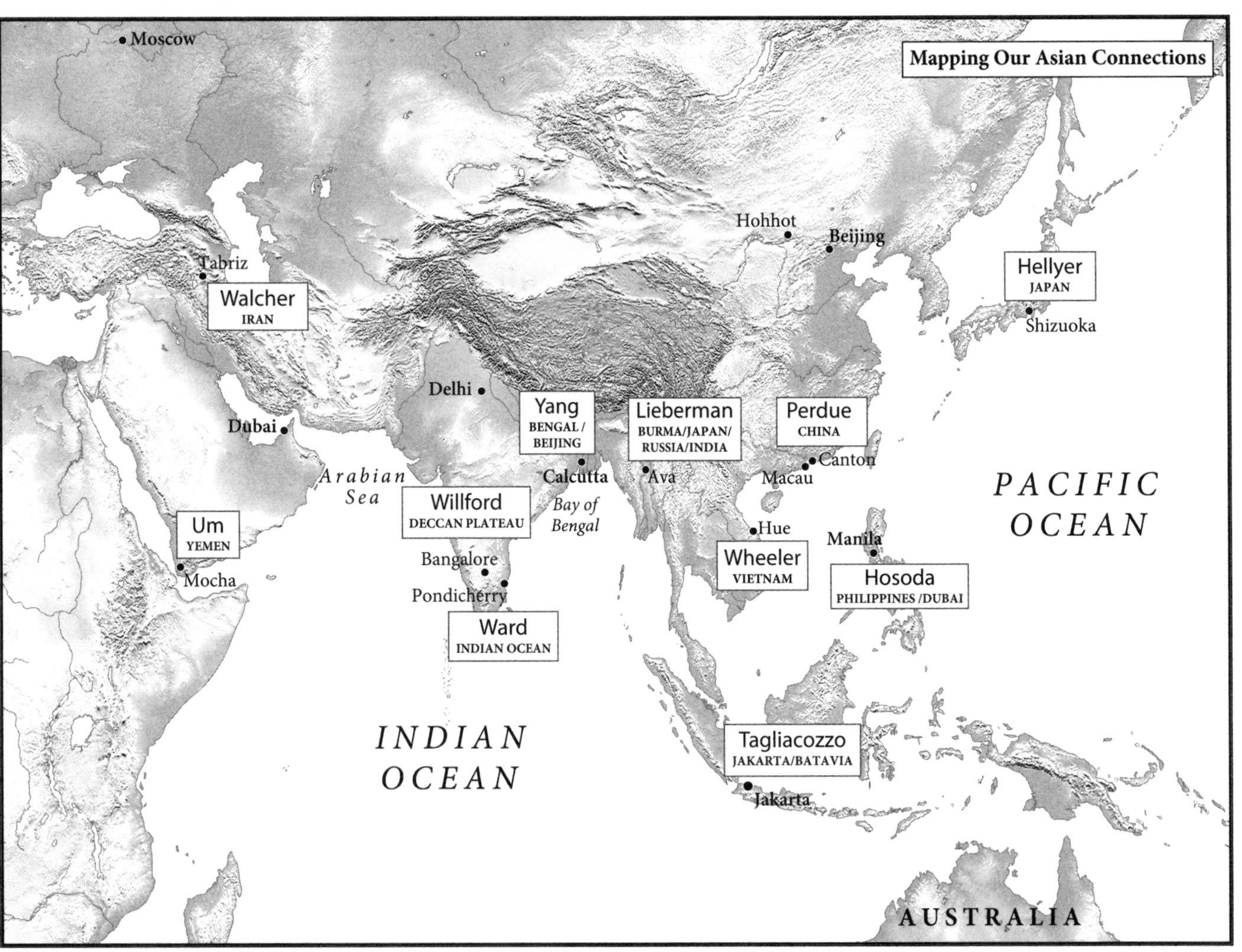
Mapping Our Asian Connections
Moscow
Tabriz
Walcher
IRAN
Hohhot
Beijing
Hellyer
JAPAN
Shizuoka
Delhi
Dubai
Yang
BENGAL / BEIJING
Lieberman
BURMA/JAPAN/ RUSSIA/INDIA
Perdue
CHINA
Canton
Macau
Arabian Sea
Calcutta
Ava
PACIFIC OCEAN
Willford
DECCAN PLATEAU
Bay of Bengal
Um
YEMEN
Mocha
Hue
Manila
Wheeler
VIETNAM
Hosoda
PHILIPPINES /DUBAI
Bangalore
Pondicherry
Ward
INDIAN OCEAN
INDIAN OCEAN
Tagliacozzo
JAKARTA/BATAVIA
Jakarta
AUSTRALIA

Introduction

Structuring Moments in Asian Connections

PETER C. PERDUE, HELEN F. SIU, ERIC TAGLIACOZZO

The *Asia Inside Out* project aims to redefine conventional understandings of the vast land and sea regions stretching from the Middle East and South Asia, across the seas of Southeast Asia, and up the East Asian coast to China, Korea, and Japan. Until recently, humanists and social scientists have generally carved up this region based on criteria defined by land-based, state-centered entities, or by civilizational criteria determined by religious or linguistic communities. Thus, the conventional definition of East Asia implies separate histories of China, Korea, Japan (and sometimes Vietnam), as determined by national and imperial boundaries and by common allegiance to the classical Confucian traditions (Tsunoda and De Bary 1958; De Bary et al. 1999). South Asia conventionally includes those territories that formed part of the Mughal and British empires with certain shared cultural essences and histories (Embree 1988). These territories have now become nation-states, primarily Pakistan, India, Bangladesh, Nepal, and Sri Lanka. Southeast Asia is sometimes seen as a leftover category in between South and East Asia, or as a particular hybrid of Muslim, South Asian, and East Asian traditions, or even as a distinctive region marked by contrasts between hills and lowlands, or land masses and seas (Reid 1988, 1993; Lieberman 2003, 2009). Each of these regional definitions has stimulated valuable traditions of research, yet they remain embedded in institutional structures for the production of area studies knowledge.

Many analysts, however, have questioned these regional and national definitions, from a variety of perspectives (Ludden 2003; Gupta and Ferguson 1992; Pomeranz 2002). None of the above-mentioned regions or nation-states is homogeneous by any criterion, whether linguistic, cultural, religious, economic, or historical. The boundaries of these nation-states and empires have shifted over time with various historical articulations of power and control, and they have always included diverse and mobile peoples within them. A distinguished scholarly tradition has examined long-distance continental Eurasian trade and its associated cultural and religious transformations (Hansen 2012). Moreover, a newer focus on ocean systems and littoral settlements, which spill over from land to seas, has altered interpretations of landed societies (Braudel 1973; Lewis and Wigen 1997; Chaudhuri 1990; Hamashita, Selden, and Grove 2008; Wong 1999).

Large theoretical paradigms encompassing regional space have always had to exclude much of the diversity of the region they explain. G. William Skinner's powerful and now classic model of Chinese regional space, for example, defined eight or nine macroregions composing the space of China Proper (Skinner 1985), but it did not extend to the territories considered political or ethnic frontiers by the Chinese empire (Perdue 2005; Crossley, Siu, and Sutton 2006; Millward 2007; Lewis 2009; Duara 2009). Similarly, Louis Dumont's *Homo Hierarchicus* (1980) privileged timeless religious principles over class, ethnic, and regional differences in historical South Asia. Nicholas Dirks, on the other hand, demonstrated that colonial encounters shaped the caste system, long considered a cultural essence and symbol of Indian society (Dirks 2001). Furthermore, by delineating India's expanded footprint in support of British imperial operations in the Indian Ocean arena in the late nineteenth and early twentieth centuries, Metcalf (2007) delved broadly into historical details to decenter a dominant imperial construct. Models of Southeast Asia based primarily on Java, for example, like Clifford Geertz's *Agricultural Involution* (1963), did not work as well even for lowland rice areas in the rest of the region, not to mention the analytical omission of the impact of colonial extractions, migrations to the "outer islands," and the problematic concept of "dual economy" (White 1983). Divisions between highland and lowland peoples, from the ethnography of Edmund Leach to the "Zomian" theory of Willem van Schendel and James Scott, did not exclusively refer to conventional Southeast Asian territories alone, but applied to much larger regions, including parts of contemporary South and East Asia (Leach 1954; van Schendel 2002; Scott 2009). An entire generation of historians and anthropologists has stressed contingencies in colonial encounters, in shifting characters of traders and networks, and fluid cross-border alliances and imaginations (Stoler 1989, 1995; Fiskesjö 2002; Tagliacozzo 2005; Ho 2006; Blussé 2011). In short, most efforts to generalize about Asian regions have been either too small (they fit only one portion of an important imperial or national space) or too large (they extend beyond conventionally understood regional and cultural boundaries) to fit within the traditional definitions of Asian regions.

Besides the conceptual issues on historical linkages, contemporary global developments have also called into question the adequacy of spatial definitions of Asia created in the post- World War II era. These positivist social science paradigms took for granted a certain grand narrative of nation-states. The key actors in this narrative were communities and populations tied to well-defined national territories. It unnecessarily marginalized or even neglected the analytical significance of mobile populations such as traders, migrants, and refugees (Malkki 1995). Asian peoples, products, and concepts have always traveled across land and sea routes, but since the 1990s the scale, speed, and intensity of global interactions have increased dramatically (Harvey 1990; Appadurai 1996; Ong 2006). Theorists may debate whether late twentieth century globalization has challenged state-centered institutions or has strengthened them, but a historically more nuanced appreciation of global flows would enrich even the most opposing viewpoints.

Chinese migrants since the sixteenth century left the mainland to settle and trade abroad, primarily in Southeast Asia (Wang 2000; Tagliacozzo and Chang 2011; Sinn 2012). The globalization of the Chinese diaspora began in the nineteenth century with the participation of Chinese migrants in gold rushes and indentured labor in the Americas. In recent decades the Chinese diaspora has extended to all the settled continents of the world: Africa, Europe, Russia, and the Americas. Each of these mobile populations has unique cultural logics and identities (Ong and Nonini 1997; Ong 1999; Riemenschnitter and Madsen 2009). South Asians have likewise moved well beyond their traditional destinations in the Indian Ocean region and British imperial possessions (Xiang 2007). Filipinos, for example, are as likely to be found in Dubai, Taiwan, Hong Kong, or mainland China as they are in the United States

Historical Trade Circuits

Date palm merchant house, Oman. (Photo by Helen F. Siu)

Historical Chinese fishing net, Kochi. (Photo by Helen F. Siu)

Guangxi women from the hills. (Photo by Helen F. Siu)

(Constable 1997, 2003). Japanese-Brazilian migrants in Japan (Roth 2002), South Asians in the Gulf area, and African and Arab traders in Yiwu, Guangzhou, and Hong Kong (Simpfendorfer 2009; Mathews 2011) have increasingly been a focus of scholarly attention. These multiple human and commodity flows spill over all boundaries defined by national or cultural borders and have created global food chains (Bestor 2004), pan-Asian popular cultures (Iwabuchi 2002) and "inter-referencing cityscapes" (Roy and Ong 2011).

But we have not reached a stage of idealized neoliberal globalization, in which all peoples and places are flattened out into a single global consumer culture. Historical, economic, and cultural legacies still strongly affect global trade and cultural interaction. Regional studies done by scholars versed in the particularities of a space and tradition still have a vital role to play in shaping our awareness of global developments (Watson 2006; Hendry 2000; Liechty 2003; Mazarella 2003; Tsing 2005; Condry 2006; Ren 2011; Xiang, Yeoh, and Toyota 2013). But the regions we study need a much more interactive, collaborative style of research than the traditional area studies approaches have provided. Instead of viewing regions, cultures, and peoples as physically bounded units occupying continents and polities, we need to focus on multilayered, interactive processes that embrace both land and sea routes and incorporate political dynamics of empires, nation-states, neoliberal markets, and postsocialist global engagements at relevant historical junctures.

This first volume of our three-volume series, ranging from Yemen to Japan, assembles chapters by historians, art historians, and anthropologists. We asked each author to focus on a particular date that indicates important processes and movements throughout the region. Each author concentrates on key sites and periods which designate major routes, networks and processes spanning the sixteenth through the twentieth centuries. All these regions experienced mobility for many centuries, but the direction and scale of movement shifted significantly at key turning points. The authors have generally not chosen conventional benchmark dates, which usually coincide with times of imperial conquest, major discoveries and/or colonial expansions, or world economic crises and debilitating wars. Instead, they highlight less obvious but equally significant inflection points when certain major cultural processes changed direction. Furthermore, the spaces they discuss often do not coincide with conventionally defined imperial administrations, and they span both land and sea. By exploring particular sites over extended periods of time, these essays question the adequacy of conventional dates and spatial conceptions.

Collectively, they encompass Asia at the largest scale of continental and maritime exchange, religious transformation, and military conquest.

The first three chapters address key turning points in religious, economic, and political formations in the early to mid-sixteenth century. In each of these polities, transformations extended well beyond the imperial boundaries. The Safavid victory in 1501 over rival Central Asian confederations set in motion new directions for the lingering influence of Central Asian military traditions on Eurasia. Victor Lieberman describes the mid-sixteenth century as the "onset of a more or less coherent early modern phase" in the formation of four different states: Burma, Japan, Russia, and North India. Likewise, the Portuguese acquisition of a leasehold in Macau in 1557 makes better sense when seen alongside concurrent developments of Ming policy toward Mongols on the northwestern frontier and toward the maritime trading confederations called "dwarf pirates" (or *wokou*) on the southeast coast of China at the same time.

In Heidi Walcher's chapter, 1501 at first seems to be a conventional date for the start of modern Iranian history, but it looks different when viewed as an event in wider Asian histories. Establishing the Safavid capital in landlocked Tabriz meant that the empire had a predominant orientation toward Central Asia, with little maritime control. Since Tabriz had been a capital of the Il-Khanids since 1263, the influence of Mongol and Timurid cultural orientations strongly shaped Safavid geopolitical consciousness. Twelver Shiism was the most distinctive feature of Safavid rule, directing its diplomatic efforts toward finding allies against the Sunni Ottomans and ultimately leading to active contacts with Europe. The exaltation of absolute monarchy, however, had its roots not only in Shiite ideology, but also in earlier imperial ideals of Timurid and earlier Sassanid traditions.

Walcher thus questions the critical distinctiveness of 1501 as a founding date for modern Iran by showing significant continuities with earlier regimes. She also undermines later national concepts of space, arguing that the Safavids did not control many regions of their empire securely. Iran was a "conglomerate of regions" rather than a coherent entity. Cultural exchanges also spread widely across Eurasia, including extensive imports of Chinese porcelain and the widespread use of Persian as a lingua franca. These arguments show the large multiregional reach of Iran extending beyond Safavid borders, stressing the centrality of the region as a zone in between Europe and China.

Victor Lieberman singles out the mid-sixteenth century as a time of critical transformation of four "states": the aforementioned Burma, Russia, Japan,

Vegetable seller, Bangalore. (Photo by Helen F. Siu)

Chinese produce in Nizwa market, Oman. (Photo by Helen F. Siu)

Marketing Mao on Cat Street, Hong Kong. (Photo by Helen F. Siu)

and India. Each state dramatically increased its central powers through military conquests, leading to the establishment of long-lasting empires that defined their early modern experience. The factors that encouraged this greater integration included relatively favorable global climate, expanded international trade, increasing agricultural productivity and population growth, well-stocked currency supplies, and new technologies of firearms alongside bureaucratic paper production. Cultural links between the new conquering elites and the subject population also increased. They defined core regions of the polities dominated by one ethnic group, surrounded by others who looked for closer ties to the metropolitan centers. While other authors in this volume track interactions across land and sea between single ports and regions, Lieberman stresses the integration of large continental states responding to common global trends. Even though he preserves the conventional definitions of states as landed polities, he points to remarkable parallels in their development and stimulates further study of comparison and interaction across the early modern Eurasian world.

Peter C. Perdue examines the years when Ming China granted the Portuguese a leasehold on Macau, Chinese pirate-merchants surrendered to a Ming official, overseas Chinese settlement rose in Southeast Asia, and officials began to arrange a settlement to end Mongol raids on the northwest frontier. He argues that an integrated account of the relationships of empires to their border regions sees them all as part of growing global exchange relations. Many aspects of these trading relationships built on earlier precedents, including delegation of powers to merchant communities and establishment of foreign merchant settlements and border trading posts. The two new actors in sixteenth-century Asia were the Portuguese and Spanish, who inaugurated a global silver economy, and overseas Chinese merchants in Southeast Asia. Some Ming officials promoted exclusion of outsiders and emigrants from the social space of the empire, while others argued for greater encouragement of foreign trade in order to improve the livelihood of peoples in frontier regions. The victory of those who advocated more open trade initiated China's extensive involvement in global economic exchange. China's engagement increased in the seventeenth through nineteenth centuries.

The chapters by Um, Wheeler, and Ward approach developments in three major maritime-oriented polities from the seventeenth through eighteenth centuries. Because of the impact of global factors, including climatic change, firearms, agricultural production, and trade, these states created more integrated and centralized political and cultural entities which endured into the nineteenth century. Nancy Um discusses the transformative effects of 1636 and 1726 on Yemen's position as a producer of coffee and as a major port. The arrival of Zen Buddhism in Vietnam in 1683, as Charles Wheeler argues, decisively turned the history of coastal Vietnam in a different direction for centuries thereafter. Kerry Ward, continuing this maritime perspective, describes the different trade routes which converged in 1745 on Pondicherry, linking merchants from Europe to East Asia.

Nancy Um describes the shifting position of Yemen in global coffee trade networks from 1636, when the Ottomans abandoned efforts to rule the state, to 1726, when production of coffee expanded to other parts of the world, like Dutch Java. At first new markets opened as the Ottomans withdrew, but later, as Javanese production competed for markets in Amsterdam, Yemen's strategic position declined. Yemen, located on a node connecting land and sea routes, served as an important index of both local commercial and cultural consciousness, and also of the broader transformations of global trade.

When the imams of Yemen monopolized the coffee trade, they attracted merchants from Europe, the Ottoman realms, and India, exporting beans both east and west. Yemen was a southern extension of Ottoman rule in the seventeenth century, but its formidable resistance to Ottoman expansion gave it an autonomous role at the center of world markets. The coffee emporium in the town of Bayt al-Faqih centralized all trade from the highlands of Yemen, allowing the imams to profit from high demand for the drink by Arabs, Turks, Indians, and Europeans. Notably, the different communities did not trade at the same times, and the imams prevented Europeans from active participation in the market, in order to give financial benefits to the Ottomans and respond to protests against European cultural influence. The intermediate position of Yemen in the conflicting demands of world trade demonstrates how European, Middle Eastern, and Asian trade routes converged on key sites at particular moments, making them the focus of commercial and geopolitical attention.

Charles Wheeler singles out the date 1683, when the Qing dynasty completed the conquest of Taiwan and the monk Nguyen Thieu brought Zen Buddhism to Vietnam. The Qing victory meant the end of the Zheng confederation centered on Taiwan, but not the end of cultural connections in the South China Sea. Wheeler shows the existing linkages of religion and economy through the story of this migrant monk. Living in a "water frontier,"

Nguyen Thieu extended his contacts across state boundaries, a maritime mirror of Safavid cross-continental connections. His success was also dependent on a longer history of the settlement of Ming refugees from Qing rule in Vietnam. The Ming refugees, who had extensive privileges under Vietnamese rule, grew to be wealthy traders in port cities and Cochin China. They served as conduits for Chinese culture from the southeast coast, as monks promoted the formation of syncretic religious communities spreading from Fujian to Vietnam and from Korea to Japan. This model of an international Buddhist community declined in the nineteenth century, but revived in the twentieth century under Thich Nhat Hanh, the globally famous Vietnamese Buddhist with acolytes around the world, including China. Thus from the date of 1683 we can trace expanding ripples of economic and religious contact that encompassed the Southeast Asian maritime region, as well as the Qing imperial realm.

Kerry Ward relies on the diary of a Tamil interpreter living in Pondicherry, southeastern India, to provide a snapshot view of wide-ranging trade networks that crossed the Indian Ocean in all directions. From the African coast and through the Middle East and Southeast Asia, scholars, pilgrims, traders, and laborers moved on ships in closely connected communities. While some densely populated regions, like Java, primarily turned away from the sea, others, like a number of islands of the Indian Ocean, necessarily depended entirely on trades in cowrie shells and other maritime products. Across the vast reaches of this "water frontier"—even larger than the one previously described as connected to the Vietnamese monk Nguyen Thieu—British, French, and Dutch powers attempted to exert military and commercial influence. Severe weather conditions in this year obstructed much shipping activity, but the constant influence of monsoons and currents ensured that the time-honored patterns of trade endured. There was no unified cultural notion of historical or calendar time, but the climate (experienced as seas and monsoons) created shared perception of times. This chapter, one of the most intensively sea-focused studies in the volume, encourages us to view oceans as parallel to land-based polities, showing that human interactions across the seas follow related patterns to those on land.

In more recent times, larger-scale global processes, including weather, imperialism, and trade, similarly found their reflection in local sites and times. The next three essays look at the late nineteenth and early twentieth centuries, which featured the rise of new global powers, like the United States and Japan, rapid commodity production and industrialization in Asia, and the great expansion of trans-Pacific trade that had already given rise to visible port cities (Blussé 2008). Although many of the interdependencies of the pre-industrial Asian order persisted, racialism and Orientalism, with their deeply rooted convictions of the inferiority of Asian peoples, held an increasingly stronger grip both on world markets and on geopolitical decisions.

According to Robert Hellyer, the crucial links to global markets that set off Japan's dramatic economic growth began with the opening of major tea export trade in 1874. Anand Yang reexamines the well-known events of the Boxer Rebellion in China in 1900 through the eyes of an Indian soldier who implicitly called into question the role of one empire in promoting the conquest of another one, all in the name of civilization. Eric Tagliacozzo argues that already by 1910, and only at a shallow depth beneath the surface of Dutch control, the movement toward a postcolonial era of Indonesia had already begun.

Robert Hellyer begins with the critical year of 1874, when Japanese tea exports to the United States first surpassed those of China. Although historians of the Meiji restoration of 1868 often stress the triumph of a powerful industrializing national state, Hellyer shows that Japanese tea producers creating a new export industry depended heavily both on British and American distributors and on Chinese technical expertise. The Japanese tea industry was a truly transnational enterprise, drawing all its participants into tighter webs of interdependence. On the other hand, British competitors from India and Ceylon effectively exploited racial prejudice, flooding American markets with advertisements depicting Chinese and Japanese green teas as unhealthy and adulterated and praising the cleanliness and scientific production methods of the British plantation black teas. The temporary Japanese success, followed by the rise of Indian tea, illustrates clearly the intertwining of racial prejudice, industrial production, and the ideology of science in shaping the preferences of American consumers vis-à-vis global markets.

Anand Yang's chapter also highlights the role of racial distinctions, giving us a rare view of imperialist war from the subaltern's perspective. Gadadhar Singh, an Indian soldier in the British army's expedition against the Boxer Rebellion of 1900, left an account in Hindi of his experiences that strikingly rebukes the Western imperialist justifications of the war. Far from seeing the Boxer expedition as a war of good Christians against evil pagans, Singh displayed genuine empathy for the Chinese as people who, as Buddhists, shared religious principles with Indians. He knew the English language literature on the Boxers, and he drew on especially revealing conversations with Americans and Irish, who like him had experience as British colonial subjects. In his view, they expressed implicit support for Indian independence and skepticism about the pretenses to a civilizing mission of the British leaders of the expedition. In Singh's account, we see the emergence among common soldiers of a new concept of pan-Asian solidarity against Western imperialism. Yang's analysis demonstrates that awareness of common Asian identity, supported by ancient religious and economic achievements, transmuted easily into anti-imperialist sentiments that pervaded Asian societies in the early twentieth century (Bose 2006).

Eric Tagliacozzo's essay complements Yang's analysis with a view of the colonial apparatus of Indonesia from the top in the year 1910. By this time, Dutch techniques of systematizing knowledge, patrolling boundaries, and supervising the local people's customary practices seemed to have reached their peak. Cartography, ethnography, railroads, steamships, and police patrols filled in the porous spaces that had plagued the border regions in the nineteenth century. The colonial view of Indonesia displayed apparently impregnable confidence and omniscience. Yet it was a fairytale. Soon Dutch rule would collapse under the impact of Japanese attacks and a burgeoning indigenous nationalism. Although the world portrayed by Tagliacozzo can appear as a closed system, confined to the colonial producers of knowledge, he also describes acute awareness of international hierarchies, as the Dutch kept a close watch on the progress of their British neighbors, allies, and competitors. Even when colonial Asia seemed to be carved up into solid blocs and frozen into ruling structures, the seeds of collapse were germinating in areas where the colonizers could not see adequately.

The twentieth and twenty-first centuries, often regarded as eras of radical modernity, continued the trends of previous eras. Andrew Willford describes the contest in contemporary Bangalore between assertions of monocultural linguistic identity and the embedded memories that stem from the city's cosmopolitan locus at the crossroads of a number of empires, trade routes, language communities, and pilgrimage routes. The Filipino "visitors" to Dubai described by Naomi Hosoda took advantage of its status as an open city to gain greater opportunities for social mobility. Other Filipinos were confined by contract-worker status into more proscribed roles. By 2008, these Filipino "visitors" had flooded into the city beyond the reach of government control, creating a thriving, fluctuating new community of global travelers. Thus the unceasing processes of mobility beyond borders continue older traditions of travel and exchange, while expanding into new spatial and cultural dimensions.

Willford, in contrast to those who describe a proliferation of intercultural mingling in the contemporary world, stresses contrary tendencies toward narrower linguistic identification. Bangalore, unlike most of the other sites explored here, lies in the interior of a continent, not on the coast, but it experienced the same multiple crisscrossing stimuli as its maritime counterparts. The city of Bangalore, which had occupied for centuries a central node of multiple states, languages, and religious cults, became the capital of the linguistic state of Karnataka in 1956. Since that time, conflicts between Kannada speakers and the Tamil minority have flared up, featuring attacks on poorer Tamil workers and riots over a court decision awarding river boundary rights to the neighboring Tamil state. Even though Bangalore is renowned for its cosmopolitan high-tech development, the local politics of the state indicate persisting strains. Local communities try to preserve fictitious fantasies of a monocultural past in the face of the dissolving acids of global capitalism. Bangalore's tensions, similar to those in other Asian world cities such as Mumbai (Hansen 2001) and Hong Kong (Mathews 2011; Siu 2008) are simultaneously global, national, and local, like all the other interactions in this volume.

Migrants now cross thousands of miles by air instead of land or sea. Their journeys take hours and days instead of months or years, and they move between independent nations instead of empires, but their experiences still reflect centuries of history. Hosoda describes the plight of Filipino workers trapped within the borders of Dubai, in the United Arab Emirates, in 2008 because of a change in visa regulations. This incident once again reveals hidden processes of economic and cultural movement. Dubai gained a reputation as an "open city" in the Filipino media because it seemed to offer unusual opportunities for employment and the chance to enjoy a cosmopolitan, glamorous urban life. The realities were quite different. Filipinos found themselves crammed nine to a room working very long hours, in an uncertain environment. But they quickly learned self-reliance, grasping at new opportunities to create new identities, and few wanted to return home quickly. Their experience on a global scale is remarkably similar to that of Chinese rural migrants who moved to coastal China in recent decades

Twenty-First-Century Landscapes of Power

China Pavilion, Shanghai Expo. (Photo by Helen F. Siu)

Emirate Towers, Dubai. (Photo by Helen F. Siu)

Infosys: India's IT future. (Photo by Helen F. Siu)

(Pun 2005; Gaetano and Jacka 2004; Chang 2008). Both kinds of migration offered risks and opportunities, and both changed the identities of the migrants and the spaces they occupied. We can more easily examine the psychological effects of migration in contemporary studies than in historical sources, but constants remain in all these pioneering frontiers. These include the attraction of new places for young people, the willingness to take risks, the mixed results that migrants find on arrival, and their personal conflicts over when or whether to return home.

These three volumes together will examine the historical processes spanning wide geographical areas which shaped the people, places, and institutions that make up the modern Asian world. In all of these historical processes, significant turning points marked shifts from one era to another, as different political structures rose and fell, economic waves moved up and down, and people in motion changed their destinations in response. These significant moments transcend simple divisions of land and sea, political regimes, or religious and cultural boundaries. These empirical studies have deep theoretical implications. We highlight the historical global alongside contemporary flows and mobilities in order to place the bounded, statist units of positivist social science in a larger framework. By focusing on these critical periods, places, and peoples of historical and modern Asia, we hope to provide scholars and general readers with new perspectives on the long-term processes that have shaped the contemporary world.

References

Appadurai, Arjun. 1996. *Modernity at Large: Cultural Dimensions of Globalization.* St. Paul: University of Minnesota Press.

Bestor, Theodore C. 2004. *Tsukiji: The Fish Market at the Center of the World.* Berkeley: University of California Press.

Blussé, Leonard. 2008. *Visible Cities: Canton, Nagasaki, Batavia, and the Coming of the Americans.* Cambridge, MA: Harvard University Press.

———. 2011. "Junks to China: Chinese Shipping to the Nanyang in the Second Half of the Eighteenth Century." In *Chinese Circulations: Capital, Commodities, and Networks in Southeast Asia,* ed. Eric Tagliacozzo and Wen-Chin Chang, 221–258. Durham, NC: Duke University Press.

Bose, Sugata. 2006. *A Hundred Horizons: The Indian Ocean in the Age of Global Empire.* Cambridge, MA: Harvard University Press.

Braudel, Fernand. 1973. *Capitalism and Material Life: 1400–1800.* New York: Harper.

Brook, Timothy. 2008. *Vermeer's Hat: The Seventeenth Century and the Dawn of the Global World.* New York: Bloomsbury Press.

Chang, Leslie T. 2008. *Factory Girls: From Village to City in a Changing China.* New York: Spiegel & Grau.

Chaudhuri, K. N. *1990. Asia before Europe: Economy and Civilisation of the Indian Ocean from the Rise of Islam to 1750.* Cambridge: Cambridge University Press.

Condry, Ian. 2006. *Hip-Hop Japan: Rap and the Paths of Cultural Globalization.* Durham, NC: Duke University Press.

Constable, Nicole. 1997. *Maid to Order in Hong Kong: An Ethnography of Filipina Workers.* Ithaca, NY: Cornell University Press.

———. 2003. *Romance on a Global Stage: Pen Pals, Virtual Ethnography, and "Mail Order" Marriages.* Berkeley: University of California Press.

Crossley, Pamela Kyle, Helen F. Siu, and Donald S. Sutton, eds. 2006. *Empire at the Margins: Culture, Ethnicity, and Frontier in Early Modern China.* Berkeley: University of California Press.

De Bary, William Theodore, Irene Bloom, Wing-tsit Chan, Joseph Adler, and Richard John Lufrano. 1999. *Sources of Chinese Tradition.* 2nd ed. New York: Columbia University Press.

Dirks, Nicholas. 2001. *Castes of Mind: Colonialism and the Making of Modern India.* Princeton, NJ: Princeton University Press.

Duara, Prasenjit. 2009. *The Global and Regional in China's Nation-Formation.* London: Routledge.

Dumont, Louis. 1980. *Homo Hierarchicus: The Caste System and Its Implications.* Complete rev. English ed. (translator Mark Sainsbury). Chicago: University of Chicago Press.

Embree, Ainslie, ed. 1988. *Sources of Indian Tradition.* Vol. 1, *From the Beginning to 1800.* New York: Columbia University Press.

Fiskesjö, Magnus. 2002. "The Barbarian Borderland and the Chinese Imagination—Travellers in Wa Country." *Inner Asia* 4 (1): 81–99.

Gaetano, Arianne, and Tamara Jacka, eds. 2004. *On the Move: Women in Rural-to-Urban Migration in Contemporary China.* New York: Columbia University Press.

Geertz, Clifford. 1963. *Agricultural Involution: The Processes of Ecological Change in Indonesia.* Berkeley: University of California Press.

Gupta, Akhil, and James Ferguson. 1992. "Beyond 'Culture': Space, Identity, and the Politics of Difference." *Cultural Anthropology* 7 (1): 1–23.

Hamashita, Takeshi, Mark Selden, and Linda Grove, eds. 2008. *China, East Asia, and the Global Economy: Regional and Historical Perspectives.* London: Routledge.

Hansen, Thomas. 2001. *Wages of Violence: Naming and Identity in Postcolonial Bombay.* Princeton, NJ: Princeton University Press.

Hansen, Valerie. 2012. *The Silk Road: A New History.* Oxford: Oxford University Press.

Harvey, David. 1990. *The Condition of Postmodernity*. Oxford: Basil Blackwell.

Hendry, Joy. 2000. *The Orient Strikes Back: A Global View of Cultural Display*. Oxford: Berg.

Ho, Engseng. 2006. *The Graves of Tarim: Genealogy and Mobility across the Indian Ocean*. Berkeley: University of California Press.

Iwabuchi, Koichi. 2002. *Recentering Globalization: Popular Culture and Japanese Transnationalism*. Durham, NC: Duke University Press.

Leach, E. R. 1954. *Political Systems of Highland Burma*. Cambridge, MA: Harvard University Press.

Liechty, Mark. 2003. *Suitably Modern: Making Middle-Class Culture in a New Consumer Society*. Princeton, NJ: Princeton University Press.

Lewis, Mark Edward. 2009. *China's Cosmopolitan Empire: The Tang Dynasty*. Cambridge, MA: Belknap Press of Harvard University Press.

Lewis, Martin W., and Kären Wigen. 1997. *The Myth of Continents: A Critique of Metageography*. Berkeley: University of California Press.

Lieberman, Victor B. 2003. *Strange Parallels: Southeast Asia in Global Context, c. 800–1830*. Vol. 1, *Integration on the Mainland*. Cambridge: Cambridge University Press.

———. 2009. *Strange Parallels: Southeast Asia in Global Context, c. 800–1830*. Vol. 2, *Mainland Mirrors: Europe, Japan, China, South Asia, and the Islands*. Cambridge: Cambridge University Press.

Ludden, David. 2003. "Presidential Address: Maps in the Mind and the Mobility of Asia." *Journal of Asian Studies* 62 (4): 1057–1078.

Malkki, Liisa. 1995. "Refugees and Exile: From 'Refugee Studies' to the National Order of Things." *Annual Review of Anthropology* 24: 495–523.

Mathews, Gordon. 2011. *Ghetto at the Center of the World: Chungking Mansions, Hong Kong*. Chicago: The University of Chicago Press.

Mazzarella, William. 2003. *Shoveling Smoke: Advertising and Globalization in Contemporary India*. Durham, NC: Duke University Press.

Metcalf, Thomas R. 2007. "Introduction: Empire Recentered." In *Imperial Connections: India in the Indian Ocean Arena, 1860–1920*. Berkeley: University of California Press.

Millward, James. 2007. *Eurasian Crossroads: A History of Xinjiang*. New York: Columbia University Press.

Ong, Aihwa. 1999. *Flexible Citizenship: The Cultural Logics of Transnationality*. Durham, NC: Duke University Press.

———. 2006. *Neoliberalism as Exception: Mutations in Citizenship and Sovereignty*. Durham, NC: Duke University Press.

Ong, Aihwa, and Donald Macon Nonini. 1997. *Ungrounded Empires: The Cultural Politics of Modern Chinese Transnationalism*. New York: Routledge.

Perdue, Peter C. 2005. *China Marches West: The Qing Conquest of Central Eurasia*. Cambridge, MA: Belknap Press of Harvard University Press.

Pomeranz, Kenneth. 2002. "Political Economy and Ecology on the Eve of Industrialization: Europe, China, and the Global Conjuncture." *American Historical Review* 107 (2): 425–446.

Pun, Ngai. 2005. *Made in China: Women Factory Workers in a Global Workplace.* Durham, NC: Duke University Press.

Reid, Anthony. 1988. *Southeast Asia in the Age of Commerce, 1450–1680.* Vol. 1, *The Lands Below the Winds.* New Haven, CT: Yale University Press.

———. 1993. *Southeast Asia in the Age of Commerce, 1450–1680.* Vol. 2, *Expansion and Crisis.* New Haven, CT: Yale University Press.

Ren, Xuefei. 2011. *Building Globalization: Transnational Architecture Production in Urban China.* Chicago: The University of Chicago Press.

Riemenschnitter, Andrea, and Deborah L. Madsen, eds. 2009. *Diasporic Histories: Cultural Archives of Chinese Transnationalism.* Hong Kong: Hong Kong University Press.

Roth, Joshua. 2002. *Brokered Homeland: Japanese Brazilian Migrants in Japan.* Ithaca, NY: Cornell University Press.

Roy, Ananya, and Aihwa Ong, eds. 2011. *Worlding Cities: Asian Experiments and the Art of Being Global.* Oxford: Blackwell.

Scott, James C. 2009. *The Art of Not Being Governed: An Anarchist History of Upland Southeast Asia.* New Haven, CT: Yale University Press.

Simpfendorfer, Ben. 2009. *The New Silk Road: How a Rising Arab World is Turning away from the West and Rediscovering China.* Basingstoke: Palgrave Macmillan

Sinn, Elizabeth. 2012. *Pacific Crossing: California Gold, Chinese Migration, and the Making of Hong Kong.* Hong Kong: Hong Kong University Press.

Siu, F. Helen. 2008. "Positioning 'Hong Kongers' and 'New Immigrants'." In *Hong Kong Mobile: Making a Global Population,* ed. Helen F. Siu and Agnes S. Ku, 117–147. Hong Kong: Hong Kong University Press.

Skinner, G. William. 1985. "Presidential Address: The Structure of Chinese History." *Journal of Asian Studies* 44, no. 2: 271–92.

Stoler, Ann Laura. 1989. "Rethinking Colonial Categories: European Communities and the Boundaries of Rule." *Comparative Studies in Society and History,* 31 (1): 134–161.

———. 1995. *Capitalism and Confrontation in Sumatra's Plantation Belt, 1870–1979.* 2nd ed. Ann Arbor: University of Michigan Press.

Tagliacozzo, Eric. 2005. *Secret Trades, Porous Borders: Smuggling and States along a Southeast Asian Frontier, 1865–1915.* New Haven, CT: Yale University Press.

Tagliacozzo, Eric, and Wen-chin Chang, eds. 2011. *Chinese Circulations: Capital, Commodities, and Networks in Southeast Asia.* Durham, NC: Duke University Press.

Tsing, Anna Lowenhaupt. 2005. *Friction: An Ethnography of Global Connection.* Princeton, NJ: Princeton University Press.

Tsunoda Ryusaku, and William Theodore De Bary, eds. 1958. *Sources of Japanese Tradition.* New York: Columbia University Press.

van Schendel, Willem. 2002. "Geographies of Knowing, Geographies of Ignorance: Jumping Scale in Southeast Asia." *Environment and Planning D: Society and Space* 20: 647–668.

Wang, Gungwu. 2000. *The Chinese Overseas: From Earthbound China to the Quest for Autonomy.* Cambridge, MA: Harvard University Press.

Watson, James L., ed. 2006. *Golden Arches East: McDonald's in East Asia.* 2nd ed. Stanford, CA: Stanford University Press. First published 1997.

White, Benjamin. 1983. "'Agricultural Involution' and Its Critics: Twenty Years After." *Bulletin of Concerned Asian Scholars* 15 (2): 18–32.

Wong, R. Bin. 1999. "Entre Monde et Nation: Les Régions Braudéliennes en Asie (Between Nation and World: Braudelian Regions in Asia)." *Annales* 56 (1): 5–41.

Xiang, Biao. 2007. *Global "Body Shopping": An Indian Labor System in the Information Technology Industry.* Princeton, NJ: Princeton University Press.

Xiang Biao, Brenda S. A. Yeoh, and Mika Toyota, eds. 2013. *Return: Nationalizing Transnational Mobility in Asia.* Durham, NC: Duke University Press.

I

1501 in Tabriz

From Tribal Takeover to Imperial Trading Circuit?

HEIDI A. WALCHER

Tracing the question of one of the most consequential or decisive dates in Iranian history, 1501 [907][1] would make a compelling and logical date, understood as the year of the founding of the Safavid dynasty by Ismail I, by capturing Tabriz and proclaiming Shiʿism as the official religion of his rule. Most historians, even those working on other periods (like this author), and probably also theologians, political scientists, and art historians concerned with Iran would agree. In a certain sense it can be read almost as an "official" date; it has become a practical textbook date and even in a revisionist approach to the history of wider Iran[2] it would probably not completely lose a certain relevance. Even if one considers with skepticism the condensation of vast time periods and geopolitical spaces or the concept of accessing broad, long-term historical trends through a single date, in an Iranian context 1501 would still resonate with a certain meaning and evoke specific historical frameworks, identities, and trends. Moreover, the heavy weight of 1501 in marking a new era in Iranian history is extremely persuasive, as it neatly fits into the axiom of 1500 as indicating the beginning of the "early modern period." In European historiography, by overwhelming consensus, 1500 marks a new epoch, because of the synchronous convergence of such events as the Reformation, early capitalism, and the opening of sea routes to Asia and the Americas.

Accepting the inception of modernity in the non-European world as concurrent with these overall global trends promotes the notion of an "early modern period" in Asia and the Middle East, beginning at the same time.

However, linking this date (1501) and place ("early modern Iran" in its broadest sense) to Asia raises many questions, provides very few answers, and offers no straightforward narrative nor anything close to a new paradigm or model. The cultural and historical space of Iran has always interacted with both directions—Europe and Asia. On the one hand, most Iranians would consider themselves Middle Eastern or Asian and momentarily cheer for the Asian rather than the European football team.[3] In 1905, many Iranians decisively identified with Japan's military victory against Russia, hailing this as a major if rare success for a small Asian state against the superpower of the time. On the other hand, since the mid-1800s Europe has become so central to Iranian politics and developments that, from the perspectives of late nineteenth-century Iranian history or twentieth-century historiography, Asia is not necessarily the first point of reference.

A widely accepted historical canon understands the Ottoman, Safavid, and Mughal states as a world system with innate cultural and regional interdependencies. Applying the term "civilization" to this system implies a specific cultural cohesion, commonality, and patterns of political-commercial interaction, including far-reaching networks of naval ties to Southeast Asia and sub-Saharan Africa. (i.e., Dale 2010, 3) Most discussions of these three states focus on the period beginning with the late sixteenth century, a phase of intensive interaction also with Europe. While in the late 1400s and early 1500s an active transregional exchange from the Bosporus to the Amu Darya and beyond existed, it followed older historical patterns. The rhythms and scope of these exchanges were different from those of a century later, when sea routes and central imperial control had changed their parameters. Thus, how the diverse regions of Iran in the early 1500s were precisely linked to patterns of interaction beyond the system of the three empires and tied into wider Asia remains a more intricate and open-ended discussion. Examining historical precedents and geographical connections, this chapter aims to suggest a few tentative critical thoughts.

In tracing historical developments and attempting to define caesurae, epochs, or phases of change, single big events marking a clear-cut point of departure and measuring changing rhythms of time, place, or trends serve as numerical markers for timelines. 1501 in Tabriz has been and can be read precisely as such a marker, especially from frameworks of national or religious history. Yet if interpretations and perspectives of national history are dissolved, this date and place lose precision and perhaps even relevance. Despite its indisputable ideological and political meaning, 1501 is in fact an ambivalent date, denoting more a variable point of reference and an unpredictable origin rather than a clear-cut point of departure. It might be used as an auxiliary aid to pursue questions about the complex interactivity of communication, exchange, interdependence, and transition in Asia, covering people and territories from the Persian Gulf to the South China Sea. Marking a point in time half a century before the worldwide commercial boom of the late sixteenth century, driven heavily also by European players, 1501 in a transnational as well as an Iranian or western Asian context is an unwieldy date.

The trans-Asian relations of Iran are more apparent in earlier periods, such as the Il-Khanid or Timurid times of the thirteenth to fifteenth centuries. Later, also, more concrete ties, traceable through larger documentary evidence, emerge in the post-Tabriz period since the 1590s, when the center of the Safavid state had become more stable, and territories under its rule were more effectively linked to global maritime networks along the seam of the Persian Gulf. Nader Shah's 1739 seizure of the Mughal throne in Delhi provides a tangible example of Persia reaching into South Asian territory. The export of the first chests of opium to Batavia in 1869 marks Iran's rising role in supplying the opium trade to China (and Europe). Almost any year in the late nineteenth century—when the pace of modern transport and the volume of the exchange of goods, people, and ideas had reached unprecedented scales and when the material matrix of commodities and communication is more quantifiable or tangible—demonstrates more direct and active Asian contact. The argument for wider Iranian interaction with Asia in the early 1500s is, however, more circumstantial, even though it followed earlier patterns. This examination of links to Asia in 1501 thus attempts to trace aspects different from quantifiable commodities, specific trading communities, or commercial connections by discussing spaces of premodern historical, cultural, political, and geographical interdependencies.

This discussion will thus limit its focus to the very early 1500s, or the first few decades of what has been called the "classical period" of Safavid rule (1501–1590), summarizing the "revolutionary phase" (1447–1501) (Babayan 2002, 143). At the time, the occupation of Tabriz was a local event, whose consequences over a *longue durée* were uncertain. 1501 in Tabriz has thus a different tempo and geographical pattern than the later Safavid period. As a landlocked city, it lies at the very fringes of what in historical and geographical terms has been considered Western Asia, and thus it lacks easy links to East or South Asia. Current and historical geopolitical understandings and definitions further complicate the task. Since the artificial creation of the term "Middle East," based on British and American policy considerations of the early twentieth century, implicit politico-ideological and religio-ideological notions compound or distort the question of geographic and geopolitical alignments (Lewis and Wigen 1997, 35–103; Adelson 1995, passim). Because of this influence, Iran has become somewhat marginal to the current definition or understanding of Asia as a geographical, political, or cultural-economic entity. The various (often contradictory) layers of geographic and political names shall not be untangled conclusively here. Yet once wider Iran, including the Persian Gulf, is taken out of the construct of a "Middle East" or textbook narratives of the "Making of the Modern Middle East," its situation at the very southwestern rim of Asia and its geostrategic position midway between the Atlantic coast of Portugal and the East China Sea deserves a different framework. One of central Iran's most important links to Asia (as well as the Atlantic world) since the early modern period has been its maritime connection through the Persian Gulf. Yet from the land-based rule of the Safavids, particularly in the pre-Isfahan period up to 1598, the control of maritime affairs was indirect and tenuous. Iran today also exhibits a longstanding North–South bias, with wealth and especially power concentrated in the urban centers of the north. In the early modern period, land-based frontiers and transit routes held conspicuous primacy. The maritime connection through the Persian Gulf always existed, but only gained economic primacy and centrality in Safavid policy in the mid-sixteenth century, about five to six decades after the installation of the Safavid monarchy in 1501. And even then, the Safavid strategy of enforcing hegemony in the Persian Gulf approached it much like another land-based region (Chaudhuri 1990, 112–148).

Although Ismail I's zeal and the primacy of religious ideology may have been a specific regional phenomenon, in terms of the time–space frame of this discussion, we may also interpret 1501 as a dynastic starting point, a means of pinpointing new political and religious frameworks and economic developments. In this sense it fits neatly into the time frame termed the "early modern period," which sees the concurrence of new intellectual, technical, and economic processes launched by the Renaissance and the opening of new sea routes to South Asia and the Americas. A parallel case is Babur's 1503 conquest of Kabul, which facilitated his seizure of Agra in 1526, founding the Mughal dynasty (see Lieberman essay in this volume). In chronology, 1501 in Tabriz thus fits into the notion of large-scale global changes between the 1500s and 1600s. At the same time, pursuing horizontal continuities in the framework of Asia and its local or regional dimensions, 1501 looks less like a starting point and more like a time of transition or a catalyst of earlier trends that both repeats earlier trends as well as transforms them. Questioning the meaning of 1501 as a starting point for a specifically Iranian trajectory may also subvert dynastic frameworks, including conventional presumptions, posing the question: how Safavid was early Safavid Iran?

The Military Victory—or the 1501 Event

In 907, the Year of the Dog, or July/August of 1501, the young Ismail, spiritual and military leader of the extremist messianic Safaviyya order, won a battle at the village of Sharur in the Araxes Valley of Nakhichevan against the vastly larger forces of the Aq Qoyunlu Sultan Alvand Bayandur, who had controlled the northeastern third of the late tripartite Aq Qoyunlu state.[4] This military success allowed Ismail to seize the Aq Qoyunlu's capital of Tabriz. For Ismail and his tribal Qizilbash warriors, who followed his spiritual and military claims with divine reverence, this was a decisive victory in territorial as well as psycho-religious terms.

Ismail's father had been killed in battle by his brother-in-law Yaqub Aq Qoyunlu in 1488. Ismail was brought up in hiding, protected by the Safaviyya brotherhood's innermost supporters in Lahijan (Khvāndamīr [1370] 1991, 31–34; Roemer 2003, 215). At age seven he received the compelling title *vali allah* ("lieutenant of god"), elevating him to a status almost equal to the first Shiʿi caliph Ali.[5] In 1499, when the ruling members of the Aq Qoyunlu were in the midst of their own power struggles, he made a bid for power. By the spring of 1500, he had gathered thousands of messianically driven military followers from sympathizers and devotees of the Turcoman tribes in Azerbaijan and Eastern Anatolia. The division of the Aq Qoyunlu's state aided Ismail's ambition. With the defeat of his enemy's larger forces and the occupation of the important Turco-Iranian city of Tabriz, he gained a major strategic advantage, also facilitating his grab of royal power. Taking the place of grand master of the Safaviyya Sufi order (following the 1494 death of his brother), Ismail had secured the absolute spiritual and political power to which his father and grandfather aspired (Woods 1976, 173; Roemer 1986, 189; Khunjī [1382] 2003, 252–308).

The Relevance of Tabriz

Ismail I's occupation of Tabriz had an innate logic. Besides its role as the regional center of Azerbaijan and headquarters of the ruling power, it had an economic and strategic infrastructure as well as historical stature. Although the town of Ardabil, as the Safaviyya order's place of origin and ancestral shrine, carried a certain sanctity, it had neither the function nor the strategic advantage or historical eminence of Tabriz (Mazzaoui 1972, 43–44).

The topography of extensive mountain massifs around Tabriz and the local river system places the city at the junction of the corridor stretching from the south along the eastern banks of Lake Van and the Sahand mountain massif to Transcaucasia as well as the transit route along the northeast passage, making it a congenital capital of the provinces of Azerbaijan and northern Iran. Tabriz had assumed a geopolitical function already in Sasanian times, although it lost its influence in the fourth century. By the time of the Arab conquest, it apparently was a town with minor relevance. Most of the Arab geographers in the tenth and eleventh centuries refer to Tabriz as a small town, which until the Mongol invasion had largely regional importance. A series of recent articles discuss the relevance of Tabriz in scholarly, artistic, religious, commercial, and political functions from the Il-Khanid to the Aq Qoyunlu period, attesting by the end of the fifteenth century Tabriz's traceable influences throughout Iran as far as Egypt and links to commercial networks from China to Europe (Pfeiffer 2014, 11 and passim). Hülegü's destruction of Baghdad in 1258 changed the territorial function of Azerbaijan and the position of Tabriz as urban center. Tabriz had become the political capital of the Il-Khanids, officially first under Abaqa's rule in 1263, and had experienced great development under Ghazan Khan since 1295. Since then it had carried the epithet *Dar al-Saltanah* ("Abode of the Monarchy"), which it regained under Ismail and held until the nineteenth century. The Timurids moved their political capital eastwards to Samarkand, but had held Tabriz since 1387 as a strategic and administrative center of what was still known as the "throne of Hülegü."[6] The Jalayrids, local successors to the Il-Khanids, used Tabriz as a residence, as did the rulers of the Turcoman tribal confederations, the Qara Qoyunlu and Aq Qoyunlu, in the competition to succeed the Timurids from 1375 to 1501.

As the urban headquarters of the Aq Qoyunlu's nomadic court, Tabriz emerged as a political, cultural, and religious center, counting among the "great Islamic capitals of the age." Husayn Abivardi Fayzi, who traveled there in the late 1400s, extolled the city, along with Cairo, Istanbul, and Herat, as one of the "four thrones" (Woods 1976, 146, 279). Early Safavid accounts styled it "paradise-like." Based on these early accounts, twentieth-century scholars continued to assess it as one of the most important cities between Istanbul and India, with only Tbilisi, Isfahan, Baghdad, and later Tehran in the same category (Amīnī 2000, 163, 176; Minorsky and Bosworth 1998, 41–49).

Tabriz in 1501, then, functioning as a stepping stone to the creation of long-term dynastic rule, carried unmistakable historical and symbolic implications. "His Majesty took his place in the Royal capital," commented Hasan Beg Rūmlū (1934, 26, 227). It was easily the political and cultural center of a territory reaching from the Eastern Mediterranean to Transoxania and the southern Caucasus to the Arabian Sea, and also for this reason it was periodically a site of contestation between the Ottomans and the Safavids. Controlling Tabriz was a crucial precondition in Ismail's vying for power with the Aq Qoyunlu and to create a state following Timurid and Mongol models. Ismail's 1501 occupation of this city thus implied a number of generally understood references to historical or dynastic antecedents as well as larger territorial and political implications. Proclaiming that "a brave champion will conquer all lands: all Asia Minor (Rum), China, Khurasan, and Syria,"[7] Ismail made clear that his territorial ambitions aimed to repeat those of his various predecessors who had claimed Tabriz, with explicit territorial aspirations from the Mediterranean to at least northwestern China.

Subduing Tabriz as his political headquarters, with the aim of taking possession of the western Turcoman and eastern Timurid territories, he crowned himself there as the ruler with the consequential imperial Iranian title *pād-i shāh* ("king of kings"), held before him by his grandfather Aq Qoyunlu Uzun Hasan, minted coins in his name, and, by having the names of the twelve Imams read in the *khutbah* (Friday prayer), proclaimed Twelver Shiʿism as the official religion of his rule. He is also said to have introduced the practice of the ritual cursing of the first three Sunni caliphs and coerced the population to convert from a Sunni to an Alid ritual and identity (i.e., Rūmlū 1934, 26–27; Glassen 1972, 261–262). All of these were programmatic gestures declaring new religio-ideological directions and expressing ambitions beyond a short-term raid. The occupation of Tabriz opened access to a crucial network of political infrastructure and resources. Its subjugation was a proclamation of far larger ambitions and the first step from a regional militant Sufi brotherhood to an urban-based, coercive state power.

The Religious Implications

One of the most consequential parts of Ismail I's declaration in Tabriz was the religious dogma tied to his kingship. The imposition of what emerged as Twelver Shiʿism was one of the singularly most important leitmotifs defining the rationale, success, and legacy of Safavid rule. The military victory and capture of the city of Tabriz also marked the prelude to the change in the religio-political landscape with which the later imperial Safavid state (and its successors) was to identify and legitimize itself. Over the following decades a new religious idiom developed that framed Safavid Iran not just in religious and theological, but also political, cultural, and societal terms. In the long run, it created a contrapunctual anti-Sunni counterdefinition, which nonetheless adhered to an Islamic macrostructure but created a deliberate religious polarity against internal imperial neighbors, who proclaimed a Sunni identity, even though this was no closure of commercial exchange, cultural multiplicity, and political relations.

One of the central elements reverberating around the date of 1501 is the extremism and zeal of Ismail and his devotees, which over the following few decades imposed a new religious identity by the use of sheer force, zealous propaganda, and missionary activities. Ismail was the crucial figure in this, both in zeal and self-reference. Following the occupation of Tabriz, he was hailed by his followers as the living emanation and manifestation of God, the representative of the savior (Twelfth Imam or *mahdī*) and the source of absolute truth (i.e., Minorsky 1942, 1026; Woods 1976, 182).

In one of his Turkic verses, Ismail declared:

> I am God's eye [or "God Himself"!]; come now, O blind man gone astray, to behold Truth (God).
>
> I am that Absolute Doer of whom they speak. Sun and Moon are in my power.
>
> My being is God's House, know it for certain. Prostration before me is incumbent on thee, in the morn and even. (trans. Minorsky 1942, 1047)

As reincarnation of Ali, he claimed infallibility and was paid divine reverence by devotees. However, in this early phase, Ismail's Shiʿism was still rudimentary and basically limited to the profession that Ali had been the rightful successor of the Prophet, or what has been termed "Qizilbash Islam" (Babayan 1994, 137; Babayan 2002, 145). The cult of Ali had been very closely tied to the evolution of Sufism in the lands of Iran from the thirteenth century onward, as well as to the principle of the "perfect spiritual leader" *(murshid-i kāmil).* Many of the tribes in the region, in part reacting to an expansive Ottoman hegemony, were attracted to the extremist mystical ideas of the numerous heterodoxies circulating in Anatolia at the time, many venerating Ali as a divine figure and believing in various forms of the incarnation of god in the leaders of Sufi brotherhoods. Yet, the imposition of this version of Shiʿism (or perhaps better "Alism") was imbued with the milieu and zeitgeist by which Ismail was conditioned: the Sufi cults and ideals of divinely inspired leadership, his own personal zeal, but also by political intuition. Installing Shiʿism as his official religion and message mobilized the forces of a dynamic religious ideology in the service of the Safavid movement, creating a focus and a common goal or foe (both abstract and real) that aided the cohesion in the early scramble for supremacy against his Aq Qoyunlu relatives, forging a compelling basis for the Safaviyya order's claims to absolute power. The declamation of Ali's singular righteousness entailed an unmistakable religio-ideological direction and by implication a delineation of a more specific territorial but also internal identity.

In wider Asia this meant new religio-ideological premises which forced age-old interactions, the rhythm of transregional patterns, commercial and political fence lines, competitions, and alliances to adapt to them.

While there were a great number of followers and sympathizers of Ismail's militant chiliasm also in Anatolian territories claimed by the Ottomans, the response of the population was not just one of acceptance. The new ruler's coercion created hardship and death as well as a wave of refugees to Ottoman domains, India, and Central Asia. Still, Ismail's decision to impose Twelver Shiʿism as an official religion had crucial ramifications in creating the basis for the long-term development of a Safavid state and shaping what is now considered modern Iran, determining identities and politics to this day. It laid the foundations for the development of what in the twenty-first century we know as Twelver Shiʿism (in terms of theology, jurisprudence, politics, and religious practices).

Ismail's successors initiated the methodical patronage of a Shiʿi establishment, including the institutionalization of certain religio-political offices, the formation of a field of Shiʿi jurisprudence and orthodox theology, the patronage of shrines and institutions, and the founding of large religious endowments, some of which still act as extremely wealthy financial organizations in today's global money markets.

The religio-political position of the Safavids and their specific ideological orientation, as well as their absolutist monarchical aspirations, shaped the political geography and with it the fluidity of East-West relations. It engendered diplomatic efforts in search of alliances against Ottoman interference in trade routes and commercial affairs, prompting, for example, active diplomatic contacts between Europe and Safavid Iran, which had precedents already under Timurid or Aq Qoyunlu rule (i.e., Kauz 2005, passim; Keçik 1976, 70, 97, 103, 148; Matthee 2003a, 105).[8]

Military Campaigns—Conquests until 1514

Although it did not cause the immediate collapse of the Aq Qoyunlu tripartite state at one stroke, the 1501 occupation of Tabriz was a decisive moment that played up Ismail's claim as divinely guided leader and military commander, providing the critical momentum for further conquests along the western and eastern frontiers.

Ismail spent the following years consolidating his power over the central Iranian provinces from Iraq in the West to Khurasan in the East.[9] In 1510 [916] after the battle of Marv against the Uzbek Shaybani Khan, the Safavids could claim the city of Herat, which in historical and cultural terms was at least as important as Tabriz and which, continuing Timurid practice, became the Safavids' eastern capital and the seat of the heir-apparent (Dale 2009, 205–207). There is little doubt that Ismail aspired to gain control over Transoxania, but he was unable to subdue the Uzbeks. These early conquests were fought with the force of militant religious fervor, scorched-earth methods, and savage brutality, entailing towers of enemy skulls and even acts of cannibalism (Bashir 2006, passim).

In fact, tracing the axis of period and place of the Safavids' rise in a trans-Asian perspective, the 1510 conquest of Herat as the eastern capital is perhaps even more crucial than 1501, as Herat functioned as an eastward crossroad and facilitated the fusion of western and eastern Iran, without which the Safavid ruling project might not have succeeded.[10]

Military success combined with messianic propaganda attracted a continuous stream of recruits and supporters from Anatolia, who arrived bearing the fanaticism of a revolutionary fighting spirit that fuelled Safavid raids

Miniature page from the partly fictitious *Tarikh-i alam-aray-i Shah Ismail* (The world adorning history of Shah Ismail), showing a battle between Ismail and Abu'l-Khayr Khan, produced in Isfahan, c. 1688. (Freer Gallery of Art, Smithsonian Institution, Washington, DC: Gift of Martha Mayor Smith and Alfred Mayor in memory of A. Hyatt Mayor, F2000.3)

far into western Anatolia (Roemer 1986, 219–222). The establishment of a militant Shiʿi state on the eastern Ottoman borders, inhabited by Turcomans who sympathized with the extremist Safavid propaganda and the spiritual, quasi-divine leadership of Ismail, was from Ottoman perspectives an overt threat. The Ottomans (then the rising hegemonic power) felt provoked by the acutely growing followership of Ismail's religio-militarist movement among the Anatolian tribes, now the dominant element at the eastern Ottoman frontier and the same groups that had supported their rise to power. A further provocation was Ismail's overt interference in the Ottomans' own war of succession following the death of Bayezit II. Immediately after having gained security on the throne, Sultan Selim I (1512–1520) prepared the expedition against Ismail. (Supposedly, he took as model Mehmed II's campaign against Uzun Hasan in 1473.) In a dogged campaign in which thousands of people were killed, he also ordered the annihilation of all potentially disloyal Shiʿis in Ottoman domains.

Ismail's apotheosis, implying infallibility and military successes, led to the disaster of the Battle of Chaldiran in the fall of 1514 [920]. Selim's troops, vastly outnumbering the Safavids, fought with the latest artillery, which Ismail and his partisans deemed craven and unnecessary. Selim briefly took possession of Tabriz (on September 7 [17 Rajab]). But given practical military realities and sympathies for the Safavid message among his sprawling troops, which possibly endangered their loyalty, Selim withdrew.[11] His withdrawal saved the early Safavids as well as their hold on Tabriz until Shah Tahmasp I (1524–1576) moved his headquarters farther away from Ottoman frontiers to Qazvin.

For Ismail, the battle's outcome was nonetheless a calamity, whose psychological ramifications were more serious than the actual loss of territory. It shattered his reputation for divine nature and invincibility, especially so for the Qizilbash (Babayan 2002, 301, 323). Except for one further annexation in the Caucasus, Ismail did not again lead his troops into battle (despite Uzbek raids and the rise of the Mughals in the East), which meant a halt to Safavid expansion for several decades. Numerous serious later crises caused by the unabated hostilities among the inner Qizilbash factions, the recurrent Uzbek challenges in Khurasan, the ongoing military confrontations with the Ottomans, and the repeated crises of succession (Roemer 2003, 275–291) left it uncertain whether the Safavids would survive as a viable force. Much of the vigor of the personal cult and the extremism of Ismail I's regime dissipated upon his death in 1524, though the ideological drive for an absolute and divinely inspired kingship survived (Savory 1960, 91–105).

Absolute Kingship, Long-Term Implications, and Standard Interpretations

Ismail's 1501 coronation facilitated the transition from Mongol-Timurid principles of rule and Sufi cults of authority to a synthesis of pre-Islamic Iranian kingship and Shiʿi ideas of legitimacy. By the 1510s he had emerged as the successor to the Turcoman Aq Qoyunlu rulers, leaving the early Safavid system close to their system of state and political outlooks. The organization of his early regime greatly resembled a theocracy with the domination of a strong military element. (Babayan 1994, 158).

The Safavids devised a genealogy of their descent from Ali while also claiming that Husayn, Ali's second son, had married the daughter of the last Sasanian king, Yazdigird III. Using these claims, the Safavids linked the house of Ali to the pre-Islamic Iranian monarchical traditions. The divine right of the Iranian kings thus continued to be part of the legitimacy and charisma of the Safavid rulers. This process of Iranization (hand-in-hand with the imamization of Twelver Shiʿism) is outwardly reflected by two further moves of the capital from Tabriz to Qazvin (1548) and eventually to Isfahan (1598). In political-bureaucratic terms, the Safavids (though struggling with this) achieved the lasting amalgamation of Iranian political and administrative conventions with the Turkish military-tribal prerogatives. The old Iranian principle of absolute kingship, now in the Safavid version, mediated the tension between both elements. It reified the ancient Iranian monarchical system, which persisted until 1979 (except for the idea of god's incarnation in the shah, which disappeared with the Safavids between 1722 and 1736.) Absolute kingship built the historical case for the strong centralism of the modern Iranian state's bureaucracy.

Yet, in our attempt at anatomizing the relevance of time and space, 1501 emerges as an aggregate of several historical antecedents, including reverberations of Il-Khanid rule and the imperial notion of the Timurid as well as the pre-Islamic Sasanian empires. Sasanian ideas of kingship were crucial to the later formation of the Safavid monarchy. The Ottoman sultans, for example, referred to the Safavid shahs as to the Aq Qoyunlu shahs with titles from the *Shāhnāmah* (i.e., Jamshid, Faridun, Kaykhosrow) and as "shah or sultan of

Iranian lands" or "the lord of the Iranians" (Navā'ī 1977, 578, 690, 700–701). In essence, one could argue that what has been labeled wider Iran, in its Turkic as well as Iranian influences, is much less about a state than about the relationship of the population to its king.

The Safavids have been credited with achieving an enduring dynastic state for the first time since the seventh-century Arab conquest of Sasanian Iran, thereby paving the way for a modern nation-state. Considering, however, that lasting political and cultural patterns had been created by the vast territories of the Saljuqs, Il-Khanids, and Timurids as well as the shorter-lived rule of the Qara and Aq Qoyunlu in the west, from which the Safavid period was not a total departure, we may dispute the cohesiveness of Safavid rule. The Timurids, in political orientation, terms of legitimacy and rulership, imperial ambitions, and geographical horizons, particularly eastward to Central Asia and the Punjab but also westward towards the shrine-cities of Iraq, remained a persuasive precedent for the Safavids' vision of an imperial state (Szuppe 1997, 320, 322).[12] Having a Timurid blueprint in mind, Ismail's grip of supremacy (despite the disaster of Chaldiran) laid the basis for a lasting centralized and expansionist state (i.e., Manz 1989, 2; Quinn 2000, 86, 99, 123; Burton 1997, 23–39). This is why the taking of Tabriz in 1501, however tenuous in the early years, has been interpreted as creating the basis for the transformation of a religio-tribal military occupation into a cohesive state (and with this, the territorial and cultural frame for what emerged as modern Iran).

1501 thus brought into conclusive power the movement of the Safaviyya order, founded by Shaykh Safi al-Din Ardabili (1252–1334) as a Sunni Sufi brotherhood. With this, it brought to political conclusion the profession of a militant, millennial Shi'i allegiance that had evolved under the position of Ismail's father and grandfather as the order's supreme spiritual and military leader. Claims of descent from the house of the Prophet further reinforced the sacred origin of the Safavid leaders. Despite widespread antinomian ideas and the Alid cult, the majority of the people of the Persian-speaking domains were not Shi'is before the rise of the Safavids. Much emphasis has been given to the synthesis of kingship and Islam by which Safavid ideological hegemony decisively changed the religious identity of Iran. Before that, cultural traditions in literature, sciences, art, and historical practices of administration and bureaucracy formed the central common ground for the peoples of the wider Iranian world. Ismail transformed the principle of "a charismatic millennial leadership" into a Shiʿi theocracy with himself as the god-king. The Shiʿitization subsequent to 1501 remained a long and complex process, but irreversibly changed Iran's dominant religio-political matrix to a Twelver Shiʿia identity. Ismail also created a precedent of Islamic-Iranian millennial leadership which, it can be argued, reappeared even in the twentieth century, as represented by figures like Khomeini or even Ahmadinejad.

Deliberating the Date—Transition and Transformation

In the *Encyclopaedia of Islam* Roemer declared, "under Isma'il, Iran became a national state for the first time since the Arab conquest," a statement which both reinforced and reflected standard interpretations. Elsewhere he noted that, regardless of whether one considers it the beginning of modern Iranian history or not, 1501 "certainly heralds a new era" (Roemer 2003, 189–190). Following standard twentieth-century interpretations and narratives of Iranian history, 1501 is thus a conventional as well as predictable date. It works as a useful summary point in vast surveys of world histories, generally marking a point of departure. It is also a perfect date for partisan court chroniclers and historians of military history or dynastic achievements and a definitive event which marks the onset and prepares the ground for a "golden age."

While 1501 works to flag such an unmistakable beginning of all the trends outlined above, considering earlier patterns and precedents makes 1501 appear much less as a date that inaugurated a completely new order. Rather, it denotes a point of transition, both in terms of time and space. Shaykh Jābirī Anṣārī, an administrator and chronicler of Isfahan, noted in his late nineteenth-century universal history on "Isfahan and the whole world" for the year 907, "in Azerbaijan shah Ismail had the *khutbah* read in the name of the Imams of the Twelver-Shiʿa. And the shah beat with 7,000 *Qizilbash* Sufis the 70,000 troops of Mirza Alvand. Discovery of the Island St. Helena in the Atlantic" (Jābirī Anṣārī [1321] 1942, 171). This statement does not resound with a big bang, nor does it give 1501 the importance assumed in the historiography since the twentieth century, where it has become a touchstone to denote the inauguration of a new system and era. It sounds rather like a lapidary affirmation of a noteworthy event.

There are several reasons for this. First, the structure and scope of this chronicle in many ways followed the tradition of Islamicate universal histories, starting with early Muslim history but also providing a narrative of Sasanian events. Further, there are the implications of the meaning and specific perspective of Isfahan in the nineteenth century, by which time Iran's attention was fixed towards Europe and the Atlantic system as a primary point of political, economic, and cultural measurement. Jābirī Anṣārī attempted to not only to relate but frame his time and place as crucial in the events of the "whole world." This, by the nineteenth century, was defined by modern events located in Europe rather than Asia. The European "discovery" of an island in the Atlantic, hence, had much greater relevance than the concurrent 1501 Uzbek victory against the Mughals. Late Qajar sensibilities and views of the Safavid period had, again, specific dynastic and ideological implications which reverberate in this kind of annual entry. Lastly, the Safavids identified themselves not just along the lines of a universal history, but rather of a *heilsgeschichte* (history of salvation), which in this early phase of the 1500s operated with ideas of divine predestination and cyclical notions of time.[13] Most Safavid narratives and chronicles generally begin with the founding of the order by Shaykh Safi al-Din in the mid-thirteenth century and the brotherhood's succeeding shaykhs, rather than with Ismail's taking of worldly monarchical power. Some chronicles emphasize the genealogy leading to the descendants of the prophet and his nephew Ali; some begin with Adam and the creation.[14] The fusion of Ismail's self-proclamation as messianic fulfillment in Timurid and pre-Islamic notions of rulership support the principles of *heilsgeschichte.* In hagiographic narratives, using dreams as authoritative and divine indicators, these histories stress the predetermination of Shaykh Safi's mandate in an auspicious beginning, which merely entails the predestination of Ismail's kingship in a much longer cycle of time and historical fulfillment that saw its renewal in the rise of Abbas I in the 1590s.[15] Rūmlū, for example, recounted that Ismail fought altogether five battles, the one at Sharur against Mirza Alvand being simply the second of these (Rūmlū 1934, 90). Considering the period since the initial attempts by Ismail's grandfather and father to fuse spiritual and political-military supremacy, beginning in the mid-fifteenth century, 1501, even from the perspectives of Safavid writers, indicates a point of transition in a predestined trajectory of divine providence rather than a beginning.

Without Safavid teleology—that is, their transformation from a Sunni-Sufi order to an absolutist divine monarchy with imperial-territorial and religio-ideological prerogatives—or with the historical hindsight of a national history in mind, 1501 loses precision or significance, emerging as time condensed to a point in the timeline of a calendar. As a mere agreement of an

Deniz Atlas. (Walters Art Museum)

astronomical-calendrical calculation, it may have a certain neutrality, but looked at from any other perspective—whether geographical, nationalist, astrological, didactic, or from the wider historical context—it sustains limited or variable relevance and assumes multiple meanings, breaking up into different contexts of time and space. Stripped of preconceived connotations, 1501 in an Iranian-Asian context is thus a rather vague date, which at best summarizes earlier trends of political and imperial ambitions.

Beyond Iran-zamin—or, Linking Early Safavid Iran to Asia

Discussed in terms of transregionalism and wider Asian interdependencies, 1501 also looks like an incongruous date. It is about half a century before the grand economic and political changes engendered by new shipping technology, the upshot of the discovery of the New World, and fast-growing intercontinental trade, the analysis of which has been at the center of the discussion of world history in the past few decades. By the end of the sixteenth century, Safavid Iran was inexorably drawn into these global trends. But comparing 1601 (or even just 1551) with 1501 using categories like the volume of trade, commodities exchanged, processes of institutionalization, cultural productivity, mobility of people, size of trading communities, number of European travelers, or types of surviving documents, the beginning of the 1500s appears to belong to a different era.

Despite the militant messianic effusion and the victorious coronation in Tabriz, it was uncertain whether the victory and following military successes up to 1514 would form a turning point or rather become a passing phase in the struggle for supremacy of various Turcoman federations between eastern Anatolia and the Uzbek steppe. The 1514 defeat at Chaldiran could easily have been the end of the Safaviyya movement. The taking of Tabriz by Ismail I is thus one local incident in the period labeled "the age of discovery," shortly after Columbus's arrival in the Americas (1492), Vasco da Gama's first voyage to India (1498), and/or the later Portuguese capture of Malacca (1511). However, about a century before the 1602 incorporation of the Dutch East India Company and five to seven decades before the worldwide commercial boom entailing a short phase of great economic wealth and grand monarchical power in wider Iran, facilitated by the much-acclaimed rule of Shah Abbas I (1588–1629), 1501 seems again rather distant from more tangibly documented transregional interactions in central and eastern Asia.

In the early 1500s, enforceable absolute royal power was a goal rather than reality, and in 1501 Ismail I with his followers could have only hoped to be part of the beginning of the kind of imperial system created by his descendants (Dale 2010, 87). In more realistic terms, the early Safavid project was part of the immediate struggle for absolute supremacy with the rival tribal confederacies of the Aq Qoyunlu, the Uzbeks in the east, and Ottomans in the west. Yet taking these coordinates of time and place as point of transition and catalyst of earlier patterns of power and geography opens a different perspective on transregionalism in the direction of Central and eastern Asia.

The Timurid and Aq Qoyunlu systems, as closest imperial predecessors to the Safavids, entailed a vision of power and state that carried tangible continuities and reverberations—in political aspirations as well as geographical, economic, cultural, and ideological terms. Establishing imperial rule over the territory reaching from Iraq to Transoxania, the Timurids had demonstrated the possibility of such power in real terms. Their military support had been drawn from territories further east in Central Asia. Like the Safavids, they spoke a language different from the majority of their subjects in central Iran (even though they adhered to Islam, spoke Persian, and were literate) (Liu 2010, 87–96; Manz 2007, 178–207). Timurid rule, using deliberate allusions, again itself followed the dynastic aspirations and territorial ambitions of the preceding Il-Khanids (Manz 2007, 1, 9). For Timur Lang, the reification of Mongol rule included the goal of annexing northern India and China, which facilitated the continuation of these earlier relations (Roemer 2003, 94). The Timurid state, with its claims to Mongol territorial demarcations and imperial goals, was unmistakably in the mind of Ismail and his Qizilbash devotees as well as his monarchical successors.[16] The Timurids had left a model of empire, a military system, and a structure of relations between the central power and the provincial and urban elites which reverberated during Aq Qoyunlu rule and was taken up by the early Safavids. Safavid accounts extolled Timur Lang's "charisma" and his contacts with the early Safaviyya shaykhs, and recent historians have emphasized messianic elements in Timurid sovereignty reflected, for example, in the title "Lord of the Conjunction" (Moin 2012, 54). Timurid continuities are likewise traceable in Safavid literary and historiographical traditions,[17] miniature painting and book illustrations, or modes of craftsmanship (Quinn 1996, 145–146; Melville 2008, 29–38). The Timurid illumination workshops thriving in Herat survived under early Safavid patronage in Shiraz and Tabriz. Painters, in fact, were deliberately brought there by Ismail. These workshops provide material examples of early Safavid links to Khurasan and further east.

All this entailed mental maps based on lasting memories of interactions with the Chaghatai domains of Central Eurasia, reflected in a rhetoric of reaching further east. Ismail, using wordplay, took the penname Khaṭā'ī, meaning "sinner"[18] but also "China" and "lotus flower." He proclaimed, "Khaṭā'ī is of divine nature, that he is related to Muhammad Mustafā" and

"my name is Valī Shāh Ismā'īl; my surname is Khaṭā'ī." Evoking both erotic longing as well as physical-territorial possession, he declared: "Since I have set my heart on the curls *(chīn)* of your white face, the clime of (the white) Byzantines, Chin and Khita belong to Khaṭā'ī."[19] In another verse he salutes "beautiful Shiraz and the attractive land of China . . . "your gazelle eyes take a levy from the kingdom of Khotan, and your august locks tax the Emperor of China . . ." (trans. by Minorsky 1942, 1028, slightly modified; Birdoǧan 1991, 109). Frequent allusions to "Khotan" or a "Khotan Turk" in his verses, following time-honored metaphors for the beloved, again expressed erotic attraction and desire, but they also refer to an aspired ideal place of origin and one to be conquered and possessed (Minorsky 1942, 1028).[20] Although to some extent resonating with established literary tropes, these allusions can also be read as lands stretching at least to the northern frontiers of China, which were explicitly on Ismail's horizon, even if far-flung or exoticized.

Even if we reduce such phrases to literary style and wordplay, they also imply territorial ambitions, political, artistic, and intellectual culture, commercial interactions, cultural symbolism, and (imperial) visions referring to Central and eastern Asia. After all, at that time the space reaching westwards to the Mediterranean was controlled by the Ottomans and Mamluks and presented the Safavids with different, more immediate frontiers (repeating Chingisid and Timirud-Chaghatai precedents). Considering Ismail's ambition of realizing Mongol and Timurid ideas of rule from China to Iraq, to which the Aq Qoyunlu also aspired, one could thus argue that 1501 forms a "summary" of that idea.

Il-Khanid elements also materialized in the Safavid domains. Recent research on Il-Khanid rule in Iran emphasizes the process of the merging of Mongol practices and Iranian-Islamic models of government, in which tax and provincial administration as well as military practices were less an Iranian-Islamicate system adopted wholesale by Mongol rulers of a nomadic background, but in many ways a Mongol regime with its own methods. Trans-Asian relations via Central Asia were particularly close during the Mongol

---

Opposite page: Miniature from *Divan* (collected poems) by Shah Ismail Khat'ai (Shah Isma'il). Manuscript from Tabriz, c. 1520. (Arthur M. Sackler Gallery, Smithsonian Institution, Washington, DC: Purchase—Smithsonian Unrestricted Trust Funds, Smithsonian Collections Acquisition Program, and Dr. Arthur M. Sackler, S1986.60)

period, with annual exchanges of envoys. The Great Khans' acknowledgement of the Il-Khanids as "prince(s) of the western regions" had an impact on the latter's administrative and cultural system. Specific administrative organizations of the royal household, for example, survived as long-term institutions and were still practiced under late Safavid rule (Liu and Jackson 1992, 435–436. Melville 2006, 159, 164).

Perhaps Trans-Asian connections also ought to be framed less in historical precedents (counter-dynastic frames), or actual, measurable routes (land or maritime), but in frames of diverse cultural transmissions. Relations between the Great Khans in China and the Il-Khanids also produced a cultural exchange with diverse influences on the arts and sciences. This included geographical information resulting in navigation charts and maps, the introduction to China of sciences from Islamized western Asia such as mathematics, alchemy, medicine, pharmacology and geometry, or Persian translations of Chinese medical works, and lasting Chinese influences on artistic visions and the iconography of the wider Iranian world (Liu and Jackson 1992. Allsen 2009:150). The employment of Muslim outsiders in high positions of the Chinese military or tax administration, the founding of Muslim communities in China, and imports of cobalt from Iran are other standard examples of this exchange. Chinese porcelain and local pottery, traded on both land and sea routes, give the most tangible evidence of exchange between wider Iran and East Asia before and after 1501.

Art historians have argued that Chinese ceramics, preserved in considerable quantities, dominate our understanding of inter-Asian trade and its repercussions in Southwest Asia in the premodern period (Stanley 2010, 108). While this exchange is well documented in the early Islamic period, the circulation of these kinds of artifacts increased dramatically by the late sixteenth century, creating an intricate interaction of commercial interchange, including the establishment of local productions of ceramics, exchange of patterns, copies, and imitations from China to Europe. Two of the most prominent examples are the early large consignments which reached southern Iran during the Ming naval expeditions of the early fifteenth century in Chinese bottoms and the famous collection of 1,162 Chinese porcelain pieces in the *Chini-khanah* of the Shrine of Ardabil, which Shah Abbas I donated as part of a *vaqf* (endowment) in 1611.[21] While not neatly tied to 1501, Chinese blue-and-white porcelain obviously indicates direct exchange

Aq Qoyunlu unloading porcelain. (Topkapı Palace Museum, Istanbul)

between wider Iran and China via land and sea routes. Yet porcelains might be seen not just as concrete commodities but also as objects to which are attached notions of value, and transmitters of images that transcend paths of commercial exchange, where more abstract concepts like worldviews and cultural spaces are mediated. Thus, explorations of space and time along immaterial cultural elements like millennialism,[22] Sufism, conceptions of kingship, calendrical conventions, astrology, dream cultures, or literary traditions like the *Shāhnāmah* are additional components of eastward loops to western Asia.

Another element in tracing boundaries and transregionalism in western Asia is language, which circumscribes cultural domains that facilitate social and intellectual linkages, at least among the elites. Although Turkish was spoken from the Bosporus to Bukhara, Persian functioned as a lingua franca along the Silk Road network between the fourteenth and sixteenth centuries, playing an influential role even at the Yuan court in China and maintaining a tangible role through Ming rule and later. Marco Polo supposedly managed to communicate in Persian on his travels in China (Liu 2010, 87–96; Boyle 1974, 175). Persian used to be the administrative and cultural language of the region extending over Anatolia, Central Asia, and North India. Indian courts developed distinct literary styles that were also influential in Iran until the early twentieth century, fashioning what became known as "Indo-Persian culture," with distinct influences also in historiography, architecture, and mysticism (Alam 2000; Riazul Islam 1957). Although Ismail I wrote his poetry in Turkish, Persian functioned as a political and cultural instrument, used from Istanbul, Mesopotamia, and the Arab littoral of the Persian Gulf to Bengal and Transoxania, facilitating a plausible degree of communication and mobility for traders, missionaries, clerics, literati, exiles, émigrés, artists, and conquerors with their troops.

Route Directions—Land and Sea Interdependencies

Enumerating route itineraries involves a certain tedious listing of place names without giving them meaning or reflecting the realities of terrain and movement. But beyond showing things like trade or pilgrimage connections, routes imply hierarchies of places, polities, and markets, and for the purpose of this discussion also imply, if superficially, horizontal continuities of time and place.

Research over the last decades, accompanied by fierce debates, has established the predominance of Asian commercial networks and economies in an early modern global system of which Safavid Iran was a part. With the rise of the Dutch and British, if not earlier, the changing networks of the Atlantic system drifted more into the consciousness of the Safavids, including the Persian Gulf as place of commercial exchange, wealth, and power. However, by 1501 the Persian Gulf was not a primary concern in Azerbaijan, the new urban headquarters of Tabriz, after all, being much closer to the Caspian Sea than the Persian Gulf. The legacy of the Safavids' Il-Khanid and Timurid predecessors, and their own Turcoman origin in Eastern Anatolia, embraced a cultural origin and geographical memory that emphasized a focus and orientation rooted in the land routes along the old Silk Road network, involving long-established transit lines, joining urban centers and tribal regions much more than maritime connections. How the interchange along the land-based routes worked at the time is more difficult to establish.

It has been argued that the Mongols' destruction of Baghdad and the Mamluks' military confrontations with the Crusaders caused the decline of routes through the Persian Gulf while aiding the rise of the Red Sea route (Forêt and Kaplony 2008, 1–5; McChesney 2003, 129–156; Alam 1994, 203). Economic historians have argued that Iranian trade with India and further east was especially high at the end of the 1400s (Frank 1998, 83). For Tabriz, all this meant a gain of importance and wealth in east-west trade, particularly under the Timurids and Aq Qoyunlu, who facilitated active traffic between Western and Central Asia, and connecting beyond them to China and East Asia through Samarkand or Bukhara and Herat, which was a nexus also for land routes to India via Kabul and Qandahar (Roemer 2003, 158).[23] In the early 1500s, this pattern seems to have still dominated trade with the West and changed only with the commercial boom of the 1550s and later Safavid attempts at manipulating trade routes to counteract Ottoman interference and boycotts.

One of the few contemporary accounts of a journey from Samarkand to China is the *Khiṭāynamah* of a merchant, Alī Akbar Khiṭā'ī, who traveled in 1500 from Samarkand to China, returned in 1516, wrote down his experiences in what resembles the format of a guidebook, and as a Sunni dedicated it to the Ottoman Sultan. He described the structure of China's government, historical events, religions, social affairs, monetary issues, and military and civil institutions. Doubts have been expressed whether Alī Akbar actually ever went further than Khotan. Yet, even if he never did reach central China, his report reveals the routine utility of that northern land route as well as the relevance of relations between Central Asia and China in the early 1500s, when both territories claimed by the Uzbeks and the Safavids were subject to intense political upheavals (Khiṭā'ī [1372] 1993, 21–193; Lin 1983, 58–78). Another random but concrete example of connectedness is the Mughal Shah Babur's description of Kabul in the early 1500s, which noted products of Khurasan, Rum, and China in its markets and, discussing Khotan and Kashgar, stressed these places' ongoing connections both East and West (Beveridge 1970, 160).

Routes of transit obviously assume a crucial function in questions about the workings of transregionalism. Western networks linking wider Iran to Ottoman territories and Europe as well as Eastern routes to South and East Asia all lead through Iranian lands, whether along the northern fringes over land or the southern ones along the sea. In the late Safavid period the central trade routes are reasonably well documented even though many of them were much older. These include the Jaddih-yi Atabeg (named after the leaders of Luristan of the fourteenth century) from the Persian Gulf through the Zagros Mountains leading to central Iran (that is, Iraq 'Ajam). The western routes connected Tabriz and the more central and southern cities to Anatolia and Syria via Aleppo, Bursa to Izmir. The northern routes led via Tabriz and

Transcaucasia to Russia, through the western Caspian to Europe and the Baltic. The route to Central Asia passed by the western Caspian coast or Astarabad to Semnan, Nishabur, the shrine city Mashhad, to Marv, from there passing the Oxus River to Bukhara, or coming there from the North Indian plains via Qandahar. The southern routes led via Isfahan, Shiraz, and Yazd to the ports of the Persian Gulf such as Gambru (Bandar Abbas), Hormuz, and Basra.[24] This network remained more or less in operation with little modernization until the early 1900s.

Information about trade routes to the East before the big commercial boom of the late sixteenth century is less abundant, although directions and urban nexuses seemed to have remained fairly continuous. Valerie Hansen, again dispelling the idea of a single route of trade by scrutinizing archeological records, recently argues that in commercial and numerical terms the Silk Road, meaning the many "overland routes leading west out of China through Central Asia to Syria and beyond," was not significant, and that what has been called the Silk Road economy shrank after 755 (Hansen 2012, 111, 232, 235, 241). While stressing small-scale trade, she argues that it was the infrequent movement of envoys, artists, refugees, and the Chinese military which made all those people transmitters of culture, religion, and technology. Undoubtedly soldiers and envoys moved between wider Iran and China during the Mongol and Timurid regimes. This movement supports the idea that trade is not the only medium propelling interaction and exchange.

The consolidation of Ottoman power in the Arab provinces since 1517 enabled greater Ottoman control of commercial routes and transactions, which particularly affected the Levantine–Persian Gulf axis. The Portuguese occupation of Hormuz (1515–1622) unsurprisingly had crucial ramifications on the patterns of trade in the Persian Gulf, drawing southern Iraq and central Iran more directly into a system involving increasingly European players and taking new geographical directions. The rapid growth in maritime trade and circulation of money obviously increased the importance of the Persian Gulf and ocean trade for the Safavids, but in the early 1500s it had not yet completely replaced the relevance of local or long-distance land routes. Nor did it render contacts to the dynamic trade networks of Central Asia less relevant. Unlike the Ottomans, the Safavids never strove to become a naval power, but rather negotiated a tenuous dominance with the adjoining coastal rulers (and/or foreign naval powers). To be sure, since the 1550s the Safavids were acutely aware of the emerging importance of the Persian Gulf and its maritime connections. Despite the growing importance of maritime connections particularly to South Asia, land and sea routes in the early 1500s operated with a degree of interdependence and adaptability. Routes and directions depended on accessibility as affected by political conditions and seasonal practicalities, or local competition over material and political gain.[25]

Orders of Space—Hegemonies and Regions

Enforcing the hegemony of the center of power over the frontier provinces, continually challenged by the Ottomans, Uzbeks, and Portuguese, the shah certainly needed to display credible military power and an enforceable administrative system, but he depended just as much on the cultivation of relationships with the local elites and tribal groups along the peripheries as well as a certain degree of negotiation over the modalities of these relations. During the Tabriz phase in the early 1500s, dominated by ongoing military confrontations, relations between the still-changing frontiers and long-distance travel seemed volatile. The working of the relations between the center and the periphery implied a degree of mutuality of interest. As the Afghan invasion of 1722 shows, mere coercion did not work indefinitely; instead, persuasion and cooption of local tribes and provincial urban elites were one method of maintaining a centralizing system of power. Although standard views, molded by twentieth-century nationalist perspectives,[26] have emphasized the Safavids' centralization as a major success, the actual nature of the early-sixteenth-century state's central power along the border provinces ought to be reexamined. Dependencies were not always unilateral, and local interests, identities, and economics did not succumb completely to the force of an absolutist centralization, particularly in places heavily contested by the Ottomans or Mughals. The fluctuations in loyalties and prevailing local interests maintained a dynamic rather than static situation. Attempting to analyze early sixteenth-century frontiers as a process, they appear less as sharp demarcations than multidimensional regions, which were shaped and motivated not just by the hegemony of the center, but by the often tribal nomadic populations and local elites, as well as the physical environment and topography, which facilitated or limited accessibility and transit.[27] Similarly, provincial urban centers, though bound by liabilities to the Safavid royal center, had different and changing gravities and regional networks in a polycentric system. Tabriz and its wider province, after losing its royal position in 1548, took on a more regional function. Herat, crucial in mediating connections to Central Asia and India, was much closer to Sistan, Makran, the Hindu Kush, and Samarkand than to the early Safavid capitals Tabriz or Qazvin, but as second capital directly influenced demarcations and access to the East.

Circulating maps depicting Safavid territories usually do not reflect such ambiguities of political power, but rather frequently tend to convey a clear, unmitigated territorial hegemony along unambiguous lines. A more critical examination of the realities behind such lines may explain some of the geography beneath it as well as sharpen our understanding of transregionalism between wider Iran and eastern Asia and how it worked at in the early 1500s. One of the difficulties remains that there are hardly any geographical works from the Safavid period.[28] However, the questioning of representations or indeed the provincial realities behind border demarcations in wider Iran also raises questions about basic premises of geographical nomenclature. By the early 1500s, wider Iran had various geopolitical names. It was referred to not only as *Iran* but mostly *Iran-zamin,* (earth, terrain of Iran), *Kishvar-i Iran* (clime or country of Iran), *Mamalik-i Iran* (private provinces of Iran), *Mamalik-i Mahrusah* (protected domains), or *Shahanshah-i Iran* (king of kings of Iran),[29] which implied, first, the relationship between the country and the king, but also a more polycentric, changeable regionality rather than closely confined and rigid borderlines categorically controlled by a central power. While Ismail I embraced an absolute, divinely mandated rule along Timurid and Mongol lines of territory, in 1501, wider Iran was understood less as a coherent geopolitical entity than as a conglomerate of various regions, including Armenia, Georgia, Iraq ʿAjam and Iraq ʿArab,[30] Khuzistan, Fars, Kirman, Mekran, Nedha, Sistan, and Khurasan. The Mughal shah Babur, for example, talks about the two Iraqs, in which he also counted Tabriz, and Ismail himself talks about the Mulk ʿAjam (kingdom of ʿAjam) (Beveridge 1970, 16, 219; Minorski 1942, 1045, 1035). The case is further complicated by the fact that many of these are names of regional as well as geopolitical entities. The *Ahsan al-tawārīkh,* for example, delineated Ismail's realm as comprising Azerbaijan, Iraq ʿAjam, Khurasan, Fars, Kirman, Khuzistan, and for a shorter time also Diyarbakr, Balkh, and Marv (Rūmlū 1934, 90; for regions of Central Asia see McChesney 2009, 277 n1).

Regions and urban centers were more likely to define political allegiances and long-distance relations in the northeast, which by the late sixteenth century—until Abbas I's reconquest of Herat and Balkh in 1598/9 (1007)—was still claimed by the Uzbeks. Similarly, the western borders consisted not simply of a Safavid and Ottoman side, but were shaped by Baghdad, Khuzistan, Kurdistan, Armenia, and Georgia. Hegemony over the territories running through these regions was fiercely contested by both sides, and remained undefined in territorial, political and ethnic terms until the twentieth century.

There is evidence of trade and interchange with northwestern Chinese frontiers, but what lands beyond Khotan meant to the Aq Qoyunlu or the early Safavid milieu is unclear. The nineteenth-century separation of Iran and Afghanistan has furthermore blurred central Iran's earlier land links farther east. The Il-Khanids in any case had referred to Khurasan as reaching from Mazandaran to the Indus; for the Timurids, Khurasan and Turan were one space. From the Mughal perspective, Khurasan could be everything north of India, and other texts generalized Khurasan as lands from the Oxus and Qandahar to Qazvin. By 1511 Ismail saw the Oxus River as the Uzbek border (Rūmlū 1934, 154; Khvāndamīr [1370] 1991, 139).

Crucial in tracing such interdependencies, principles of transregionality, and an Asian perspective of Iranian lands in the early sixteenth century are geographical considerations, routes, and "anti-routes" (i.e., Ispahani 1989). Atlases and maps frequently delineate Safavid eastern boundaries along Khurasan, Sistan, and Makran in a straight line.[31] This seems to be a peculiar cartographic construct, although it also appears in other early modern European maps (i.e., Alai 2005, 77, 118). Undoubtedly there existed serious geographical constraints or anti-routes shaped by extreme topographic, geographic, and climatic conditions, but there is little doubt that these eastern perimeters as well were regions or transitional zones, flexible, permeable, even changeable, rather than straight, unambiguous demarcation lines. Ambitions of local leaders and mountain and tribal populations were crucial in mediating communication and trade beyond delineations drawn by real or projected political hegemony. A major challenge of the early 1500s was to balance the aspirations of a centralizing regime and those of diverse provincial peripheries, which were shaped by a combination of geography, negotiated loyalties with the urban elites and nomadic populations, and fluctuating degrees of hegemony. One good example of this balance is the geographically and climatically difficult region of Baluchistan before the demarcations drawn in the nineteenth and twentieth centuries (Ispahani 1989, 148–151). Qandahar, also along the eastern frontiers, frequently changing status between the Safavids and the Mughals while governed by a local elite (i.e., Riazul Islam 1957, 13–19), or the tribal rulers of Khuzistan and Luristan are other examples of tributary states mediating transregional traffic in sometimes difficult geoclimatic regions.

Safavid rule has been portrayed as a coherent dynastic entity, both in time and space, with a clearly definable beginning (1501) and end (1722–1736). In this trajectory, 1501 functions as a specific signpost, describing a religio-cultural and political entity in a distinctly circumscribed territory. However, when thinking in terms of wider Asia (rather than an Ottoman-Safavid-Mughal-system or a "premodern Middle East"), the working of Safavid centralism, its administrative system, its creation of borders, and the operating of its lines of communication ought to be reconsidered. Taking as base a coherent, centralist, and imperial state that moreover functioned supposedly as a predecessor to the modern nation-state, the territorial and political delineations of Safavid Iran have been considered along explicit boundaries. Nonetheless, the western frontiers were under continuous dispute with the Ottomans, and areas like Qandahar were claimed and intermittently ruled by the Mughals. Although some geotopographical environments, with extreme climatic conditions, seem to be rigid and highly impermeable, mobile groups have surmounted even stark geographic barriers, as in Khuzistan and along the Zagros Mountains or parts of what geographically is known as Baluchistan. Thus border areas of *Iran-zamin* in the early 1500s marked more fluid transitions in geographical, dynastic, socio-political, and cultural terms.

Populations that inhabited transitional territories or lands on both sides of the border often either mediated, or in appointed offices, influenced communication, movement, and access along established trade routes. Numerous regions were administered as vassal states through local governors (Röhrborn 1966, 73–94). Such territories were often difficult to access, frequently differed in terms of language, culture, or religion, and occasionally functioned as buffer states. Khuzistan, for example, was partially controlled by the Arab Musha'sha' tribe, the Lurs, or the Kurds, who moved between both Ottoman and Safavid sides and were used by both powers as buffer zones. Many of these tributary states were later absorbed with more stringency into Safavid sovereignty, thereby losing a more flexible or quasi-autonomous status. The local rulers of Khuzistan maintained external loyalty to the Safavids after annexation by Ismail I with Baghdad in 1508/9 [914], administered their own administration as governors *(valīs)*, and paid taxes to the Safavid center, but they maintained a strong autonomous status, even during the phase of high central control under Abbas I (Matthee 2003b, 265; Kasravi [1330] 1951, 47–69).[32] Conversely, Bitlis at the Ottoman border as well as eastern Sistan defected again from Safavid control. Gurjistan (Georgia) is another example of negotiation with local rulers. When the Ottomans challenged Safavid control, it could only be held by Tahmasp I when the Georgian king came to his court, professed to Islam, and was then installed as governor (Roemer 2003, 287–288). The situation was similar along the Persian Gulf. Since 1602, when Portugal was expelled by Abbas I, Bahrain, for example, was ruled indirectly through tribal clans like the Huwala clan or by the urban-based Shaykh of Bushire (Cole 1987, 182–187). The manipulation and displacement of whole groups of populations was an additional method of influencing and negotiating peripheral as well as internal loyalties. It was this dynamic, rather than a static or unilateral hegemony, which, particularly in the early 1500s, shaped accessibility and transit through Central and East Asia as well as the Persian Gulf. Examining access and exchange with regions like Mawar al-nahr (Mawarannahr) and eastwards, while also understanding trans-Asian frontiers as permeable and negotiable, gets beyond the peculiar notion of Safavid Iran as "wedged in" between the imperial states of the Ottomans and Mughals.

Under these considerations, wider Iran in 1501, through historical memory, cultural traditions, and language, appears as a multiregional part of the circuit of central and inner Asia. Interpreting Tabriz in 1501 in relation to East Asia, in a sense, reflects a view of Asia from the outside in. At the same time, when the political idea of Iran was summarized by the establishment of a more clearly defined Safavid imperial state, wider Iran was located exactly in the center of the southern band of Eurasia, reaching from the Portuguese Atlantic to the coast of Fujian. It is this centrality that has constructed the centripetal position of these multiple regions and always given Iran (in its widest definition) a crucial role in geopolitics. In this position, Iran has invariably been an intermediary and actor between Europe and Asia, a role which it attempted to occupy with its first diplomatic contacts in the late 1500s and which it still plays successfully today. The weight which Iran's center gave to western or eastern connections respectively was (and still is) largely guided by pragmatic expediency about wider geopolitical and economic realities. Following close relations with China and India under the tenure of Ahmadinejad, new president Rouhani's latest turn to revive relations with Europe and the United States may be interpreted as the most recent example of utilizing this position between East and West.

Notes

1. Dates in brackets refer to the date according to the Islamic lunar calendar *(hijrī qamarī).*

2. A deliberately vague periphrasis, referring to prenational Iran, also implying cultural and political connections to the neighboring regions. One of the early attempts to come up with the term "Persianate" (world, culture, etc.) was Marshall Hodgson's use in a 1970 article. For various reasons, the concept gained trendy currency in recent years. While the scholarly and ideological-popular notions attached to this term as well as its fuzziness could support the general argument about Safavid boundaries as processes and diachronic transitions proposed here, this discussion's actual utilization of the term would remain largely rhetorical, rather than adding substance or proof to the argument. While the term carries great possibilities to transcend national-dynastic limits, and while there are historical reasons for the term and the principles it involves, it also carries ideological implications. "Persianate" expands the concept of Iran, but does not explain trans-Asian or intra-Asian links, not even if we cite Persian as the lingua franca in use from Iraq to Xinjiang. A broader, more inclusive term, "Persianate," can make an effective replacement of dynastic or national frameworks, but is not necessarily explanatory or useful in understanding preconceptions of twentieth-century national historiography. For one essay on the spread of Persian, see Fragner 1999.

3. Strangely, this was pointed up to me by a Tehrani, who by all means supports the FC-Bayern.

4. For details, see Woods 1976, 175, 181. He argues that there were attempts at peace negotiations before the battle, but Mirza Alvand, his relative, refused to accept Ismail's Alid credo and consequent prerogatives (Qumi [1383] 2004–2005, 1: 69).

5. Nephew and son-in-law of the prophet Muhammad; as such the fourth caliph and first Shiʿi imam, considered by the Shiʿis as Muhammad's only legitimate spiritual and political successor.

6. Rendered as "fief" by Minorsky, including areas of Azarbayjan, Gilan, Shirvan, Darband and parts of Asia Minor. Sadiq Isfahani notes it reached from "Hamadan to the extreme borders of Rum" (1832, 16).

7. Minorsky here transliterated *"beg (bag-igit),"* which can also be rendered as "prince" or "an outstanding leader" (1942, 1021, 1040, 1051). To eastern Turkic (Chaghatai) influences as mere literary tradition see (idem, 1010, 1012).

8. For early Italian visitors to Ismail's court, see Aubin 1995.

9. I.e., the battle against Sultan Murad Aq Qoyunlu near Hamadan, 1503; against Husayn Kiya and Muhammad Karra, 1504–05; taking Diyarbakr in 1507 [913]; annexing Iraq later the same year and Khuzistan the following year.

10. Timur took Herat in 1380, replacing the regional Kart rulers a few years later. It achieved its greatest cultural prosperity and influence under Sultan Husayn Bayqara 1469–1506. It changed hands between the Safavids and the Uzbeks; despite its crucial strategic importance, the Safavids' hold over the city remained tenuous, until they eventually lost it through the revolt by the Afghan Abdali tribe in 1716. From then, western Iran never really regained stable hold over Herat, which leads to the question to what extent the Safavids really had managed a long-term fusion of western and eastern Iran.

11. Selim withdrew to Amasya, taking Diyarbakr and northern Kurdistan from there.

12. The suggestion of the relevance of Timurid and Aq Qoyunlu legacies to the Safavids is certainly not new, yet further research into the precise continuities in the early 1500s may bear interesting results on wider interpretations of Iranian history.

13. The notion of the Safavids as the beginning of a nation connects to the teleology of a *heilsgeschichte,* which is one reason why Safavid "greatness" has been so compelling, both in the ideological context and narrative of the Pahlavis as well as the Islamic Republic, the former stressing the monarchical, the latter the religious achievements. W. Hinz's "Iran's rise to a nation-state," while really covering the fifteenth-century history of Uzun Hasan and the early Safavid Shaykhs to 1499, aimed to justify the treatment of this particular period, but also reflected twentieth-century projections of this idea in a peculiar twist. He equated the "ingenious" leader Reza Shah Pahlavi (1925–1941) to Ismail I as founder of the empire with maternal Aryan roots. The pre-Ismail phase of the fifteenth century thus prepared the way for the national renewal of Iran and "Aryan Persiandom," in contrast to the "alien rule" over Iran by previous Turkic rulers. Here Ismail changes from the renewer of Islam to the renewer, or at least facilitator, of the pre-Islamic empire (Hinz 1936, 7, 74, 125).

14. E.g., Y. Huseyni-Khatunabadi (see Melville and Quinn 2012, 257; also 224–6, or Amīnī 2000).

15. E.g., Khvāndamīr [1370] 1991, 3–64; Turkman [1334] 1956, vol 2. In fact, in most Safavid chronicles, the taking of Tabriz makes a rather brief episode in a presumably

predestined trajectory of Ismail's escape from prison in Fars, the leaving of Lahijan, to the crossing of the river Kur, the battle against Shirvan Shah, the taking of the forts of Baku and Gulistan, which all preceded Tabriz and continued with his further conquests until the 1514 defeat at Chaldiran (i.e., Qumī [1383] 2004–2005, 1: 10–70; also Wood 2004, 89). Most accounts place these also clearly in the path that begins with his father's and grandfather's attempts to gain temporal and spiritual power. The only one who gives a detailed eulogizing account of the battle and the capture of Tabriz is Khvāndamīr ([1370] 1991, 63–67; Mazzaoui 1972, 71–82; also Amīnī 2000, 163–184). On cycles of time in the Safavid period see Babayan 2002, 3–39.

16. The Uzbeks followed the same vision of recreating the empire of Timur Lang (Roemer 2003, 282).

17. Interestingly, Khvāndamīr concludes his long history of the Mongols, Timurids, and Uzbeks with Ismail's life and career. Quinn and Melville have stressed the continuities of Timurid historiographical traditions in those of the Safavids (Melville and Quinn 2012, 209, 213, 225; see also Moin 2012, 23–55).

18. It is generally assumed that the penname is to mean "sinner." Sümer (1992, 56 n.112), points out that Ismail adopted this penname paying respect to Herati poet and friend of Sultan H. Bayqara, ʿAlī Shīr Navāʾī, acclaimed as most outstanding poet of Chaghatay Turkish. Yet this still does not explain why Ismail used sinner. [Thanks to Prof. Chr. Neumann for this reference].

19. "Chin" and "Khita" are Persian names for "China."

20. This kind of metaphorical use of China (or *chīn*) is not Ismail's original invention, but follows a long tradition in medieval and later Persian (and probably Turkic) literature. There possibly also resonates an allusion to Sadi's "Khatʾai Turk" and Hafiz's famous ghazal about the "Shirazi Turk" (Ingenito 2014, 97). *Chīn* could refer to eastern Turkestan as well as China, the latter also called *Māchīn* or *Khitaī*.

Muhammad Sadiq-Isfahani (1832, 22–25, 45, 92), writing in the early seventeenth century, probably based in India, described China, following older traditions, as a great country in the East, "named after Chín, the son of Japhet," who was the son of Noah. The capital of Māchīn was Tanktāsh, and Khaṭāʾī was an acclaimed region in the East reaching to about Transoxania *(mawar al-nahr)* of which the capital was Khánbáligh (today's Beijing). Both regions he considered in the first and second climes. He also gave distances there via Samarkand, Kashgar, and Khotan, as well as longitudes and latitudes.

21. He also brought 300 Chinese potters to Iran to improve the local production of Chinese-style ceramics. On the other side, these wares became a major economic factor during the late Ming period in the seventeenth century (i.e., Pope 1956, 19; Newman 2006, 69).

22. Examples could be Subrahmanyam 2001, or Murata 1999, discussing Sufi texts in China, finding that almost all of them were Persian. See also Moin 2012; Green 2012.

23. While under Uzbek rule at that time, Bukhara and Samarkand were still major centers for trade to India and Indian merchants in the seventeenth and eighteenth centuries.

24. For one of the most important routes to the Persian Gulf see Floor 1999, 67–94; also Harrison 1942, 113–129.

25. Alam, for example, has stressed the competitiveness of land and sea routes in the commercial system in Central Asia (1994, 215) and Frank stressed that the Indian Ocean maritime and continental trade were not asymmetric but moved parallel (1998, 82, 88).

26. There are numerous allusions as well as explicit statements to the notion of the Safavids preparing a national base (i.e., Mazzaoui 2003:6). There is a strong current of this also in German histories on the Safavid period.

27. There seems to be a continuity of this system until the nineteenth century, which only changed with European quests for indisputable, legally binding demarcations since the late 1900s.

28. See Minorsky 1980, 161–62; Alai 2005, 51. Most of the available maps on Safavid Iran, more or less contemporary, were produced in Europe, the earliest ones still based on Ptolemaic maps published and printed in Venice, Cologne and Amsterdam (Alai 2005, 1–119).

29. Other terms since the Timurids were *Moluk-i Iran* (rulers of Iran), *Shahriyar-i Diyar-i 'Ajam* (kings of the land of 'Ajam), *Sipahsalar-e Iran* (generalissimo of Iran), *Ahwal-i Iran* (conditions of Iran), as well as *Iran and Turan.*

30. Iraq consisted of two geographical regions, Iraq-i 'Ajam and Iraq-i 'Arab. For a vaguely visual approximation of this pattern see the reprint of a 1266 world map by Kashghari in Forêt and Kaplony 2008, figs. 7.1 and 7.2). Many of these designations follow the geographies of the early Arab geographers.

31. I.e., see maps of the Safavid state in Dale 2010, 63, 187. A much better sense of the situation is reflected by a map of the area from Makran to Tashkent in Alam 1994, 221.

32. The conversion of privately owned lands into crown lands directly controlled by the court was one measure to increase the control of the ruling center.

References

Adelson, Roger. 1995. *London and the Invention of the Middle East: Money, Power, and War, 1902–1922.* New Haven, CT: Yale University Press.

Alai, Cyrus. 2005. *General Maps of Persia, 1477–1925.* Leiden: Brill.

Alam, Muzaffar. 1994. "Trade, State Policy and Regional Change: Aspects of Mughal-Uzbek Commercial Relations, c. 1550–1750." *Journal of the Economic and Social History of the Orient* 37 (3): 202–227.

———, ed. 2000. *The Making of Indo-Persian Culture.* Delhi: Manohar Press.

Amīnī, Ibrāhīm ibn Mīrak Jālāl al-Dīn. 2000. *Futūṭāt-i shāhī: tārīkh-i Ṣafavī az āghāz tā sāl-i 920 h.q.* Ed. Muḥammad Riżā Naṣīrī. Tihrān: Silsila-i Intishārāt-i Anjuman-i Āsār va Mafākhir-i Farhangī.

Aubin, J. 1995. "Chronique persanes et relations italiennes: notes sur les sources narratives du regne de Šâh Esmâ'il Ier," *Studia Iranica,* 24: 247–259.

Babayan, Kathryn. 1994. "The Safavid Synthesis: From Quizilbash Islam to Imamite Shi'ism," *Iranian Studies,* 27(1–4): 136–161.

———. 2002. *Mystics, Monarchs, and Messiahs, Cultural Landscapes of Early Modern Iran.* Cambridge, MA: Harvard University Press.

Bāfqī, Muḥammad Mufīd ibn Maḥmūd. 1989–1991. *Mukhtaṣar-i Mufīd. Kitāb-i musamma bih Mukhtaṣar-i Mufīd.* Ed. Muḥammad Mufīd Mustawfī Yazdī. Wiesbaden:. L. Reichert.

Barendse, R. J. 2000. "Trade and State in the Arabian Seas: A Survey from the Fifteenth to the Eighteenth Century." *Journal of World History* 11(2): 173–225.

Bashir, Shahzad. 2006. "Shah Isma'il and the Qizilbash. Cannibalism in the Religious History of Early Safavid Iran." *History of Religions* 45(3): 234–256.

Beveridge, A. S. 1970. *Babur-Nama.* New Delhi: Oriental Books Corporation.

Birdoğan, Nejat. 1991. *Alevilerin Büyük Hükümdarı šah Ismail Hatai.* Istanbul: Can Yayınları.

Boyle, J. A. 1974. "Some Thoughts on the Sources for the Il-Khanid Period of Persian History." *Iran: Journal of the British Institute of Persian Studies* 12: 185–188.

Burton, Audrey. 1997. "Descendants et successeurs de Timour: la rivalité territoriale entre les régimes ouzbek, safavide et moghol." in Maria Szuppe, ed. *L'héritage timouride: Iran-Asie central-India, quinzième/dix-huitième siècles,* 23–39. Tachkent: IFEAC.

Chaudhuri, K. N. 1990. *Asia before Europe: Economy and Civilisation of the Indian Ocean from the Rise of Islam to 1750.* Cambridge: Cambridge University Press.

Cole, Juan R. I. 1987. "Rival Empires of Trade and Imami Shi'ism in Eastern Arabia, 1300–1800." *International Journal of Middle East Studies* 19(2): 177–203.

Dale, Stephen. 2009. "The Later Timurids c. 1450–1526." In *The Cambridge History of Inner Asia: The Chinggisid* Age, ed. Nicola Di Cosmo, Allen J. Frank, and Peter B. Golden, 199–217. New York: Cambridge University Press.

———. 2010. *The Muslim Empires of the Ottomans, Safavids, and Mughals.* Cambridge: Cambridge University Press.

Floor, Willem. 1999. "The Bandar Abbas Isfahan Route in the Late Safavid Era (1617–1717)." *Iran. Journal of the British Institute of Persian Studies* 37: 67–94.

Forêt, Ph., and A. Kaplony, eds. 2008. *The Journeys of Maps and Images on the Silk Road.* Leiden: Brill.

Fragner, B. 1999. *Die "Persophonie." Regionalität, Identität und Sprachkontakt in der Geschichte Asiens.* Berlin: ANOR.

Frank, Andre Gunder. 1998. *ReOrient: Global Economy in the Asian Age*. Berkeley: University of California Press.

Glassen, Erika. 1970. *Die frühen Safawiden nach Qazi Ahmad Qumi*. Freiburg: Klaus Schwarz Verlag.

———. 1972. "Schah Isma'il und die Theologen seiner Zeit." *Der Islam* 48: 254–268.

Green, N. 2012. "Empires, Frontiers and Renewers, 1400–1800." In *Sufism: A Global History*. Malden, MA: Wiley-Blackwell.

Hansen, Valerie. 2012. *The Silk Road: A New History*. Oxford: Oxford University Press.

Harrison, J. V. 1942. "Some Routes in Southern Iran." *The Geographical Journal* 99 (3): 113–129.

Hillenbrand, Robert. 2003. "The Sarcophagus of Shah Isma'il at Ardabil." In *Society and Culture in the Early Modern Middle East: Studies on Iran in the Safavid Period*, ed. Andrew Newman, 165–190. Leiden: Brill.

Hinz, Walter. 1936. *Irans Aufstieg zum Nationalstaat im fünfzehnten Jahrhundert*. Berlin: de Gruyter.

Hodgson, Marshall, G. S. 1970. "The Role of Islam in World History." In *International Journal of Middle East Studies*, 1(2): 99–123.

Ḥusaynī Astarābādī, Ḥusayn ibn Murtażā. [1366] 1987. *Tārīkh-i sulṭānī: az Shaykh Ṣafī tā Shāh Ṣafī*. Ed. Iḥsān Ishrāqī. Tihrān: ʿIlmī.

Ingenito, Domenico. 2014. "'Tabrizis in Shiraz are worth less than a dog:' Saʿdī and Humām, a lyrical encounter", 77–127. In *Politics, Patronage and the Transmission of Knowledge in 13th–15th Century Tabriz*, ed. J. Pfeiffer Leiden: Brill.

Ispahani, Mahnaz Z. 1989. *Roads and Rivals: The Political Use of Access in the Borderlands of Asia*. Ithaca, NY: Cornell University Press.

Jābirī Anṣārī, Muḥammad Ḥasan. [1321] 1942. *Tārīkh-i Iṣfahān va Ray va hamah-i jahān*. N. pl.: Ḥusayn Imādzadah.

Kasravī, Aḥmad. [1330] 1951. *Tārīkh-i pānṣad sālah-yi Khūzistān. Intishārāt-i Bungāh-i Maṭbūʿātī-yi Gūtenbirg*

Kauz, Ralph. 2005. *Politik und Handel zwischen Ming und Timuriden; China, Iran und Zentralasien im Spätmittelalter*. Wiesbaden: Reichert Verlag.

Keçik, Mehmet Şefik. 1976. *Briefe und Urkunden aus der Kanzlei Uzun Ḥasans*. Freiburg: Klaus Schwarz Verlag.

Khiṭāʾī, ʿAlī Akbar. [1372] 1993. *Khiṭāynāmah: sharḥ-i mushāhadāt-i Sayyid ʿAlī Akbar Khaṭāʾī, muʿāṣir-i Shāh Ismāʿīl Ṣafavī dar Chīn*. Ed. Īraj Afshār. Tihrān: Markaz-i Asnād-i Farhangī-i Āsiyā.

Khunjī, Fażl Allāh ibn Rūzbahān. 1992. Tārīkh-i ʿĀlam ārā-yi Amīnī. Tārīkh-i ʿĀlam-ārā-yi Amīnī. Persian text edited by John E. Woods with the abridged translation by Vladimir Minorsky, *Persia in A.D. 1478–1490* (Turkmenica 12); revised and augmented by John E. Woods. London: Royal Asiatic Society.

———. 1382 [2003]. *Tārīkh-i 'Ālam ārā-yi Amīnī. Sharḥ-i ḥukmrānī-i salaṭīn-i Āq Qūyūnlū wa ẓuhūr-i Ṣafavīyān.* Ed. Muḥammad Akbar 'Ashīq. Tihrān: Markaz-i Nashr-i Mīrās-i Maktūb.

Khvāndamīr, Amīr Maḥmūd. [1370] 1991. *Tārīkh-i Shāh Ismā'īl va Shāh Ṭahmāsb-i Ṣafavī: Ẕayl-i Tārīkh-i Ḥabīb al-siyar.* Ed. Muḥammad 'Alī Jarrāḥī. Tihrān: Nashr-i Gustarah.

Levi, Scott. 1999. "The Indian Merchant Diaspora in Early Modern Central Asia and Iran." *Iranian Studies*, 32(4): 483–512.

Lewis, M., and K. Wigen. 1997. *The Myth of Continents: A Critique of Metageography.* Berkeley: University of California Press.

Lin, Yih-Min. 1983. "A Comparative and Critical Study of Ali Akbar's Khitay-nama with Reference to Chinese Sources." *Central Asiatic Journal* 27: 58–78.

Lisān al-Mulk Malik Sipihr. [1323] [1905]. *Tārīkh va jughrāfiyā-yi Dār al-salṭanah-yi Tabrīz.* Tā'līf Shāhzādah Nādir Mīrzā. Tihran:. Kitābkhānah-yi Iqbāl.

Liu, Yingsheng. 2010. "A Lingua Franca along the Silk Road." In *Aspects of the Maritime Silk Road: From the Persian Gulf to the East China Sea,* ed. Ralph Kauz, 87–96. Wiesbaden: Harrassowitz

Liu, Yingsheng, and Peter Jackson,. 1992. "Chinese Iranian Relations–Mongol Period." In *Encyclopaedia Iranica,* ed. Ehsan Yarsharter, 5: 434–436. Costa Mesa, CA: Mazda Publishers.

Mancke, Elizabeth. 1999. "Early Modern Expansion and the Politicization of Oceanic Space." *Geographical Review*, 89(2): 225–236.

Manz, Beatrice F. 1989. *The Rise and Rule of Tamerlane.* Cambridge: Cambridge University Press.

———. 1994. *Central Asia in Historical Perspective.* Boulder, San Francisco, Oxford, CO: Westview Press.

———. 2007. *Power, Politics, and Religion in Timurid Iran.* Cambridge: Cambridge University Press.

Matthee, R. 2003a. "Anti-Ottoman Concerns and Caucasian Interest: Diplomatic Relations between Iran and Russia 1587–1639." In *Safavid Iran and Her Neighbors,* ed. Michel Mazzaoui, 101–128. Salt Lake City: University of Utah Press.

———. 2003b. "The Safavid Mint of Huyayzeh: The Numismatic Evidence." In *Society and Culture in the Early Modern Middle East: Studies on Iran in the Safavid Period,* ed. Andrew Newman, 265–291. Leiden: Brill.

Mazzaoui, Michel M. 1972. *The Origins of the Safawids; Shi'ism, Sufism, and the Ghulat.* Wiesbaden: F. Steiner.

———, ed. 2003. *Safavid Iran and Her Neighbors.* Salt Lake City: University of Utah Press.

McChesney, R. D. . 2003. "The Central Asian Hajj-Pilgrimage in the Time of the Early Modern Empires." In *Safavid Iran and Her Neighbors,* ed. Michel Mazzaoui, 129–156. Salt Lake City: University of Utah Press.

———. 2009. "The Chinggisid Restoration in Central Asia: 1500–1785." In *The Cambridge History of Inner Asia: The Chinggisid Age*, ed. Nicola Di Cosmo, Allen J. Frank, and Peter B. Golden, 277–302. Cambridge: Cambridge University Press.

Melville, Charles. 2006. "The Keshig in Iran: The Survival of the Royal Mongol Household." In *Beyond the Legacy of Genghis Khan,* ed. Linda Komaroff, 135–164. Leiden: Brill.

———. 2008. "Between Tabriz and Herat." In *Iran und iranisch geprägte Kulturen,* Studien zum 65. Geburtstag von Bert G Fragner, ed. Markus Ritter, Ralph Kauz, Birgitt Hofmann. Wiesbaden: Reichert Verlag.

Melville, Charles, and Sholeh Quinn. 2012. "Safavid Historiography." In *Persian Historiography*, ed. Charles Melvielle, 209–257. Series: History of Persian Literature, vol. 10. London: I. B. Tauris.

Minorsky, V. 1942. "The Poetry of Shah Isma'il." *BSOAS* 10(4): 1006a–1053a.

———, ed. 1980. *Tazkirat al-Muluk, A Manual of Safavid Administration.* Cambridge: Cambridge University Press. Originally published 1943.

Minorsky, V., and Bosworth, C. E. 1998. "Tabriz." In *Encyclopaedia of Islam,* First edition (1913–1936), 7, 583–593: Leiden: Brill.

Moin, A. Afzar. 2012. *The Millennial Sovereign, Sacred Kingship, and Sainthood in Islam.* New York: Columbia University Press.

Murata, Sachiko. 1999. In *The Heritage of Sufism: The Safavid & Mughal Period.* Vol. 3, *Late Classical Persianate Sufism (1501–1750),* ed. L. Lewisohn and D. Morgan, 343–352. Oxford: Oneworld Publications.

Navā'ī, 'Abd al-Ḥusayn, ed. [1347] 1969. *Shāh Ismā'īl Ṣafavī: asnād va mukātabāt-i tārīkhī hamrāh bā yād'dāshthā-yi tafṣīlī.* Tihran: Bunyād-i Farhang-i Īrān.

———. [1536] 1977. *Asnād va mokātabāt-i tārikhi-yi Irān az Tīmūr tā Shāh Ismā'īl.* Ṭihrān: BungāhTarjumih va Nashr-i Kitāb.

Newman, Andrew. 2006. *Safavid Iran: Rebirth of a Persian Empire.* London, New York: I. B. Tauris.

Pfeiffer, Judith. 2014. *Politics, Patronage and the Transmission of Knowledge in 13th–15th Century Tabriz.* Leiden: Brill.

Pope, John A. 1956. *Chinese Porcelains from the Ardebil Shrine.* Washington, DC: Smithsonian Institution, Freer Gallery of Art.

Quinn, Sholeh A. 1996. "The Dreams of Shaykh Safi al-Din and Safavid Historical Writing." *Iranian Studies* 29(1–2): 127–147.

———. 2000. *Historical Writing during the Reign of Shah 'Abbas: Ideology, Imitation, and Legitimacy in Safavid Chronicles.* Salt Lake City: University of Utah Press.

———. 2003. "The Timurid Historiographical Legacy: A Comparative Study of Persianate Historical Writing." In *Society and Culture in the Early Modern Middle East: Studies on Iran in the Safavid Period,* ed. Andrew Newman, 19–31, Leiden: Brill.

Qumī, Aḥmad Ibrāhīmī Ḥusaynī. [1383] 2004–2005. *Khulaṣat al-tavārīkh.* Ed. Iḥsān Ishrāqī. Tihrān: Dānishgāh-i Tihrān. Originally published 1980–1984.

Riazul Islam. 1957. *Indo-Persian Relations: A Study of the Political and Diplomatic Relations between the Mughul Empire and Iran.* Tehran: Iranian Culture Foundation.

Roemer, Hans Robert. 1986. "Chapters 1–5." In *Cambridge History of Iran.* Vol. 6, *The Timurid and Safavid Periods,* ed. P. Jackson and L. Lockhart, 1–350. Cambridge: Cambridge University Press.

———. 2003. *Persien auf dem Weg in die Neuzeit: Iranische Geschichte 1350–1750.* Würzburg: Ergon Verlag. Originally published 1989.

Röhrborn, Klaus-Michael. 1966. *Provinzen und Zentralgewalt Persiens im 16. und 17. Jahrhundert,* Berlin: de Gruyter.

Rūmlū, Ḥasan. 1931–34. *Aḥsan al-tawārīkh. A chronicle of the early Ṣafawīs, being the Aḥsanu't-tawārīkh of Ḥasan-i-Rūmlū.* Persian & English. Vol. 1, 1931; vol. 2, 1934. Ed. and trans. C. N. Seddon. Baroda: Oriental Institute.

Ṣādiq Iṣfahānī, Muḥammad Ṣādiq ibn Muḥammad Saliḥ. 1832. *The Geographical Works of Sadik Isfahani.* Translated by J. C. from Ouseley coll. London: Oriental Translation Fund, (J. Murray).

Savory, Roger. 1960. "The Principal Offices of the Safavid State during the Reign of Isma'il I (907–30/1501–24)." *BSOAS* 23(1): 91–105.

Schottenhammer, A., R.; Ptak, R., et al. 2009. *Pferde in Asien. Geschichte, Handel und Kultur.* Wien: Verlag der ÖAW.

Sohrweide, H. 1956. "Der Sieg der Safawiden und seine Rückwirkungen auf die Shiiten Anatoliens im 16. Jahrhundert." *Der Islam* 41: 95–223.

Subrahmanyam, Sanjay. 1992. "Iranians Abroad: Intra-Asian Elite Migration and Early Modern State Formation." *The Journal of Asian Studies* 51(2): 340–363.

———. 2001. "Du Tage au Gange au XVIe siècle: une conjoncture millénariste à l'échelle eurasiatique." *Annales. Histoire, Sciences Sociales,* 56(1): 51–84.

Sümer, F. 1992. *Safevî Devletinin Kuruluşu ve Gelişmesinde Anadolu Türklerinin Rolü: Şah İsmail ile Halefleri ve Anadolu Türkleri.* Ankara: Türk Tarih Kurumu.

Stanley, Tim. 2010. "Patterns of Exchange in the Decorative Arts between China and South-west Asia." In *Aspects of the Maritime Silk Road: From the Persian Gulf to the East China Sea,* ed. Ralph Kauz, 107–116. Wiesbaden: Harrassowitz.

Szuppe, Maria. 1992. *Entre Timourides, Uzbeks et Safavides: questions d'histoire politique et sociale de Hérat dans la première moitié du XVIe siècle.* Paris: Association pour l'avancement des études iraniennes.

———. 1997. "L'évolution de l'image de Timour et des Timourides dans l'historiographie safavide du seizième au dix-septième siècle." In Idem. *L'héritage timouride. Iran-Asie central-India, quinzième / dix-huitième siècles,* 313–331. Tachkent: IFEAC.

Thomas, T. Allsen. 2009. "Mongols as Vectors for Cultural Transmission." In *The Cambridge History of Inner Asia: The Chinggisid* Age, ed. Nicola Di Cosmo, Allen J. Frank, and Peter B. Golden, 135–156. New York: Cambridge University Press.

Turkmān, Iskandar Beyg Munshī. [1334] 1956. *Tārīkh-i ʿālamʾārā-yi ʿAbbāsī.* Tihrān: Maʾassasah-i Maṭbāʿāt-i Amīr Kabīr.

Wood, Barry D. 2004. "The Tarikh-i Jahanara in the Chester Bratty Library: An Illustrated Manuscript of the 'Anonymous Histories of Shah Ismaʾil.'" *Iranian Studies* 37(1): 89–107.

Woods, J. E. 1976. *The Aqqoyunlu, Clan, Confederation, Empire: A Study in Fifteenth/Ninth Century Turko-Iranian Politics.* Minneapolis, MN: Bibliotheca Islamica.

2

1555

Four Imperial Revivals

VICTOR LIEBERMAN

After advancing up the Irrawaddy Valley at the end of the rains in 1554, the Burmese ruler Bayin-naung surrounded Ava, capital of Upper Burma, by land and water. Its dispirited defenders offering only feeble resistance, in January 1555 the city fell to artillery and ground assaults. Thus, for the first time since the early 1300s—when warring polities had supplanted Burma's first unified empire, that of Pagan—the entire Irrawaddy basin came under a single sovereignty. Thereafter, apart from two brief interregna, Lower and Upper Burma would remain united until the British arrived (U Kala 1932, 280–286; *Nidana* 1912, 155–156; Lieberman 2003, ch. 2).

In 1555, Ivan IV began work on St. Basil's Cathedral in Moscow to commemorate his victory three years earlier over the Tatar khanate of Kazan on the middle Volga. In 1556, Ivan completed his conquest of the Volga basin by annexing the khanate of Astrakhan on the Caspian shore. Ever since Kiev, Russia's first historic polity, fell to the Mongols in 1240, the Russian plain had been fragmented and subject to predation from the eastern steppe. But with these victories, Muscovy reversed the historic relation between steppe and sown and began to transform itself from a regional kingdom into the world's largest multiethnic empire (Pavlov and Perrie 2003, 41–53; Martin, 1995, chs. 5–11).

Returning from exile, the Mughal warrior Humayun entered the plains of North India in 1554 determined to revive the imperial project of his father. Humayun seized Delhi, capital of Hindustan, and by the middle of the next year had established his authority across most of North India. Thus was founded, or refounded, the Mughal empire, whose armies continued to add territory to 1690, and whose legacy the British would invoke. The late fourteenth-century unravelling of North India's first pan-regional Muslim polity, the Delhi Sultanate, had initiated an era of interregional warfare. But now Humayun's victories—like those of Bayin-naung and Ivan IV in these very years—dramatically reversed that devolutionary trend (Richards 1993, 11–12; Asher and Talbot 2006, 114–123, 290; Jackson 1999, 272–277, 296–325).

In the Japanese isles, 1555 saw no seminal event. Five years later, however, Oda Nobunaga, launching a surprise attack in pouring rain against a rival warlord, seized the strategic district of Owari in the chief island of Honshu. By his death twenty-two years later, Nobunaga was well on his way to uniting all of Japan. That task was completed by his followers Toyotomi Hideyoshi, who pacified the islands by 1592, and Tokugawa Ieyasu, who in 1603 founded the shogunate that would endure to 1868. Like Burma, Russia, and North India, Japan had known a brilliant unification in the late first or early second millennium that yielded to persistent post-1350 polycentrism. Nobunaga's victories therefore fit a larger pattern of sixteenth-century recentralization (Asao 1991; Totman 1993, ch. 4).

These synchronized revivals in regions with vastly different politico-cultural systems that had little or no contact with one another raise questions as difficult as they are basic: why did all four realms collapse and remain fragmented in the centuries before 1555? Why did all recoalesce in the sixteenth century? What elements did these reunified polities inherit from earlier states? Why did each restored polity exceed any previous formation in territory and solidity? And why did integration continue to gather strength to 1700 and beyond? Here I consider four realms, but as I have sought to show elsewhere, they were emblematic of broader Eurasian patterns (Lieberman 2003; 2009).

Synchronized Growth, Synchronized Disorder, c. 1000–1450/1500

The short answer to the first question is this: all four realms collapsed between 1240 and 1467 in part because economic growth aggravated longstanding institutional weaknesses. But this formula poses new puzzles: why was economic expansion broadly coordinated in different parts of Eurasia? Why did growth, which had nurtured unifications in the late first and early second millennia, suddenly become politically corrosive in the thirteenth and fourteenth centuries? If growth was indeed coordinated, why did local states falter at different times between 1240 and 1467?

In the tenth or eleventh century, the Irrawaddy basin, the Russian plains, and much of South Asia entered a phase of marked agrarian and commercial vigor. In Burma, for example, Buddhist monasteries and lay elites promoted extensive irrigation and reclamation projects. At first these were concentrated near the chief city-state of Pagan, but in the mid-1100s, as population began to exceed carrying capacity, Burmese turned to frontier areas west of the Irrawaddy. Supported by new agrarian and commercial wealth, in and around Pagan sprouted one of Asia's foremost Buddhist centers, while the once-diminutive city-state expanded to embrace most of the Irrawaddy basin and the south coast. As the region's first extensive polity, Pagan was a "charter state" because it provided a territorial, institutional, and religious charter for later kingdoms (Aung-Thwin 1985; Hudson, Lwin, and Maung 2001; Lieberman 2003, 88–119).

The same may be said of Kiev, whose chronology roughly paralleled Pagan's. In the tenth century, an archipelago of trading outposts arose along the Dnieper route linking the Baltic to Constantinople, with Kiev as the pivot. Between c. 1100 and 1240, trade also expanded with Eastern Europe and the Mideast, while Kievan princes and peasant communities, particularly on the frontiers, extended cereal farming and stock rearing. We thus find a branching network of princely cities, secondary towns, and small rural settlements in the basins of the Dnieper, Dniester, Bug, and Volga, where ruling lineages that derived from Kiev continued to regard that city as the premier seat of a collective family enterprise (Martin 1995, chs. 1–4; Franklin and Shepard 1996; Lieberman 2009, 130–147).

Unlike Pagan and Kiev, the Delhi Sultanate was not the first serious polity in its region, North India having supported major empires since the fourth century BCE. Founded in 1206, the Sultanate also began notably later than Pagan or Kiev. Yet as India's first extensive Muslim empire whose conventions inspired a host of successor polities, Delhi too was a charter state. Moreover, North India benefited from a sustained period of economic vitality no less pronounced than in the Irrawaddy basin and the Russian plain. After c. 900, cultivation advanced rapidly, as did long-distance trade, particularly along trade and migration corridors. In fact, the Delhi Sultans were only the most successful in a series of mobile warrior groups who expanded from the dry zone corridors of Inner Asia and the Deccan to dominate agrarian India, typically locating their capitals, like Delhi, on the agrarian-pastoral interface (Jackson 1999; Wink 2001; Lieberman 2009, 681–686).

These broadly coordinated flowerings reflected, in distinct local combinations, the intertwined effects of the Medieval Climate Anomaly (the MCA) and Eurasian commercial expansion, reinforced possibly by disease domestication.

Set in motion by increased solar radiation, by changes in the heat economy of ocean currents, and perhaps by a reduction in volcanism, the MCA, 900/950–1250/1300, raised northern hemispheric temperatures anywhere from .8 to 2 degrees C. By increasing water vapor in the tropical atmosphere and by magnifying land-sea thermal contrasts, the MCA dramatically enhanced the volume and reach of monsoon rains in both South Asia and mainland Southeast Asia. Such conditions facilitated in Upper Burma the extension of both irrigated and rain-fed agriculture, and in South Asia the extension of cultivation, the breeding of horses in rain-fed pastures, and closer pastoral-agrarian integration (Buckley et al. 2010; Sinha et al. 2010; Lieberman 2011; Cook et al. 2010; Lieberman 2009, 687–691; Lieberman and Buckley 2012). On the Russian plains, the MCA extended the growing season by a precious three to eight weeks and permitted cultivation at more northerly latitudes (Trouet et al. 2009; Mann et al. 2009; Lieberman 2009, 144–146).

In each region, agrarian and demographic growth encouraged population growth, market integration, surplus extraction, and by extension, charter state formation. But insofar as the MCA favored market activity in most of Eurasia, climatic change also promoted, indirectly at least, an increase in multilateral long-distance trade, both overland and by sea. Symptomatic of rising Eurasian mercantile demand, and at the same time stimulating that demand, were wider flows of bullion and bulk goods and new systems of merchant organization, textile production, and navigation (Abu-Lughod 1989; Wade 2009; Kuroda 2009; Stearns 2010, 29–56). Commercial revenues were central to the political economy of Kiev, and played a significant, if ancillary, role at Pagan and Delhi. Commerce, moreover, provided a principal channel for the transmission of those universal religious and high cultural motifs—Buddhist, Orthodox Christian, Muslim—that defined elite charter culture.

Finally and more speculatively, smallpox domestication may have helped to coordinate growth in the Irrawaddy basin and on the north Pontic shore. To follow William McNeill, isolated areas, lacking regular exposure to smallpox and too thinly populated to sustain domestic chains of infection, suffered horrific die-offs among all age cohorts whenever they were exposed. But in the late first and early second millennia in both coastal Southeast Asia and Russia, local population growth and more frequent trade with Eurasian cores where smallpox had long been established may have allowed that malady (and perhaps measles) to become an endemic, economically tolerable disease primarily of children (McNeill 1976; Fenner et al. 1988).[1]

If such dynamics helped to generate charter states, in the thirteenth and fourteenth centuries Pagan, Kiev, and the Sultanate all collapsed because, as I suggested, cultural and political vulnerabilities were exacerbated by sustained economic growth. Everywhere the end of the MCA brought tensions to a head.

In each charter realm, capital-centered elites inhabited a literate religious universe substantially divorced from the pretextual, oral culture of the general population. In Burma, for example, various forms of Buddhism and Hinduism enjoyed lavish court patronage but in the villages Buddhist monasteries were rare, literacy in Burmese not to mention Pali was yet less common, while shaman-mediated spirit cults dominated ritual life. Likewise, in Kiev, Orthodox Christianity, which derived from Byzantium and Bulgaria, was an almost exclusively urban, elite phenomenon divorced from the still-pagan countryside (Kaiser 1980). In thirteenth-century North India, the usual elite/mass divisions were reinforced by the Muslim invaders' principled aversion to non-Muslim practices at all social levels. In all three realms, intertwined with horizontal cleavages of this sort were ethnic and linguistic—what might be termed vertical—fissures. Even in the Irrawaddy basin, which was arguably the most well-integrated culturally of the three realms, surprisingly few provincial residents identified with the customs, language, and ethnicity of the imperial center (Lieberman 2003, 114–118; 2009, 174–175, 670–172). Compared to later periods, such features entailed a certain brittleness, for they impeded efforts to harness local energies to imperial projects, to instill normative visions of social order and religious orthodoxy, and to fend off external challenges.

By post-1500 standards, moreover, all three polities were poorly monetized, obtaining much of their revenues as in-kind taxes or labor services and rewarding supporters with land grants that were inherently devolutionary. The Sultanate was least disadvantaged in this regard, but even there, without adequate coinage, the throne was forced to abandon experiments with military salaries (Lieberman 2009, 646–47; Jackson 1999, 303–305). In a peculiar twist to this general problem, in lieu of cash donations Pagan kings sought to acquire religious merit for felicitous reincarnations by making such lavish gifts of tax-free land to the monkhood that by 1300 up to two-thirds of all cultivable acreage had been alienated (Aung-Thwin 1985).

No less critical, Pagan, Kiev, and the Sultanate faced severe problems of territorial overextension. All were what I term "solar polities," wherein a central sun held in unsteady gravitational orbit provincial planets, whose sovereignty often rivaled that of the capital and whose autonomy grew with distance. In 1169 and 1203, outlying princes sacked Kiev, while from the 1280s, Lower Burma's port cities revolted against Pagan. The Delhi Sultanate's ill-considered southern conquests precipitated revolts that in a mere thirteen years, 1334 to 1347, stripped away control over the entire Deccan, the far south, and Bengal (Martin 1995, ch. 4; Lieberman 2003, 121; Asher and Talbot 2006, 41–45).

Economic growth magnified such weaknesses by awarding resources to autonomous actors, especially on the frontier, where reclamation and long-distance trade tended to concentrate. In the twelfth century, the Dnieper trade to Constantinople, Kiev's lifeline, declined vis-à-vis new routes beyond Kiev's direct control to Hungary, Poland, the Baltic, and the Volga. What is more, virtually all agrarian colonization occurred outside the old Kievan core. Between 1064 and 1237, as new masonry buildings multiplied across Russia, the share constructed in the provinces, as opposed to Kiev, rose from 17 to 83 percent (Miller 1990). Likewise, Lower Burma could throw off northern control in large part because it profited more directly than the interior from rising Indian Ocean and Chinese maritime trade (Wade 2009). Ultimately, one could argue, even Pagan's problem of religious lands was a function of economic growth, insofar as by 1200, after more than two centuries of reclamation, Pagan, located in a dry zone, began to run out of fresh irrigable lands. Without that ecological ceiling, continued religious donations would not have threatened the royal fisc, and coastal trade would not have destabilized the state as rapidly as it did.

Consider too external invasions as a spur to charter collapse and the relation of such invasions to economic growth. Everywhere invasions by militarized frontiersmen widened internal fissures. Thus, in India, the 1398 sack of Delhi by the Turko-Mongol warrior Tamerlane eclipsed what remained of Sultanate power.[2] In Russia, not only did the Mongols in 1240 obliterate the enfeebled Kievan federation, but to the mid-1400s, Mongol-Tatar overlordship precluded Russian recentralization (Ostrowski 1998). At Pagan, Mongol attacks from 1287 exposed Upper Burma's weakness and abetted coastal defection. Worse, Tai-Shan warriors migrating from South China and northern Vietnam founded principalities in the hills surrounding Upper Burma, which they raided repeatedly to 1527. Directly by weakening Upper Burma, and indirectly by diverting attention from the coast, Tai-Shans helped forestall reintegration of the basin until the events with which this essay began (Lieberman 2011).

If frontier incursions capitalized on sedentary weaknesses and if they benefited from changes internal to Turko-Mongol and Tai societies, in a wider sense, they also fed on pan-Eurasian economic vitality. As I have argued elsewhere, Eurasian prosperity between c. 1000 and 1300 favored Turko-Mongol and Tai expansion in three ways. First, the MCA climate seems to have been particularly kind to Inner Asian and Tai-Shan birthrates vis-à-vis those of settled agrarian populations. Second, as sedentary societies in China and Southeast Asia widened their commercial and political interaction with frontier peoples, they unwittingly provided the latter with the cultural skills, including literacy, new military technologies, and administrative expertise, necessary to subjugate and rule settled domains. In effect, agrarian societies unwittingly enhanced the power potential of their "barbarian" neighbors. Third, superior mobility and long-distance ties often let Turko-Mongols and Tais profit more directly from burgeoning pan-Eurasian trade than their agrarian counterparts (Lieberman 2003, 122–123, 240–244; 2009, 585–591, 685–691; 2011).

By the same token, after 1346 the Mongol-mediated transmission of the Black Death along steppe caravan routes to the Crimea, whence the disease entered Europe and doubled back into Russia through newly expanded trade circuits, can be seen as a hideously unwelcome, economically ruinous byproduct of commercial expansion characteristic of the thirteenth and fourteenth centuries (Benedictow 2004, 211–215; Langer 1975).

Although the Black Death apparently spared Southeast Asia and India, in the late 1300s and 1400s most of Eurasia suffered bullion shortages, which reflected inter alia the inflation of labor costs that attended the Black Death in key mining areas, technical difficulties in Central European silver mines, and an end to Yuan silver exports. In one region after another, the ensuing "bullion famine" erected new barriers to monetization of the political economy, while impeding private investment and trade (Lieberman 2009, 188, 420, 558, 691–692; Kuroda 2009; Atwell 2002).

But arguably the most potent coordinating agent of charter collapse was the sharp shift from the MCA to the Little Ice Age (the LIA) that began in the late 1200s, intensified in the mid- and late fourteenth century, and continued for most of the fifteenth century. By reducing the volume and reach of monsoon rains and by introducing appreciably less benign climate to Russia and indeed all of northern Europe, the LIA dramatically reversed the agrarian benefits of the MCA. Droughts in mainland Southeast Asia and central India in the mid- and late-fourteenth century were unmatched in duration, and possibly severity, by anything since at least the sixth century CE. In both Russia and monsoon Asia, falling rural production and population helped to produce that reduction in revenue, the ensuing intensification of elite factionalism, and that heightened vulnerability to external domination which together defined the fourteenth and fifteenth centuries (Buckley et al. 2010; Lieberman and Buckley 2012; Lieberman 2011; Sinha et al. 2010; Jackson 1999, 296–325; Trouet 2009; Mann 2009; Lieberman 2009, 189–195, 692; Kremenetski et al. 2004).

In sum, charter collapse was overdetermined. Insofar as MCA-assisted economic growth aggravated longstanding internal weaknesses and contributed, directly or indirectly, to frontier invasions, to the Black Death, and to fourteenth-century cleavages, climate may have been the single most influential mechanism of Eurasian synchronization. But because political and economic dynamics were locally contingent, and because global climatic shifts varied somewhat in their regional effects, political chronologies in Burma, India, and Russia between c. 1240 and 1450 remained broadly, not strictly, aligned.

The main point is that some combination of these factors continued to favor political fragmentation well into the sixteenth century. Pagan split between a rump Upper Burma state at Ava, various Tai-Shan hill principalities, two Middle Burma kingdoms, and a Pegu-centered coastal polity, all of which brutalized and allied with one another with bewildering regularity. Alongside a rump Delhi Sultanate, South Asia saw successor states arise at Jaunpur, Bengal, Malwa, Bahmani, and Vijayanagra. Most Kievan lands fell under either Lithuania or the Mongol-Tatar Kipchak khanate, which in turn devolved into the khanates of Kazan and Astrakhan. Weakened by Lithuanian and Tatar demands, an unforgiving economy, and multiple inheritance patterns, the 13 Kievan domains of 1240 had devolved by 1400 into some 250 petty states, among which Moscow was at best primus inter pares (Lieberman 2009, 192, 213).

How did Japan, to which I referred at the outset, fit this schema? The Japanese islands followed a broadly similar trajectory, but according to a more leisurely rhythm that derived from geographic and climatic insularity.

Aided by unusual warmth from c. 200 to 700 CE (which contrasted with cooling during most of this period in Europe and southern Asia), by iron tools and new rice strains from Korea, and by extensive high culture borrowing from China, Japan between the seventh and ninth centuries developed a literate, Chinese-style Mahayana Buddhist realm. As an institutional and territorial model for subsequent generations, this was a charter polity equivalent to the somewhat later empires of Pagan, Kiev, and the Delhi Sultanate.

Like those entities, Japan's new order, with its capital at Heian (later known as Kyoto), was extraordinarily elitist, literate only at the apex of society, poorly monetized, and territorially uneven. But whereas Pagan, Kiev, and the Delhi Sultanate lasted only 200–300 years, the essential features of the Heian imperial order—including its central institutions and state-temple relations—endured with relatively modest changes for some 600 years, from c. 700 to the late thirteenth century (Farris 2006; Souyri 2001; Adolphson 2000). This extraordinary stability reflected at least three factors: 1) The Heian court effectively forbade claims to provincial sovereignty, which crippled other charter states. 2) After the initial domestication of Chinese culture, the court severely reduced continental contacts. This eliminated both the threat of commercial centrifugalism, such as weakened Pagan and Kiev, and the danger that continental invaders would exploit internal fissures. 3) In part because of unfavorable weather and devastating smallpox epidemics (in turn a function of limited continental exposure), Japanese cultivation, population, and commerce developed very slowly, if at all, for much of the era from 670 to 1250—even as smallpox domestication and the MCA were promoting rapid growth in our first three realms.[3] If such conservatism strained the tax system, on balance it aided Heian because it deprived provincial elites and other autonomous agents of the resources needed to challenge central authority in the manner of Burmese governors or Kievan princes (Farris 2006; Lieberman 2009, 391–398).

Conversely, what finally dissolved the Heian-based order was a resumption of economic growth from the late 1200s. Well before 1280, the eagerness of Heian elites to convert public lands and revenue into private resources had opened a space for provincial warriors, samurai, who, in return for titles and revenue rights, defended the landholdings of their Heian court patrons. As warrior services became ever more critical and as warrior control over local resources grew more secure, leading samurai gradually displaced their social superiors, establishing in 1338 a ruling coalition of military families known as the Ashikaga shogunate. But much as they had sidelined aristocratic courtiers, this new leadership became vulnerable to challenges by yet more humble, locally based warriors. The basic problem for Ashikaga leaders, as for their civilian predecessors, was that they lacked reliable mechanisms to tap provincial wealth once the economy began to grow again. By the fourteenth century, smallpox was being domesticated. To boost tax revenues, local warriors encouraged agrarian innovation and market exchange. Under warrior patronage or on their own initiative, peasants developed more efficient labor routines, crops, and tools. After c. 1400, climate apparently improved. In contrast to our other realms, neither Mongol incursions nor the Black Death checked this revival.[4] The economic dynamism nurtured by these varied factors favored ever-more-ambitious local actors, including corporate villages and militant Buddhist leagues, but most particularly warrior networks in direct control of land and markets. After 1467, when the Ashikaga shogunate finally imploded, Japan dissolved into some 200 feuding domains led by self-made military magnates known as *daimyo* (Farris 2006; Souyri 2001; Totman 2000, chs. 5, 7; Berry 1994).

In other words, Burma, Russia, North India, and Japan all reached the same destination in the fifteenth century, a condition of competitive polycentrism, but according to rather different chronologies. The first three realms grew rapidly for 200 to 300 years, fragmented in the thirteenth or fourteenth century, and remained divided during an extended phase of economic retrenchment. Japan's political economy evolved sluggishly to the late 1200s, only to begin rapid, destabilizing growth that consumed central authority in the late 1400s. Yet in a larger sense, in all four realms economic expansion outpaced political adaptation.

Political and Military Spurs to Reintegration, c. 1450–1650

Starting in the second half of the fifteenth century and accelerating to the seventeenth century and beyond, a mix of charter legacies, cyclic renewal, and truly novel dynamics inaugurated what I term early modern integration. For the first time Japan now marched to the same drummer as the other three areas. Why, then, these coordinated revivals?

In each realm, an ideal of unity survived from the charter era. Ivan IV, for example, claimed (with considerable anachronism) that he was reassembling the lands of his blessed Kievan forebears (Pavlov and Perrie 2003, 47–52). In Japan, where neither the ideal of a unified state nor the ultimate locus of sovereignty in the emperor had ever been displaced, sixteenth-century unifiers instinctively sought to seize the imperial seat of Heian/Kyoto. Likewise, the early Mughals saw Delhi, capital of the sultans whose imperium they strove to reassemble, as the center of Muslim India (Asher and Talbot 2006, 118, 131, 196–197).

Notwithstanding this persistence of charter ideals, the duration and severity of charter state collapse meant that would-be unifiers, outside India at least, no longer had a workable institutional blueprint. With little realistic idea of what their experiments would yield, they were obliged to begin an arduous, generations-long task of assembling new networks from the ground up. Driving such experiments was an iron Darwinian imperative: as warfare grew in scale and expense and statelets by the score were cannibalized, only the most imaginative and efficient could hope to survive.

The campaigns of 1552 to 1592 with which this essay opened testified to the success of military and administrative reform during the previous three or four generations. But by posing problems of territorial coordination on a novel scale, and in most cases by precipitating wars with yet more powerful rivals, those victories initiated yet another phase of ad hoc improvisation. In short, in each realm the entire period c. 1450 to 1650 saw rapid experiment and fundamental innovation. This is not to claim, of course, that administrations froze after 1650, merely that by 1650 each new system had consolidated itself.

Thus, in the Irrawaddy basin, the First Toungoo Dynasty (1486–1599) joined the manpower of the interior, where it sponsored elaborate reclamation and irrigation projects, to the burgeoning commercial wealth of the coast, where it moved its capital. Having reunited the basin in 1555 with the help of Portuguese firearms, the dynasty collapsed in the 1590s through ill-judged efforts to subjugate Siam and Laos. Learning quickly from those mistakes, the Restored Toungoo Dynasty (1597–1752) jettisoned extravagant territorial claims and returned the capital to Upper Burma but retained control of the maritime south through complex gubernatorial reforms. In the 1630s, the restored dynasty also instituted the first basin-wide cadastral surveys, overhauled provincial taxes, and expanded sharply the ranks of military and civilian servicemen, known as *ahmu-dans*. Reflecting primarily military objectives and exceeding in ambition and efficiency anything available to Pagan, in essence these centralizing measures would remain in place to 1825 (Lieberman 1984).

Between c. 1450 and 1580, Moscow triumphed over Tatar khanates and Russian rivals because, among other initiatives, it embraced European-style firearms, vastly expanded cavalry prebends, devised new gubernatorial controls, imposed Tatar-style taxation on the Russian countryside and, alone among Russian principalities, adopted royal primogeniture. Seventeenth-century expansion against Poland, Sweden, and the Ottomans imposed military burdens more continuous and more technically daunting than anything Toungoo Burma, not to mention ancient Kiev, faced. In response, the new Romanov Dynasty (1613) accelerated the transition from steppe cavalry to European-style infantry, strengthened military and fiscal chanceries, and in 1649 extended and regularized serfdom. As a nonmarket structure that sought to guarantee labor services and taxes and that would endure into the nineteenth century, serfdom was broadly analogous to the Burmese *ahmu-dan* system. Despite or because of shifting cultural paradigms, under Peter the Great (r. 1682–1725) and his successors, rationalization of the state and militarization of the caste-based social order only intensified (Martin 1995; Hellie 1971; Lieberman 2009, 214–228, 282–306; Hughes 1998).

During the Warring States era (1467–1568) local *daimyo* created Japan's first consolidated proprietary domains, radically increased agrarian and commercial taxation, and formed massive armies of peasant foot-soldiers—armies up to twenty-five times larger than their thirteenth-century counterparts—whose epic battles culminated in the Tokugawa reunification. Although the Tokugawa faced no foreign threats, the shogunate sought to preclude renewed domestic resistance by taking direct control of key urban and economic zones, subjecting dependent *daimyo* to strict controls, disarming the peasantry, and—reminiscent of Burmese *ahmu-dan* service and Russian serfdom—minimizing mobility among status groups on whose taxes elite income and state operations rested. Again, these reforms, in place by 1650, would continue in essential respects to the nineteenth century (Hall et al. 1981; Totman 1993; Lieberman 2009, ch. 4).

Building on the work of the Lodi kings, who from the mid-1400s had tried to revive Delhi's authority, and of the brilliant Indo-Afghan leader Sher Shah Sur, the early Mughals curbed the hereditary appropriation of military benefices, sought to draw *zamindar* landholders into a unified hierarchy, and collected unprecedented military revenues through cadastral surveys, high-quality coinage, and tax rates based on decennial averages of local yields and prices. Against the armies of Akbar (r. 1556–1605), who more than any other ruler shaped the new Mughal order, no North Indian kingdom or coalition of kingdoms could stand. Recurrent seventeenth-century campaigns also achieved more effective control over the Deccan than the Delhi Sultans could boast (Richards 1993).

Economic Spurs, Direct and Subtle, c. 1450–1650

In a word, in all four zones, intensifying competition between c. 1450 and 1650 drove hegemonic polities to extract ever more resources from progressively larger territories. In internal structure these new systems may not have resembled one another very closely, but in local terms each was unprecedentedly effective. Yet if political and military pressures spurred reintegration, in every instance that process was synergistic with two other powerful dynamics, namely, multifaceted economic expansion and accelerated cultural circulation. Consider each in turn.

In some ways, post-1450 economic growth was merely a cyclic recovery that mimicked charter-era expansion. Insofar as population losses had forced the abandonment of marginal lands, per capita and per acre productivity rose, at least until earlier population ceilings reappeared. A return of somewhat warmer weather for much of the period c. 1450–1630 also favored agrarian renewal, in South and Southeast Asia by strengthening the monsoons, in Russia by again extending the growing season. In Japan, too, warmer climate for much of the fifteenth and sixteenth centuries helped raise yields on established fields and permitted cultivation of hitherto marginal lands in north Honshu. To some degree, this novel climatic coordination between Japan and other regions contributed to their unprecedented political synchronization (Lieberman 2009, 417–418). By 1450, moreover, the worst effects of the Black Death in Russia had passed.

To such quasi-cyclic factors must be added truly novel elements. In Burma between c. 1350 and 1700, new irrigation projects and political support joined stronger monsoons to increase sharply the planting of new high-yield, late-maturing *indica*-rice strains. The novel cultivation of cotton, which responded to rising domestic and Chinese demand, and later of tobacco, maize, and peanuts brought prosperity to districts unsuited for rice (Lieberman 2003, 141–145, 175). In Japan, whereas earlier reclamation had focused on restricted upland valleys, from 1467 to 1651 at least forty-nine projects transformed expansive, fertile sedimentary basins. From the late 1300s, Japanese farmers also began adopting high-yield, early-ripening, drought-resistant Champa rice, as well as better fertilizers and new water control techniques. As also may have been true in seventeenth-century Burma, in advanced sectors of Japan, modified systems of landholding encouraged innovation by providing stronger family incentives. Together with more double-cropping and crop specialization, such changes facilitated a transition from what Conrad Totman terms the "age of dispersed agriculturalists" to the "age of intensive agriculture" (Totman 2000, pts. 2, 3; Lieberman 2009, 425–427; Hall et al. 1981). In Russia by the early 1500s, renewed population pressure, military demands, and Lithuanian example spurred the introduction of a three-field system of crop rotations on monastic and noble estates, whence it spread by the seventeenth century to the lands of military servitors and some peasants. Compared to slash-and-burn agriculture, three-field rotations reduced fallow, improved fertility, and integrated pasturage and husbandry more effectively, inaugurating, according to one authority, an agrarian transformation more far reaching than anything Russia would experience until Soviet collectivization (French 1983). Buoyed by more efficient irrigation and labor inputs, in 1400 agriculture in much of South India and the Punjab also entered a 300-year expansionary phase, while from the late 1500s reclamation led by an emergent Muslim gentry transformed Bengali jungles into one of Asia's great rice granaries (Subrahmanyam 1990; Eaton 1993; Lieberman 2009, 690–694).

Cereal yields per acre varied considerably, with Japan and Russia forming the extremes of high and low productivity. But in each case, judged again by local standards, agrarian vitality became marked. Between 1400 and 1650, by best estimates, in Upper Burma acreage rose by 40 percent, and population by well over half. Such Russian data as are available point to population growth far stronger than in Burma (Lieberman 1991; 2009, 218; Hellie 1971, 87, 379). In Japan between 1300 and 1600 arable land rose by 60 percent, and population by a remarkable 270 percent (Farris 2006, 262–263; Lieberman 2009, 425–426). In India population grew from c. 145,000,000 in 1500 to 175,000,000 in 1700 (Lieberman 2009, 694).

In turn, agricultural/demographic growth spurred domestic commerce. A larger aggregate and possibly per capita surplus, rising urban demand, and elite insistence on cash taxes and rents swelled the volume of goods that peasants and middlemen brought to market. At the same time, more diverse crops and a turn to handicrafts by land-scarce peasants increased the variety—and consumer appeal—of market offerings. Inevitably, trade spurred, and profited from, falling transport costs, as seen, for example, in the upgrading of Tokugawa shipping routes and highways, in improvements to the trunk road from Bengal to the Punjab, and in an expansion of commercial fleets along the Irrawaddy. In all four regions from the mid-1400s well into the eighteenth century, we thus find not only "extensive growth," in which output rises through the sheer addition of production units, but "Smithian growth," in which wider exchange, specialization, and economies of scale improve productivity within a conservative technological framework. Overall, between 1400 and 1700, in Gilbert Rozman's schema of commercial/urban integration, Burma probably advanced from Stage D to Stage E, Russia from Stage C to Stage F, and Japan and North India from Stage D to Stage G (the highest level, "national marketing"). Everywhere cash transactions, money-lending, and commutation grew more common, as coins spread to humble strata and money values more often expressed social relations (Lieberman 1991; 2009, 8, 35, 67, 176–177, 219–220, 296–298, 418–429, 450–455, 560–561, 694–696; Rozman 1976).

International trade also rose sharply after 1450/1500, rapidly eclipsing pre-1300 levels, which is hardly surprising, given that much of China, Southwest Asia, and Europe joined in this fresh expansionary phase and that New World bullion began lubricating global exchange. With Europe and the Mideast, Russia traded furs, hemp, and flax for silver and manufactures. After c. 1500, China's burgeoning population acted as a commercial pump for all of East Asia, sucking in silver from the New World and Japan and bullion, spices, cotton, and forest exotica from Southeast Asia, while sending to its neighbors streams of bronze cash, silk, and porcelain. In return for bullion and handicrafts, India supplied Southwest and Southeast Asia with industrial crops and great quantities of cotton textiles (Reid 1988–1993; Lieberman 2009).

By land and sea, long-distance exchange reinforced domestic growth in at least five ways: 1) In response to global demand, major improvements in silver mining and smelting techniques after 1533/1557 in Japan and the New World decisively ended Eurasia's long "bullion famine." Without the ensuing increase in liquidity, in all four of our regions monetization, and by extension commodification and urbanization, would have been severely hindered. 2) Exports stimulated both agrarian (e.g., rice, cotton, flax) and handicraft sectors. 3) Imported manufactures encouraged diversification and labor intensification by luring peasant producers and stoking consumer demand. 4) A host of crops—cotton and new rice strains from India; Champa rice; and the aforementioned New World tobacco, maize, peanuts as well as chilies, tomatoes, and (of growing demographic importance to Japan) sweet potatoes—entered along maritime routes. 5) Trade facilitated the transfer of new technologies, including the Mideastern waterwheel, dome arch, draw loom, and accounting procedures to India; European financial, mining, and manufacturing techniques to Russia; and Chinese nautical, engineering, metallurgical, mining, ceramic, and textile technologies to both Japan and Southeast Asia.

In short, international trade joined climatic amelioration, Eurasian-wide demographic recovery, and agrarian reorganization to intensify economic growth in all four zones after 1450 or 1500.

By its very nature, such growth conferred a cumulative political advantage on privileged districts—Upper Burma, the Volga-Oka interfluve in Russia, the Inland Sea-Kanto axis in Japan, the Indo-Gangetic plain—over more marginal areas. Even if core and periphery grew at the same pace, the core's initial economic superiority ensured a self-reproducing absolute advantage in manpower and wealth. Yet in fact, at least to 1650, growth rates in the core normally exceeded those in outer zones. Furthermore, the development of national markets, which implied a concentration of higher level commercial functions in the capital region, meant that where frontier colonization or overseas trade became an engine of growth (as in post-1650 Burma and Russia), the center retained major advantages. Favored districts could then pyramid their powers both of coercion (military superiority) and attraction (patronage and cultural display).

Not only the scale, but the nature of each political economy changed after the charter era. Variations in the extent of commodification notwithstanding, in all four realms we find movement from subsistence to market production, from in-kind to cash taxes, and from land grants to salaries and commercial favors. By their very nature, such changes enhanced the efficiency of central collection and redistribution. Bulky or perishable in-kind taxes were of limited use—what was a Burmese king in 1365 supposed to do with local gifts of a pig, an ox, beer, and pots of rice curry? (Lieberman 1991)—but cash taxes could be transmitted over great distances and disbursed according to uniform procedures. By the same token, cash awards to provincial officials or military personnel carried less risk of political entropy than land grants, while specialized wage labor was generally more efficient than corvée. In Burma, a post-1500 shift from land to cash religious donations essentially solved the problem of land alienation that had crippled Pagan. In Japan, a combination of more effective extraction and a larger revenue base meant that, by one calculation, the Tokugawa shogunate in 1700 collected more than twenty times more agrarian revenue than its tenth-century predecessor. In India, too, Mughal cash revenues vastly exceeded those of the Delhi sultans (Lieberman 2009, 69, 222, 429, 455, 694, 697).

More broadly, the state's enhanced patronage and regulatory ambition and the growing economic importance of tax revenues and market access obliged provincial elites to seek alliance with a central coordinating body. One key to centralization, therefore, lay in the growing inclination of local elites to support, indeed to help create, an administration that could protect long-distance exchange, improve commercial regulation, limit tolls and transaction costs, simplify legal jurisdictions, and share tax revenues. Thus centralization often was more a matter of bottom-up initiatives and local-central negotiation than of top-down imposition. After a century of commercial integration in the Irrawaddy basin, the ease with which Bayin-naung subdued Ava and Tai-Shan states reflected, in part, a recognition by far-flung elites that political coordination was in everyone's material interest. A similar *daimyo* calculus probably eased the path of Tokugawa Ieyasu.

Economic expansion, international trade in particular, also provided two technical aids to coordinate Eurasian state-building, namely, paper and guns. Along with cumulative institutional reform, these features allowed the state, like the economy, to start after c. 1550 from a higher technological level than its charter predecessor. Paper-making reached Japan from China at an early date, but in the Tokugawa era, marked price reductions permitted a vast expansion in official archives. In the eleventh century, paper, and in the fifteenth century, paper manufacture spread from the Mideast to India, where a torrent of Mughal records produced what has been termed a "paper empire." So, too, in Muscovy, where paper arrived from eastern Europe, chancery scribes in the mid-1500s developed archives central to the imperial project (Bloom 2001, 41–42, 217; Richards 1993, 3; Lieberman 2009, 226, 293, 456, 647–650).[5]

Although they had appeared earlier, firearms had a major impact only from the early or mid-1500s, and along with Japanese and New World silver, may have been the principal agent of late-sixteenth-century political coordination. As noted, Portuguese matchlocks and cast-metal cannon contributed to Bayinnaung's victories in Upper Burma and the Tai-Shan hills. Thereafter, the value of guns to the Burmese army only increased as the quality of Arab and European imports improved. In Japan, whose advanced metallurgy allowed high-quality local imitations soon after Portuguese introduced matchlocks in 1543, the new weapons became a major feature in *daimyo* armies as early as 1575 and probably hastened national unification by several decades. The Mughals, whose realm Marshall G. S. Hodgson (1974) termed a "gunpowder empire," used light cannon and matchlocks, derived from Central Asia, to good effect as early as 1526. Whereas in postunification Japan a pacific environment allowed firearms technology to stagnate, the Mughals continued to upgrade their arms into the eighteenth century. This was yet more obviously true of Moscow, whose Western-style cannon aided the 1552 victory at Kazan, and whose life-and-death contests with Sweden and Poland after 1600 obliged officials constantly to imitate, at enormous financial and human cost, the latest in European guns, fortifications, and infantry drill (Lieberman 1984; 2009, 222–224, 285–291, 421–422, 697–698; Hodgson, 1974).

In each region (including Japan to 1600), firearms created a virtuous circle: only the wealthiest, most innovative polities could afford the new weapons, which facilitated acquisitions of fresh territory and wealth, which facilitated weapons modernization. Thus firearms reinforced the cumulative advantage that economic growth in a more general sense conferred on privileged commercial districts.

Cultural Circulation

Consider, too, the relation of economic growth to cultural circulation and the extent to which popular identification with central norms of language, ethnicity, and religion provided psychological support to new political projects. Cultural integration drew on diverse dynamics, including social emulation and autonomous religious impulses. Yet by itself, multifaceted economic change was a particularly potent solvent of social and spatial isolates. This was true along agricultural frontiers—in Lower Burma, southern Russia, northern Japan—where settlers tied more or less closely to imperial culture overawed alien populations. It was yet more obvious in long-settled districts, where the growing surplus nurtured ever-more-elaborate trade and educational circuits that privileged the cultural and political claims of central places. From the capital and provincial towns, for example, elite patterns of speech, dress, deportment, and religious observance diffused into the hinterland, as seen in the contraction between c. 1500 and 1700 of minority languages and ethnicities in the Irrawaddy basin, Honshu, and central Russia. Moreover, in Burma and Japan after c. 1500, proliferating religious schools, government demands for local record-keepers, and the growing commercial utility of writing fostered a marked rise in literacy and numeracy. Whereas in the charter era only a tiny capital elite had been literate, by 1700 probably a third of Burmese and Japanese males could read simple materials. Symptom and spur to this trend was the appearance of kingdom-specific literatures using vernacular languages and/or demotic writing systems and exploring an unprecedented variety of genres and themes (Lieberman 2009, 27–28, 70–74, 226–241, 293–294, 431–438, 476–477). In Burma and Japan as well as in Russia (notwithstanding markedly lower literacy rates in the latter realm), cultural/linguistic uniformity aided capital efforts to improve provincial communications and to regularize fiscal exactions.

At the same time, as expressed in folktales, songs, paintings, texts, and popular rituals, increasingly standardized religious and ethnic traits tended to assume a political character. It was only after c. 1250 in Japan, and 1400/1450 in Burma and Russia, that modified versions of charter religious traditions began to penetrate the countryside. Theravada and Christian orthodoxy were inherently sympathetic to imperial centralization insofar as they idealized the ruler as font of morality and bulwark against anarchy and sanctioned royal supervision of local personnel, both lay and religious, in the name of salvation. On the borders of Muscovy, where Orthodox Russians fought Muslim and Catholic non-Russians, religion/ethnicity fused easily with political loyalty; but, if the religious element was less conspicuous, similar tendencies towards politicized ethnicity transformed allegiances along the north Japanese, the

Burmese-Siamese, and the Burmese-Mon frontiers. By enlisting men from different provinces against a common foe, by increasing frontier reliance on the crown, and by nurturing xenophobic tales of communal danger and salvation, warfare provided a recognizable "other" against which group sentiment could be directed. As the Time of Troubles in Russia (1598–1613), the Mon interregnum in Burma (1740–1752), and Japanese-Ainu relations demonstrated, deeply felt popular sentiments afforded early modern states greater resilience, a higher degree of popular identification with the center, a sharper sense of cultural distinctiveness and cohesion than were available to their charter-era predecessors (Lieberman 1984, ch. 5; Dunning 2004; Howell 2005).

Less dramatic than politicized ethnicity, but arguably no less supportive of central power, were autonomous local movements of ethical and religious socialization. Such movements promoted notions of communal order and discipline, in effect systems of nonstate governance, which helped to compensate for yet scarce central resources and on which more visible official efforts often depended (cf. Gorski 2003). Thus, for example, in Japan after c. 1450, by seeking to curb antisocial behavior, to distribute tax burdens, and to safeguard family livelihood, an ethic of family obligation and mutual surveillance rendered self-governing villages *(so)* the building blocks of *daimyo* and eventually Tokugawa power. The expanded *ahmu-dan* system in Toungoo Burma provided a comparable infrastructure for rural pacification. Even in largely illiterate Muscovy, after c. 1500 a deepening of popular Orthodox sensibilities joined government tax demands to engender novel programs of communal self-governance and peasant self-policing that provided a social and attitudinal foundation for serfdom (Lieberman 2009).

What about cultural integration in Mughal India? The elitism and relative novelty of the Mughals' Perso-Islamic heritage joined India's vast size and the persistence, indeed revitalization, of regional traditions to preclude the same level of vertical and horizontal acculturation that we find in Burma, Russia, or Japan. In the early and mid-1700s, Perso-Islamic imperial culture proved quite unable to prevent imperial disintegration. And yet, compared to their Delhi predecessors, the Mughals' enhanced authority benefited from three cultural trends, all of which reduced the sharp cleavage between conquest elite and subject population that we find under the Delhi sultans: (1) Liberal intellectual currents and fiscal necessity led Akbar, in particular, to court non-Muslim elites and to promote expressly eclectic religious expressions. (2)

The incomparable prestige and utility of Muslim court conventions encouraged sustained imitation by non-Muslim elites. (3) At a popular level, Islam entered into fruitful dialogue with South Asian religions and language (Lieberman 2009, ch. 6).

State Influences on Economy and Culture

In myriad ways, then, economic and cultural modification of the local environment, often imperceptible capillary changes, encouraged political centralization. But surely the lines of causation ran in the opposite direction as well. That is to say, limited though early modern state capacities remained, as its authority grew, each state used those powers, intentionally and unintentionally, directly and indirectly, to render the economic and cultural environment more favorable to central projects. State formation and local processes of social integration were therefore reflexive and mutually constitutive.

Insofar as royal interventions were self-conscious, they reflected a mix of motives, including autonomous religious commitments and social visions. Yet pressures of interstate competition were normally paramount. This was particularly clear in economic matters, because typically the vast bulk of central revenues went to the army, and fiscal reform normally either anticipated or came in the immediate aftermath of major campaigns. To enhance their tax base, Toungoo and Muscovite rulers encouraged reclamation and colonization, welcomed foreign merchants, monopolized key imports and exports, and sought to dominate lucrative trade routes. Indeed, in both realms it is fair to say that territorial expansion between c. 1450 and 1700 followed a primarily mercantile logic. Likewise, to enhance their fiscal base, *daimyo* improved domestic transport and promoted official trading schemes, new crops, reclamation, and riparian control.[6] The Mughals sponsored similar projects, a 1665 edict declaring, "The [ruler's] entire elevated attention and desires are devoted to the increase in the population and cultivation of the Empire" (Ludden 1999, 96).

Often, however, unintended actions had as marked an economic impact as deliberate policy. In each region, unification and pacification, although preeminently political acts, encouraged trade by linking distant markets, introducing greater uniformity of weights and currency, and widening legal jurisdictions. By concentrating people and expenditure in capital cities, governments in all four realms, without necessarily planning to do so, offered private producers expanded market access. Everywhere cash taxes also had the effect, if not the objective, of boosting commodity production. Much the same could be said of new protections for peasant tenures in seventeenth-century Burma and Japan.

Similarly, in art, literature, language, dress, and deportment, Pegu, Ava, Moscow, Kyoto, Edo, Agra, and Delhi functioned as arbiters of taste for local elites in ways that at times were unanticipated. Often the impulse to cultural standardization came not from the throne, content to rule a polyglot realm, but from upwardly mobile provincials eager to imitate court language and art forms so as to enhance their local standing. The widening flow of written documents between the provinces and the capital had similar, if often unintended, homogenizing cultural effects, which in turn, I have suggested, helped to promote psychological identification with the throne. To this must be added cultural interventions self-consciously designed to elevate official norms, including efforts to promote particular dialects, etiquettes, clothing styles, and artistic forms; to purify and standardize texts; to unify religious rituals and personnel; to integrate provincial social hierarchies; and to marginalize or suppress communities—Mons in Burma, Christians in Japan, Old Believers in Russia—who were considered politically and/or religiously suspect.

Concluding Perspectives

For roughly a thousand years, the regions under review experienced a series of increasingly well-coordinated political cycles whose rhythms were governed by climate change, interstate imperatives, and tightening international linkages. Charter histories were only loosely coordinated, with some 500 years separating the foundation of the Heian state and the Delhi Sultanate, and with Kiev collapsing some 230 years before the Ashikaga shogunate. But after 1450 a more genuinely universal, synchronized constellation of forces promoted reunification in all four realms within a narrow time span, from 1552 to 1592. By 1650, Burma, Russia, and Japan all had developed unprecedentedly mature, stable administrative/social systems whose essential features would persist into the early nineteenth century. Even in India, Mughal conventions remained influential long after the empire's effective demise.

Space prevents a closer consideration of post-1700 history, but enough has been said to suggest that this combination of enduring recentralization, quickening commodification, firearms-based warfare, rising textuality, and more encompassing cultural identities defines the period from 1450/1500 to 1800/1850 as a more-or-less coherent phase in each realm under review. Starting with recovery from postcharter breakdowns and ending with European irruptions in Southeast Asia, Japan, and South Asia, these years anticipated, however weakly, more sustained integrative processes in the late nineteenth and twentieth centuries. Now Jack Goldstone (2004, 2008) has argued against use of the term "early modern" to characterize pre-1800 societies outside Britain on the grounds that the principal feature of true modernity, namely the use of "engine science" to support industry, was not the inevitable outcome of universal processes, but a contingent phenomenon unique to Britain. Yet if modernity would be unrecognizable without industry, it would be no less so without efficiently mobilized states, cohesive national territories, uniform political ethnicities, popular literacy, and commercialized economies. All these developments the centuries after 1450 clearly adumbrated. If, in the absence of European intervention, we cannot assume that these features would have culminated in an industrial-based order, neither can we see modernity as an externally derived total rupture from prior history everywhere outside Britain. By this logic, in all four societies the military events of 1552 to 1592 heralded a broader early modern transformation.

Notes

1. Smallpox had probably long been endemic in North India, but as we shall see, would become so in Japan only at a later date.

2. Admittedly, Inner Asian incursions were a double-edged sword: the Sultanate itself had been founded by invaders from the northwest.

3. The fact that during the MCA Japanese climate was unfavorable and population stagnated reinforces the link between climate and demography elsewhere. Japan's late smallpox domestication was a function of insularity, but why Japan followed a different climate regime for much of the pre-1400 era is less clear. See Lieberman 2009, 82, 395, and 395 n60.

4. Failed Mongol invasions in 1274 and 1281 probably hastened the collapse of the Kamakura shogunate, but had no long-term political or economic impact.

5. Burmese scribes, however, continued to use palm leaves, or less commonly cardboard *parabaiks*. Tokugawa Japan used wood-block printing, and in Russia moveable type appeared hesitantly from the 1550s, but printing in this period had no discernible influence on Burma or India.

6. Although inter-*daimyo* political competition continued to encourage such initiatives after 1603, military competition per se was critical only during the pre-Tokugawa period.

References

Abu-Lughod, Janet. 1989. *Before European Hegemony.* New York: Oxford University Press.

Adolphson, Mikael. 2000. *Gates of Power: Monks, Courtiers, and Warriors in Premodern Japan.* Honolulu: University of Hawai'i Press.

Asao, Naohiro.1991. "The Sixteenth-Century Unification." In *The Cambridge History of Japan,* vol. 4, ed. John Whitney Hall, 40–95. Cambridge: Cambridge University Press.

Asher, Catherine, and Cynthia Talbot. 2006. *India before Europe.* New York: Cambridge University Press.

Atwell, William. 2002. "Time, Money, and the Weather." *Journal of Asian Studies* 62: 83–113.

Aung-Thwin, Michael. 1985. *Pagan.* Honolulu: University of Hawai'i Press.

Benedictow, Ole. 2004. *The Black Death, 1346–1353.* Woodbrigge, Suffolk: Bodell Press.

Berry, Mary Elizabeth. 1994. *The Culture of Civil War in Kyoto.* Berkeley: University of California Press.

Bloom, Jonathan. 2001. *Paper before Print.* New Haven, CT: Yale University Press

Buckley, Brendan, et al. 2010. "Climate as a Contributing Factor in the Demise of Angkor, Cambodia." *Proceedings of the National Academy of Sciences,* 107: 6748–6752.

Cook, Edward, et al. 2010. "Asian Monsoon Failure and Megadrought during the Last Millennium," *Science* 328: 486–489.

Dunning, Chester. 2004. *A Short History of Russia's First Civil War.* University Park: Pennsylvania State University Press.

Eaton, Richard. 1993. *The Rise of Islam and the Bengal Frontier.* Berkeley: University of California Press.

Farris, William Wayne. 2006. *Japan's Medieval Population.* Honolulu: University of Hawai'i Press.

Fenner, Frank. 1988. *Smallpox and Its Eradication.* Geneva: World Health Organization.

Franklin, Simon, and Jonathan Shepard. 1996. *The Emergence of Rus 750–1200.* London: Longman.

French, R. A. 1983. "The Introduction of the Three-Field Agricultural System." In *Studies in Russian Historical Geography,* vol. 1, ed. James H. Bater and R. A. French, 65–81. London: Academic Press.

Goldstone, Jack. 2004. "Neither Late Imperial nor Early Modern." In *The Qing Formation in World-Historical Time*, ed. Lynn Struve, 242–302. Cambridge, MA: Harvard University Asia Center.

———. 2008. *Why Europe?* New York: McGraw Hill.

Gorski, Philip. 2003. *The Disciplinary Revolution*. Chicago: University of Chicago Press.

Hall, John Whitney, Nagahara Keiji, and Kozo Yamamura, eds. 1981. *Japan before Tokugawa*. Princeton, NJ: Princeton University Press.

Hellie, Richard. 1971. *Enserfment and Military Change in Muscovy*. Chicago: University of Chicago Press.

Hodgson, Marshall G. S. 1974. *The Venture of Islam*. Vol. 3. *The Gunpowder Empires and Modern Times*. Chicago: University of Chicago Press.

Howell, David. 2005. *Geographies of Identity in Nineteenth-Century Japan*. Berkeley: University of California Press.

Hudson, Bob, Nyein Lwin, and Win Maung. 2001. "The Origins of Bagan." *Asian Perspectives* 40 (1): 48–74.

Hughes, Lindsey. 1998. *Russia in the Age of Peter the Great*. New Haven, CT: Yale University Press.

Jackson, Peter. 1999. *The Delhi Sultanate*. Cambridge: Cambridge University Press.

Kaiser, Daniel. 1980. *The Growth of Law in Medieval Russia*. Princeton, NJ: Princeton University Press.

Kremenetski, K. V., et al. 2004. "Medieval Climatic Warming and Aridity as Indicated by Multiproxy Evidence from the Kola Peninsula, Russia." *Paleogeography, Paleoclimatology, Paleoecology* 209: 113–125.

Kuroda, Akinobu. 2009. "The Asian Silver Century, 1276–1359." *Journal of Global History* 4: 245–269.

Langer, Lawrence. 1975. "The Black Death in Russia." *Russian History* 2: 53–67.

Lieberman, Victor. 1984. *Burmese Administrative Cycles*. Princeton, NJ: Princeton University Press.

———. 1991. "Secular Trends in Burmese Economic History, c.1350–1830, and Their Implications for State Formation." *Modern Asian Studies* 25: 1–31.

———. 2003. *Strange Parallels: Southeast Asia in Global Context, c. 800–1830*. Vol.1, *Integration on the Mainland*. Cambridge: Cambridge University Press.

———. 2009. *Strange Parallels: Southeast Asia in Global Context, c. 800–1830*. Vol. 2, *Mainland Mirrors: Europe, Japan, China, South Asia, and the Islands*. Cambridge: Cambridge University Press.

———. 2011. "Charter State Collapse in Southeast Asia, c. 1250–1400, as a Problem in Regional and World History." *American Historical Review* 116: 937–963.

Lieberman, Victor, and Brendan Buckley. 2012. "The Impact of Climate on Southeast Asia, circa 950–1820: New Findings." *Modern Asian Studies* 46: 1049–1096.

Ludden, David. 1999. *An Agrarian History of South Asia.* Cambridge: Cambridge University Press.

Mann, Michael, et al. 2009. "Global Signatures and Dynamical Origins of the Little Ice Age and Medieval Climate Anomaly." *Science* 326: 1256–1260.

Martin, Janet. 1995. *Medieval Russia 980–1584.* Cambridge: Cambridge University Press.

McNeill, William. 1976. *Plagues and Peoples.* Garden City, NY: Anchor Press.

Miller, David B. 1990. "Monumental Building and Its Patrons as Indicators of Economic and Political Trends in Rus', 900–1262." *Jahrbucher fur Geschichte Osteuropas* 38: 321–355.

Nidana Ramadhipati-katha. 1912. ed. Phra Candakanto. Pak Lat, Siam. Unpublished Mon translation by H. L. Shorto.

Ostrowski, Donald. 1998. *Muscovy and the Mongols.* Cambridge: Cambridge University Press.

Pavlov, Andrei, and Maureen Perrie. 2003. *Ivan the Terrible.* London: Pearson/Longman.

Reid, Anthony. 1988–1993. *Southeast Asia in the Age of Commerce.* 2 vols. New Haven, CT: Yale University Press.

Richards, John. 1993. *The Mughal Empire.* Cambridge: Cambridge University Press.

Rozman, Gilbert. 1976. *Urban Networks in Russia 1750–1800 and Premodern Periodization.* Princeton, NJ: Princeton University Press.

Sinha, Ashish, et al. 2010. "A Global Context for Megadroughts in Monsoon Asia During the Past Millennium." *Quarternary Science Reviews* 30: 47–62.

Souyri, Pierre. 2001. *The World Turned Upside Down.* New York: Columbia University Press.

Stearns, Peter. 2010. *Globalization in World History.* London: Routledge.

Subrahmanyam, Sanjay. 1990. *The Political Economy of Commerce.* Cambridge: Cambridge University Press.

Totman, Conrad. 1993. *Early Modern Japan.* Berkeley: University of California Press.

———. 2000. *A History of Japan.* Malden, MA: Blackwell.

Trouet, Valerie, et al. 2009. "Persistent Positive North Atlantic Oscillation Mode Dominated the Medieval Climate Anomaly." *Science* 324: 78–80.

U Kala. 1932. *Maha-ya-zawin-gyi.* Vol. 2, ed. Saya Pwa. Rangoon: Burma Research Society.

Wade, Geoff. 2009. "An Early Age of Commerce in Southeast Asia, 900–1300 CE," *Journal of Southeast Asian Studies* 40: 221–265.

Wink, Andre. 2001. "India and the Turko-Mongol Frontier." In *Nomads in the Sedentary World,* ed. Anatoly Khazanov and Andre Wink, 211–233. Richmond, Surrey: Curzon.

3

1557

A Year of Some Significance

PETER C. PERDUE

In 1557, the Ming dynasty granted the Portuguese a leasehold on the town of Macau, initiating China's regular contact with the global economy. The Ming had granted the Portuguese trading rights in 1554. Francis Xavier, the first Jesuit missionary to proselytize in Asia, had died two years earlier while waiting on a small island near Macau for permission to reach the Chinese mainland. Xavier was later beatified, and a lavish procession in 1621 proclaimed him the patron saint of Macau (Brockey 2007, 1). In 1555 the first Jesuit visited Canton from Macau, and Matteo Ricci was invited to Macau from India. He finally reached Beijing in 1583.

In the same year, the notorious Chinese pirate-merchant Wang Zhi surrendered to the Ming official Hu Zongxian. He was one of the main leaders of the confederations of "dwarf pirates" *(wokou)* who had raided and traded along the southeast China coast since the early sixteenth century. Wang's surrender, followed by intensive military campaigns by the great Ming general Qi Jiguang and the lifting of the ban on foreign trade in 1567, eventually brought relative peace to the region and allowed foreign trade to flourish.

The Ming removal of the ban on overseas trade also stimulated Chinese migration abroad. Chinese had already settled in places like the Ryukyus and Palembang in the fifteenth century, and they sailed to Malacca, Ayudhaya, and

Champa, but in the late sixteenth century Chinese merchants helped to stimulate the rise of the great entrepots of Hoi-an, Manila, Phnom Penh, Patani, Banten, and Batavia. By 1600 there were several thousand Chinese in each of these ports. Their commercial power continued to rise during the seventeenth and eighteenth centuries (Kuhn 2008).

In 1571, silver mines opened in Potosi in modern Bolivia and the Spanish seized Manila. Thus began the great silver flow that linked the New and Old Worlds. At the same time, Chinese from the mainland, who had already formed a large proportion of the maritime merchant-pirate networks, emigrated in larger numbers to Manila and other Southeast Asian cities, setting up regular trading links based on the flow of New World silver and exports from China.

In China's northwest, during the 1550s and 1560s, a Mongol federation led by Altan Khan had repeatedly raided the frontier garrisons, while also requesting licenses to trade, which were usually rejected by the Ming. In 1570, high officials worked out a settlement allowing one of Altan Khan's grandsons to "surrender" to the Ming, and regulated trade relations were established. Also around this time, the building of the true Great Wall began.

The developments of these decades were an intertwined set of events engaging officials, missionaries, merchants, pirates, and others from many regions, but most scholars only tell this story from the point of view of one country. They separate the Portuguese story from the *wokou* story, and they separate the *wokou* story from the pacification of the northwest frontier. Even views of the *wokou* differ sharply between Japanese and Chinese scholars. We need a more comprehensive overview of the crucial changes in these decades that linked China to the rest of the world. The rise and fall of the *wokou*, the arrival of the Portuguese, the settlement of raiding on the northwest frontier, and Chinese overseas migration were interconnected processes in these critical decades in the mid-sixteenth century.

Merchant-Pirates or Pirate-Merchants? The Rise and Fall of the *Wokou*

For two hundred years, the Ming dynasty attempted to enforce a ban on overseas trade, rejecting the active engagement in maritime trade of its predecessors, the Song and Yuan dynasties. Zhu Yuanzhang (r. 1368–1399), the dynastic founder, who came from a peasant family in agricultural Anhui, distrusted and feared the wealthy commercial gentry of the lower Yangzi valley. In addition, his rivals during the wars for control of the new dynasty had enlisted followers who raided along the southern coast. Zhu Yuanzhang sponsored the building of defensive walls along the coast, and enacted the first ban on overseas trade in 1397 (Wiethoff 1963, 30). All people who transported cattle, textiles, currency, weapons, humans, and other goods across the borders by land or by sea were to be punished by beatings and confiscation of their goods. Merchants engaging in "private" (*si*) trade were regarded as "traitors" (*jian*) who endangered the security of the state.

The third emperor, the Yongle emperor (r.1403–1424), sponsored the famous large-scale expeditions of Admiral Zheng He into the southern seas, but these were primarily diplomatic and military missions intended to reassert Chinese maritime power in regions where the Yuan had tried to establish dominance (Wade 2005). After 1433, however, the maritime expeditions ceased, as the rulers in Beijing turned their attention toward military threats from the northwest frontier. They also tried to reinforce defensive stances on the southeast coast, building fortifications, destroying large boats, and tightening up on prohibitions against foreign trade.

Ming policy officially endorsed only registered tribute trade missions from recognized states, and regarded "private" (*si*) unregistered trading voyages as no different from piracy. Astute local officials recognized, however, that many merchants did not engage in violent raids, and that excessively strict enforcement of the trade ban would drive poor fishermen and peasants into criminal activity. Even during the strict prohibitions of the fifteenth century, some voices still spoke out against excessive constraints on trade. Although the fundamental ideology of the dynasty exalted the farmer and demeaned the merchants, social and economic practice, particularly in the prosperous south, often contravened pronouncements from Beijing. Provincial and local interests in Guangdong, Fujian, and Zhejiang found the profits from maritime trade attractive, both for filling the treasury and for filling their own purses. Local gentry became sponsors of illegal trading expeditions, giving the merchants investment capital, a base to store goods, and political protection.

From the early sixteenth century, the pressure of growing illegal private trade instigated further debates at the court. Proponents of a stricter trade ban argued that overseas trade by both foreigners and native Chinese threatened the established agrarian social order, since mobile seafarers were beyond control by families or local administration. Proponents of liberalization accepted the basic principles of the Ming agrarian order, but argued for flexible application on the local level, so that inhabitants of regions along the coast who lacked sufficient arable land could make a living from the sea.

We may describe the contrast between these views as one of dogmatism versus realism, or the "logic of theory" versus the "logic of practice" (Perdue 2009). This distinction is applicable to policy debates about both the southern coastal traders and the northwestern nomads. Those who followed the logic of theory invoked abstract, unchanging principles to explain human behavior and justify policy proposals. In their view, barbarians would always be violent and savage, and the only appropriate response was to use military force. The empire should take revenge for the humiliation of attacks by nomads and pirates by launching large-scale, centralized military campaigns. Only total victory could be justified morally and as security policy. Negotiations and monetary incentives could never modify their behavior.

Those following the logic of practice argued for small-scale experiments to test the barbarians' sincerity. Their opinion of nomads and pirates was equally contemptuous, but they argued for solving conflicts individually, on a local basis. For example, if opening horse markets or coastal trade led to a reduction in raids, they would use the resources from trade to build up coastal defenses, without indulging in expensive campaigns. Weng Wanda, for example, one of the authors of the Ming Great Wall strategy, argued that Mongols could respond to appeals to their self-interest, and it was possible to negotiate with them. Critics of these policies attacked their proponents as corrupt opportunists, while the realists responded that grandiose plans for large-scale operations were utopian and impossibly expensive. The debates at court often turned into personalized factional disputes far removed from the merits of specific policies, as each side leveled charges of immorality and malfeasance at the other.

Zhu Wan's Failure and Lin Xiyuan's Local Power

During the early sixteenth century, shortly after the intensification of restrictions on trade, the scale and intensity of raids along the coast increased dramatically. In 1547, Zhu Wan was appointed to the powerful position of Grand Coordinator for Coastal Defense, including jurisdiction over the Fujian coast, with the mission of eradicating coastal piracy (Goodrich and Fang

1976, 373; Higgins 1981). When he arrived in Zhangzhou, he was alarmed to discover that military preparedness and discipline were at very low levels and, even more disconcerting, that wealthy families and gentry had formed a "web of complicity" in illegal trade with foreigners for some time, building large boats which they sailed as far as Malacca and Japan (Higgins 1981, 9). These "Chinese pirates in caps and gowns" (*yiguan zhi dao*) were the key instigators of illegal trade and local violence. As he insisted, "the pirates and gentry are like host and guest for each other" (Higgins 1981, 175). The three key centers for this activity were Zhangzhou and Quanzhou in Fujian, and the outpost of Shuangyugang on an island near Ningbo. As Zhu Wan noted,

> Every year in the months when the southern winds blow, foreigners come to anchor at Shuangyugang, including those from the Japanese islands, the Folangji [Portuguese], Pahang, and Siam. The traitors [*jianren*] from the interior have regular business with them and then disperse; it gets worse from year to year; there is unbelievable poison spreading all along the coast. (Zhu 1997 3.38)

Shuangyugang became an international arms trading post, and through it foreign weapons, including Portuguese breech-loading artillery pieces, called *folangji*, passed from the Portuguese into the hands of both pirates and Ming troops.

Reports to Zhu Wan indicated the close relationship between foreign traders and local elite households. The gentry acted as "harboring hosts" (*wozhu*), offering warehouses for the merchants to store their goods and accepting deposits of funds from the maritime expeditions. But the local gentry often refused to return the deposits from the traders, calling in government troops to drive them away. In retaliation, the merchants raided the mainland bases and killed their former business associates. This was a form of brutal early capitalism, often verging on violence, profitable but risky for both sides. As the writer of *Mingshi Jishi benmo* summarized the situation:

> The foreigners always relied on local merchant households to manage the illicit trade. The merchants, in search of illegal [*jian*] profit, took responsibility for smuggled goods worth from several thousand up to 10,000 taels. When the foreigners pressed for repayment, the merchants evaded them. The foreigners also relied on high-ranking gentry households to manage their trade, and the gentry deposits were greater than those of the merchants. The foreigners occupied nearby islands and demanded their

> loans back, but after a long time with no repayment, their supplies were exhausted, so they came and went on the seas as pirates. As troubles arose, some were killed and wounded. The gentry households, concerned about this, urgently wanted to drive them away, so they urged the authorities to take action, saying, "the foreigners have ensconced themselves on nearby islands, and are killing and plundering, yet the officials have not sent out even one soldier to drive them away. Is this the proper way to defend against the pirates?" The authorities then sent out troops, but leaked information in advance, so as to collect bribes. Afterwards goods came again just as before. As this went on for a long time, the pirates became very angry, stating . . . that they must recover their gold and treasure before they would return home. So they squatted on the islands and would not leave. And they drew in support from coastal people who suffered from poor livelihoods, officials who had lost their positions, and scholars who had not fulfilled their ambitions. All of them colluded with the pirates and followed their leadership, as they frequently attacked the coastal districts. These [Chinese pirates] usurped the title of "king," or notables, and their lineages, families, and lands were all entered in the registers with no complaint. No one dared to touch them. (Gu Yingtai 1937, 55, 43; Higgins 1981, 163–164)

This fascinating report reveals the underlying support of local society for the illegal trade and the way in which local scholar-gentry could both profit from illegal trade and manipulate Ming prohibitions for their own advantage. They could brazenly refuse payment to foreign traders and call in Ming troops to drive out their creditors, while at the same time gaining profits once the ineffective campaigns were over. In retaliation, the foreign traders occupied offshore islands and raided the countryside. Foreign raids were both "revenge and retribution for broken promises" and efforts to recover lost investments (Higgins 1981, 165). From many local Ming officials' point of view, illegal trade itself was only a moral violation to which they could turn a blind eye, but the resulting violent conflict needed larger repressive measures from the central government.

Zhu openly attacked this close-knit network of local gentry and overseas traders by prohibiting anyone from going out to sea, reinforcing the *baojia* mutual responsibility system, and directly assaulting the base at Shuangyugang. He succeeded in destroying the harbor, but he aroused great local opposition. The traders at Shuangyugang moved their business to Fujian, where Zhu once again attacked and captured over two hundred of the leaders, beheading many of them. But his enemies had him impeached for killing innocent traders without imperial approval, and Zhu was dismissed and subjected to investigation. He committed suicide in 1549 before the investigation was completed.

Zhu's narrow-minded dedication to elimination of piracy refused to allow for the benefits of trade. He knew very well that the primary livelihood of the people of coastal Fujian was illegal trade, but he had little sympathy for their plight. He stated, "The people who live in Zhangzhou, Quanzhou, and other places on the coast, conduct trade on the high seas with foreigners as their occupation. Their regular business is murder and robbery" (Wiethoff 1963, 137; Zhu 1997, 2.29a). Zhu represented very well the dogmatic logic of theory that characterized entire populations as bandits while ignoring the economic causes that drove them into illegal behavior. He denounced all the local officials of Fujian as people who "all have ties to barbarians and robbers, and they continually break the law" (Zhu 1997, 5.10; Wiethoff 1963, 101–102). He attempted to expose their involvement in illegal trade in order to stamp out the practice.

The editor of one local gazetteer took a diametrically opposed position, indicating greater sympathy by those who knew the local population well: "There is very little arable land in Fujian, but its population is very dense. The poor soil cannot support even half of the population. For this reason the most powerful people are forced to pursue the profits that the sea offers" (*Haicheng xianzhi* 1633, 5.3a cited in Wiethoff 1963, 137).

One of Zhu Wan's main targets was the eminent scholar and overseas merchant Lin Xiyuan (Goodrich and Fang 1976, 920–921; So 1975, 68). A native of Dong'an Fujian, he passed the *jinshi* exam in 1517 and rose to high official rank, earning respect for his efforts at enacting famine relief. He himself proposed policies to repress pirate raids (Chen, 1964, 165, 16b–20b.) He also argued strongly for intervention in Annam when the Vietnamese usurper Mac Dangdung took the throne, and he promoted the reclamation of lands on the Sino-Vietnamese border. But Lin was found guilty of exceeding his authority and dismissed from office. He found his second career in his hometown by joining the profitable though illegal overseas trade. He acted as "harbor host" for local traders near Amoy by selling their goods on commission in local markets, and he built for himself a large fleet of ocean-going junks, providing capital for captains to trade with Southeast Asia. He was described as the "overlord" (*tuhao*) of the district, an immensely wealthy man who carried out justice independently, protected by his local allies. Zhu denounced him as a "local king" who abused his talents: "local officials hated and feared him, and could do nothing about him. He wrote 'Lin Fu' on his gate, listened to people's complaints without permission, put up unauthorized proclamations, and constructed large ships called 'ferries' (*duchuan*) to carry the bandits' goods and defy prohibitions on trade" (Chen, 1964, 205.685–695).

Lin also promoted trade with the Portuguese at sea, arguing that the foreigners brought prosperity to the region and helped in the suppression of piracy:

> When the Folangji [Portuguese] came to China, they brought pepper, sapan-wood, ivory, sapan oil, garu-wood, sandal wood, and other incense to exchange with the people on the frontier at a particularly reasonable price. As to foodstuffs and daily necessities they had to get from us, such as rice, flour, pigs and chicken, they paid the people twice the market price. Therefore, the frontier people were happy to trade with them . . .
>
> The Folangji have never invaded our land nor slaughtered our people nor plundered our treasures. Furthermore, when they first came to China, they chased away the bandits on our behalf because they were afraid that they might be involved. The bandits became scared and did not dare to cause any trouble . . . Thus we see that the Folangji have not been pirates but have been warding off pirates on our behalf. I can by no means see the reason why the government insists on punishing them. (So 1975, 69 n104; Lin 1997, 5, 30–34. Trans. by So)

In Zhu Wan's view, by contrast, the Portuguese were no different from the local pirates. They were only more threatening because they supplied foreign weapons: "The folangji, calling themselves kings, boasted that 'The firearms *(niaochong)* we will use to attack you are so large that they will pulverize this city wall'" (Zhu 1997 quoted in Higgins 1981, 191–192.)

Zhu's critics, however, argued that these "Portuguese" were really only innocent traders from Malacca, with no pretensions to dominate the region. Zhu was impeached for killing these innocent traders (Higgins 1981, 191, 195; Zhu 1997 2b; Gu 1937, 55.590).

None of Zhu Wan's efforts to shut down the trade could touch Lin; instead Zhu Wan suffered demotion and investigation, while Lin Xiyuan survived and became celebrated in the local temple. The power of Lin and other local gentry indicates that these elites had strong connections with mercantile interests spanning the East Asian coast, and they had supporters at the court in Beijing who could remove inconveniently dedicated officials who threatened their position.

According to his defenders, Zhu Wan was "pure, energetic, stern, honest, and bravely carried out his duties." (Higgins 1981, 198; Zhang Tingyu, ed. 1975 j.205, p. 5405, my translation.). Only the power of local families succeeded in having him impeached on trumped-up charges. But we may also fault him for his rigidity toward the intricate imbrication of trade with local society and his determination to use only coercive measures to break this tenacious interdependency. His failure reflected not only court intrigue, but an unrealistic campaign to keep a dynamic commercial society isolated from the irresistible pressures of world trade.

Wang Zhi (d. 1559) and Hu Zongxian (1511–1565)

The relationship between Wang Zhi and Hu Zongxian illustrates another outcome of this conflict between Beijing's efforts to crack down on illegal trade and the defensive power of local elites. Wang Zhi, who rose to become the chief leader of the pirate confederations attacking the China coast, was originally a merchant from Huizhou prefecture in Anhui (Goto 1927; Wills 1979; So 1975, 107–110). Hu Zongxian, the supreme commander of the Ming military attack on the pirates, came from the same prefecture as Wang Zhi. He used his personal connections to capture Wang Zhi in 1557, but the emperor overruled him when he tried to spare Wang's life. Wang was executed in 1559, but several years later Hu himself was dismissed for having been too friendly with Wang Zhi, arrested, released, arrested again and imprisoned, and died in jail. The two men stood on opposite sides of the battle between the Ming and the pirates, but the tumultuous factional politics of the Ming court determined the fates of both of them. Their close involvement with each other in international trade and politics showed again the blurred lines between local gentry, overseas merchants, pirates, and local officials in this coastal region.

The actual movements of Wang Zhi are unclear, and the main source about him was written by his enemy Hu Zongxian, so it is difficult to judge the reliability of his account. Hu Zongxian may have exaggerated Wang Zhi's importance in order to claim more credit for his capture, but his general description of Wang Zhi's career seems accurate (Goto 1927).

Huizhou, located quite far inland, without extensive river networks, nevertheless produced a large number of merchants who engaged in long distance trade. Known as "Xin'an merchants," they expanded their connections from local markets to wider networks reaching to the coast and beyond

(Zurndorfer 1989; Fujii 1953–1954). Wang Zhi began business as a salt merchant, but after going bankrupt he turned to overseas ventures financed by local gentry. Wang had traveled to Japan, and he may have had connections with the Portuguese. Once again, the island of Shuangyugang, close to Ningbo, served as a base for him as well as smugglers from many other nationalities (Wiethoff 1963, 158). Wang participated in illegal coastal trade as it rose in importance in the 1520s, making connections with Portuguese, Chinese, and Japanese traders. Chinese gentry with bases on land served as hosts for the traders, storing their goods and investing in voyages. When local government retaliation escalated the violence, at some point Wang Zhi fled to southern Japan. Xu Hai was one of the main leaders of the pirates in the 1550s, and Wang Zhi may have been one of his subordinates. When Xu Hai was killed in 1556, Wang rose to a leadership position.

Although Hu Zongxian and other Chinese sources described him as the "pirate king," based in Satsuma, Japan, it seems implausible that he exerted total authority over the many different pirate groups. Under the name of "Shingoro," he was named as the leader of pirate groups based in northern Kyushu, while another man, "Shinsiro," led the groups in southern Kyushu. A stele inscribed in Dinghai xian, Zhejiang, mentions Shingoro as the leader of attacks with thousands of men along the coast. The *Mingshi* claims that in 1553 he led up to 20,000 men in hundreds of ships in these attacks. In 1555, Hu Zongxian sent envoys to Japan to talk to Wang Zhi, hoping to negotiate with him. Wang Zhi at this time remained in his base in Japan and did not participate in attacks on the coast. Hu released Wang's family from prison and promised to pardon Wang for previous attacks and relax prohibitions on trade. Wang initially believed Hu's promises and sailed with his ships to Zhoushan island near Shanghai.

Critics, however, attacked Hu's proposals for bringing on more disastrous raids, and they suspected that Wang Zhi had paid Hu a bribe of several hundred thousand taels. Hu lost the support of his patrons at court and, fearing for his own career, changed his approach. He went back on his word to Wang Zhi, saying that he would allow the court to decide about whether or not to execute Wang Zhi.

In a great victory led by Hu Zongxian, the Ming troops in 1557 defeated the pirates at Dinghai xian, executing hundreds of them and capturing more than eighty alive, including Wang Zhi. Although Hu Zongxian had induced Wang Zhi to come to China, promising him favorable conditions if he surrendered, he betrayed him and captured him alive. Hu had counted on the emperor

Ming soldiers fighting pirates, from Qiu Ying, *Wakō Zukan*. (Tōkyō Daigaku Shiryō Hensanjo 1974)

pardoning Wang Zhi, but other critics at court attacked Hu's proposal as too lenient. After Wang Zhi's execution, Hu Zongxian himself fell under suspicion for his moderate approach. Hu, as a local man closely tied to the mercantile culture of the south, was vulnerable to attacks from those who rejected overseas trade in principle. Ultimately both Wang Zhi and Hu Zongxian fell victim to those at court who rejected all compromise with the merchant pirates.

The defeat and execution of Wang Zhi, however, did cut down sharply on the pirate attacks in the 1560s. The most important factor in ending piracy, however, was the reopening of legal trade in 1567, along with the new presence of the Portuguese in Macau.

The Role of the Portuguese

The Portuguese first came into contact with Chinese merchants when they arrived at Malacca in 1511. They had already been ordered by their king to "inquire about the Chijns, whence they come, and from how far, and the merchandise they bring, how many of their ships come each year, and the form and size of their ships, whether they return in the same year they come, whether they have factors or houses in Malacca or any other country, whether

they are weak or warlike, whether they have weapons or artillery . . . and if they are not Christians, in what they believe or what they worship, and what customs they observe, toward what place their country extends and upon whom they border" (Chang 1934, 33). Clearly the Portuguese were intensely curious about the Chinese, since there had been almost no direct reports about China since Marco Polo, and they regarded them as significant rivals in trade and war.

Relations got off to a good start at first. At Malacca in 1511, the Portuguese gave protection and aid to five Chinese junks in attacks against the Malaccan king. The king of Malacca, after losing his territory to the Portuguese attack, sent an embassy to Beijing asking for aid, but the emperor refused to give him assistance. In the early years, Chinese traders in Southeast Asia and the new Portuguese arrivals shared information and profits, and Portuguese regarded the Chinese as a "very good people" who "desired peace and friendship with the Portuguese" (Chang 1934, 38).

When the Portuguese proceeded to Chinese territory, however, they soon ran the risk of being confused with pirates. Landing at Tunmen, an island in the mouth of the Pearl River, they negotiated with the local commander to be allowed to proceed to Canton. In 1517, they were received in Canton and allowed to stay on shore pending a response from Beijing. Ambassador Tomé Pires, a former apothecary who had engaged in the drug and spice trade in India, briefly visited Canton in 1517 and returned in 1520 to head for Beijing (Goodrich 1976, 1123). Meanwhile, the fleet commander, Fernão Peres, opened trade with the Chinese in Quanzhou. He had established good relations with local merchants and had the promise of getting approval from Beijing.

His brother, Simão d'Andrade, however, undid much of Fernão's good work by building a fort on Tunmen, mounting artillery, and hanging a sailor there (Zhang Tingyu, ed., 1975 325.8b; Chang 1934, 47). When Tomé Pires arrived at Beijing, court officials accused him of many offenses committed in Canton: arriving in the first place without permission, refusing to pay customs duties, preventing other foreign traders from doing business, constructing fortresses on Chinese soil, spying, and taking Malacca by force. The Zhengde emperor was tolerant, arguing that the Portuguese needed time to learn Chinese customs, but when the emperor died in 1521, the hardliners at court, with the support of the new emperor, launched their attack. The Cantonese censor He Ao described the Portuguese as "cruel and crafty," with arms superior to other foreigners. They had fired cannon in Canton, and trading with them would inevitably lead to violence (*Zhang Tingyu 1975:* j. 325.8b, my translation). Now the Portuguese had become irrevocably identified with pirates in the minds of those hostile to foreign trade. Pires and his embassy were sent to Canton and imprisoned, led in chains to the provincial surveillance office. A battle between Portuguese and Chinese ships near Tunmen exacerbated tensions, leading to the expulsion of the Portuguese from Canton. Pires probably died in prison in Canton in 1523.

Yet the trade continued, because both sides profited from it. Paul Freedman (2008) has described the great interest in Asian spices in European markets and the large price differentials between local markets in Asia and those in Europe. Portuguese could obtain pepper from India at low prices and sell it in Chinese markets for four times the price they could obtain in Malacca. But similar large profits were also available in China for the intermediaries in the trade. The Portuguese joined with Chinese, Malays, and others in profiting from this intra-Asian trade. Customs duties in Canton reached several tens of thousands of taels monthly.

The Cantonese population and its officials ardently supported the foreign trade, but the Portuguese, by fortifying Tunmen Island, had identified themselves in the eyes of the court as no different from the pirates raiding the rest of the coast. Chang Tien-tse argues that the Portuguese, unlike other Asians and Europeans, "regarded trade and piracy as almost identical," but in fact this attitude was widely shared across Asia and Europe in medieval and early modern times (Chang 1934, 66). In an era where there were no disciplined navies under control of nation-states, violence was simply one of the "protection costs" all merchants had to anticipate paying in the interest of reducing risks to their cargoes and securing profits (Lane 1987, IX:234). Although they did not arrive in Southeast Asia at a propitious time for legal trade with China, they arrived fortuitously just as pirate attacks along the coast of China were increasing. Like the other pirate-traders, they carried on profitable illegal trade for the next thirty years (Chang 1934, 66, 68).

Zhangzhou, Quanzhou, and Ningbo replaced Canton as the primary center of illegal trade, and the Portuguese, like others, established bases on islands near the large towns. It was the backing of local merchant gentry in the towns that protected this trade. People like Lin Xiyuan, mentioned above, openly defended trade with the foreigners, but others simply engaged in it tacitly. Portuguese could disguise themselves as Malays and Siamese, sailing on Asian ships, mixing with the multicultural confederations of the seas (Gu 1807, 119.14a). As Zhu Wan had discovered when he captured illegal traders, the crews of these ships included Chinese, Japanese, Portuguese, Southeast Asians, and even Africans (Nakajima 2009).

Cantonese officials argued strenuously for reopening the port to foreign trade simply to support local administration and relieve economic depression. In 1530, Viceroy Lin Fu, representing the Cantonese maritime interest, argued that banning trade from Canton would hurt the local population and drive the traders to Fujian: "Since the officials have driven off foreign ships from Annam, Malacca, etc., they have moved to Zhangzhou, where they anchor freely beyond our control. The result is that profit flows to Fujian, and the markets of Canton are empty" (Wiethoff 1963, 75; Gu 1807, 120.14b–15a). He insisted on the great benefits available to rich and poor alike from participation in the spice trade, as well as its importance for the fiscal stability of local government.

Lin also made the same argument that his Qing successors would make, pointing out that goods imported through Canton could go directly to the Imperial Household. Just like Europeans of the time, the Ming court demanded large quantities of spices, so this was an attractive temptation (Gu 1807, 120.4). Lin succeeded in reopening Canton foreign trade. Although the Portuguese were still officially banned, through contacts with local agents they carried on indirect exchanges.

By the 1540s, the Portuguese had established a small base on an island thirty miles west of Macau, carrying on smuggling with tacit local approval. In 1554, Leonel de Souza negotiated with the Chinese officials for legalized

An Unusual View of the Praya Grande by an unknown Chinese artist around 1830. (Photo courtesy of the Peabody Essex Museum)

trade, providing for payment of customs duties. Chinese and Western sources differ on the reasons for this agreement. Chinese official sources state that the Portuguese were merely admitted into the existing town in 1553 when their goods were damaged by a storm. The Portuguese later claimed that they were allowed to build a city on Macau in return for defeating a powerful pirate chieftain. Lin Xiyuan's letter, cited above, and Semedo's account of 1643 both give the Portuguese credit for driving out local pirates, in return for which they were allowed to settle in Macau. By 1563, the Portuguese had 900 people living in the city, but the predominant population consisted of thousands of other Asian foreigners and very few Chinese.

During the rest of the sixteenth century, the city grew rapidly, becoming the primary coastal port for Chinese trade with the world. The lifting of foreign trade restrictions in 1567 and the founding of Manila in 1571 allowed access to many countries, and the Portuguese were in the best position to be intermediaries between China and Japan, Manila, Siam, Malacca, Goa, and Europe. The Spanish were excluded from Canton, so the Portuguese had a monopoly of Manila trade. Silver rose to become the primary vehicle of commerce in the

1580s, replacing the barter trade. This was the golden age of Macau's trade until attacks by the Dutch and Spanish in the seventeenth century.

Altan Khan and Northwest Trade

On the northwest frontier at the same time, Ming officials, under pressure from traders and raiders, also shifted from prohibition to legalized border trade. I and other scholars have discussed the settlement of the conflict with the Mongolian chieftain Altan Khan in detail elsewhere, so I will only summarize the events here, with a few additional comments (Perdue 2005a, 2005b; 2009; Waldron 1990; Goodrich 1976, 6–9; Pokotilov 1976). Altan Khan became the leader of the twelve Tümed tribes north of the border with Shanxi in 1531. He and his brother led repeated raids against the Chinese settlements in order to obtain silk, food, and clothing. He constantly asked for permission to bring tribute missions to China, but when these requests were refused he continued his raids. The Jiajing emperor and his officials viewed with suspicion and contempt not only the Mongol raiders, but also many of the Chinese settled on the northwest frontier. They ordered, for example, in official documents that the character for "barbarian" (*yi*) be written as small as possible. A brief attempt to open fairs to trade Mongol horses for silk was shut down in 1551, when the emperor prohibited all trade with Mongols on pain of death. One powerful argument against trading with the barbarians was that many Chinese had settled in territory under Altan's control, and Altan demanded grain supplies for them as part of trading relations. These Chinese, like those who had gone overseas, were regarded as traitors, criminals, and fugitives, undeserving of support by the dynasty.

In 1547, just as Zhu Wan arrived in the south to prosecute intensified restrictions of coastal trade, the leading official Zeng Xian proposed large-scale military campaigns to drive out the Mongols from the Ordos region, at a total cost of 3.75 million taels (Waldron 1990; Perdue 2000; Higgins 1981, 179). Zeng's mobilization for the campaign alienated the local population by drafting forced laborers and requisitioning cooking pots and farm tools to make weapons. As in the south, lobbyists at court criticized Zeng Xian, leading to his execution and the abandonment of the recovery campaign. Zeng's abortive efforts drove more Chinese to seek refuge with Altan Khan. The army deserters, criminals, refugees, and hard-pressed farmers of the northwest, like their fellow Chinese on the south coast, moved beyond the jurisdiction of the agrarian empire to find better conditions of life in the mobile frontier. Around 1555, with the help of these Chinese settlers, Altan began building a new city, Köke Khota (modern Hohhot, the capital of Inner Mongolia), as he incorporated new populations into his regime. It was his equivalent of the island bases of the pirate merchants of the coast.

The person who achieved a sustainable settlement of the northwest frontier conflict was Wang Chonggu, Governor-general of Shaanxi, supported by the Grand Secretary Zhang Juzheng. In 1570, when Altan Khan's disgruntled grandson sought asylum in Datong, Wang Chonggu outlined a peace settlement that would establish regular trade, including tribute embassies, give Altan Khan the honorary title of "Submissive King" (Shunyi Wang), and ask him to return the main Chinese deserters. The Ming could obtain horses for the military while the Mongols gathered supplies of silk, fur, grain, clothing, and cooking pots. The settlement promoted the commercialization of the frontier, as merchants flocked to Köke Khota and other fairs along the border. The northwest became a relatively peaceful zone for the first time in over fifty years.

Parallels and Contrasts

The interactions of trade and diplomacy in the two regions shared many common features. In both areas, local officials with pragmatic views of the non-Han population led negotiations that brought peace and profit to the border populations through the establishment of legal and regulated trade. Han Chinese and non-Chinese mingled in the region, as some Chinese moved beyond the borders of the empire, and some non-Chinese settled in the interior. The military and commercial balances between the Ming and its rivals differed, but the outcomes were broadly similar.

Unlike the southeast, the Ming succeeded in the northwest without the ability to carry out military conquests or induce genuine surrender by the Mongols. Altan Khan and the Mongols remained quite independent of Ming rule, and their territory included many Chinese migrants as well. In this region, trade flows were more unbalanced, as silver flowed to the frontier garrisons and from there out into the steppe border, along with Chinese goods. In return, the Ming received only low-grade horses. The trade was more like a regularized system of protection payments than an equal exchange for the court. But local settlers and merchants did profit from peaceful exchange, so the security benefits were worth the price. The Ming indirectly promoted greater cultural exchange among the Mongols, as well, in the form of sedentarization and the sponsorship of Buddhism. Altan Khan had begun building his city before the trade settlement, and Lama Buddhism had persisted in southern Mongolia since the end of the Yuan period. But Wang Chonggu and Altan Khan both found advantages in strengthening the position of Buddhism.

The Ming officials believed that Buddhism would pacify the warlike nature of the Mongols, create sites of settlement and trade, and foster closer cultural exchange. Mongol princes indeed hired Chinese craftsmen to build temples in Mongolia and Kokonor and agreed to donate horses and camels to monasteries instead of sacrificing them to their ancestors. In 1578, Altan invited Sodnam Gyamtsho of the Gelugpa sect in Lhasa to visit him at the first major temple built in Kokonor and gave him the title of "Dalai Lama" (Oceanic Teacher, in Mongolian). The Dalai Lama declared Altan to be the reincarnation of Khubilai Khan, and the grandson of Altan Khan became the first Mongol to take the post of Dalai Lama in 1586.

In Southeast Asia, Chinese cultural influence was exerted directly by migration and transfer of Chinese practices to the overseas Chinese community, but these traits did not necessarily transfer to other Southeast Asian populations. In the northwest, the effects were more indirect, as there were fewer migrants, and the Mongols adopted Buddhism for their own purposes. Nevertheless, in both regions, Han Chinese and other cultural traditions interacted more closely, encouraged by trading relationships and flows of people beyond the empire's borders.

Conclusion

Studies of the northwest frontier, the southeast coast, and overseas migration usually fall apart into separate monographs and separate chapters of textbooks. But to write an integrated history of China's participation in the emergence of the first global economy, we need to tie them together.[1] Decisions about the northwest frontier, the primary focus of dynastic strategic thinking, had implications for the southern coast; the silver imports from the south financed the building of the Great Wall; and Chinese emigrants extended commercial and "soft power" beyond the continental borders.

No single date can sum up a complex socioeconomic process, and the Portuguese were not the major actors in the opening of either frontier. But they deserve some special attention, because they were the new boys on the block. All the other elements of frontier policy—garrisons, merchant provisioning, the walls, regulated trade, protection payments disguised as "tribute"—had ancient precedents. The Portuguese, followed by the Spanish and other Europeans, added the first new element: a global economic link created by silver. Macau, the first foreign-controlled border town linking China to the wider world, became the key node. Hong Kong, Shanghai, and many others followed in its wake. The second new element was the large-scale migration of Chinese out of the mainland into Southeast Asia, which further integrated the regional trading system, as commodities and humans moved in and out of East and Southeast Asia in larger amounts and in new directions. Chinese and Europeans together created the modern world economy.

This period initiated China's engagement with the world economy, including the New World, and the same was true of Europe. For the first time, the flows of key commodities like silver, spices, tea, porcelain, and sugar tied together Eurasia, the New World, and Africa. But we can ask more questions about the cultural consequences of economic contact. Did Chinese and European connections with the American continents generate radically different views of the globe, or were the new peoples added on to existing knowledge of Southeast Asia, South Asia, and Eurasia? European historians consistently describe the sharp newness of the "wondrous possessions" of the Americas as a radical shift in early modern consciousness (Greenblatt 1991). Historians of China tend to minimize the impact of this global trade. Perhaps both perspectives are excessively one-sided, but we could think about new ways to address the subject comparatively. Nicolás Wey-Gómez, for example, argues that Columbus and the early explorers saw themselves as heading not only West, but *South*. That is, they were seeking the riches of the tropics, and they defined the New World in terms of inherited preconceptions about equatorial peoples, including racial, ecological, and economic prejudices:

> Columbus also intended to sail *south* to a tropical part of the globe that he and his contemporaries had some reason to identify initially as legendary India . . . The assumptions Columbus carried with him as he sailed south concerning the nature of the lands and peoples he sought to find were of pivotal importance for the development of the complex ideas and practices we associate with early modern colonialism . . . to the extent that five hundred years after Columbus' death we continue to wrestle with

> the divide between the "developed" nations of the north and the "developing" nations of the south, we too are heirs to an intellectual tradition whose ancient notions of place paved the way for recent colonialism. (Wey-Gómez 2008, 3, 57)

Chinese, especially in south China, had had long experience with the tropics, and much closer ones than northern Europeans, but they, too, had their prejudices about southern peoples, from the aborigines of Taiwan and the southwest to the Vietnamese. This meant that when the Europeans arrived in tropical waters, they seemed like just another one of the many peoples who had crossed these seas and not a challenge to existing trade routes and cultural contacts. We could analyze the "metageographical" concepts of Asians and Europeans more insightfully if we looked at how both societies viewed the global South, instead of opposing East and West (Lewis and Wigen 1997).

We also need to examine comparatively the concurrent presence of contacts on both northwest and southeastern frontiers and the connections between them, in China and Europe. The northwest frontier always held primacy in Chinese geopolitical and economic thinking (with the partial exception of the Southern Song). Whenever dynasties placed their political centers in the north, they focused their policy discussions on the threat of the steppe nomads. Maritime peoples of the south were a supplement or byproduct. But Western Europeans also engaged with northern and southern frontiers in their own fashion. The primary enemy for most Europeans was in the south and east, in the Islamic world. The Islamic world was richer, more urbanized, and more militarily powerful than Europe through most of the medieval and early modern period. Of course, the unity of the Mediterranean world, as described by Braudel and others, often overcame religious and military conflict, just as conquest dynasties of China periodically united the steppe and settled worlds. But European views of the Islamic world generally shaped how they constructed their global trade routes and cultural interactions in analogous ways to how the Chinese reacted to Central Eurasia as the forge from which they built other foreign relations.

In short, we need to study Chinese frontiers as connected and comparable with each other; we should include the Chinese beyond the mainland as part of the story just as much as the non-Han within the empire; and we should put China in the world by exploring comparisons and connections on economic, political, and cultural dimensions.

Notes

1. The *Cambridge History of China* volumes on the Ming dynasty barely mention the emigration of Chinese from China. They treat Inner Asia and the world economy in completely separate chapters (Twitchett and Mote 1998, 8: chs. 4, 8). Wolfgang Franke claims that Chinese sources ignore "the dependence of Fujian coastal population on fishing . . . which led to overseas emigration as early as the Ming period" (Twitchett and Mote 1998, 7: 777). In fact, as noted, local writers knew very well that Fujianese were actively engaged in overseas trade.

References

Brockey, Liam Matthew. 2007. *Journey to the East : The Jesuit Mission to China, 1579–1724*. Cambridge, MA: Belknap Press of Harvard University Press.

Chang Tien-tse. 1934. *Sino-Portuguese Trade from 1514 to 1644: A Synthesis of Portuguese and Chinese Sources.* Leiden: E. J. Brill.

Chen Zilong, ed. [1638] 1964. *Huangming Jingshi Wenbian.* Taibei: Guolian tushu chuban youxian gongsi.

Freedman, Paul H. 2008. *Out of the East: Spices and the Medieval Imagination.* New Haven, CT: Yale University Press.

Fujii Hiroshi. 1953–1954. "Shin-an Shonin No Kenkyu." *Toyo Gakuho* 36 (1–4): 1–44.

Goodrich, L. C., and Chaoying Fang. 1976. *Dictionary of Ming Biography, 1368–1644*. 2 vols. New York: Columbia University Press.

Goto Shukudo. 1927. "Wako-O O Choku [Wang Zhi]." *Rekishi Chiri* 50 (1, 2, 4): 32–40, 106–126, 289–309.

Greenblatt, Stephen. 1991. *Marvelous Possessions: The Wonder of the New World.* Chicago: University of Chicago Press.

Gu Yanwu. 1807. *Tianxia Junguo Libingshu.* (np): *Fuwenge.*

Gu, Yingtai. 1937. *Mingshi Jishi Benmo 80 Juan.* Congshu Jicheng Chubian. Shanghai: Shangwu.

Haicheng xianzhi. 1633 edition.

Higgins, Roland. 1981. "Piracy and Coastal Defense in the Ming Period: Governmental Response to Coastal Disturbances, 1523–1549." Ph.D. dissertation, University of Minnesota.

Kuhn, Philip A. 2008. *Chinese among Others : Emigration in Modern Times.* Lanham, MD: Rowman & Littlefield.

Lane, Frederic C., 1987. "Technology and Productivity in Seaborne Transportation," in Frederic C. Lane, Benjamin G. Kohl and Reinhold C. Mueller. *Studies in Venetian Social and Economic History*, Variorum Reprint. London: Variorum Reprints, 1987.

Lewis, Martin W., and Karen Wigen. 1997. *The Myth of Continents: A Critique of Metageography*. Berkeley: University of California Press.

Lin Xiyuan. 1997. *Tong'an Lin Ciya xiansheng wenji*. Jinan: Qi Lu shushe.

Nakajima Gakusho. 2009. "Maritime Trade in the East China Sea and Transition of Western Style Firearms During the 1540s." Paper delivered at the annual meeting of Association of Asian Studies, Chicago, March. .

Perdue, Peter C. 2000. "Culture, History, and Imperial Chinese Strategy: Legacies of the Qing Conquests." In *Warfare in Chinese History*, ed. Hans van de Ven, 252–287. Leiden: Brill.

———. 2005a. *China Marches West: The Qing Conquest of Central Eurasia*. Cambridge, MA: Harvard University Press.

———. 2005b. "From Turfan to Taiwan: Trade and War on Two Chinese Frontiers." In *Untaming the Frontier: Interdisciplinary Perspectives on Frontier Studies*, ed. Bradley J. Parker and Lars Rodseth, 27–51. Tucson: University of Arizona Press.

———. 2009. "Commerce and Coercion on Two Chinese Frontiers." In *Military Culture in China*, ed. Nicola Di Cosmo, 317–338. Cambridge, MA: Harvard University Press.

Pokotilov, Dmitrii. 1976. *History of the Eastern Mongols During the Ming Dynasty*. Philadelphia, PA: Porcupine Press.

So, Kwan-wai. 1975. *Japanese Piracy in Ming China During the Sixteenth Century*. East Lansing: Michigan State University Press.

Twitchett, Denis, and Frederick Mote. 1998. *The Cambridge History of China*. Vols. 7–8, *The Ming Dynasty, 1368–1644*. Cambridge: Cambridge University Press.

Wade, Geoff. 2005. "The Zheng He Voyages: A Reassessment." *Journal of the Malaysian Branch of the Royal Asiatic Society* 78 (1): 37–58.

Waldron, Arthur. 1990. *The Great Wall of China: From History to Myth*. Cambridge: Cambridge University Press.

Wey Gómez, Nicolás. 2008. *The Tropics of Empire : Why Columbus Sailed South to the Indies*. Cambridge, MA: MIT Press.

Wiethoff, Bodo. 1963. *Die Chinesische Seeverbotspolitik und der Private Uberseehandel von 1368 Bis 1567*. Hamburg: Gesellschaft für Natur- und Völkerkunde Ostasiens.

Wills, John E., Jr. 1979. "Maritime China from Wang Chih to Shih Lang." In *From Ming to Ch'ing: Conquest, Region, and Continuity in Seventeenth-Century China*, ed. Jonathan D. Spence and John E. Wills, Jr., 201–238. New Haven, CT: Yale University Press.

Zhang Tingyu, ed. 1975. *Mingshi*. Taibei: Xin wenfeng chuban gufen youxian gongsi.

Zhu, Wan. 1997. *Piyu Zaji: 12 juan,* Siku Quanshu Cunmu Congshu. Ji Bu ; 78. Jinan: Qilu shushe chubanshe.

Zurndorfer, Harriet Thelma. 1989. *Change and Continuity in Chinese Local History: The Development of Hui-Chou Prefecture 800 to 1800*. Leiden: E.J. Brill.

4

1636 and 1726

Yemen after the First Ottoman Era

NANCY UM

Spanning the meeting-point of the Red and Arabian Seas, Yemen has connected the larger maritime network of the Indian Ocean to that of the Mediterranean Sea since antiquity. In the seventeenth and eighteenth centuries, this maritime position took on new dimensions as Yemen emerged as the central site for cultivation and trade of the coffee bean, which had become a lucrative commercial item with the increasing popularity of coffee as a social habit from Europe to Asia. In 1636, under attack by rebel imams, the Ottomans withdrew from their last foothold in Yemen, at the port of Mocha. Yemen's coffee trade flourished for nearly a century after this date. But after 1726, when the first major Dutch shipment of coffee arrived in Europe directly from Southeast Asia, Yemen's coffee business went into decline. Although Yemen's preeminent commercial role was short lived, this segment of time represents an important moment in the globalized history of the early modern southern Arabian Peninsula.

When the Ottomans controlled Yemen, beginning in 1538, the region was knit with its Mediterranean neighbors to the north, at the far limit of territories under the aegis of Istanbul. After the Ottomans fled, the region moved into a more fluid position, politically detached from the demands of Mediterranean powers, but still economically intertwined with them, as well as related spheres to the south and the east. As such, the consequences of the Ottoman departure from Yemen in 1636 set the ground for its later seventeenth- and eighteenth-century commercial history. The Ottomans are key to this investigation because they established Yemen's coffee market and then struggled to control it after their forced departure, even attempting to ban Europeans from the market, although these efforts eventually failed. These two years bracket a period of transformation of coffee from an exclusive African-Arabian product to a global commodity produced in many centers.

Rather than tracing its economic history, this paper posits coffee as a mobile object of exchange, subject to shifting spheres of demand, but also production. In this manner, I echo the contours of Robert Hellyer's paper in this volume that explores the cultivation of American tastes for Japanese green tea in the late nineteenth century, but with China as the commercial model. Using these two stimulating beverages as examples, we both explore production and consumption patterns within an interregional network of exchange in and out of Asia. In particular, this paper tracks the dimensions of desire for coffee from a wide regional perspective and hones in on the ways in which Yemen's coffee market served as a site for cross-cultural contestation and competition. These issues were increasingly pressing at a moment when it was not just the coffee bean that was in transit, but also the plant that was being cultivated across world regions from the Arabian Peninsula to the islands of the Indian and Atlantic Oceans.

With coffee as a conceptual lens, one can locate Yemen's shifting place within the multiple, overlapping, and mutable networks with which it corresponded. Although this paper is not explicitly art historical, in that it does not deal with objects or architecture as the focus of study, it is implicitly linked to the interests and goals of art historians by centering the concepts of space and visibility. While using sources that are mainly textual, this paper locates historical processes and temporal change within a tangible material and spatial matrix. Moreover, the geographic scope oscillates between wider regional processes and events and a honed localized view of the specific space of the Yemeni coffee market in Bayt al-Faqih. By doing so, this microhistory becomes nested and fixed within a much larger spatial network and the scale of political change comes down to the ground.

The First Ottoman Era, 1538–1636

Yemen's commercial coffee history begins when the Ottomans first harnessed the bean as a commodity and developed it as a major item of Red Sea and Mediterranean trade. Additionally, as described by historian Giancarlo Casale, the sixteenth-century Ottoman occupation of Yemen and its subsequent seventeenth-century loss constituted the respective beginning and end of active Ottoman policies of Indian Ocean exploration and engagement. Here, I draw on Casale's research on the Ottoman Red Sea and Indian Ocean (2009), while also extending the perspective offered by his work. I do this by considering how the Ottoman departure from Yemen reverberated far outside Istanbul in the postoccupation site of the southern Arabian Peninsula in the seventeenth and eighteenth centuries.

The Ottomans set their sights on Yemen in 1525, when the corsair Selman Reis offered the opinion that Yemen would yield great profits as a territory. By that time, the last sultan of Yemen's Tahirid dynasty (1454–1517) had been killed and the lowland areas were being controlled by the *levend,* "a fractious band of Levantine and Circassian mercenaries left behind from the last Mamluk expedition there." By contrast, the northern highlands were under expanded Zaydi rule.[1] Selman Reis encouraged Ottoman interest in the region by identifying Yemen as "a land with no lord, an empty province" (Casale 2009, 43). Hadim Suleyman Pasha, the governor of Egypt, then formally established Ottoman power in Yemen in 1538, on his return journey from an unsuccessful attack against the Portuguese at Diu on the Indian coast. This moment ushered in a period of Ottoman rule that lasted almost one hundred years. With Yemen, as well as the port of Suakin in modern Sudan, Massawa in Eritrea, and Jidda in Saudi Arabia, under Ottoman control, the Red Sea functioned as "an Ottoman lake" through the beginning of the seventeenth century.

While in 1525 Selman Reis had adequately enumerated Yemen's possible profits as an Ottoman territory, he had sorely misjudged Yemen's tractability as a province. Indeed, the divisive nature of local politics made Yemen an easy target to invade, but a difficult terrain to rule. Local resistance would prove insurmountable, eventually causing the Ottomans to flee after less than one hundred years. Among many obstacles to Ottoman control, two Zaydi imams posed the biggest threats. The first, al-Mutahhar b. Sharaf al-Din (d. 1572), who was a de facto imam of Thila, took many cities under Ottoman control beginning in 1566, only to be thwarted a few years later by Koca Sinan Pasha, who arrived from Egypt with large numbers of troops.[2] Another more significant Zaydi revolt against Ottoman rule emerged in 1598, when Imam al-Mansur billah Qasim b. Muhammad (r. 1598–1620) and his son pushed the Ottomans from the inland regions of Yemen and eventually isolated them on the coast. The Ottomans finally left Yemen in 1636 via the port of Mocha, their last foothold on the southern Arabian Peninsula.

After this point, the Ottomans continued to hold key Red Sea sites, such as Suakin, Massawa, and Jidda, but withdrew from the active Indian Ocean forays that Casale described for the sixteenth century. Even so, the Ottomans recognized that Yemen was key to their territorial and economic ambitions. As historian Jane Hathaway has described, Sultan Mehmed IV considered attacking Yemen again in the 1670s, due to fears of Qasimi expansion into the Hijaz (2005, 125). Additionally, as will be detailed below, the Ottomans continued to communicate with the Qasimis after their expulsion, with the interest of intervening in local commercial policies. Eventually, the Ottomans returned to Yemen's Red Sea coast in 1848 and reoccupied parts of the region until 1918.

The Rise of the Qasimis

After the 1636 Ottoman departure, a local family of Zaydi imams descended from al-Mansur al-Qasim established themselves as Yemen's rulers in place of the Ottomans. Although they hardly receive notice in most historical studies of the Middle East or the Indian Ocean, the Qasimis of Yemen won a remarkable and mismatched faceoff between a small Shiʿi state and the large expansionist force of the Sunni Ottomans. For this reason, the Qasimis looked to the unprecedented military victories that allowed for the foundation of their imamate as a source of pride long after the Ottomans had left (Hathaway 2005, 114).

As Heidi Walcher has shown in this volume for Safavid Iran and Tomislav Klaric (2008) has demonstrated for early modern Yemen, major political shifts entail a reconfiguration of geographic boundaries that may not be represented readily through common methods of cartographic depiction. For many of these geographic shifts represent subtle changes in the relationship between regions or the blurring of perceived spatial limits, which cannot be rendered simply through lines drawn on a map. Before the Qasimi period, the Zaydi imamate had always been localized, with imams ruling from landlocked northern centers with the compliance and support of the surrounding tribes.[3] In direct contrast to this regional model, the Sunni states of Yemen, such as the Ayyubids, Rasulids, and the early modern Tahirids controlled the southern territories and engaged in communication with outside states via maritime trade and diplomacy. After Imam al-Muʾayyad Muhammad (r. 1620–1644) expelled the Ottomans, the Qasimis turned their backs on the longstanding model of regional authority and engaged in territorial expansion beyond the traditional Zaydi areas, thereby tying together regions that had been previously separated politically and linking the Zaydi north to the Sunni south.

Eventually, the third Qasimi imam, al-Mutawakkil Ismaʿil (r. 1644–1676) brought all of lower Yemen and the eastern stretch of Hadramawt under his rule, with what Hathaway called "a new geopolitical assertiveness" (2005, 116). He engaged in military campaigns and oversaw extended tracts of land outside of the traditional localized Zaydi bases in northern Yemen. Under these expanded conditions, the Zaydi imamate was pressed to adopt administrative mechanisms that were based on the model of previous Ottoman institutions, such as new strategies of taxation and a standing army, which no Zaydi imam in Yemen had held before (Haykel 2003, 50–56). Additionally, as Haykel has eloquently shown, the territorial expansion of the Qasimis allowed for greater connections between Zaydi scholars in the highlands and Sunni Traditionist ones in the lowlands, leading to their widening impact on the former's scholarship and legal opinions. With these major shifts, the Zaydi imamate itself transformed.

For these reasons, the year 1636 marked a moment of structural transformation for Yemen, and also for Yemeni Zaydism. In many ways, the geographical divisions that had defined Yemen's terrain for centuries were inverted after the departure of the Ottomans. Rather than a stark political and religious break between the north and the south, the two areas were tied together and ruled by a Zaydi imam. This new expanded role of the Zaydi imam opened up Yemeni Zaydism to new influences, facilitating a move away from its core doctrinal tenets. Additionally, the Zaydis then came into close contact with outside states through control of the lowland ports.

Coffee Stories

Originally, coffee grew wild in Ethiopia, but the roots of its consumption as a beverage date to the early fifteenth century in Yemen, likely in Sufi circles.

Although local authorities treated it with suspicion and passed legislation against it in places like Mecca, Cairo, and Istanbul, coffee caught on quickly as a social habit in the Arab and Ottoman worlds (Hattox 1985). Initially, small quantities of wild Ethiopian beans were garnered for export until Özdemir Pasha, the enterprising officer who spearheaded campaigns along both sides of the Red Sea, fostered coffee farming in Yemen in order to handle the increased demand for this cash crop, as Tuchscherer has proposed (2003, 54).[4] From the late sixteenth century forward, Yemen emerged as the major cultivator and exporter of the bean to a world that was increasingly thirsty for it.

The Ottomans were responsible for spurring the development of Yemen's coffee cultivation and export industry in the sixteenth century, but the local coffee trade escalated after they departed, in order to cater to a widening global demand. In the late seventeenth century, Yemen became a veritable world center for the sale of this precious commodity. The fortunes of merchants residing in cities like Cairo and Amsterdam hinged upon the Yemeni coffee market, at least for a brief time. For that reason the Qasimi dynasty has been referred to as the "Coffee Imamate" (Haykel 2003, 16). But this position was unstable, particularly after coffee cultivation spread to locations outside of the immediate region.

It is important to unravel the three strands of coffee's history—the history of the coffee bean as a commodity, the liquid history of the beverage and its consumption as a social habit, and the botanical history of the coffee plant. It is often the case that the stories of the bean and plant are folded into the lively narrative of the caffeinated drink's dispersal. While clearly related, these three trajectories may not be overlaid seamlessly. The Arabic etymology is instructive. The term that describes the drink *(qahwa)* is distinct from that which refers to the bean *(bunn),* suggesting that the object of consumption may have lived a very different social life during its commodity stage. Moreover, while the plant derived from Africa, both the cultivated bean and the hot, dark beverage entered the global realm from Yemen, but the production and consumption spheres became splintered soon after coffee was cultivated outside the immediate region. The coffee-studies pioneer Steven Topik describes the contemporary ramifications of this split: "For much of coffee's history, coffee-growing countries have been rural and illiterate while coffee-drinking countries and urban coffee-drinking intellectuals led the world into the Age of Enlightenment" (2009, 83). Thus, the history of coffee combines the story of an agricultural product, a commodity, and a beverage. To tell its story, we need to untangle its various spheres of circulation.

The Yemeni Coffee Market

While the Ottomans spearheaded coffee cultivation in Yemen in the sixteenth century, the Qasimi imams instituted major structural changes in the way that coffee was distributed and sold in the seventeenth century. Here a few words about Yemen's topography are necessary. Coffee grows at high altitudes where rainfall is adequate and temperatures optimal. In Yemen, ranges of mountains curve around the peninsula from the north to the south. These mountains were terraced to accommodate coffee bushes while effectively allowing runoff water to trickle down the agricultural slopes. Under the Ottomans, the coffee market appears to have been surprisingly unregulated. Coffee was sold at the ports of export or at the highland points of production and processing, with the intermediation of Indian Baniyan brokers (Brouwer 2006, 41–42). The coffee bales then exited Yemen via the Red Sea or by overland caravan.

The Qasimis instituted a structure that allowed for closer regulation and monitoring of the coffee market. One cannot say when it began, but sometime between 1640 and 1683 a centralized coffee emporium was established in the town of Bayt al-Faqih, which sits strategically in Yemen's lowland Tihama region that stretches along the border of the Red Sea.[5]

The town is situated ideally at the base of the coffee-growing mountains, but also located squarely between the three coastal ports that handled export shipping. It is closest to the port of al-Hudayda, but accessible to the northern port al-Luhayya and the southern port Mocha, each by a journey of a few days. It is likely that Imam al-Mutawakkil Isma'il, who instituted major commercial reforms in Yemen, established Bayt al-Faqih as the Qasimi coffee emporium, but local sources provide no details about it. It is clear, however, that this centralized coffee emporium was established so that coffee sales could be managed and controlled more closely by the imam's officials. As recounted by the French merchants who arrived in Yemen in the early eighteenth century, the coffee market in Bayt al-Faqih was a panoptic space with the city's governor seated on a dais in the center overseeing daily transactions (La Roque 1726, 98). Fees were levied at the point of purchase, Bayt al-Faqih, and then additional duties were added when the coffee bales were transported through the ports, allowing for the maximum profit on this precious commodity. For a period of more than forty years, bridging the late seventeenth century and the first quarter of the eighteenth century, the coffee market

Ports and emporia of seventeenth- and eighteenth-century Yemen. (Barry Levely)

at Bayt al-Faqih served as the global emporium for the coffee bean, called by the Danish historian Kristof Glamann the "centre of a trade of a world-embracing character" (1958, 191).[6]

Agents shipping for Jidda and Cairo were the main clients of the coffee market in Bayt al-Faqih, with the majority of bales sent from Yemen's ports northward to Jidda, destined for Egypt and further Mediterranean distribution, including to Europe (Kawatoko 2001).[7] Beginning in the first decades of the seventeenth century, coffee was also exported from Yemen to the east, for the Iranian and Indian markets (Matthee 1994, 5–6). Although English and Dutch merchants arrived in Yemen initially for a stake in the western Indian Ocean trade and not for coffee alone, it became a desired item for both by the end of the seventeenth century, when the habit had garnered a committed Western following and coffeehouses could be found in most major European cities.[8] In the first quarter of the eighteenth century, this prized commodity became the major European interest in Yemen and also spurred the merchants associated with the French, Swedish, and Ostend East India Companies to arrive on the Arabian coast.

While Bayt al-Faqih served as the centralized site for coffee sales, merchants used three different ports for export. Those shipping for the Cairo market via Jidda used the northern ports of al-Luhayya and al-Hudayda primarily. Those shipping to the Persian Gulf market used all three ports of al-Luhayya, al-Hudayda, and Mocha. European merchants shipping via Indian Ocean channels used Mocha almost exclusively.[9] Although India was rarely intended as the final destination point for Yemeni coffee, Indian merchants were key to its trade at Bayt al-Faqih. Namely, the Baniyans—Hindu and Jain merchants from Gujarat, the northwest region of India—played a major role as brokers for the coffee trade, as well as the general overseas and wholesale trade of Yemen in the seventeenth and eighteenth century.[10] During the post-Ottoman era, they were regular inhabitants in Yemeni cities as merchants and brokers who also inspired controversy over both their economic visibility and their religious difference (Haykel 2003, 125–126; Um 2009, 162–184).

The first quarter of the eighteenth century also witnessed the rise of European coffee cultivation in colonial territories and then Yemen's loss of its near monopoly on the coffee bean. In 1707, the Heeren XVII of the Dutch East India Company, or VOC, ordered the Batavia administration to stimulate local coffee cultivation.[11] Sizeable quantities of adequate quality were finally harnessed in 1711. By 1726, Dutch imports of coffee in Amsterdam were dominated by Javanese beans, rather than Yemeni-grown ones (Knaap 1986, 36). In 1714, the French obtained coffee plants for cultivation on the island of Réunion (Île Bourbon) and then later on Martinique (Campbell 2003, 67–68). In the 1730s, the coffee grown in the French territories in the West Indies and Indian Ocean and shipped via Marseille began to arrive in the

Mediterranean ports of Egypt, the Levant, and Anatolia. This shift represented a major reversal in the global flow of coffee exports, with European middlemen funneling the trade and transit of coffee grown in colonial plantations destined for Muslim consumption (Tuchscherer 2003, 56). So this era marked a transitional period in coffee's global availability, as well as foregrounding the increasing role that European cultivation would play in global coffee markets. Yemen's coffee industry continues into the modern era, but its central role in the global coffee trade was irrevocably compromised by these developments.

Ottoman and European Competition in the Southern Arabian Marketplace

As described above, the expulsion of the Ottomans from Yemen in 1636 marked the end of their efforts to engage directly in the Indian Ocean sphere. It also marked the end of their control over the lucrative coffee market. Ottoman merchants, both Turkish and Arab, continued to profit from the precious bean, but they did so at the will of the Qasimi imam and his governors, who controlled the local market tightly, and also with the assistance of agents at Bayt al-Faqih who would ship coffee to Jidda for transfer to the north. While much has been written about European interest in the Yemeni coffee market at this time, less is known about Ottoman involvement. Hathaway has provided a general picture of a situation in which "the Ottomans were at the virtual mercy of the Qasimi imam who derived a healthy profit from the coffee trade." According to the Ottoman court historian Mustafa Naima (1655–1716), the Ottomans lamented contributing to the treasury of their ousters, the Qasimis, as they continued to rely upon them for this prized commodity (Hathaway 2006, 168).

But a second turning point occurred in the first decades of the eighteenth century, a time of crisis in the Yemeni coffee market, when prices were on the rise.[12] The Ottomans influenced the Qasimis to limit European purchases on the market, albeit ineffectively, culminating in a ban ordered in 1719. These price increases are often explained as a result of European direct purchases of coffee, which were expanded via Indian Ocean channels during this time. But it is difficult to determine how much of an effect the European trade actually had on the coffee market because earlier comparative figures, as well as ones for Cairo and Persian Gulf sales, are either undocumented or incomplete. Moreover, certain external factors, such as years of bad crops and complications in transit must also be taken into account when considering fluctuations in price. As economic historian Mehmet Genç has stated, "after 1702, the relationship between the demand and price of coffee becomes both complex and ambiguous" (2001, 163).

But for the purposes of this investigation, the actual effect of European sales on the Yemeni coffee market is less important than the *perception* that the European commercial presence was the principal cause for the rise in prices at Bayt al-Faqih. Once again, Hellyer's work on the Japanese tea market is instructive. In the nineteenth century, a vibrant cross-cultural sphere of production, advertising, and marketing that encompassed Japan, the United States, China, and India formed American opinions regarding the quality of tea and its health effects. These perceptions were key factors in the marketability of tea and ultimately drove the demand for it, whether or not they were based on solid data. In the case of Yemeni coffee beans, we know that individual merchants in Cairo could use the European presence in Yemen's coffee market to increase their profits strategically. According to Raymond, they engaged in a kind of "psychological warfare" by deliberately overestimating the amount of coffee that Europeans had purchased in Yemen and underestimating their own supplies in order to raise the value of their coffee bales once they arrived in the Egyptian marketplace (1980, 42). Thus it is not surprising that merchants at Bayt al-Faqih blamed the Europeans for the rise in coffee's price. Indeed, the arrival of a European boat in Mocha's harbors would cause the price of coffee at Bayt al-Faqih to skyrocket, at least momentarily.

It is well known that Ottoman officials attempted to limit European purchases of coffee in Cairo and other cities in the Mediterranean. In 1703 and then, in 1706, they instituted an outright ban on exporting coffee outside of the boundaries of the empire (Buti 2001, 221–222; Raymond 1980, 44; Tuchscherer 2003, 57). While this ban, in addition to other Ottoman attempts at limiting coffee's sale and consumption, was unevenly enforced and regularly circumvented, it nevertheless represents the fact that the Ottomans saw coffee as an important local commodity that should not be provided for the free consumption of Europeans (Genç 2001, 163–164). The present essay relies upon a combined reading of local Arabic sources, in conjunction with commercial and travel records of the Dutch, English, and French, to show how the Ottomans tried to inspire the Qasimis to implement a similar ban in Yemen. Their efforts were ultimately ineffective, but still represent the extension of Ottoman interest in the southern Arabian marketplace long after their seventeenth-century departure.[13]

My goal is to show how the interests of various merchants and states collided in Yemen, particularly at Bayt al-Faqih, the sole location where the Mediterranean coffee trade and its Indian Ocean counterpart overlapped. While both markets ultimately supplied Europe, they represent two distinct trajectories of the coffee bean, which each operated according to its own spatial, temporal, and economic logic. The different players in the coffee market placed multiple demands on the imam, as its overseer, at the moment when coffee itself was being transformed as a commodity that was no longer solely Yemeni, but in the process of becoming global.

Ottoman Envoys in Yemen

In his account of the first French missions to Yemen in 1708 to 1712, Jean de la Roque wrote about a French doctor, Monsieur Barbier, who was sent to the interior highland court to treat Imam al-Mahdi Muhammad (r. 1698–1718), who was suffering from an ear infection.[14] (La Roque 1726, 203) During his three-week-long stay at the court in al-Mawahib in 1712, he witnessed an Ottoman envoy that came from Istanbul via Egypt. The ambassador, who appeared with a large retinue and many gifts, complained that European coffee sales had diminished the supply going to Egypt and had caused the price of this precious commodity to increase. He also objected to the fact that Europeans received a preferential customs rate on their purchases in Yemen. According to the French observer, Imam al-Mahdi did not welcome this Ottoman intervention in his policies and seemed to desire the quick departure of the delegation. It is impossible, however, to ascertain what actually transpired between the imam and the Ottoman envoy, as this information came to the French through a secondhand source at the court. Regardless, there were no ramifications to the European coffee trade that year—the French shipped as many bales as they had in a previous season—so it does not appear that al-Mahdi acted upon any Ottoman demands.

The Ottoman concern over competition in Yemen's coffee market escalated over the following years, as indicated by multiple envoys dispatched to the Qasimis. Of these embassies, the best-documented one was sent in 1719 and described by a Yemeni chronicler, Muhsin b. al-Hasan, also known as Abu Talib.[15] According to Abu Talib, an Ottoman ambassador from Jidda arrived at the court of Imam al-Mutawakkil al-Qasim (r. 1718–1727) in Sanaa with a letter from the Sultan in hand. His goal was to convince the imam to prohibit the European trade of coffee in Yemen, which was "in the general interest of Muslims." The letter added that non-Muslims should not to be allowed to live in Mocha[16] and threatened in stark terms that travelers from Yemen would be forbidden from proceeding to Jidda by sea if this demand were not obeyed (al-Hasan 1990, 405). After consideration, al-Mutawakkil, unlike al-Mahdi before him, agreed to comply and sent the messenger away satisfied with many gifts.[17] Although the passage alludes to the ensuing dissatisfaction of the merchants affected, the issue then disappeared from the chronicle.

This embassy was also noted in the Ottoman sources from Cairo studied by Raymond, which mention a *kapıcı başı* that was sent to Yemen in 1719 to demand that Europeans be excluded from the coffee market there (Raymond 1973, 1: 150). This mission was apparently supported by the sharif of Mecca as well. According to these records, the imam of Yemen agreed to make a considerable quantity of 30,000 to 35,000 fardes of coffee available for the Jidda market the following year, although nothing was said about limiting the European stake in the trade. Although these two accounts differ in details, we can discern from them that the Yemeni imam made efforts to appease the Ottoman ambassador of 1719 and that officials in Cairo believed that the mission had been a success.

Yet perspectives from Yemen reveal that these decisions were hardly simple, straightforward, or conclusive. Rather, over the months following this envoy's visit, a series of discussions and negotiations took place between the imam of Yemen and local Dutch and English merchants about not only whether they could purchase coffee in Yemen, but also how and where they should do so. In this regard, the *dag registers,* or daily logbooks of the VOC, offer a helpful perspective. The Dutch merchants convey that on September 3, 1719, a messenger from the imam in Sanaa came to their house in Mocha, transmitting the Ottoman complaint that the European trade had raised coffee prices too high, thereby preventing them from purchasing it. Additionally, the Ottoman envoy voiced concerns about the Dutch and English houses, which were said to be large and equipped with artillery and expressed the fear that they could take the city by siege with little warning. The Dutch immediately wrote a letter to the imam stating that these claims were untrue. Even so, five days later, another letter came to the Dutch, this time from Bayt al-Faqih, with the news that Imam al-Mutawakkil had sent a letter to that city's governor telling him not to allow the "hat wearing nations" to purchase any coffee (September 8, 1719, VOC 9116, ff. 37–38).

The previous year, 1718, was described by Glamann as an uncommonly bad year for coffee, when there was "an abnormally great demand and also an abnormally small supply" due to a poor harvest (1958, 197). Additionally, in May 1719, a ship from Ostend had arrived to trade in Yemen for the first time, which alarmed the other European groups in the city, and was undoubtedly noted by other merchants at Bayt al-Faqih as well (VOC 9103, ff. 95–96). It appears that the Ottomans were reacting to the dire problems of the past year, when the diminished supply of beans was further exacerbated by the increased presence of European merchants at the coffee emporium.

Although the Dutch are solitary observers of these events at the port and their sources are invaluable to the historian, one should not accept their subjective framing of them in a wholesale way. The VOC merchants at Mocha were alarmed by this infringement on their trading rights and wrote to the imam in outspoken terms about the immediate need to restore the privileges outlined in their trade treaty. But, in fact, the imam's 1719 ban on European coffee sales would have had little effect on European trade, at least at the outset. September was the low season for European trade. All Indian Ocean ships bound for the east and the south had left the port in August. Only a few European merchants, such as the Dutch and some English merchants, remained at the port of Mocha during this low season. Similarly, no European merchants were present in Bayt al-Faqih, although, at that time, that city was filled with agents, provisioned with chests of silver from Jidda to purchase coffee destined for the north. They were busy buying up the old beans from the past year and waiting eagerly for the new harvest to arrive from the highlands in the coming weeks. Although the European merchants at Mocha would stay abreast of news from the coffee emporium, they were unable to buy significant quantities of coffee until their silver arrived for the new trade season, beginning with the arrival of their ships from both Asia and Europe in January.[18] Moreover, they would have wanted to avoid the increased prices that stemmed from the influx of Cairene capital during this time. Undoubtedly, the imam was aware of this particular schedule for trade, for he was deeply invested in it. His own ships had left for Surat a few weeks earlier, on August 23 (VOC 9116, f. 34).[19]

Moreover, as we continue reading the Dutch *dag register*, the imam's ambivalence about his own newly imposed ban becomes clear, for he began modifying it almost as soon as the Ottoman messenger had left his court.[20] On September 26, a letter arrived from the imam to the Dutch in Mocha as a response to theirs from a few weeks earlier. While he assured them that they were not guilty of any misconduct, he still prohibited all Europeans from buying coffee in Bayt al-Faqih, but did allow them the minor concession to purchase coffee beans in Mocha. This concession was hardly appealing to the Dutch because coffee in Mocha was only available in small quantities that were marked up in price and often of poor quality. Anyone who was interested in buying significant quantities would do so in Bayt al-Faqih.

For that reason, the Dutch continued to argue for their right to buy coffee in Yemen's central coffee emporium in a long letter to the imam, dated September 27, 1719. In it, they not only rejected the ban on coffee purchases at Bayt al-Faqih, but also responded to claims that were not commercial, but rather sumptuary in nature. It is clear that concerns about their economic presence were collapsed almost indistinguishably with those about the visible presence of non-Muslims in on the Arabian Peninsula, one of the key Ottoman concerns. For instance, the Dutch attempted to mollify the charges about the size and weaponry of their houses in Mocha and Mawzaʿ (an inland town which was used as a vacation spot by European merchants at this time), the number of horses that they owned and how often they rode them, and the critical issue of their relations with local women. They threatened that the imam must reinstate the original terms of their trade treaty or they would leave the city and it would become deserted like Aden. At the same time, they wrote a letter containing all of the same points to the wazir and governor of Bayt al-Faqih, Salih b. ʿAli al-Huraybi. To al-Huraybi, however, they added that it was not them but the English who caused the problems, thereby blaming their European competition for these complications.

As the debate between the Dutch and the imam continued, the latter eventually yielded his position. On November 13, the imam conceded by allowing them to buy coffee in Bayt al-Faqih as long as they did not go in person, but purchased it via Baniyan brokers. The Dutch accepted this compromise, which represented almost a full restitution of their privileges. Yet they were still awaiting the arrival of their ships in the coming months. Nonetheless, the two concessions that the imam offered are telling. They reveal clearly that the imam's goal was not to exclude Europeans from Yemen's coffee market. To the contrary, he was content with limiting their visibility there. The observant agents at Bayt al-Faqih who were shipping for Jidda and Cairo conveyed not just beans to their northern counterparts, but also information. By limiting the European presence in Bayt al-Faqih, a site of direct interface between these various merchant groups, the imam could continue to profit from the European trade in Yemen, while maintaining the fragile illusion that he had kept his promise to the Ottoman sultan. In this way, the imam was trying to negotiate the Mediterranean interests of the Ottomans, while still managing the demands of the active Indian Ocean trade, in which Europeans played a considerable, although not singular, role. The imam wanted to uphold his trade agreements with the Europeans, while also keeping them out of the watchful eye of the Ottoman sultan's agents and informants.

In the following weeks, these concerns died down considerably. In December, Qasim al-Turbati, a local merchant who had gone up to Sanaa, informed the Dutch that the imam was no longer concerned about this issue, which was, by that point, articulated entirely in sumptuary terms. Al-Turbati stated that all talk of "artillery, horses, and whores" had disappeared from the imam's court (December 11, 1719, VOC 9116, f. 57). On January 13, 1720, two Dutch ships came into the harbor, and during the next month the Dutch sealed their first purchase of coffee at Bayt al-Faqih for the year through Baniyan brokers. When the English East India Company ships arrived in the spring, they, however, were dissatisfied with working through their brokers and attempted to regain permission to send their own representatives to buy coffee directly. On May 12, 1720, the governor granted this to Edward Say, the English factor, who then sent the writer Thomas Hartnett to the coffee emporium (May 16, 1720, IOR G/17/1, pt. 1, f. 8r). Hartnett shipped bales of coffee from that city to Mocha in June. So, within eight months, the short-lived ban on European purchases of coffee was completely lifted, just in time for the height of the European coffee trading season. When the Dutch closed their books for the year in July 1720, they had purchased 1,771,742 lbs. of coffee, a significant quantity indicating that the events described above did not have a major impact on their trade.

Conclusion

The events surrounding the unsuccessful 1719 ban on European purchases of coffee in Yemen are unique because they represent the only instance in which the imam agreed to Ottoman demands even initially and also because they are relatively well documented from different sources. In the following years,

Ottoman envoys continued to arrive in Yemen with similar concerns. For instance, five years later, in March 1725, the Dutch heard that some Turkish merchants from Egypt had arrived in Sanaa again asking that Imam al-Mutawakkil allow them to have sole rights over coffee sales at Bayt al-Faqih, which he did not agree to (March 25, 1725, VOC 9119, ff. 150–151). This mission differed from the two that were described above because it seems to have been executed on the initiative of individual merchants rather than the Ottoman state and been targeted at all merchants, rather than just the Europeans, which would include those from the Persian Gulf as well. Apparently, dissatisfied with the imam's negative response, those merchants took matters into their own hands. A couple weeks later, on April 5, a Dutch letter reported that some "Turkish" merchants had tried to prevent them from buying coffee at Bayt al-Faqih. The local governor asked the Dutch to remain in their rented home, rather than appearing at the coffee market, in order to curb any possible conflicts (VOC 9119, f. 156). Later that year, in December, the Dutch heard that another Turkish envoy had arrived at the court in Sanaa, again trying to intervene with European coffee purchases. This envoy also went to Bayt al-Faqih to talk to the governor there (December 7, 1725, VOC 9120, f. 36). The sheer recurrence of these envoys signals that their missions were not being carried out effectively and hence required repetition.

However, the Ottomans stopped sending these envoys soon after this last account. By 1726, they had clearly realized that their efforts against European coffee sales were ineffective. At this time, they had also lifted similar injunctions in the Mediterranean (Genç 2001, 164). In March 1726, the news arrived in Mocha that seven Dutch ships full of coffee were sent from Asia to Europe, a quantity that far outweighed that which they had purchased in Yemen the previous year (March 27, 1726, VOC 9120, ff. 53–54). Although the initial consignment of coffee successfully cultivated in Java had been shipped fifteen years earlier, the 1725 shipment had been the first to yield a significant quantity and thus caused worried rumors to spread among Mocha's merchants and officials (Knaap 1986, 37). The Dutch remained at the port for many more years in order to boost the demand for Javanese beans on the European market by keeping the price of Yemeni coffee high.[21]

Rather than constituting a classic case of east-west confrontation around the Indian Ocean rim, the events described above demonstrate the liminal status of the three parties that each stood to lose or profit from various sets of shifting arrangements within the southern Arabian marketplace. The Ottomans were a major superpower that was surprisingly ineffective at controlling commercial affairs outside of, as well as within, their borders. The Qasimis were quite conciliatory toward European merchants, whose local presence they were eager to retain. Dutch and English merchants were not operating in a protocolonial framework in which their trade impact unfolded in a straight line toward colonial rule; rather, they held a relatively fragile position in Mocha and were often more concerned with the trade activity of their European counterparts than that of Muslim or Asian ones.

This essay began with the year 1636, when the first Ottoman occupation of Yemen ended, as an important turning point for the southern Arabian Peninsula. But it concludes with 1726, another key year for Yemen, the moment when knowledge about the success of offsite coffee cultivation arrived on the Arabian Peninsula. Accordingly, this year also marked the beginning of a steep and rapid decline in Yemen's global contributions of this highly sought-after commodity. As such, these two years serve as brackets that trace the transformation of coffee from its status as a plant cultivated in Africa and Arabia to its new incarnation as one that was actively farmed in the Atlantic and Indian Ocean realms. These years also highlight the elasticity of Yemen's place in the global networks that it participated in. Before 1636, it represented the southern limit of the Ottoman world dominated by the Mediterranean-oriented interests of Istanbul. But then, in the later seventeenth century and into the eighteenth, the Qasimi imam of Yemen was situated at the center of a global matrix, caught between the competing interests of the Mediterranean world, as represented by Ottoman economic demands, and Indian Ocean ones, as represented by the Mocha trade.

Notes

The author wishes to thank Eric Tagliacozzo and Helen Siu for the kind invitation to participate in Asia Inside Out. Thanks are also due to conference participants and audience members in Hong Kong and at Wellesley College, who commented intelligently on this essay at earlier stages and helped guide its revision. Mary Youssef generously took time to discuss the intricacies of the Arabic sources. Thanks also to Barry Levely for the map.

1. As one of three major subbranches of Shiʿi Islam, Zaydism, which emerged in the ninth century, has been represented by two communities historically, one in Yemen and the other in Tabaristan on the Caspian Sea. When the Caspian Zaydi

community declined in the twelfth century, the Yemenis became the dominant representatives of Zaydism into the modern era.

2. Al-Mutahhar was technically unable to assume the position because of a physical handicap. According to Blackburn, he was a "de facto imam" for the purposes of military engagement and political leadership (2000, 3).

3. The Zaydi concept of the imam is much broader than that of the other Shiʿi groups, the Twelvers and the Ismaʿilis, and succession does not follow lineal descent. For Zaydis, the imam must be a descendant of the Prophet through Fatima and ʿAli, possess scholarly erudition and be capable of defending the community, in addition to other criteria.

4. Although the Ottomans held the ports of Massawa and Hergigo in Abyssinia, they had only limited access to the interior regions.

5. In 1640, Wurffbain was still purchasing coffee in Mocha (Brouwer 2006, 42). The first dated mention of the coffee market in Bayt al-Faqih appears in a Dutch source from 1683 (VOC 1406). However, Bayt al-Faqih was also subject to the wider political upheavals. It was briefly controlled by a certain Amir Zayd, who took the city in the name of the wazir Zayd b. ʿAli Jahhaf, but then Imam al-Mahdi Muhammad reclaimed it in 1097/1685–1686 (Zabara 1985, 385).

6. However, the port of Mocha, which played a relatively minimal role in the coffee trade, has largely overshadowed the inland center's reputation as a place for coffee sales. In fact, the name Mocha coffee is a bit of a misnomer, signifying the port from which coffee was shipped, but not the place where it was grown or purchased (Brouwer 2006, 56–57; Um 2009, 36–47).

7. Raymond has shown that few merchants from Cairo ventured south of Jidda or maintained direct contact with Yemeni counterparts in this era. Rather these northern merchants were served by agents that worked from Bayt al-Faqih. We know very little about this group of agents, but a Yemeni merchant named Saʿd al-Din al-ʿUdayni was likely one of them (Raymond 2002; Um 2009, 89–91).

8. When the Dutch and English initially began to purchase coffee in Yemen in the seventeenth century, it was intended for transshipment in the Arabian Sea, mainly for the Persian Gulf and western Indian markets. The European market opened up to coffee shipments in the 1660s (Matthee 1994).

9. The English also negotiated for the right to transport their coffee beans from Bayt al-Faqih to al-Hudayda, but only used that option when there was a shortage of camel drivers from Bayt al-Faqih or when their ships arrived in Yemen late in the season, as they did in 1721.

10. In his short but important study on the Baniyans in Yemen, R. B. Serjeant attempted to excavate the earliest textual citations to the community, which date to the fourteenth century, with Ibn al-Mujawir's mention of Hafat al-Baniyan (the Baniyan quarter) in Aden. One may find scattered references to the Baniyans, or even less discriminately, Indian merchants, in sources that predate the Qasimi era. But it is clear

that the Baniyan merchants emerged as a major unified block of merchants in the trading world of Yemen in the seventeenth and eighteenth centuries, when the textual references to their Arabian presence increase notably (Serjeant 1983a, 432–435).

11. According to Leupe, the Dutch transported coffee plants from South Asia to Indonesia beginning in 1696. By 1699, they had cultivated them successfully in Java. Other sources, including Yemeni lore, surmised that the Dutch smuggled coffee plants out of Yemen against the imam's orders (Leupe 1859, 56; Baghdiantz-McCabe 2008, 206).

12. For instance, Tuchscherer has shown that the number of Turkish merchants participating in Cairo's Red Sea trade between the years 1708 and 1730 witnessed a sharp decline (1991, 328) While this trade encompassed more than coffee, declining coffee revenues must have played a role in this drop. Dutch sources indicate that coffee prices rose considerably since the year 1717 and English sources record a steady increase for the period from 1710–1745 (Chaudhuri 1978, 360; Knaap 1986, 36).

13. Not all Ottoman diplomatic visits of the time were related to the coffee question. In 1114/1702–1703, Salim Pasha sent his brother Ahmad Agha to the imam's court in al-Mawahib. He stayed for a while and then passed through Sanaa (where he was entertained), ʿAmran, and finally left from al-Luhayya (al-Hasan 1990, 305).

14. La Roque's book was immediately popularized and translated into English and German. Along with a narrative of the French missions, it provided a lengthy appendix about coffee. La Roque did not travel to Yemen, but used letters and interviews with the ship crewmembers and merchants that made the two journeys. For more on the medical treatment of the imam of Yemen by foreign doctors see Um, forthcoming.

15. Abu Talib stated that the ambassador arrived in 1133/1720–1721, whereas the VOC records say that he arrived in 1719 (1131 AH). When the English documents begin in 1720, they show that the crisis was almost resolved by that point. I use the earlier Dutch date, which is corroborated by English and Ottoman documents, rather than Abu Talib's dating. Abu Talib was writing retrospectively and other dates in his text are incorrect by a year or two, such as that of Aurangzeb's death, which was recorded in 1117/1705–1706, but actually happened in 1118/1707. Glamann described an embassy that arrived in Yemen in July 1719. However, Glamann interpreted the information based on the erroneous assumption that the Ottomans were still occupying Yemen at that time (probably drawing from van den Broecke's early seventeenth-century account). For that reason he described the Ottoman sultan's inability to exert control over the Yemeni market as an internal problem of authority. To the contrary, this was a case of a foreign state trying to intervene in local commercial affairs (Glamann 1958, 188, 192). Also, in passing, Serjeant mentioned an Ottoman embassy that had arrived at the imam's court to complain about the European trade, but gave no date (other than stating that this happened some time before the year 1737) or citation (Serjeant 1983b, 79).

16. This issue was one of contention between Ottoman jurists, who were Sunni adhering to the Hanafi school of legal interpretation, and Shi'i Zaydi ones. Hanafis believed that non-Muslims should not live anywhere on the Peninsula, while Zaydis deemed it permissible for non-Muslims to live in Yemen, but not in the vicinity of the holy cities. As Haykel has shown, this issue was hotly debated within Yemen at this time, between the two camps of strict Zaydis and Sunni-oriented scholars (2003, 115–126).

17. The Dutch clarified, saying that the messenger was sent away with lots of Spanish reals and many bales of coffee as a gift, although they heard different accounts of the quantities of each (Sept 16, 1719, VOC 9116, f. 39).

18. On September 21, information and samples of coffee arrived in the Dutch house in Mocha from Bayt al-Faqih, sent via Indian Baniyan brokers. Although this did not constitute a direct transaction, it indicates that Indian brokers were still working with European merchants to inform them of the state of the market in spite of these new restrictions (VOC 9116, f. 40).

19. The Qasimi imams owned two ships, which are documented as early as the imamate of al-Mahdi Muhammad (r. 1698–1718) through al-Mansur al-Husayn's period (r. 1727–1748). It is unlikely that they were built in Yemen, however. These ships are never mentioned in the local Arabic chronicles, but appear often in the commercial records of the Dutch and English, as do the names of the ships' *nakhudhas*, or sea captains (Um 2009, 91–95).

20. The Ottoman ambassador set sail from the port of al-Luhayya on September 25 (VOC 9116, f. 40).

21. Although VOC officials discussed the possibility of closing down the Mocha factory as early as 1724, it was not closed down officially until 1739 (VOC 9113; Glamann 1958, 208–209).

References

al-Hasan, Muhsin b. (Abu Talib). 1990. *Tarikh al-yaman fi 'asr al-istiqlal 'an al-hukm al-'uthmani al-awwal,* ed. 'Abd Allah Muhammad al-Hibshi. Sanaa: Al-Mufaddal Offset Printers.

Baghdiantz-McCabe, Ina. 2008. *Orientalism in Early Modern France: Eurasian Trade, Exoticism and the Ancien Régime.* New York: Berg.

Blackburn, J. R. 2003. "The Era of Imam Sharaf al-Din Yahya and his son al-Mutahhar." *Yemen Update* 42: 3.

Brouwer, C. G. 2006. *Al-Mukha: The Transoceanic Trade of a Yemeni Staple Town as Mapped by Merchants of the VOC, 1614–1640: Coffee, Spices and Textiles.* Amsterdam: D'Fluyte Rarob.

Buti, Gilbert. 2001. "Marseille entre Moka et café des îles: espaces, flux, réseaux, XVIIe–XVIIIe siècles." In *Le commerce du café avant l'ère des plantations coloniales:*

espaces, réseaux, sociétés (XVe–XIXe siècle), ed. Michel Tuchscherer, 213–244. Cairo: Institut français d'archéologie orientale.

Campbell, Gwyn. 2003. "The Origins and Development of Coffee Production in Réunion and Madgascar, 1711–1972." In *The Global Coffee Economy in Africa, Asia, and Latin America, 1500–1989,* ed. W. G. Clarence-Smith and S. Topik, 67–99. Cambridge: Cambridge University Press.

Casale, Giancarlo. 2009. *The Ottoman Age of Exploration.* Oxford: Oxford University Press.

Chaudhuri, K. N. 1978. *The Trading World of Asia and the English East India Company, 1660–1760.* Cambridge: Cambridge University Press.

Genç, Mehmet. 2001. "Contrôle et taxation du commerce du café dans l'Empire ottoman fin XVIIe—première moitié du XVIIIe siècle." In *Le commerce du café avant l'ère des plantations coloniales: espaces, réseaux, sociétés (XVe–XIXe siècle),* ed. Michel Tuchscherer, 161–179. Cairo: Institut français d'archéologie orientale.

Glamann, Kristof. 1958. *Dutch-Asiatic Trade, 1620–1740.* The Hague: Martinus Nijhoff.

Hathaway, Jane. 2005. "The Mawzaʿ Exile at the Juncture of Zaydi and Ottoman Messianism." *American Jewish Studies Review* 29 (1): 111–128.

———. 2006. "The Ottomans and the Yemeni Coffee Trade." *Oriento Moderno* 26 (1): 161–171.

Hattox, Ralph. 1985. *Coffee and Coffeehouses: The Origins of a Social Beverage in the Medieval Near East.* Seattle: University of Washington Press.

Haykel, Bernard. 2003. *Revival and Reform in Islam: The Legacy of Muhammad al-Shawkani.* Cambridge: Cambridge University Press.

India Office Records (IOR), Mocha Factory Records. G/17/1, pt. 1. British Library, London.

Kawatoko, Mutsuo. 2001. "Coffee Trade in the al-Tur Port, South Sinai." In *Le commerce du café avant l'ère des plantations coloniales: espaces, réseaux, sociétés (XVe–XIXe siècle),* ed. Michel Tuchscherer, 51–65. Cairo: Institut français d'archéologie orientale.

Klarić, Tomislav. 2008. "Le Yémen au XVIIe siècle: territoire et identités." *Revue des mondes musulmans et de la Méditerranée* 121–122: 69–78.

Knaap, G. J. 1986. "Coffee for Cash: The Dutch East India Company and the Expansion of Coffee Cultivation in Java, Ambon, and Ceylon 1700–1730." In *Trading Companies in Asia, 1600–1830,* ed. J. van Goor, 33–50. Utrecht: Hes Uitgevers.

La Roque, Jean de. 1726. *Voyage to Arabia the Happy by way of the Eastern Ocean, and the Streights of the Red-Sea: Perform'd by the French for the first time, A.D. 1708, 1709, 1710.* London: G. Straham.

Leupe, P. A. 1859. "Invoering der koffijkultur op Java, 1700–1750." *Bijdragen tot de taal-, land-, en volkenkunde van Nederlandsch-Indië* 7: 53–71.

Matthee, Rudi. 1994. "Coffee in Safavid Iran: Commerce and Consumption." *Journal of the Economic and Social History of the Orient* 37: 1–32.

Raymond, André. 1973. *Artisans et commerçants au Caire au XVIIIe siècle.* 2 vols. Damascus: Institut français de Damas.

———. 1980. "Les problèmes du café en Égypte au XVIIIe siècle." In *Le café en Méditerranée: histoire, anthropologie, économie, XVIIIe–XXe siècle,* 31–71. Aix-en-Provence: Institut du recherches méditerranéennes.

———. 2002. "A Divided Sea: The Cairo Coffee Trade in the Red Sea Area during the Seventeenth and Eighteenth Centuries." In *Modernity and Culture: From the Mediterranean to the Indian Ocean,* ed. L. T. Fawaz and C. A. Bayly, 46–57. New York: Columbia University Press.

Serjeant, R. B. 1983a. "The Hindu, Baniyan Merchants and Traders." In *San'a': An Arabian Islamic City,* ed. R. B. Serjeant and R. Lewcock, 432–435. London: World of Islam Trust.

———. 1983b. "The Post Medieval and Modern History of San'a' and the Yemen, ca. 953–1382/1515–1962." In *San'a': An Arabian Islamic City,* ed. R. B. Serjeant and R. Lewcock, 68–107. London: World of Islam Trust.

Topik, Steven. 2009. "Coffee as a Social Drug." *Cultural Critique* 71 (Winter): 81–106.

Tuchscherer, Michel. 1991. "Les activités des Turcs dans le commerce de la mer Rouge au XVIIIe siècle." In *Les villes dans l'empire ottoman: activités et sociétés,* ed. D. Panzac, 321–364. Paris: CNRS.

———. 2003. "Coffee in the Red Sea Area from the Sixteenth to the Nineteenth Century." In *The Global Coffee Economy in Africa, Asia, and Latin America, 1500–1989,* ed. W. G. Clarence-Smith and S. Topik, 50–66. Cambridge: Cambridge University Press.

Um, Nancy. 2009. *The Merchant Houses of Mocha: Trade and Architecture in an Indian Ocean Port.* Seattle: University of Washington Press.

———. 2015. "Foreign Doctors at the Imam's Court: Medical Diplomacy in Yemen's Coffee Era." In *Transcultural Networks in the Indian Ocean, 15th–18th Centuries: Europeans and Indian Ocean Societies in Interaction,* a special issue of *Genre: Forms of Discourse and Culture* 48(2).

VOC Archives, Mocha Records. The National Archives. The Hague, Netherlands.

Zabara, Muhammad. 1985. *Nashr al-'arf li-nubla' al-yaman ba'd al-alf.* Vol. 2. Sanaa: Markaz al-Dirasat wa al-Buhuth al-Yamani.

5

1683

An Offshore Perspective on Vietnamese Zen

CHARLES J. WHEELER

Nations work themselves out in time as well as space. Take the year 1683, for example. Anyone who studies Chinese history regards the date as being more important than most others. Why? Because, in that year, a great armada under the conquering Qing Dynasty landed on the island of Taiwan and defeated the last of the Ming Loyalist resistance to Manchu rule led by the descendants of the legendary merchant warrior Zheng Chenggong or Koxinga. Thus, the year marks a watershed in Chinese history, a punctuation in the nation's long chronology. At this place in time, viable Han (Chinese) resistance to the Manchu-led enterprise to conquer China—which had begun nearly a century before, overthrew the Ming Dynasty in 1644, and quickly overran most of China, only to spend another four decades struggling to consolidate their dominion over the country's southern maritime—ended. In this light, 1683 marks the end of the beginning of a new Qing order in Chinese history and the end to any practical hope of restoring the old Ming one (Wakeman 1985). Chinese history's arrow thereafter drew some of its trajectory from 1683.

This is not the only way we conceptualize the Chinese national timeline or interpret the place and significance of 1683 on it. A second and much older interpretation identifies the year as a watershed in the history of China's engagement—or rather, disengagement—with the world beyond its extended shores. The idea owes much to the work of historians like John King Fairbank and, through him, Hosea Morse (Fairbank 1953; Morse 1910–1918; Cohen 1984, 102). Soon after his victory on Taiwan, the Kangxi Emperor issued his edict "opening" the Chinese coast to state-sanctioned sea trade, which set in motion a series of policy reforms that restructured China's management of shipping and trade. These new policies set the parameters of China's maritime commercial relationship with the world overseas into the nineteenth century—a world into which Chinese began to pour after 1683, and a world from which people sailed to do business in China in ever increasing numbers. Historians have generally viewed the Qing government's new policy regime after 1683 negatively, as a bad precedent that reinforced the agrarian giant's unwillingness to grasp the geostrategic significance of growing maritime-based commerce, social interaction, and military power along its southern shores (Fairbank 1953). In another sense, then, one might also mark 1683 as the beginning of the end for the Qing, and the whole imperial order with it, which began to stumble in the face of Western challenges in the nineteenth century before it collapsed in 1911, thanks in part to ineffective maritime policies.

Of course, we could imagine 1683 in other ways. If one accepts the idea of the Zheng regime as a protostate (Carioti 1996), then 1683 marks the end of a long contest between two visions of Chinese trading empires—one which relied solely on the fruits of commercial enterprise at sea, and another which subordinated maritime trade to the larger complex interests of the agrarian empire. Despite its defeat, however, the Chinese maritime continued to grow, explosively so after 1683, in fact. The influence this had on the relationship between China's political center and its south-coastal regions, increasingly connected to compatriots and commercial resources beyond the center's reach, lives with us today. The Qing annexation of Taiwan signals an unprecedented projection of Chinese sovereignty into the sea—less because of the island itself and more because of the strategic Taiwan Straits, through which inter-Asian shipping traffic must pass. The effect of this maritime projection has been gradual, but it did contribute to a Mahan-centered vision of power that intellectuals like Liang Qichao embraced almost as soon as the American admiral produced his thesis on the naval basis of world power. It remains very much alive today, especially in diatribes against the American presence on the island and in the Straits, celebrations of PRC naval operations in the Indian

Ocean, and the growing perception of China seas as *Chinese* seas. Given the percentage of shipping that flows through the South China Sea, and China's militarization there, 1683 continues to shape China. Eventually, it will affect the whole world.

These three facets of 1683 point to long-term effects that extend well beyond the narrow national perspective that has shaped conventional interpretations of this date so far. The Zheng defeat and new Qing commercial order reshaped local, intraregional, and interregional relationships all along the great arc of maritime Asia—and through this hemispheric stream, the rest of the world. Indeed, the multiple chains of consequences leading from the events of 1683 lead well beyond the domains of Chinese geopolitics, commerce, or Chinese overseas communities where conventional studies dwell. Sometimes, these consequences even transcended people, places, and things that we deem Chinese. Thus, 1683 influenced the world in surprising ways.

Through religion, for example, the consequences of 1683 changed East Asia and change the world today. In that year, Master Nguyen Thieu—in Chinese pronounced *Yuanshao*—one of Vietnam's most important Zen masters, arrived at the court of a Vietnamese lord. There, he introduced a new school of practice that eventually transformed Buddhism in Vietnam and, in the very long run, the world—the expression of which remains evident in photos of Master Thich Quang Duc's self-immolation in 1963 and the globally popular teachings of Master Thich Nhat Hanh. Nguyen Thieu thus provides an excellent example of the full extent of 1683's impact, when we view it from a long-term and wide-ranging perspective, grounded in the context of the social groups that shaped both the event and the historical geography of its influence. By reconstructing the larger "social field of the sea" in which he operated, we can begin to see how the collapse of one trading empire, the Ming Loyalist regime under the Zheng clan, invigorated the expansion of another trading empire, which in turn encouraged a compact between Chinese sea traders and missionary-minded monks that projected Zen lineages from their bases in southern China into the Asian maritime. These monks and their disciples carried more than religion with them; in the course of their circulations, they transported religious commodities, translated cultural knowledge and technical expertise, and even transplanted sectarian politics.

This interaction moved both ways, of course. In time, however, the patterns of religious circulations began to change, as the social geography around them changed. The great transoceanic flows that transformed Zen across eastern Asia during the seventeenth century broke up into smaller circuits, which encouraged the localization of Zen practice that forgot its more cosmopolitan origins. Colonialism and global economy encouraged a return to larger scales of monastic interaction in the twentieth century. This inspired the international Buddhist congresses that in turn influenced the highly nationalistic character of Buddhist-led social and political movements in Vietnam, and in turn shaped the thinking of antiwar activists and Christian intellectuals worldwide. Nguyen Thieu's influence continues to this day in the diffused society of disaporic Vietnamese and the cosmopolitan Buddhism of his best-known dharma descendant, Thich Nhat Hanh.

The Myth and the Master

Biographies of Nguyen Thieu and histories of his school's origins usually rely most heavily on the biography that Vietnamese court historians wrote about him in the middle of the nineteenth century, in a biographical compilation entitled *Dai Nam liet truyen,* or "Biographies of the Eminent in Dai Nam." The court authors appear to have collected their biographical data from inscriptions and texts that one can still find at temples in and around Hue and Binh Dinh in Central Vietnam (for the most complete set, see Nguyen 1996, 1: 91–163). From these biographies, we learn very little about the master's early years. The story begins in China, in the coastal prefecture of Chaozhou in eastern Guangdong province. At the age of nineteen, Ta Nguyen Thieu—pronounced *Xie Yuanzhao* in Mandarin Chinese—"left his family" to study under Zen master Kuangyuan Benguo at a monastery called Baozi (V: *Chua Bao Tu*). The biographers provide no information about his birth year, his master, or the location of his monastery. In 1677, Nguyen Thieu sailed aboard a Chinese merchant ship to Qui Nhon, a port city in the Vietnamese domain of Cochinchina, where a Chinese merchant community thrived. Two years later, he established a monastery that he named Thap Thap Di Da, "Ten Stupa Amitabha Monastery," for the Buddha of the Pure Land and the ten ancient Cham stupas that sat behind the compound's walls. His religious work apparently impressed the lord of Cochinchina, because he invited Nguyen Thieu to the royal capital of Phu Xuan (near modern-day Hue) and asked him to serve his court as the "master of the realm" or *quoc si* [C: *guoshi*], an advisory position with a long tradition in Vietnam.

During his years as the court's Buddhist master, Nguyen Thieu worked to promote his school of practice, whose name is the same as one of his popular Vietnamese aliases, *Hoang Bich*—pronounced *Huangbo* in Mandarin. His membership in the Huangbo branch of the Linji (V: *Lam Te*) school of Southern Zen ties him to a network of principal Huangbo temples that lay principally in Fujian, a province with a long history of sea trade with Central Vietnam, Cochinchina's core region. There, he founded and restored a number of monasteries, many of which still exist today. In 1688, the Chinese master traveled to China on behalf of his Vietnamese lord in order to gather Buddhist images, sutras, and the records of Zen patriarchs. He also tried "to recruit eminent monks," most importantly Shilian Dashan, the colorful abbot of a wealthy monastery in Guangzhou (*DNLT* 1: 205; for a biography, see Jiang 1999). Dashan accompanied Nguyen Thieu to Cochinchina in 1695 and spent a year and a half working to "establish the correct Dharma" before he returned to China. To the court biographers, this was an important achievement, because they also place Dashan among the royal biographies (*DNLT,* 1: 207; *DNLTTB,* 260–262). To be precise, the Guangzhou master transferred the dharma lineage of Lam Te or Linji, and thereby established a clear master-disciple genealogy between Lam Te practitioners in Vietnam and the original master Linji in ninth-century China. Because of this, in part, Lam Te/Linji became the most popular school of Zen in Vietnam. This includes Nguyen Thieu's own school, whose temples can be found in Vietnamese-speaking communities worldwide.

Sometime after Dashan's voyage, Nguyen Thieu retired to Ha Trung Monastery outside the Nguyen capital, where he continued to develop his teachings. He lived there until he died, in 1712 we are told. The master received many posthumous honors, including a great stupa that the Cochinchinese court erected at his burial site in the royal monastery of Quoc An in 1729. The emperors of the Nguyen dynasty (1802–1945), who descended from the Nguyen lords who ruled Cochinchina, continued to venerate him.

Nguyen Thieu's religious legacy reached beyond his popular school. Historians acknowledge the role that he and Dashan played in the cultivation of Lieu Quan. As a youth, the young Vietnamese received dharma transmission from Dashan during his visit and studied with disciples of both Dashan and Nguyen Thieu, most importantly the latter's student Tu Dung. Soon after, he began to develop his own school of practice, the first Zen lineage created by a Vietnamese. The Lieu Quan school quickly grew and attracted the support of the Nguyen Thieu court. Today, it is also one of the most popular schools of Zen in the Vietnamese-speaking world and has many branches worldwide (including the internationally famous school of Zen master Thich Nhat Hanh; on Lieu Quan, see Thich 1971, 162–176).

Why did Nguyen go to Cochinchina? The standard biographies do not say. Worse, they break down under close scrutiny. His religious accomplishments were genuine, of course. But his alleged relationship with Shilian Dashan is most likely false. Contemporaneous accounts of Dashan's voyage make no mention of Nguyen Thieu, including Dashan's own memoir, which identifies only two Fujianese men, whom a Japanese source identifies as sea merchants (*HWJS*, 1: 1; *KIHT*, 2: 1744). Nguyen Hien Duc, in his study of Buddhism in Cochinchina, discovered that Nguyen Thieu left the capital before the mission departed for China and sailed south to Dong Pho, a Chinese market for sea trade and center of Ming Loyalism, where he resettled. In fact, he never left Dong Pho. Professor Duc discovered the former court master's grave under one of his other names, Sieu Bach, in a monastery he founded there in 1698 (Nguyen 1996, 1: 104–119).

Why did Nguyen Thieu leave his prestigious position in the royal capital for a sparsely populated and heavily malarial netherworld of renegades, feuding Cambodian princes, Vietnamese generals, and Ming Loyalist warlords? Nguyen Hien Duc argues that the master had no alternative, because the court implicated him in a failed coup against Lord Nguyen that took place in early 1694 (Nguyen 1996, 1: 29; on the coup see *DNTL*, 108). This may be true, but the answer does not explain why the Vietnamese court supported the appointment of Nguyen Thieu disciples to abbacies in Cochinchinese monasteries, positions that required court approval at precisely the time of the master's relocation south (Wheeler 2007, 322). Nor does it explain why the master chose to hide in Dong Pho, a town on the frontiers of rebellion-prone Cochinchina, where Vietnamese officials must have been sensitive to the security of a territory filled with non-Vietnamese subjects. Why not sail back to China? The court's posthumous praise for Nguyen Thieu—twenty-seven years after his alleged death—raises questions, too.

We may resolve the questions about Nguyen Thieu's origins, his reasons for migrating overseas, and his migration to Dong Pho by placing him back into the context of the social world that helped to create him. The trouble is, such a world isn't readily available, because it did not sit neatly within the boundaries of land, nation, ethnicity, region, or even religion. His was largely a world at sea. It moved through the currents of this ocean world that flowed in a great arc across the Asian littoral from northeast to southeast. For a few decades in the late seventeenth century, the principal agents of this maritime social world—sea merchants, recalcitrant Ming sympathizers, and their local patrons—created a unified field of action that offered monks like Nguyen Thieu the opportunity to create a new kind of Buddhism overseas. Thanks to these patrons, and their institutional networks, Zen Buddhism experienced a moment of evangelism that transformed the religious landscape of the Vietnamese-speaking world. The catalyst in this process of religious conversion arrived in 1683, with the arrival of the legendary Ming Refugees.

The Legend of Vietnam's Ming Refugees

Across the sea, as Nguyen Thieu settled into his new position serving Cochinchina's monarch, a Qing fleet sailed toward Taiwan. There, the Qing admiral Shi Lang received the surrender of Zheng Keshuang, king of Dongning. Keshuang's grandfather, the colorful merchant/warrior Zheng Chenggong, created this renegade regime from a coalition of Ming Loyalist officials and soldiers sustained by the commerce of Fujianese sea traders whose armed fleets patrolled the seas and dominated the commerce of Chinese merchant colonies between Malacca and Nagasaki. They used their commercial power to defy the Manchu conquest of China and, when that failed, create a maritime Chinese state. But Taiwan fell, and the regime surrendered. One of the Zheng fleets did not follow suit, however. In a report to his emperor, Shi Lang stated: "the ships of Yang Yandi are now in Cambodia [Jianbuzhai] in Cochinchina [Guangnan]" (Fu 1966, 1: 61). By "Cambodia," the admiral meant southern Cambodia, which in the 1600s meant the Mekong Delta, better known today as southern Vietnam or the Saigon region. Weak state power and internecine conflict left the territory largely ungoverned at the time, creating opportunities for ambitious neighbors. Cochinchina was a de facto Vietnamese kingdom, which first arose in north-central Vietnam around 1600 and expanded south until, by century's end, it had overrun the Mekong Delta region and reached the Gulf of Thailand (hence the transformation into *Cambodia* in *Cochinchina*). They were not the only outsiders with designs on Cambodia, however. Shi Lang reported that the Zheng regime, when faced with defeat on Taiwan, had considered moving its government there—some suggested Manila, others Cambodia—but in the end they chose surrender. Yang, the leader of the Zheng southern fleet, persisted (Chen 1960, 454). Before its king had even surrendered, he and his sailors threw in their lot with the Vietnamese and started a new life in the Mekong.

The story of Yang Yandi (V: Duong Ngan Dich) and his Ming "refugees" is the stuff of legend in Vietnam. Histories of Vietnam generally interpret this event as a pivotal moment in the story of *Nam tien,* the "March South," a classic piece of settler mythology in which Vietnamese fulfill a form of manifest destiny that leads them out of the Vietnamese "fatherland" in the Red River Delta in the tenth century inexorably south to the Mekong and the Gulf of Thailand seven centuries later (e.g., Dang 1994). As with Nguyen Thieu's biography, retellings of this momentous arrival draw mainly from the writings of court historians serving the Empire of Dai Nam, whose Nguyen emperors descended directly from Cochinchina's Nguyen lords. Most notable among them is the nineteenth-century official Trinh Hoai Duc (*GDTTC,* 75–76; *DNTL,* 1: 95; *DNLT,* 195–199). According to the *Veritable Record* (or *thuc luc*), Yang and his officers led "over 3,000 soldiers and over fifty ships" in the spring of 1679 "into the harbors of Tu Dung and Da Nang Bay" in modern-day central Vietnam. "Vassals of the fallen throne of the Ming," Yang and his sailors "righteously refused to accept servitude to the Qing," and therefore went "seeking vassalage" under a new monarch (*DNTL,* 1: 95).

An earlier source written in 1776 provides less information but claims that Yang "ordered the white flag of surrender" raised to signal their submission. In his account of the Ming refugees, Trinh Hoai Duc, who helped to supervise the nineteenth-century imperial account, reports that he drew on a much earlier telling written by the Cochinchinese literati Nguyen Khoa Chiem (Dao Duy Anh, preface, in *GDTTC,* 11). The author paints a bleaker picture of Yang's plight. His fleet reduced by storms from "more than two hundred" naval vessels to "only fifty," and his sailors forced to "drink dew and raindrops" and "eat the leather hides of their shoes," Admiral Yang "ordered his troops to raise white flags of surrender," divided his fleet between Tu Dung and Da Nang, and sent his lieutenant Huang Jin ashore to take a letter to Lord Nguyen. "We beg your kingdom to accept our surrender," Yang wrote. "We want to become servants of your court" (Nguyen 1987: 301–302).

Lord Nguyen reportedly "didn't have the heart to resist," according to Nguyen Khoa Chiem. He accepted their surrender. The lord then "sent an edict to the Kingdom of the Khmer [Cambodia], with an order to allow Yang and his troops to settle and live inside the boundaries of the Khmer kingdom as subjects" of the Nguyen lord (*DNTL*, 1: 91; see also *GDTTC*, 75; Le 1776, 1: 96; Nguyen 1987, 302). Of course, more than sympathy may have tempered the lord's decision. An official reasoned:

> The land of Dong Pho . . . in the country of Cambodia, has open fields that are fertile for thousands of miles, and the court has yet to find the time to manage it. It would be better if we used the strength of this band to go and open that territory.

Lord Nguyen "followed the advice" and "handed court officials the order to go to the land of Dong Pho" (*DNTL*, 1: 95). The move proved fortuitous. Soon after they settled there, the Ming Loyalists "cleared the wilds, and set up market towns." Soon, "the trading ships of the Qing [Chinese] people and of the Western countries, Japan and Java gathered." As a consequence, "Han [Sinitic] customs spread in the territory" (*DNTL*, 1: 95; *GDTTC*, 75–76). According to Trinh Hoai Duc, Yang and his band of Ming Loyalists spearheaded the Vietnamese conquest and colonization of southern Cambodia and its transformation into southern Vietnam. This story has helped to distinguish the Ming Loyalists from other Chinese in Vietnam and to celebrate them in Vietnamese history as political refugees turned "pioneers" who helped fulfill Vietnam's territorial destiny.

If the story of Yang Yandi and the Ming refugees *seems* to possess the stuff of legend, it *does,* at least in certain key aspects. Chen Chingho drew together Chinese, Japanese, English, and French accounts to show conclusively that the old corsair and his fleet arrived on the shores of Cochinchina in December 1682, not 1679 as the Vietnamese histories allege (1960, 449–50). Yang and his crew were no strangers to Cochinchina, the Mekong, or the Cambodian coast, either. As the Zheng southern fleet, Yang's ships patrolled the seas from the Gulf of Thailand to China's Guangdong province from their base in Longmen on the Gulf of Tonkin (Nguyen 1987, 301; *KIHT,* 1: 452–3). For years, the Longmen fleet bottled up the Pearl River Delta that served Guangzhou and Macau, preying on ships and collaborating with smugglers until the Qing ejected them in the mid-1670s (Chen 1960, 440–446; Peng 1959, 19). Clearly, Yang's social world circulated far beyond the shores of any single state or region.

Yang Yandi and his cohort were especially well known to the people of southern Cambodia—less for protecting merchant ships than preying on them, according to the Nagasaki customs (*KIHT* 1, 327, 338, 351, 367, 398,

422, 439). This pattern of profiting from sea trade through coercion and subversion fits the general pattern for Zheng activity throughout the larger maritime stream between Japan and Cochinchina, especially in Fujian itself (e.g., Antony 2003, 28–35). Chen Shangchuan, Yang's alleged lieutenant and a legendary figure in the history of Vietnam's Minh Huong community, never served the Zheng regime at all and probably was nothing but a career brigand (*KIHT* 1: 452–453; see his biography in *DNLT:* 1: 195–199). Surely, Yang and his "refugees" must have behaved similarly in Cochinchina—and if not, we must ask why.

The motives of the Longmen fleet look no less suspicious after their supposed resettlement in southern Cambodia. Remember, Yang anchored his fleet in two places—not only in Da Nang Harbor, which linked to Cochinchina's most important seaport, Hoi An, but also in Tu Dung Estuary at the mouth of the Huong or Perfume River, just a few kilometers downriver from the Nguyen capital. How did this look to the Nguyen court? River and coastal travel constituted Cochinchina's primary means of communication and travel (Wheeler 2006a, 136). In other words, it constituted the basis of the country's transportation infrastructure. Coastal and river brigades protected it (Wheeler 2006a, 136). Cochinchina's navy proved itself formidable in naval battles throughout the seventeenth century (Wheeler 2015). Still, imagine a fleet of fifty naval ships with 3,000 battle-hardened sailors—even hungry ones—anchoring near New York City's harbor and the mouth of the Potomac River serving Washington, DC. What would be the response? Surely, Lord Nguyen felt more than pity for these so-called refugees. Their behavior after their resettlement in Dong Pho raises more doubt. Yang's allegedly devastated soldiers broke apart into rival factions almost as soon as they set foot in their new home and jumped into the internecine conflicts then raging all over Cambodia. They started a few of their own, too. During this interlude, Ming Loyalist factions came into contact with the Nguyen, not only as allies but also as foes (Cooke and Li 2004, 40–41; Chen 1968, 414–450). While their political jockeying never really ceased, the Vietnamese did gain the upper hand by 1698, when they formally established a full government presence in the region with the *dinh* or citadel of Gia Dinh (a.k.a. Saigon or Ho Chi Minh City) and reorganized the realm's Ming Loyalist communities. Until then, the fealty of many Ming Loyalists or "refugees" in Cochinchina's southern frontier clearly remained in doubt.

If any reader still maintains that Yang and his Ming Loyalist fleet were refugees, a description of their political and social status in Cochinchina should dispel their belief. After their arrival, the Nguyen court organized the Longmen fleet into "Ming incense" villages—in Vietnamese *Minh huong xa,* a name that refers to the temple that governed the community and that invokes the idea of the incense burned in reverence to the spirit of their beloved dynasty. The court then incorporated them into a network of Ming Loyalist villages found all over the kingdom, and placed them under the authority of the Minh Huong elders of Hoi An, Cochinchina's principal seaport. As subjects of the Vietnamese lord, the Minh Huong constituted a distinct class within Cochinchinese society—a "merchant-bureaucratic elite" that functioned simultaneously as sea-trade brokers, royal bureaucrats, and cultural intermediaries. Their characteristics resemble other Chinese "créole" communities of Southeast Asia, though not as much as early modern contemporaries like the Swahili or the Huguenots (Skinner 2001; Middleton 2001; Bosher 1995). Their power derived from a set of political privileges that the Nguyen court bestowed upon them sometime during the late 1600s; these included the right to hold positions of state and nobility and intermarry with Vietnamese, own land, control foreign commercial shipping, manage the kingdom's foreign trade customs, and govern the foreign merchant community. This expansive set of privileges exceeded those enjoyed by their fellow Vietnamese, not to mention compatriot Chinese who began to sail to Cochinchina as subjects of the Qing in 1684. The sanction of Sino-Vietnamese intermarriage also set in motion a gradual shift in culture that placed them in an intermediary position between China and Cochinchina (and, later, the Vietnamese empire), a position reinforced by their continued parochial ties to Chinese through cultural institutions of kin, occupation, and native place. Altogether, these privileges offered Cochinchina's Ming Loyalists opportunities to amass great wealth and power. Perhaps, then, Nguyen court historians like Trinh Hoai Duc, himself a Ming Loyalist, inserted Yang's story in order to enshrine his community's place in the annals of Vietnamese history, in hopes of protecting their prestige, status, and power.

Moreover, Cochinchina's Ming Loyalists did not manifest themselves from a single compassionate edict by Lord Nguyen. Instead, they evolved from a set of very long, complex, and large-scale processes that took at least

150 years to unfold. It began in the 1500s, when armed Fujianese fleets, in search of clandestine trade opportunities overseas, began to establish permanent trading communities overseas. Local strongmen who understood the political as well as economic significance of new offshore sources of wealth allowed these seafarers to form permanent colonies. By century's end, "Tang Streets" appeared in Japan, Cochinchina, and elsewhere. This connected local strongmen on land with the long social stream of Chinese at sea. A Vietnamese warlord named Nguyen Hoang took advantage of this development to create an offshore market for trade between Japan and China, which financed his creation of Cochinchina. Fujianese dominated this commerce, most of all the Zheng clan. When the Tokugawa banned Japanese carrier trade in the 1630s and the Ming dynasty collapsed in 1644, the Zheng and their allies were well suited to finance their maritime regime, thanks to their control of the Chinese carrier trade between Japan and Cochinchina.

The first signs of Ming Loyalist or Minh Huong identity appear in Cochinchina as early as 1653, a full thirty years before the arrival of Yang and his refugees (Chen 1974, 40). Letters, customs reports, temple inscriptions, and imperial edicts indicate that processes of community formation were already well underway throughout the 1650s and 60s all over maritime Asia, including Japan, Korea, and Malacca as well as Taiwan and Cochinchina, where a Qing memorial of 1669 reports that "Chinese are migrating by the thousands," including "rascals who have submitted to the foreign state in order to survive" (Yu [1669] 2009; see also Zhu [1600–1682] 1995, 48–49; Lin 1987, 188; Sun 2007). In fact, when the Longmen fleet anchored off Cochinchina's shores in 1682, Ming Loyalists already dominated the country's Chinese merchant enclaves and foreign sea trade, staffed much of the Cochinchinese bureaucracy, and intermarried with Vietnamese elites. As a mythical event, Yang's arrival continues to herald a beginning, but as a historical event, the event marks a moment of fruition in an evolutionary stage of incorporation and ethnogenesis.

Like the tale of Nguyen Thieu, the story of the origin of Vietnam's Ming Refugees contains mythic elements that reveal important clues about both the subjects and also the authors who created them. Both stories are themselves the products of evolution, first spun almost as soon as the historical events unfolded, carefully woven over the course of many years, and perhaps realizing their final pattern long before the Nguyen court historians first brushed their influential narratives. By carefully deconstructing these important mythic tales, it is possible to hypothesize a reconstruction of the social world that produced the mission of Zen master Nguyen Thieu to Cochinchina, a world very much at sea.

Zen and the Art of Creating Community at Sea

The chain of developments that shaped Chinese merchant diaspora and Ming Loyalist identity in the seventeenth century trace back to the sixteenth century, not only to south-coastal seaports but also to nearby temples that inspired the Zen (or Chan) Revival. This religious renascence, and the missionary movement it later inspired, helped Chinese at sea to establish durable yet adaptable community institutions capable of sustaining elastic intersea social networks that groups like the Ming Loyalists in Cochinchina used to solve the basic problems of trade, forge cross-cultural ecumenical bonds, and secure their intermediary role between expatriate Chinese and Vietnamese elite societies. Conversely, Ming loyalists played a principal role in organizing Chinese Zen missions overseas during the late 1600s. The Chinese diaspora owes as much to Zen religious revival as it does to commercial revolution or political upheavals, and the transformation of Zen in East Asia depended upon the Chinese diaspora that first brokered it. Perhaps Nguyen Thieu migrated to Dong Pho simply because the Ming Loyalists there needed a Zen master.

Monks and monasteries helped Tang Chinese merchants forge three social commitments or bonds necessary to the function of their trade and society: first, between Chinese inhabitants of a particular Tang Chinese merchant colony; second, between Tang colonies separated by the Asian maritime; and third, between Tang colonies and their local sovereigns. Buddhist masters like Nguyen Thieu lent religious authority to Chinese sea traders seeking to legitimize the institutional commitments that created and sustained their important commercial, political, and social relationships through strategies that solved the basic problems of cross-cultural trade (Wheeler 2007). This religious function in merchant networks has been well documented in numerous cases—including the Jewish merchants of the medieval Mediterranean, Islamic merchants from Africa to Southeast Asia, Christians worldwide, and even Buddhism in Silk-Road Asia. Post-ancient Buddhism proves to be no different (Wheeler 2008). Fujianese and Ming Loyalist merchant-mariners thus employed Buddhism to do what it had done for centuries: help them create the elastic social geography that made Chinese migration possible.

Chinese Zen missionaries and their merchant patrons looked to Buddhism's transcultural authority to protect their interests in foreign environments, even to protect their non-Buddhist deities. This was possible thanks to the transcultural authority that Buddhist monks enjoyed within the Zen ecumene that encompassed maritime East Asia and also because of the syncretic doctrine within schools like the one Nguyen Thieu created, which permitted the integration of new deity forms. The nineteenth and twentieth centuries offer numerous examples of Chinese devotees of syncretic sects who sought "to label themselves as Buddhist" (Tan 1995, 154), and the same was true for Chinese colonies in other places and earlier times (e.g., Salmon & Lombard 1980). In Nagasaki, for example, the leaders of the Chinese quarter patronized the construction of Buddhist monasteries around existing Guandi and Mazu temples in order to protect them from suspicious Tokugawa officials (Baroni 2000, 32). In Cochinchina, a temple inscription dates the consecration of the bodhisattva Guanyin (*Avalokitesvara;* V: *Quan Am*) by Chinese merchants, Japanese merchants, and Vietnamese elites as early as 1640 (*PDSLTP,* c1640; Sallet 1924, 131–133). Guanyin was not new to Vietnamese, of course; indeed, they had also used the goddess in order to legitimize their claims to sea goddess temples revered by Cham, who once ruled the Center before the Vietanamese conquered them, and were still conspicuous in Cochinchina during the seventeenth century (Nguyen 1995, 49).

Monks could play a role in the introduction or evolution of non-Buddhist deities overseas, too. For example, reports of Mazu altars in monasteries and monastic worship of the sea goddess grew increasingly regular during the seventeenth century, both overseas (Baroni 2000, 32–33; Jiang 1999, 446–468; Wu 2002, 275–277) as well as in southern China (Wheeler 2007, 313). As abbot of Changshou, Dashan supervised one of the most important Mazu temples in the Chinese sea trade, the A Ma Temple of Macau (Jiang 1999, 463–468). Monks were reportedly involved in the ceremonies in Guangdong that elevated the sea goddess to Chinese imperial status in 1684, while the monk Dashan promoted the goddess overseas during his tour of Cochinchina in 1695–1696 (Wheeler 2007, 313). When the Qing court promoted Mazu, overseas traders had already adopted it into their new collective institution, the guild or *huiguan* (on the institution see Wang 2003, 121–158, 162, 178–194).

Cochinchina's Fujianese merchants formed their guild sometime between 1679 when Malacca founded its *huiguan* (Jiang 1995, 49) and 1695 when Dashan described the interior of Hoi An's *Chua Ong* or Guandi Hall (*HWJS*, 109). Two years later, the town's merchants founded another monastery, named it Kim Son, and installed a Mazu temple there, where monks obviously played a role. Eventually, Mazu and the monks began to go their separate ways. Merchants built a mariner's guild hall with a Mazu altar outside monastery walls in the early 1700s, while Kim Son temple became the Fujian *huiguan* before the end of the eighteenth century, keeping its Mazu hall (Chen 1974, 65, 95–98, 138–141). Despite the apparent institutional distance that merchants began to place between their guilds and monasteries, monks helped to introduce and legitimize their goddess to merchant communities overseas.

At the same time they created the new guilds, monks helped to promote the construction of public cemeteries and the regularization of orthodox death ritual (Wheeler 2008, 214–216; Chin 1999, 117). This was especially important to practitioners of another school of Southern Zen, Caodong Zen—*Tao Dong* in Vietnamese, *Soto* in Japanese—of which Dashan was a member (*HWJS*, 109–110; Williams 2005, 38–58). Standardized cemetery architecture and death rituals helped Hadrami merchants in the Indian Ocean give "representational shape" to their transoceanic society and created a more durable social structure, thanks to the "powerful dynamics of signification" that the graves provide (Ho 2006, 14, 25). Such an interplay between the social and sacred to create community encouraged non-Buddhist deities, like the multiple sea goddess one still finds in community after community along the coast of China and Vietnam (Wheeler 2007; 2008).

Merchants and monks came together through two important religious revivals that began in the sixteenth century and which helped to increase the adaptability of Zen practitioners to new cultural and religious environments. One was the reinvigoration of the "Three Teachings *(sanjiaoyi)*" and its syncretic ideals. This originated in sixteenth-century Fujian and quickly grew popular throughout the province and in overseas merchant colonies (Dean 1998, 16–27, 44–55, 58–60, 125–36; Franke 1989). People from all three faiths have created variations on the triad theme and instituted them in diverse ways. At the same time, Southern Zen Buddhism experienced a revival, whose advocates proposed new visions of interfaith syntheses under Zen authority (Yü 1981; Hsu 1979, 150–63). The popularity of revival Zen quickly spread throughout Southern China, including the same urban centers where the sea merchants who patronized the Three Teachings cult operated. Because of this, Zen monks often acted as a medium for broadcasting a host of nominally non-Buddhist religious ideas—and cultural practices—across East Asia, and for assimilating or accommodating local deities in host societies (Brook 1993).

The Zen Revival shaped merchant diaspora materially, because it inspired the creation of a new system of *dharma* genealogy (master-disciple lineage) that monastic communities used to devise new methods for determining monastic authority and governing monastic property. This created new incentives for missionary expansion overseas. In the sixteenth century monks in Caodong, Linji, and Huangbo lineages began to concentrate religious authority in "dharma transmission monasteries," whose abbots possessed a stamp that verified their receipt of a legitimate enlightenment transmission. By the seventeenth century, temples began to form hierarchical networks around a single governing "transmission monastery," which concentrated property in communities whose abbot could prove his enlightenment inheritance from a dharma descendant of the Buddha. This sparked competition between schools to appropriate religious authority by devising genealogies that favored one dharma lineage over another, because with higher lineage status came more monks, more property, and more wealth. When Fujianese and later Ming Loyalist seafarers began to encourage Zen masters to travel overseas for the sake of the Dharma in the middle of the seventeenth century, monastic communities were already well practiced in the art of temple expansion. Soon, a matter of religious authority took on economic and political significance.

In fact, there was a good deal at stake in these temple-building enterprises. As Chinese monks migrated into host societies, they dredged cross-cultural channels, into which flowed commodities and specialists from China. These missions comprised large groups of monastic and lay disciples, chosen for specific artistic, technical, and organizational tasks—as well as carpenters, sculptors, painters, cooks, tailors, and shoemakers. Some of these specialists sojourned, while others stayed, to do things like train local novices. This fostered a material culture that demanded its own economy. Temples regularly issued purchase orders from head monasteries in China—books, relics, clothing, ritual objects, and art. Chinese merchants supplied them, returning to China with incense woods and other prized commodities for religious consumers. To this we can also add the religious raw materials that monasteries sought in their local environments. Temple building was a costly and complex endeavor, which made it not only a religious but also economic and political enterprise.

Cultural politics potentially complicated temple building as well. After all, these missionaries and their patrons equated their temple and community building enterprises with the reproduction of Chinese, and sometimes Ming-era, cultural forms. Monks and patrons both placed a high premium on the reproduction of Chinese cultural forms, making it necessary to import expertise from home monasteries overseas, as Martin Collcutt shows for thirteenth-century Japan in the case of Rinzai—in other words Linji or Lam Te—Buddhism (Collcutt 1981, 171–220). This was especially true for Nguyen Thieu's school—also known as Hoang Bich, aka Huangbo (in Chinese) or Obaku (in Japanese)—given the premium Hoang Bich practitioners overseas placed on Chinese culture, particularly its Ming expression. As in Japan, Nguyen Thieu's early disciples chanted sutras in Fuqing dialect, chanted to Fujianese style music, prayed in Fujianese style halls, and wore robes and shoes reminiscent of the Huangbo monks of their principal monastery in the Fujianese district of Fuqing (Baroni 2000, 98–101; Thich Thien An 1971, 154–156). Ming culture grew quite popular in the host societies of Japan, Korea, and Vietnam, and this provided an entrée for both monks and merchants into elite society. It isn't surprising, then, to see strains of Ming Loyalist rhetoric migrate abroad with missionaries like Nguyen Thieu, given the number of Ming sympathizers who frequented the monasteries of Nguyen Thieu and Dashan back in Guangzhou and Macau (see discussion of Baozi Temple below).

Tones of cultural chauvinism often infused missionary zeal during the late seventeenth century; patrons of Dashan, who equated Chinese empire with civilization, celebrated the overseas mission of their master, whose enterprise promised to "spread the moralizing influence of the Son of Heaven [the emperor of China]" through his travels (preface by Chou Zhao-ao in *HWJS*, 3). Dashan gave his royal sponsor Lord Nguyen Phuc Chu the highest compliment by claiming the Vietnamese monarch had been a Chinese monk in a past life (*DNLT,* 1: 205). A Chinese patron of Dashan remarked: "How wonderful to transform the customs of far-flung places with our Chinese institutions, [and] to establish an enduring temple with overseas wealth" (preface, *HWJS,* 3). The cultural chauvinism in this passage calls attention to itself less for its sinocentrism than its similarity to missionary rhetoric in the European colonial era. Missionary masters and their disciples—whether monk, merchant, or artisan—therefore traveled as a kind of cultural junket aboard the merchant ships who carried them, bringing a complete package of Chinese (in this case mainly Fujianese) high culture. More importantly, however, we see how the expansion of monastic communities overseas promised returns of cultural capital and material wealth, both of which could be reinvested in the work of advancing sectarian interests. Thus, the cultural, economic, and political capital that temple building could generate overseas provided similar infusions at home.

So, when sea trade's political economy in East Asia changed, as it did after 1683, the members of the Tang Chinese merchant diaspora and its Ming Loyalist guard quickly adapted, thanks to the well-developed religious institutional strategy already in place, a product of evolution along multiple social streams that flowed across the sea in the seventeenth century. When their patrons introduced new rules in reaction to the Qing empire's new maritime policy regime, it appears that Ming Loyalists in Cochinchina recruited missionary-minded monks like Nguyen Thieu to build new temples and renovate old ones in order to sanctify the new institutional commitments they negotiated. This offered missionary-minded Buddhists with the opportunity to utilize their religious authority in order to expand the reach of their monastic networks into new places. But it also created new potential for conflict, including sectarian feuds. Whether pushed or pulled into the arms of the Ming Loyalists of Dong Pho, sectarian ambitions clearly played a role in the peregrinations of Zen master Nguyen Thieu.

Circulating Conflicts

Guangzhou played an important role in the overseas expansion of monasteries based in China. It turns out that Nguyen Thieu and Dashan both came from monasteries in the seaport city; both of these monasteries lay close to its western suburbs, where the foreign merchants lived, and enjoyed the patronage of wealthy Fujianese merchants and sea traders. Until recently, the location of Nguyen Thieu's principal monastery, named Baozi, remained obscure. Scholars assumed that it must have been located in Chaozhou Prefecture where he grew up. In fact, Baozi Monastery once lay "in the Western part of [Guangzhou], just outside the city wall," not far from Changshou Monastery where Dashan resided as abbot (Zheng and Dian 1974, 17–18; Cai 1997, 45; Luo 1939, 29).

It remains impossible to know whether Nguyen Thieu and Dashan were friends or foe, so complicated was their relationship and the world in which they lived. They did share one important piece of common ground, however: in addition to the Fujianese sea traders, both Zen masters enjoyed the patronage of the infamous Shang overlords. Shang Kexi, an early Chinese supporter of the Manchus, led the Qing conquest of Guangzhou in 1650. Overextended, the Qing emperor granted Shang the powers of viceroy over the city and its surrounding provinces. He and two other generals who received similar titles over other parts of southern China became known as the Three Feudatories. He and his son Shang Zhixin ruled over the region for the next two decades, until the Three Feudatories rebelled and provoked a war that led to their annihilation in 1680. The connection came to haunt Dashan in the 1690s; it did no apparent harm to Nguyen Thieu, who left China three years before the Shang fell from power.

The evidence for connection is clear. Zen master Shilian Dashan "curried favor with the King of Pingnan [Shang Kexi, one of the Three Feudatories] when he was a guest of one of [the king's] secretaries, Jin Guanxuan . . ." (Miao 1973, 2: 28a). Dashan's monastery, Changshou, and its branch monasteries (including a wealthy one in the Portuguese colony of Macau) were previously owned by Duke Anda, aka Shang Zhixin (C: *Anda gong*), who allegedly gave Dashan the monastery to use as a front in the sea smuggling racket he ran (Miao 1973, 2: 37a–39b). Nguyen Thieu appears to have been even closer to the reviled duke. The warlord's son sponsored the construction of Baozi, Nguyen Thieu's first monastery, in gratitude to the monks who chanted sutras to release his mother's soul from purgatory and provide her with merit in the afterlife (Zheng and Dian 1974, 17–18). The duke apparently maintained close ties with the monastery, because "a person named Zhong collected Shang's bones and ashes and buried them in the West Garden of Baozi Temple" after the Kangxi emperor compelled Shang to commit suicide and then ordered officials to spread the traitor's ashes over the earth (Cai 1997, 45). When he ordered Shang's suicide, Kangxi also instructed officials to close Baozi Monastery. A few years later, locals quietly reopened it (Zheng and Dian 1974, 18). Nguyen Thieu was already three years in Cochinchina by then; however, his teacher, Kuangyuan Benguo, assumed the temple's abbacy in 1682, shortly after its reopening and only months before Nguyen Thieu rose to the position of Nguyen court master. Surely Nguyen Thieu and his teacher knew about the presence of Shang Zhixin's remains and understood its significance.

The connections did not end there, of course. And along with this web of relationships—Guangzhou monks, Fujianese merchants, and a Qing viceroy—we must think back to Yang Yandi and the seafaring allies of Ming loyalism and the Zheng clan who held its banner for so long. During their rule over the Guangzhou region, the Shang clan made a good deal of money by engaging in smuggling in violation of the Qing coastal prohibition. Yang Yandi's ships played a role in this racket by stationing in the delta that served Guangzhou and Macau, preying on ships there and collaborating with smugglers until the Qing ejected them in the mid-1670s (Chen 1960, 440–446; Peng 1959, 19). Thus, the two monks shared a great deal, living in close proximity and sharing so many high profile patrons.

Whatever interests they shared, Nguyen Thieu and Dashan were by no means friends. The Guangzhou poet Pan Lei claimed that Dashan had once referred to Nguyen Thieu's teacher, Kuangyuan Benguo, as a "sinister" monk driven by envy "to the state of losing his mind." The master then wrote a book attacking Dashan, to which Dashan responded in kind. Before Nguyen Thieu's teacher could muster a counterattack, a man named Ma Xieling intervened "and they stopped fighting" (Jiang 1999, 107). This spat occurred during the late 1680s and early 1690s, long after Nguyen Thieu emigrated. It seems unlikely this truce lasted, however, because Dashan caused a public storm in 1693 so strong that it may have prompted his journey to Cochinchina and certainly contributed to his fall from grace years later. That year, the abbot published a treatise that effectively advanced all Caodong monks five generations closer to the Buddha than their Linji and Huangbo contemporaries, thanks to a clever manipulation of Zen master-disciple genealogy (Wu 2002, 137; Cai 1997, 90–92; Chen [1924] 1990, 1: 36a–b; Jiang 1999, 39–114, 163–164). This enraged Linji monastics, for the genealogical methodology would effectively raise the rankings of Caodong monks. Remember, such a move had material as well as spiritual consequences, because it affected monastic entitlements to Zen abbacies, congregations, and properties. It may have especially angered Huangbo monks, who knew that Dashan undertook the genealogical study in order to complete the work of his master Juelang Daosheng, who decades before had won a similar controversy that led to the Qing court's destruction of an important Huangbo monk's books (Mohr 1997, 345). This disaster compelled one of the monk's disciples, Yinyuan, to migrate to Japan, leading to the creation of Huangbo or Obaku Zen in Japan. The monk's early disciples in Nagasaki, where he settled, were all Chinese sea traders and customs officials working for the Tokugawa shogunate, many of whom did business in Vietnam and maintained families there (Wheeler 2007; Iioka 2009). Seen in this light, the close bond between Nguyen Thieu and Dashan implied in the Vietnamese imperial biography and popular histories seems hard to believe. Shared interests—patronage, temple building, overseas proselytization, and surviving bad associations of the past—brought the two into a conflict that projected beyond the temples of Guangzhou's western quarter and traveled along the multiple social streams that circulated at sea.

If Nguyen Thieu and Dashan did not see common cause between them, the Nguyen court surely did. There is every indication that the Nguyen court regarded the two monks, like the Ming Loyalist Chinese they served, as vital to its larger political aims. Nguyen Thieu's rise and fall coincided with a wave of temple building, renovation, and recruitment that lasted through the 1680s and 90s and utilized disciples of both Nguyen Thieu and Dashan. This great temple-building wave targeted precisely the politically sensitive areas of the kingdom where rebellions had taken place during the same period. The lion's share of these temples was built at around the time of Dashan's voyage. Most of these temples belonged to Nguyen Thieu's disciples, even after their master's fall from grace (Nguyen 1996, 1: 267, 283, 305; 2: 118, 143–144, 149, 190, 202, 254–255, 331). One of these politically-sensitive areas was, of course, Dong Pho, where the Ming refugees under Yang Yandi had settled in 1682 and where Nguyen Thieu, as an alleged escapee, founded Kim Son in 1698.

Buddhism and the Consequences of Connection

We could end the story here, and in doing so imply fruition. We could conclude by saying that the maritime colonization of Tang Chinese interests, institutions, and culture overseas led to a settling and indigenization of Guangzhou branches of Zen Buddhism, and stop there. But why stop? History has no end, and continuation offers intriguing insights into an evolutionary view of 1683 and the consequences of a particular moment of Zen connection at sea. When we do, the evolutionary track takes some rather interesting turns.

In one of the more interesting twists that are the legacy of Zen missionaries like Nguyen Thieu in Vietnam, Vietnamese patronization of Lam Te/Linji masters from China led to the legitimization of Sinic institutions of governance that reached its greatest expression in the imperial Nguyen dynasty that formed in 1802. This brand of Zen was highly syncretic, having incorporated many of the practices of the Three Teachings (C: *sanjiaoyi*) during the Zen revival of the 1600s, which translated through the generations to Lieu Quan, Nguyen Thieu's Vietnamese dharma descendant, whom the Nguyen court similarly chose to become Cochinchina's Royal Master *(quoc si)* in 1726, where he served until he died in 1745. It carried on into the next century, under the Nguyen emperors, who continued to support Zen.

By the nineteenth century, however, one can begin to imagine how the stereotype of Vietnamese Buddhism as a decadent religion by French colonial and, later, Vietnamese nationalist scholars was possible. The intersea networks of the precolonial era had changed, much to the detriment of Vietnam and its powerful Ming Loyalist merchant class (Wheeler 2006b, 192). Dashan and Nguyen Thieu's monasteries in Guangzhou disappeared, one destroyed by an angry mob, the other turned into a school (Zheng and Dian 1974, 18). Vietnamese Zen had long since narrowed in its range of interaction, its interactions with China apparently diminished. It did not last long, however. During this apparently parochial period, young monks began to seek new knowledge through new networks of information that colonialism ironically provided.

Then, in the 1920s, a new kind of internationalization and cosmopolitanism appeared, this time informed both by French colonialism and growing interaction with Buddhism in East and Southeast Asia. Monastic institutions began to interact beyond Vietnamese borders, even as nationalist expressions began to infuse Vietnamese communities from without (McHale 2004, 158–159; DeVido 2007, 259–262). This inspired Vietnamese monks to travel overseas, to imagine and promote socially engaged forms of practice, often in pursuit of a nationalist ideal of Buddhist expression, much of it encouraged through international, transsectarian interactions with like-minded monastics. The growth at first was small, but developed a good deal of force in the years following World War II. Postwar international congresses and growing access to outside information through new media inspired the first attempts to wed spirituality and social action in Vietnam during the 1950s. The effect of this international access is evident in the conceptualization of Engaged

Buddhism as articulated by Thich Nhat Hanh, a dharma descendant of the two Guangzhou masters, Nguyen Thieu and Dashan, who credits Martin Luther King, Gandhi, and numerous Christian theologians among his influences. Such access to knowledge would not have been possible without a new web of interaction made possible by a world connected by trains, planes, automobiles, cheap print, and cables—not to mention ships, albeit to a smaller degree than they had done in their heyday.

During the war and postwar years, the potential for building dense layers of networks through multiple media changed Vietnamese lives in profound ways, just as sailing ships and war had done three centuries before. The nationalist idea reached fruition within the Vietnamese Buddhist community when leaders formed a pan-sectarian, national church called the Unified Buddhist Church of Vietnam. Like Thich Nhat Hanh, many of the church's prominent leaders traced their dharma lineage to the two monks from Guangzhou. After the war, that lineage migrated overseas. The UBC exists today in the Vietnamese diaspora, where it continues to promote its national vision of a Buddhist school for Vietnamese despite intense and continued political persecution, first by the United States and South Vietnamese governments and then, after 1975, by the Communists. Technology has added new dimensions to the web, too, thanks to copiers, fax machines, mobile phones, and the Internet.

Like their two ancient masters, the dharma descendants of Nguyen Thieu and Dashan are part of a cultural crossover that has quietly unfolded since 1975. As the Vietnamese revolution ended, a refugee crisis began, and members of the Nguyen Thieu and Lieu Quan schools resettled overseas, and new branches formed in Canada, the United States, Australia, and France. All of the masters who migrated overseas endeavored to serve their beleaguered overseas Vietnamese communities—all except for Thich Nhat Hanh, whose activities and writings during the war years attracted the attention of non-Vietnamese, particularly Westerners. Master Nhat Hanh joined the growing number of Asian masters who adapted their teachings to suit Western audiences. These audiences generally know little about the role of Vietnamese national history in the development of Thich Nhat Hanh's teachings, even less so about the master's place in the history of Vietnamese Zen. In this way, descendants of Nguyen Thieu and Dashan (through Lieu Quan) have created a new kind of global Zen, complete with its own globally cosmopolitan lexicon. Branches thrive worldwide—from India to Southeast Asia and Japan;

to Buenos Aires, London, Moscow, and Abu Dhabi. They have even spread to the unlikeliest of small communities, like the town of Bellingham, Washington where I live (Kingsbury 2004). This offers the epitome of a global cosmopolitan community; monastic and lay disciples that now come from all nationalities, language families, and faiths, even while it continues to operate in national arenas through the Vietnamese diaspora.

This multivocality has produced some odd consequences lately. Hanoi allowed Thich Nhat Hanh to return to Vietnam in 2005 and even to create a branch of his Order of Interbeing in 2007 at a monastery named Bat Nha, in the country's Central Highlands. The state returned to its repressive ways, however, and closed Bat Nha in 2009, banishing most of the sect's monks and nuns and ever since repressing the remainder. This has caused an unexpected turn that brings our story full circle. It's as if the ships that carried Nguyen Thieu and Dashan have just completed their circuit and returned home. In 2009, four expelled monks resettled in Hong Kong, where they opened a small center promoting their master's practice. Since I have become a member of this community—part cosmopolitan, part nationalist, part archaic—the school has grown vigorously. By 2011, the number of monastics reached twenty, and plans are underway to exceed one hundred within the next few years, a remarkable thing in a world where religion is said to be dead. That same year, our burgeoning community moved into an unused temple complex in the mountains of Lantau Island, next to a Buddhist theme park that also seeks to make Buddhism relevant to the times, albeit in different ways.

From this mountain, just the other day, I sat and watched the morning arrive with some of the younger brothers, all of them Vietnamese. From an outcropping, high atop a mountain, I looked down to the South China Sea. My gaze crossed the expanse where ships carried Nguyen Thieu, Dashan, and many other Guangzhou monastics to the Vietnamese kingdom of Cochinchina overseas. Now, the flow moves in reverse. Two of the monastic brothers had just returned from China, whose state had placed so much pressure on Hanoi to expel Thich Nhat Hanh's order from Vietnam just two years before, because the master had loudly criticized repression in Tibet and Chinese bauxite mining in Vietnam's Central Highlands. Now, Beijing allows Vietnamese monks to travel regularly into the Chinese interior, to teach "mindfulness psychology" in Chinese cities like Guangzhou, where the first missionaries set off more than three centuries ago. Translators are working furiously, and the number of lay followers is growing quickly. The consequences of 1683 have traveled far, across vast space, lengthy time, and ever-changing social fields. The great circulation has come full circle, back to the place from whence it first embarked. But then again, no two places are really ever the same, in time or in space.

References

Antony, Robert. 2003. *Like Froth Floating on the Sea: The World of Pirates and Seafarers in Late Imperial China*. Berkeley, CA: Institute for East Asian Studies.

Baroni, Helen J. 2000. *Obaku Zen: the Emergence of the Third Sect of Zen in Tokugawa Japan*. Honolulu: University of Hawai'i Press.

Bosher, J. F. 1995. "Huguenot Merchants and the Protestant International in the Seventeenth Century." *The William and Mary Quarterly*, 3rd ser., 52 (1): 77–102.

Cadiere, Leopold. 1914. "La pagode Quac-an: le fondateur." *Bulletin des amis a vieux Hue* 2: 147–162.

Cai Hongsheng. 1997. *Qingchu Lingnan Fomen Shilue* [A historical sketch of Buddhism in early-Qing Lingnan (Guangshou)]. Guangzhou: Guangdong gaodeng-jiaoyu chubanshe.

Carioti, Patrizia. 1996. "The Zheng's Maritime Power in the International Context of the Seventeenth Century Far Eastern Seas: The Rise of a 'Centralized Piratical Organization' and Its Gradual Development into an Informal State." *Ming Qing Yanjiu* (Napoli): 29–67.

Chen Chingho. 1960, 1968. "Qingchu Zheng Chenggong zhibu zhi yizhi [The migration of the Zheng partisans to the southern borders (of Vietnam)]." *Xinya xuebao* (Singapore) 5 (1): 433–459; 8 (2): 413–486.

———. 1974. *Notes on Hoi-an (Faifo)*. Carbondale: University on Southern Illinois.

Chen Yuan. [1924] 1990. *Qingchu sengjing ji* [A record of early-Qing monastic controversies]. Shanghai: Shanghai shudian.

Cohen, Paul. 1984. *Discovering History in China: American Historical Writing on the Recent Chinese Past*. New York: Columbia University Press.

Cooke, N., and Li Tana, eds. 2004. *Water Frontier: Commerce and the Chinese in the Lower Mekong Region, 1750–1880*. Lanham MD: Rowman & Littlefield.

Dang Thu, ed. 1994. *Di dan cua nguoi Viet tu the ky X den giua the ky XIX* [The migration of Vietnamese from the 10th to the mid-19th centuries]. Hanoi: Trung tam Khoa hoc Xa hoi va nhan van Quoc gia.

DeVido, Elise Anne. 2007. "'Buddhism for This World': The Buddhist Revival in Vietnam, 1920 to 1951, and Its Legacy." In *Modernity and Re-enchantment: Religion in Post-Revolutionary Vietnam*, ed. Philip Taylor, 250–296. Singapore: ISEAS.

DNLT. Dai Nam liet truyen [Biographies of the eminent in Dai Nam], 19th century. Translated into *Quoc ngu* (colloquial Vietnamese) by Do Mong Khuong et al., 1997. Hue: Nxb. Thuan Hoa.

DNLTTB. Dai Nam liet truyen tien bien [Biographies of the eminent in Dai Nam, ancestral edition]. Translated into *Quoc ngu* and annotated by Cao Tanh et al., 1995. Hanoi: Nxb. Khoa hoc Xa hoi.

DNTL. Dai Nam thuc luc tien bien [The veritable record of Dai Nam]. Compiled by the Imperial History Officers of the Nguyen Court, ca. 1840s. *Quoc ngu* translation, 2002. Hanoi: Nxb. Giao duc.

Fairbank, John King. 1953. *Trade and Diplomacy on the China Coast: The Opening of the Treaty Ports, 1842–1854*. Cambridge, MA: Harvard University Press.

Fu, Lo-Shu. 1966. *A Documentary Chronicle of Sino-Western Relations (1644–1820).* Tuscon: University of Arizona Press.

GDTTC. Gia Dinh thanh thong chi [Union gazetteer of Gia Dinh Citadel], by Trinh Hoai Duc, c. 1820. Repr. of original Han with *quoc ngu* translation, 1998. Hanoi: Nxb. Giao duc.

Ho, Engseng. 2006. *The Graves of Tarim: Genealogy and Mobility across the Indian Ocean.* Berkeley: University of California Press.

HWJS. Shilian Dashan. 1699. *Haiwai jishi* [Overseas journal]. Ed. Chen Ching-ho, 1969. Taibei: Guangwen shuju.

Iioka, Naoko. 2009. "Literati Entrepreneur: Wei Zhiyuan in the Tonkin-Nagasaki Silk Trade." Ph.D. thesis National University of Singapore.

Jiang, Boqin. 1999. *Shilian Dashan yü Aomen chanshi: Qingchu Lingnan chanxueshi yanjiu chubian* [Shilian Dashan and Buddhism in Macau: An early edition of historical research on the study of Lingnan Zen Buddhism in the early Qing]. Shanghai: Xuelin chubanshe.

Jiang, Weitan. 1995. "Qingdai shang huiguan yu Tianhou gong [The commercial guilds and the Tianhou temple]." *Haijiao shi yanjiu* (Quanzhou), 27 (1): 45–63.

KIHT. Hayashi, Shunsai. *Ka i hentai* [The transformation from civilized (Chinese) to barbarian (Manchu)], 18th century. Repr. and ed. Ura Ren-ichi, 1958–1959. Tokyo: Toyo Bunko.

Kingsbury, Caroline. 2004. *Buddhism in Bellingham: Practice and Belief.* Devon, England: Hardinge Simpole.

Le, Quy Don. 1776. *Phu bien tap luc* [Desultory notes from the frontier]. Reprint of *Han* original with *quoc ngu* translation, 1972. Saigon.

Lin, Renhuan. 1987. *Mingmo Qingchu siren haishang maoyi* [Private maritime trade in the late Ming and early Qing]. Shanghai, Huadong shifan daxue chubanshe.

Luo, Yuanhuan. 1939. *Yuetai Zhengyalu.* Changsha: Shangwu yinshuguan.

McHale, Shawn. 2004. *Print and Power: Confucianism, Communism, and Buddhism in the Making of Modern Vietnam.* Honolulu: University of Hawai'i Press.

Miao, Quansun. 1973. "Shilian heshang [The monk Shilian (Dashan)]." 19th century. In *Yifengtang wenji* [Literary collection from Yifeng Hall], comp. Miao, *juan* 2. Taibei: Wenhai chubanshe.

Middleton, John. 2001. "Merchants: An Essay in Historical Ethnography." *Journal of the Royal Anthropological Institute* 9: 509–526.

Mohr, Michel. 1997. "Zen Buddhism during the Tokugawa Period: The Challenge to Go beyond Sectarian Consciousness." *Japanese Journal of Religious Studies,* 21 (4): 341–372.

Morse, Hosea Balleau. 1910–1918. *The International Relations of the Chinese Empire.* 3 vols. New York: Longmans.

Nguyen, Hien Duc. 1996. *Lich su Phat giao Dang Trong* [The history of Buddhism in Cochinchina]. Nxb. Thanh pho Ho Chi Minh.

Nguyen, Khoa Chiem (1659–1736). 1987. *Viet Nam khai quoc chi truyen* [The story of a Vietnamese kingdom's rise]. Repr. of original *Han* text, 1987., Taibei: Taiwan xuesheng shuju, 1987.

Nguyen, The Anh. 1995. "The Vietnamization of the Cham Deity Po Nagar." In *Essays on Vietnamese Pasts,* ed. Keith W. Taylor and John K. Whitmore. Ithaca: Southeast Asia Program, Cornell University.

PDSLTP. "Pho Da Son Linh Trung Phat [The Sacred Buddhist Mountain of Putuo]." Inscription imprint, no. 12623. Hanoi: Han-Nom Institute.

Peng, Zeyi. 1959. "Qingdai Guangdong yanghang zhidu di qiyuan [The origins of the system of foreign trade guilds in Qing-era Guangdong]." *Lishi yanjiu* 1: 1–24.

Sallet, Albert. 1924. "Le montagnes de marbre." *Bulletin des Amis a Vieux Hue,* 11 (1): 1–145.

Salmon, Claudine, and Denys Lombard. 1980. *Le Chinois de Jakarta: Temples et vie collective.* Paris: Editions de la Maison des sciences de l'homme.

Skinner, G. William. 2001. "Creolized Chinese Societies in Southeast Asia." In *Sojourners and Settlers: Histories of Southeast Asia and the Chinese,* ed. Anthony Reid, 51–93. Honolulu: University of Hawai'i Press.

Sun, Weiguo. 2007. *Da Ming qihao yu xiao Zhonghua yishi: Chaoxian wangchao zunzhou si Ming wenti yanjiu, 1637–1800.* Beijing: Shangwu yinshuguan.

Tan, Chee Beng. 1995. "Some Views on the Study of Chinese Religions in Southeast Asia." In *Southeast Asian Chinese: The Socio-Cultural Dimension,* ed. Leo Suryadinata. Singapore: Times Academic Press.

Thich, Thien An. 1971. *Zen Buddhism in Vietnam.* Rutland, VT: Charles E. Tuttle.

Wakeman, Frederic. 1985. *The Great Enterprise: The Manchu Reconstruction of the Imperial Order in Seventeenth-Century China.* Berkeley: University of California Press.

Wang, Rongguo. 2003. *Haiyang shenling: Zhongguo haishen xinyang yu shehui jingji* [Spirits of the seas: The development of Chinese sea deities and socio-economy in China]. Nanchang: Jiangxi gaoxiao chubanshe.

Wheeler, Charles. 2006a. "Re-thinking the Sea in Vietnamese History: The Littoral Integration of Thuan-Quang, Seventeenth-Eighteenth Centuries." *Journal of Southeast Asian Studies* 17 (1): 123–153.

———. 2006b. "One Region, Two Histories: Cham Precedents in the Hoi An Region." In *Viet Nam: Borderless Histories,* ed. Nhung Tuyet Tran and Anthony Reid, 163–193. Madison: University of Wisconsin Press.

———. 2007. "Buddhism in the Re-Ordering of an Early Modern World: Chinese Missions to Cochinchina in the Seventeenth-Century." *Journal of Global History* 2: 303–324.

———. 2008. "Missionary Buddhism in a Post-Ancient World: Monks, Merchants, and Colonial Expansion in Seventeenth Century Cochinchina (Vietnam)." In *Secondary Cities and Urban Networking in the Indian Ocean Realm, c. 1000–1800,* ed. Kenneth R. Hall. Lanham, MD: Lexington Books.

———. 2015. "The Case for Boats in Vietnamese History: Ships and the Social Flows that Shaped Nguyen Cochinchina (Central Vietnam), 16th–18th Centuries." In *Ships and Men,* ed. Paola Calanca et al. Paris: EFEO forthcoming.

Williams, Duncan. 2005. *The Other Side of Zen: A Social History of Soto Zen Buddhism in Tokugawa Japan.* Princeton, NJ: Princeton University Press.

Wu, Jiang. 2002. "Orthodoxy, Controversy, and the Transformation of Chan Buddhism in Seventeenth-Century China." Ph. D. thesis, Harvard University.

Yu Jin. [1669] 2009. *Da guan tang wen ji. 22 juan.* Beijing: Beijing Ai ru sheng shuzi hua jishu yanjiu zhongxin.

Zheng, Rong, and Dian Gui. 1974. [*Gengxu Xuxiu*] *Nanhai Xianzhi* [Gazeteer of Nanhai District]. Photocopy of 1910 (Xuantong 2) edition. Taipei: Chengwen chubanshe youxian gongsi.

Zhu, Zhiyu [1600–1682] 1995. *Shunshui xiansheng wenji* [Collected works of Mr. Shunshui]. 28 *juan.* [Shanghai]: Shanghai guji chubanshe.

6

1745

Ebbs and Flows in the Indian Ocean

KERRY WARD

The concept of focusing on a single year in the Indian Ocean marine environment is simultaneously more coherent and more elusive than a year centered on a terrestrial region. The regularity of the monsoonal systems and ocean currents are acknowledged as the main source of unity in the Indian Ocean, the foundation upon which thousands of years of maritime interaction have taken place. Yet Indian Ocean scholars have disagreed on the concept of unities and disunities of the Indian Ocean as a "world" and whether it constitutes a "new thalassology" (Vink 2007). Michael Pearson raises the conceptual issue of the unity of the Indian Ocean as requiring more than pointing out connections and demonstrating underlying patterns. "A history of an ocean needs to be amphibious, moving easily between land and sea." Echoing Frank Broeze, he asks the question of how far inland a maritime history can be—how far does the littoral extend? (2003, 5).

This chapter explores the sea itself as part of the natural environment, a conduit for travel, trade, and texts, an arena of conflict, and a cultural construct. As Perdue, Siu, and Tagliacozzo have pointed out in the introduction to this volume, the inclusion of ocean systems in the frame of historical analysis disrupts terrestrial-centered notions of social processes and identities. The symbiosis between land and sea is central to archipelagic Southeast

Asian societies, even the inland Javanese empires. Engseng Ho traces a single mobile diasporic society in the Indian Ocean whose unity is created through their shared stories of each other and of a single place, the Hadramawt of the southern Arabian peninsula coast, and even more locally on the coastal town of Tarim and the cultural meaning of burial as return and pilgrimage from the sixteenth century onward (2006, xix–xxvi). Extending eastwards, Denys Lombard, in his 1988 article "1988. Une outré "Mediterranée dans l'Asie du sud-est," reminds us that "wanting to understand Southeast Asia without integrating a good part of southern China into one's thinking is like wanting to give an account of the Mediterranean world by abstracting Turkey, the Levant, Palestine and Egypt" (Li Tana 2004, 2). I would like to play devil's advocate here by also suggesting that wanting to understand the Indian Ocean without integrating East Africa's coastal societies has the same effect. Although this paper concentrates on the central and eastern Indian Ocean, extending to the South China Sea, I believe that these connections across the breadth and depth of the Indian Ocean are important in furthering our understanding of "Asia Inside Out." Sugata Bose evoked the 2004 tsunami to claim that "the sense of peoples of the Indian Ocean rim sharing a common historical destiny was palpable," and it is from this perspective of human interaction that he posits the unity of the Indian Ocean in the globalized age of imperialism and anticolonialism from the nineteenth century onward (2006, 2–3). The devastation of this environmental event as a tragic marker of the unity of the Indian Ocean is in contrast to the seasonal regularity of the Indian Ocean weather patterns. Although terrestrial weather observations focus on the local, 1745 appears to have been a year of severe weather patterns in many places. One cannot see this from a single geographical point in the Indian Ocean. It takes a far-ranging perspective to put together these observations.

John Wills's *1688: A Global History* constructed a global narrative around the artificial construct of a "year" (2001). Yet the narrative ranged far beyond 1688, because events cannot be constrained within arbitrary calendrical templates. 1688 became a focal point but not the entire focus of the book. I have tried wherever possible to focus exclusively on 1745 without ranging too far or employing the benefit of hindsight. The effect of this is to render a series of stories and contexts rather than a coherent historical narrative. A year on the ocean does not reveal the significance of long-term trends on the horizon. It is more episodic, relying on the unfolding of events in terms of human observation. While long-term patterns are obscured, people and maritime social worlds become more visible. This chapter questions whether it possible to write a history of one year in the Indian Ocean that is more than a collection of flotsam and jetsam vignettes particularly in a year that is not a "turning point."

The Diary of Ananada Ranga Pillai

In concentrating on one year on the Indian Ocean, I have used the diary of Ananda Ranga Pillai as a narrative anchor. The well-known *dubash* (translator) worked for the French East India Company at Pondicherry and was particularly close to the governor, Joseph Francois Dupleix. Pillai, who came from a family of Tamil merchants and had ties throughout the region, wrote an almost daily diary for twenty-five years. Ashin Das Gupta claims that Pillai's diary is the "only surviving major document" that provides details of trading relationships in the region (1998, 362). It is a rare source, recording the ebbs and flows between the ocean and the littoral settlements. The unfolding of events is presented without the benefit of hindsight or further analysis. Events that we now understand as significant turning points do not appear as such in the diary. But what is obvious is the multiple networks and sources of information gathered about the Indian Ocean from the wide variety of shipping that entered the harbor of Pondicherry. Quotes from Pillai's diary form the navigational chart by which I set a course through 1745 in the Indian Ocean (Ramen 2007).

> Sunday, [10th] January 1745, or 1st tai of Raktâkshi.—Written intelligence came this night from Kârikâl that a vessel belonging to Tranquebar had returned from a voyage to Acheen. The tidings brought by her were to the following effect. The French ship Favori, which sailed, on 27th Purattàsi [9th October] last, from Porto Novo for Acheen, arrived at the latter place. On the 9th Arppisi [21st October], she cast anchor at Boutrian, where she landed all her goods, and the mercantile agents who were on board. She remained there until the 23rd Kârttigai [4th December], when two English ships arrived, and after an engagement captured her. (Pillai 1985, 264–265)

> Wednesday, [10th February 1745, or] 3rd Mâsi of Raktâkshi.—At 2 this morning the . . . [ship] bound for Mocha set sail, bearing the flag of the Nawâb, the ostensible owner being Mîr Ghulâm Husain. She was laden with . . . bales of blue cloths and other merchandise. (Pillai 1985, 266)

Trade Routes, Travelers, and Texts in the Malay World

Trade routes crisscrossed the Indian Ocean, linking the Red Sea to the Straits of Malacca and east to the South China Sea, from the Cape of Good Hope to the Sunda Straits. Literature abounds in multiple languages drawing on the cross-cultural aspects of oceanic encounters. Many of these stories circulated in different languages, taking on specific cultural aspects according to their contexts. For example, the *Hikayat Bayan Budiman* used typically Malay conventions regarding shipping, navigation, and gendered trading relations not common in the Persian renditions of these stories. "The heroine of the story of Siti Hasanah . . . sails to a port in some country, where she is greeted by merchants and the *syahbandar,* who make enquiries about the goods that she has brought with her. Siti Hasanah asks the merchants to wait a little, since she has not paid a visit to the ruler, that is she has not yet been granted permission to trade" (Braginsky 2004, 418–421). These stories center around sea travel and trade rather than ocean voyages of religious pilgrimage associated with the *hajj.*

Timothy Barnard argues that the only mention of a *hajj* voyage in traditional Malay literature prior to the writing of the *Tuhfat al-Nafis* in 1828, which portrays the *hajj* of the Bugis leader of Riau, was the *Hikayat Hang Tuah* that contains stories of the most famous warrior of the Malacca court in the fifteenth century (2009).The exact date for the composition of the *Hikayat Hang Tuah* is unknown, but it is in the early decades of the eighteenth century (Salleh 2006, 395–405). During these decades, Bugis mercenaries had helped the family of the *bendahara* (prime minister) of the Riau Lingga archipelago to consolidate their control of the sultanate. "The sultan granted the position of *Yang Dipertuan Muda* (viceroy) together with all real political control of the Riau Lingga Archipelago to the leader of the Bugis community and his descendants" (Barnard 2009, 65–67).

The dearth of direct representations of the *hajj* in Malay literature belies the increasingly vibrant connections between the Middle East and Southeast Asia from the seventeenth century onwards with the intensification of Islamic conversion and education in maritime Southeast Asia. Several scholars have traced generational networks of Islamic scholars across the Indian Ocean. Arab migrants from the Hadramawt were increasingly common in Southeast Asia, where the prestige of educated Sayyids who married into local elites and ruling families facilitated the spread of Islam in the region (Voll 1987;

Azra 2004). These foreign *ulama* did not necessarily wield any direct political power in their adopted homelands. Sayid Ahmad, a renowned scholar who was invited to live in Banten, married his daughter Ratu Sharia Fatimah to the crown prince Pangeran Ranamanggala, who ruled as Sultan Abulfath Mohammad Sjafi Zainul Arifin (r. 1733–1748). Sayid Ahmad had no political power in Banten, although his daughter later became effectively the female regent of Banten with the support of the Dutch East India Company (Atsushi 2010: 14–17).

One Southeast Asian scholar whose life spans 1745 is ʿAbd al-Samad al-Palimban, whose written works circulated widely in Indian Ocean Islamic networks. Known as Sayyid ʿAbd al-Samad b.ʾAbd al-Rahman al-Jawi in Arabic sources, al-Palambani's father was a Sayyid from Sanaʾa in Yemen who travelled widely in India, Java, and Sumatra. While in Palembang, he married a local woman who gave birth to al-Palembani before the family moved back to Kedah, where he held an appointment as *qadi*. Al-Palembani was educated in Kedah and Patani in southern Thailand before he was sent by his father to study in Arabia, where he lived the remainder of his life, maintaining close ties to the Jawi community in the region. His fellow students from Southeast Asia who also gained prominence as scholars in turn became teachers to several important scholars from Southeast Asia who returned to their homelands (Azra 2004, 111–113). Their voyages have not been recorded, but their texts traveled widely across the Indian Ocean. Religious travel and commerce continued to coexist in the complex indigenous and European colonial networks across the Indian Ocean in the mid-eighteenth century and would constantly change as these networks reconfigured over time.

Java and the Sea

In contrast to the mobility of people and texts across the Indian Ocean in the mid-eighteenth century, Javanese politics turned more intensely towards the inland. Luc Nagtegaal argues that the constant flows of Chinese migrants to Batavia and the surrounding plantation areas, where they labored alongside Javanese, precipitated a rural uprising against the Chinese and indigenous elites and the Dutch East India Company (VOC—*Vereenigde Oost Indische Compagnie*) itself. This had resulted in the 1740 massacre of the Chinese population in Batavia by indigenous residents and Company servants. In the aftermath, the rural rebellion spread eastward along the northeastern coastal towns of Java (Nagtegaal 1996, 220–221). This prompted Susuhanan Pakubuwana II, the ruler of the inland Kartasura Empire, to go into open rebellion against the VOC to chase the Dutch into the sea and rid Java of their presence once and for all. In Java, the Dutch, aided by their Madurese allies, defeated the Susuhanan, who in return for retaining his position ceded the northeast coast of Java and Madura to Company rule. As part of the peace treaty, the VOC also forbade the Javanese to sail outside Java, Madura, and Bali, thereby restricting Javanese trade virtually to the island (Ricklefs 1993, 21; Ward 2009, 220–221).

The Company's erstwhile ally, Cakraningrat IV of Madura, was outraged by this turn of events and what he perceived as a betrayal of his alliance with the VOC. He went into open rebellion and was formally removed as ruler of Madura by the VOC in 1745. Not long after this drastic measure, he was captured and taken to Batavia before being exiled to the Cape of Good Hope on board the VOC ship *Fortuin*. The *Fortuin* was a small supply ship that plied the oceans yearly between Batavia, the Cape, and the Netherlands. In 1745 the craft was captained by Dirk Took on the journey from Texel, departing on November 14, 1745, and arriving on July 1, 1746. On this outward journey it carried on board 150,000 guilders for trade and administration (Bruijn, Gaastra, and Schöffer 1979, 2: 372–373; 1989, 3: 500–501). On its homeward-bound journey it carried the deposed ruler of Madura, Cakraningrat IV, who, after losing sight of his homeland and crossing the Indian Ocean, would die in exile at the Cape of Good Hope on the southern tip of Africa. Even though the VOC was struggling to retain a share of the pepper trade on the Malabar coast, in 1745 the VOC granted a request by their Indonesian soldiers in Cochin to allow free passage to four *hajjis* from Cochin to Batavia in return for their labor during the journey (Barendse 2009, vol. 1; Winius and Vink 1991, 106–107).

Meanwhile in Java, "Pakubuwana II's calamitous reign" was not the result of "choosing between two mutually exclusive sources of spiritual authority: the Javanese (or Hindu-Javanese) and the Islamic" (Ricklefs 1998, 330, 337). Both were intimately connected to the ocean. Sufi scholars and texts travelled to the court across the Indian Ocean. But more foundational to the Javanese court was the relationship between Javanese kings, from the origins of the Majapahit Empire onwards, and the Goddess of the Southern Seas, Nyai Kidul. The Goddess reigned over all that is in the ocean. In the annual ritual of the *bedhaya* (court dance), the symbolized mating with Nyai Kidul imbued the terrestrial kings of Java with their supernatural power and legitimacy to rule (Ricklefs 1998, 6–13). "When the sacred *bedhaya* was danced at the start of Pakubuwana II's reign, invoking the Goddess of the Southern Ocean's very presence as the most immediate guarantor of the dynasty's fortunes, some of the mightiest forces of Java's unseen world were thus involved" (Ricklefs 1998, 13). Nyai Kidul's continued presence as the Goddess of the Southern Ocean ensured the legitimacy of the Javanese court after the 1745 move to Surakarta.

The ocean thus appears in many guises in the evaluation of Javanese politics in 1745 reaching into the very center of the island. The *Babad Tanah Jawa,* an epic poem/chronicle that describes the events of 1742 to 1745 leading up to the division of the Javanese state, depicts exile across the ocean as a disaster befalling members of the Javanese court as well as justice meted out to their enemies. Exile across the Indian Ocean, particularly to Ceylon and to the Cape of Good Hope, features prominently in the *babads* depicting this period. One group of exiles who returned to Java from Ceylon was named the "Ceylonese party" at court. Exile to the Cape of Good Hope, across the furthest reach of the Indian Ocean from Java, was considered an extremely remote journey from which return was a miraculous feat (Remmelink 1994, 214–244; Ward 2009, 193–194).

The Mascarenes, Madagascar, and Eastern Indian Ocean Networks

> Friday, [12th February 1745, or] 5th Mâsi of Raktâkshi.—This afternoon at 4, Ârumugam, son of a dancing woman, was put on board a ship, under sentence of banishment to Mascareigne. He was one of the three . . . who were incarcerated in connection with the theft in Arcot Perumâl Chetti's house . . . Vîrarâgava Nâyakkan and his son were released from confinement . . . however, they were sentenced . . . to perpetual banishment from Pondicherry, and with their families they were expelled from the bounds of the town. But Ârumugam, . . . was condemned to banishment to Mascareigne. (Pillai 1985, 266–267)

The Mascarenes to which Pillai refers were under a single French governor-general until 1746. The colony comprised the islands Île de France (Mauritius), Île Bourbon (Réunion), and the Séychelles. These islands occupied a middle space in the Indian Ocean—connected to Madagascar and the East

African coast largely through the slave trade, and to the eastern Indian Ocean through its position as a refreshment and trading post for European ships in the Asia trade. The islands population evolved into a complex ethnic and gendered hierarchy that was different from other Asian port cities because of the absence of a preexisting indigenous population prior to European colonization. One story about life on Mauritius, which became a popular legend based at least partly on fact, involved a Malagasy princess who sacrifices her inheritance to save a white man, M. Grenville de Forval, from a murder plot instigated by her father. Megan Vaughan has interpreted the story as indicating anxieties about the porous nature of social status in the colonial society (2005, 105–106). In a letter dated 1745, the aristocrat Baron Grant retold the story to his family in France:

> [Forval] received an unexpected visit from a most beautiful woman, a native of the island who . . . expressed her concern that so fine a white man as himself should be murdered . . . The sooty lady . . . was the daughter of a King and known by the title of Princess Betsy . . . [she said] "I will sacrifice for you the throne of my father . . . I will abandon my country, my friends, my customs, and that liberty that is so dear to me. My relations, who will consider me dishonoured, will detest me, and if you leave me to their vengeance, I shall be reduced to slavery which, to me, would be a thousand times worse than death." (Vaughan 2005, 105)

Grant goes on to report that Forval married Princess Betsy and they became a prominent couple in Port St. Louis because Princess Betsy's royal demeanor made her a popular figure of interest in the town (Vaughan 2005, 105–107; Larson 2000). Sources for Mauritian trade, including slave trades, are absent for the mid-eighteenth century, although indications of shipping activity linking Mauritius to Asia are widespread, as indicated by the presence of slaves from Madagascar and the Mascarenes in most ports with a European colonial presence (Allen 2010, 45–72).

The Maldives and Cowries

> [Tuesday, 27th April 1745, or] 18th Chittirai of Krôdhana.—The ship Charles, captain, M. Gossard, returned from Manilla. The merchandise which she took there belonged partly to M. de la Metrie, and partly to M. de Choisy. The captain, after firing a salute, landed. The cargo now on board consists of cowries. (Pillai 1985, 268–269)

The cowrie trade was a staple of the Indian Ocean. Cowrie shells *(Cypraea moneta)* were almost ubiquitous as a small-denomination currency throughout the Indian Ocean, and one of their main sources was the Maldive Islands south of the Indian subcontinent. Arab merchants traded cowries across North Africa and the Sahara, Indian merchants traded in cowries throughout South and Southeast Asia, and Europeans traded for cowries that were used as ballast for their ships headed for Europe, before repackaging them and re-exporting them for the slave trade in West Africa (Hogensdorn and Johnson 1986). Although the Dutch had attempted to divert the cowrie trade from their agents in Orissa and Balasore towards Ceylon, by the mid-eighteenth century they were not by any means in control of this lucrative trade. This is clearly indicated by a letter written in 1743 by a Dutch merchant about the cowrie trade on the Malabar coast:

> I have sounded these [Maldivian] envoys about the cowries and why they did not carry more of them to Ceylon . . . I think they got too little for the cowries and take them in their own vessels to Bengal and from their take rice in return. Some time ago . . . they sold many cowries to the French, who on this account sent many vessels lately to the Maldives . . . I think it is not only expedient but even necessary to maintain our friendship with this prince and open a helping hand to his vessels when they come here. (Hogensdorn and Johnson 1986, 53)

Although the Dutch were never able to impose a trade monopoly on cowries from the Maldives, they did use their influence in using their ships to protect the Maldivian sultans from their enemies in exchange for favorable treatment. In 1745, at the height of the Dutch slave trade in the Atlantic Ocean, the Dutch imported 189,863 pounds of cowries to West Africa, compared with 63,839 by the English (Hogensdorn and Johnson 1986). By the 1750s, the Dutch position in the Maldives was weakened as a result of a rebellion by Ali Raja of Cannonore, who bore the title of the "Sea King." In 1752 he abducted Sultan Muhammad Mukarram Imad-ud-din III, who died in exile at Minicoy in the Lacadives. Meanwhile, the population rebelled against their new rulers by forcing them back into the sea. The abducted Sultan's daughter gained control of the Maldives, and Maldivian vessels continued to sail to Ceylon to trade in cowries, while the King of Cannonore made overtures for French protection against the Maldivians (Hockly 1935).

Mainland Southeast Asian Coastlines and Shipping

> [Thursday, 29th April 1745, or] 20th Chittirai of Krôdhana.—The ship Notre Dame de Sœurs, captain. Felicien Da Sylva Medeiro, arrived from Macao with sugar, sugar candy, and some Chinese goods. The ship Lakshmana Prasâd, master, Sûp Sing, from Tenasserim, anchored in the roads. She has on board thirteen elephants. Another vessel, owned by the King of Siam, arrived from Tenasserim. Her name is the Nanâk . . . Her cargo consists of fifteen elephants, 81 1/2 ingots of tin, and some other goods. A ship, together with two brigantines, arrived from Balasore. (Pillai 1985, 269)

These entries in Pillai's diary hint at the diverse networks of regional shipping that traversed the Bay of Bengal. Not all ships were engaged in regional trade; smaller coastal vessels plied the waters of the Indian Ocean hugging the coastline as people moved voluntarily or involuntarily between coastal societies. Michael Charney points to the significant population movements between Bengal and the Buddhist Kingdom of Arakan during the eighteenth century. Bengali Muslims "were assigned as monastery slaves or as cultivators of monastic glebes" in the Arakan, but they commonly ran away (1999, 234–235). This account from 1777, which illustrates the porous boundaries between land, river, and sea, could easily have taken place at any time during the eighteenth century: "[They] took the opportunity to seize on a boat, and to make their escape in it. They proceeded in the boat for one day, and then quitted the boat, they landed in a woody and uninhabited part of Rakheng, and continued their route on the banks of small rivers, to avoid wild beasts and impenetrable woods—They were seven days travelling from Rekheng to Islamabad [Chittagong]" (Charney 1999, 235).

The extensive use of shipping in intraregional migration, trade, and warfare is often underplayed in mainland Southeast Asian history. The existence of elephants on board ships indicates their importance in the region not only as prestige items or beasts of burden but as weapons of war. Michael Charney's survey of Southeast Asian warfare indicates the various maritime engagements that took place in the region. During times of war, oarsmen were ordinary peasants and workers pressed into service of the kings by whom they were paid and their families maintained. An English observer of the Burmese king Alaùng-hpayà's force of 500 vessels to fight his Mon enemy in 1755 indicates a long-standing practice for sea and river warfare: "[W]hen finding it necessary to provide himself with more fighting Boats . . . as he passed by every Place, [he] gave orders . . . to call in the former Inhabitants, and obliged them to build a number of fighting Boats, in proportion to the number of the People . . ." (Charney 2004, 106).

Unlike the European system of using convicts and slaves for galley service, temporary conscription produced fitter and superior oarsmen, sailors, and soldiers. Charney (2004) indicates the shared tactics and techniques of naval warfare between the Vietnamese, Cham, Khmer, Siamese, and Burmese kingdoms. Maritime warfare was coastal and riverine and not conducted on the open seas, unlike European maritime warfare, which took place in multiple oceanic contexts. The whole region east of the Burmese coast, dubbed by Li Tana and Nola Cooke as the "Water Frontier," was transformed in the later eighteenth century, marking the emergence of two powerful new mainland kingdoms, Chakkri Siam and Nguyen Vietnam. "The concept of a 'Water Frontier' here, a fluid transnational and multi-ethnic economic zone, allows us to perceive and talk about the lower Mekong as a single region . . . a Water Frontier perspective reveals the regional significance of individual events within an appropriately wider context" (Li and Cooke 2004, xii).

Pierre Poivre's Travels around the South China Sea

Li Tana's examination of the "water frontier" begins from the middle of the eighteenth century and traces the significant increase in maritime trade with southern China along the coastal region which facilitated a huge increase in revenues in Siam and southern Vietnam (Li 2004, 3). However, references for 1745 on the cusp of this period are much more difficult to extract from the literature on this region. One source is the accounts of the "adventurer—naturalist—economist—diplomat—administrator appropriately named Pierre Poivre" (1719–1786) (Hanna and Alwi 1990, 185). The idiosyncratic nature of Poivre's career in Asia exemplifies the vulnerabilities of individuals who were not well connected and the possibilities for those whose talents were considered useful. Poivre's reputation is connected to his later career in trying to wrest the monopoly of spice production from the Dutch by illegally acquiring plant stock. But I paraphrase what happened to Poivre around 1745 because his is one of the few individual accounts of a marginal figure in this vast water frontier that centers on this year.

Born in Lyon, Pierre Poivre's intellectual talents were recognized at a young age and he was recruited to the Paris Society for Foreign Missions, where he underwent training before being assigned to Canton in 1740. His luck ran short there due to a case of mistaken identity, resulting in his imprisonment. During his incarceration he applied himself to the study of Chinese and drew the attention of a local mandarin, who secured his release and encouraged his travels in China and Cochinchina, "where he dazzled the imperial court with his linguistic and other accomplishments." He then returned to Canton and in 1745 boarded a ship for France, traveling in a convoy to avoid capture by the enemy Dutch and English. Unfortunately for Poivre, the convoy was attacked by the English in the Straits of Bangka, and during the battle a cannon ball shot away his lower right arm. The ship's surgeon had to perform an amputation during a battle in which the ship caught fire, but Poivre survived and was finally given over to the Dutch in Batavia, where the English disposed of their French prizes and the ships' crews. In Batavia, Poivre studied Malay, but as soon as possible he "took passage on a derelict craft which headed to Pondicherry by way of the Malay Peninsula . . . From Pondicherry, Poivre sailed via Isle de France and Martinique to Europe" (Hanna and Alwi 1990, 196–198).

Poivre's account of his travels provides the most detailed source on the conduct of Vietnamese sea and river warfare during the Nguyen period that spans the mid-eighteenth century. He had observed that oarsmen supplemented sail boats along the coast, and they were practiced at sailing forwards and backwards in sequence rather than in unison, as was the European technique (Charney 2004).

> A foreigner who had seen only the galleys of the king would be inclined to form a favourable opinion of Cochin China, although they seem to be designed more for pleasure than business; they are the work of art and good taste. They are exceptional and have flat floor timbers. The first I was shown during my stay in the capital had forty-eight oars and is eighty pieds [26 metres] long. There is red lacquer to the waterline, and all of the outside of the galley is black lacquer. These two lacquers are shiny and smooth as looking glass. (Poivre 1993, 700)

Despite his keen powers of observation, Poivre's failure to negotiate successfully with the Nguyen Lords resulted in his virtual expulsion and the end of immediate hopes for the French East India Company in establishing a trading post at Danang or Hoi An (Tran 2003).

While Poivre was recording his impressions of Cochin China, the Dutch were concluding a treaty with the Sultan of Perak, north of Malacca along the

Straits. The treaty bound the ruler of Perak, Sultan Malpasaar Johan Berdollat Peer Alam, to exclusive trade in tin with the VOC. The Sultan was obliged to promulgate a mandate that ships wishing to go outside must first anchor at the fort to be inspected and that he would not at any time permit anyone to smuggle tin outside (Andaya 1979, 405). Simultaneously, the VOC from their base in Malacca signed treaties with Johor with the aim of displacing the tin trade from the Bugis and aligning the Company with Malay rulers trying to wrest control in the region from overwhelming Bugis influence. These events in the mid-1740s would result in continued conflict between the Dutch and the Bugis in the region throughout the 1750s (Andaya 1983). The sheer numbers of Asian and European ships plying these waters were beyond the capacity of any single political authority to control, and "smuggling" remained endemic throughout the region.

Trade in Manila

> Tuesday, [4th May 1745, or] 25th Chittirai of Krôdhana.—This afternoon at 2, the ship Charles, captain and supercargo, M. de la Villebague, returned from Manilla, and anchored in the roadstead. The native captain is Vangâla Kumara Pillai. She is laden with . . . boxes of silver. The flowered cloths which were not sold were left at Manilla. The other goods are stated to have been disposed of to great advantage. (Pillai 1985, 269)

In 1745 trade at the Spanish colony in Manila was still recovering from the losses inflicted by the English two years earlier, when Commander George Anson captured one of the richest prizes of the Acapulco-Manila Galleon, the *Nuestra Señora de Covadonga*. Anson's ships and crew were diminished by sickness, and he had not been successful in trading with the Chinese prior to encountering the Spanish treasure ship off Cape Espiritu Santo in the Philippine Islands on 19th of June 1743. Anson's *Centurion* was successful in defeating the Spanish and, having taken possession of the ship, he sailed to Macao to sell the ship and its cargo and buy provisions for the homeward journey.

Anson's first visit to China months earlier had been the first visit to China of a warship from the Royal Navy. His presence had caused considerable discomfort for the Portuguese merchants at Macao from whom he had tried to buy provisions and the Chinese who noted the potential military power of his vessel. He released the Spanish prisoners captured from the galleon in

Macao, and provisions were provided for his ship, while the usual tonnage dues payable to the Chinese port officials were waived. "But as the HMS Centurion left the Pearl River a fleet of Chinese war junks followed her—at a safe distance—and Anunghoi Fort was bravely manned" (Coates 2009, 48–52). He then sailed for England via the Cape of Good Hope with his prize of over 1,300,000 pieces of eight, reaching England on June 15, 1744. The prize money ensured his family's wealth for subsequent generations. By 1745, Anson had invested in lavishly upgrading his country mansion, bought himself a seat in Parliament, and joined the Admiralty Board.

Weather in the Indian Ocean during 1745

> [. . . * August 1745, or . . . Âvani of Krôdhana].—A frigate bound for this, the mission of which was to communicate the intelligence of war with the English, set out from France. When approaching the Mascareigne, she missed her way during the night time, struck on a rocky cliff, and was wrecked. There were 289 persons on board of her, of whom all, with the exception of nine, were drowned. (Pillai 1985, 273–274)

> Thursday, [4th November 1745, or] 21st [sic: 22nd] Arppisi of Krôdhana.—Pondicherry was last night visited by a hurricane, which commenced immediately after sunset. It blew the whole night. The destruction caused by it cannot, even approximately, be estimated . . . During the night, however, the [Uppâru] river rose in flood, and the sluices constructed for the diversion of the water gave way . . . The water rose to the height of a cubit over the ruined buildings. Many were drowned; the cattle also perished in great numbers. The town of Pondicherry was inundated . . . In some places, the water reached up to the waist; in others up to the thigh . . . During the storm, crows, sparrows, and other birds, perished in large numbers and their remains lay floating on the water which filled the streets . . . By the grace of God, however, the morning dawned, the wind abated, and the rain ceased; and within three hours the floods had subsided . . . Had the storm continued a day longer, not a single building in the town would have remained standing. It was owing to their good deeds that God preserved the people from further injury. (Pillai 1985, 289–291)

> Tuesday, [23rd November 1745, or] 12th Kârttigai of Krôdhana.—This night, a violent gale blew for three hours. Its force, however, would be but one-fortieth of that of the hurricane which raged on the 21st Arppisi [3rd

> November]. The disturbance in the weather in this instance was held to be due to the conjunction of three causes; viz., the day in question was a Tuesday, and a new-moon day; and it was under the influence of the star Kêttai. As proof of the correctness of the statement of the sâstras on the subject, the wind blew with violence for a while, and afterwards abated. On the former occasion no one predicted that there would be a storm; but every one knew that there was to be one this day, and waited for it with trembling. God has, however, preserved us. (Pillai 1985, 292)

> Sunday, [28th November 1745, or] 17th Kârttigai of Krôdhana.—From 7 o'clock last night, until 9 this morning, a hurricane swept over the town, with much violence . . . Never before have there been three storms within the same month. What evil times may these be? (Pillai 1985, 292–293)

Painstaking research could, perhaps, reconstruct an environmental history of the Indian Ocean in any given year, even though this period precedes the formal gathering of scientific data on weather patterns. Numerous sources point to severe weather patterns in Europe, Africa, and Asia in 1745. Ships were unable to enter Table Bay at the Cape of Good Hope, and one of the ships of the return fleet was lost at sea between Batavia and the Cape. Similarly bad weather struck Macao in the period 1735–1745 when, according to the Franciscan friar José de Jesus Maria, who lived in Macao between 1742–1745, at least eleven ships were lost by storm, shipwreck, and fire (Boxer 1948). It was recorded in the Nagasaki VOC daily register on February 14, 1745: "Furthermore this winter is the severest ever. All the moats around the shogunal palace are frozen and all the ducks and geese are frozen to death." The bad weather continued with Nagasaki being hit by a large typhoon that according to the Dutch daily register "wiped out a whole street of Chinese and their whores."[1]

French-English Disputes in the Bay of Bengal

> Saturday, [5th February 1746, or] 27th Tai of Krôdhana.—Intelligence was received from Mahé that a squadron of from five to ten French ships was on its way hither, and was in all probability approaching the roadstead . . . They have at present in their possession the four French ships—from France, Acheen, Manila, and China—which are prizes taken by them last year; as also the following of their own, which arrived from England this

season; namely, five of the Company's and two of the King's. Add to these eleven, the five or six large ships which they have appropriated from those captured by them since, and the English have in all twenty-two sail; so that when their fleet encounters ours, the enemy would be about two and -a-half times the stronger. (Pillai 1985, 295–297)

[Monday], 7th February 1746, or 29th Tai of Krôdhana.—At noon, the Portuguese ship St. Louis, captain, M. Antonio-de-Caëtan, arrived here from Madras, cast anchor, and fired three guns to salute the vessels in the roads: these were returned by a like number . . . Four English sail came in pursuit of this ship . . . It appears that when the St. Louis was on her way from Chandernagore, the English sailors at Madras seized her and detained her in the roads there. When inquiry was made as to her nationality, the reply that she was Portuguese . . . Those in charge of her were asked to sell all the merchandise that was on board, and to buy goods there in exchange. They agreed to this, pretended to bargain, deceived the English, set sail, and escaped in the night . . . The goods which were brought in the Portuguese ship St. Louis were wheat, rice, and candles; it is said that there were also some sundry goods from Chandernagore. This cargo was being unloaded by boats until 2 in the morning. (Pillai 1985, 303–304)

Tuesday, 8th February 1746, or 30th Tai of Krôdhana .—The English ships which arrived yesterday are yet in the roads. They have not moved. . . . The Governor of Fort St. David . . . communicated the news to the commander of the men-of-war, supplied him with some Europeans and Carnatic sepoys, as well as three large boats, and instructed him to retaliate. He accordingly came with four ships. Anchoring in proximity to the coast, he dispatched two or three native craft, each carrying a party of 100 men composed of Europeans and natives . . . The object of the English in acting as they have done is to imitate the course followed by the French near Fort St. David, who made but a show of warlike operations, and in that respect they have outdone them. (Pillai 1985, 304–306)

Wednesday, 9th February 1746, or 1st Mâsi of Krôdhana.—Last night, at about three Indian hours after sunset, the English squadron, completely lit up, stood inshore for a while, and then moved back to its former position. The Governor, who was apprised of this, set out at once for the beach, having previously ordered the lights to be extinguished. (Pillai 1985, 307–309)

Hostilities between the French and English prompted the ambitious French governor of the Mascarenes, Bertrand-Francois Mahé de La Bourdonnais, to put together a fleet and sail from Port Louis on the Île de France (Mauritius) to Pondicherry in June 1746. Because of a lack of manpower, La Bourdonnais was forced to supplement his crews with African slaves. In an unexpected move, La Bourdonnais with his fleet of eight merchant ships was able to chase off the smaller but better-armed English fleet, which sailed for cover to Ceylon and onwards to Bengal. La Bourdonnais was instrumental in the siege of Madras that resulted in an English defeat, but he was forced to withdraw from the coast because of the onset of a severe storm which left the town vulnerable to looting. French-English hostilities at sea and along the Coromandel coast continued throughout the 1740s (Furber 1976).

Dutch East India Company Seasonal Shipping

Another nexus of European trading networks that intersected with French and English rivalries involved the Dutch East India Company shipping routes across the Indian Ocean. Archival records of the VOC voyages are almost complete—with 4,722 outward voyages and 3,359 homeward voyages. The discrepancy in these numbers can be explained by numerous shipwrecks and the disposal or rerouting of ships to the intra-Asia trade (Bruijn, Gaastra, and Schöffer 1979, x). Two outward fleets departed the Netherlands around Christmas and Easter, although the exact dates vary considerably. The Cape of Good Hope on the southern tip of Africa was the halfway point on the journeys between Europe and Asia. It was also the point from which, over time, the outward fleets from Europe split into their respective routes across the Indian Ocean to their final ports of call. The major destination was Batavia, the VOC's imperial capital on Java. Other ships were sent directly to Ceylon, and from 1750 to Bengal. Company shipping to other ports in India, China and Japan travelled via Batavia. Intermittently, ships sailed directly from Europe via the Cape to Canton (Bruijn, Gaastra, and Schöffer 1979, 62–75).

The outward fleet of four departing the various roadsteads of the Netherlands from May 12 to 27, 1744, arrived at their final destinations in stages. The *Nieuw Vijvervreugd* arrived in Batavia on December 6, 1744, probably earning her captain Hendrik Bossen and crew a sizable reward for such a fast journey. By 1746, any passage to Batavia or India that was completed within six months earned the captain and crew 900 guilders, and if they could shave another two weeks from the journey, the bonus was increased to 1200 guilders. During the 1740s, the VOC made a concerted effort to improve the sailing and navigational skills of its officers. In 1743, Governor-General Van Imoff opened the first *Académie de Marine* in Batavia to train ships' officers (Bruijn, Gaastra, and Schöffer 1979, 103).

The *Huis te Foreest,* captained by Gerrit Blauwpot arrived in Batavia on January 11, 1745, while the *Vrijheid,* captained by Adriaan van Dorp, did not enter the Batavia roadstead until April 12. The *Leeuwerik,* captained by Adriaan Laurens, parted from the rest of the fleet at the Cape and sailed directly to Ceylon, arriving on January 25, 1745. At the Cape, the *Leeuwerik* was ordered to take on seven convicts for transportation to Ceylon (Bruijn, Gaastra, and Schöffer 1987, 492–493). The VOC created a network of penal transportation and political exile across the Indian Ocean linking its major settlements (Ward 2009). The second half of the Easter fleet comprised three ships. The *Nieuwland* arrived in Batavia on April 28, 1745. The *Diemermeer* arrived in Ceylon on August 14, 1745, and *Ketel* arrived in Batavia on July 14, 1745. The *Ketel* was eventually sold in 1748 to Spanish merchants in Manila, where it was probably confined to the Asia trade.

Weather conditions partly determined the duration of journeys. The Christmas fleet of 1744 comprising six ships, four of which carried a total of nearly a million guilders in cash, was forced to return to port after hitting a storm four days out from the Netherlands and was delayed for nearly a month before departing again. Much to the relief of the VOC management, all of these ships arrived safely in Batavia between June 13 and August 17, 1745. The next part of the Christmas fleet departed the Netherlands on December 9, 1744, and arrived in Batavia between July 4 and August 18, 1745. The *Domburg,* which carried 250,000 guilders, was also carrying a woman disguised as a sailor. When her identity was discovered at the Cape, Captain Jan Verhagen allowed her to continue the voyage to Batavia as a passenger. This was not an unusual occurrence. Usually one or two women a year were found to have disguised themselves as sailors and were allowed to continue their voyages as passengers. It is probable that the ruse was in fact aided by sailors, but we do not have any biographical information about these women and their fates after their adventurous voyages to Asia (Bruijn, Gaastra, and Schöffer 1987, 494–495).

Conditions on board VOC ships spanning 1745 were not too terrible, as death rates generally stayed quite low for the year, averaging around 12–15 for ships with at least 200 souls on board. The anomaly for 1745 was the *Domburg,* which lost 60 seafarers of a total of 262 and 27 soldiers from a total of 125. The Dutch East India Company directors made a concerted effort to ensure the health of their employees on board their ships. From 1745, a series of incentives were introduced to make the job of ship's surgeon more attractive to qualified medical men. As well as being allowed a greater volume of luggage, which enabled the kind of small-scale illicit trade to which the Company turned a blind eye, ship's surgeons were paid a bonus at the end of every voyage which was further increased if the voyage was considered a "healthy" one. But the medical staff on board ships was also vulnerable to illness and death. After only his second voyage as surgeon's mate, Pieter Hogewoning died in Batavia in 1745 immediately after having made his will with his wife Lidia van der Leen, who was resident in the town (Bruijn 2009).

By 1745, VOC ships were ordered to choose, according to the weather, between Table Bay, Saldanha Bay, and False Bay as their anchorage in southern Africa. Cape Town in Table Bay was the main settlement of the Cape of Good Hope and offered ships the full complement of facilities and entertainment of a port city in the Indian Ocean. It was populated by slaves brought to the Cape via the various networks of slave trades in the Indian Ocean, and in many respects it resembled other VOC colonial port towns (Ward 2009). A total of forty-nine ships departed Europe crossing the Indian Ocean for various VOC settlements spanning departures and arrivals in 1745, while a total of thirty-two ships departed Batavia, Bengal, Ceylon, and China, crossing the Indian Ocean meeting at the Cape of Good Hope before proceeding, preferably in convoy, across the Atlantic for Europe. The return Christmas fleet was unable to enter the roadstead in Table Bay because of bad weather, being forced instead to anchor off Robben Island (Bruijn, Gaastra, and Schöffer 1987, 492–502).

The Easter return fleet of 1745 gives some insight into the perils and plight of European shipping in the Indian Ocean. Two ships, the *Standvastigheid* and the *Vlissingen,* departed Bengal on February 1, 1745, calling in at the Cape in the second week of May. Two ships departed China on February 2, 1745, and while the *Bosbeek,* captained by Laurens Siewertszoon, did not stop at the Cape, the *Overnes,* captained by Hendrik de Ruyter, anchored in False Bay for three weeks before proceeding to Europe. The *Heuvel* departed from Batavia alone on March 2, 1745, not waiting to be accompanied by the two other ships which sailed nine days later. The *Heuvel,* belonging to the Zeeland chamber of the VOC and valued at 151,405 guilders, never arrived at the Cape, having been lost somewhere on the Indian Ocean. There is no record of her fate or that of her crew and passengers. The loss of a ship was a significant financial blow to the VOC, which then had to calculate the entire loss from the voyage, not just the value of the ship itself. But ships themselves were also part of the trading world of the Indian Ocean. The two ships that departed Batavia on March 12, 1745, were spoils of war. The *Oplettendheid* was originally a French ship named the *Jason* that was captured by the English on February 5, 1745, and brought to Batavia, where it was sold to the VOC before being renamed and fitted out for the return voyage less than a month later. The *Toevalligheid* was also a French ship, the *Hercules,* captured and sold by the English during the same transaction (Bruijn, Gaastra, and Schöffer 1989, 372–379).

Conclusion

The very nature of Indian Ocean cultural interactions ensures that there is a multiplicity of marking time across regions, cultures, languages, and religions. The year known as 1745 in Christian calendars coincided with the following years across Asia: in the Islamic calendar 1157–1158; in China, Qianlong 9, or the "wood rat" and "wood ox" years; in Japan, Enkyo 2; in the Buddhist calendar 2289; in the Thai solar calendar 2288; in the Burmese calendar 1107; in the Bengali, 1152; and in various Hindu calendars—Bikram Samwat 1801–1802, Shaka Samvat 1667–1668, and Kali Yuga 4846–4847.[2] This is far from an exhaustive or completely accurate list. Even the Gregorian Christian calendar was not consistent during the eighteenth century, with the calculation of the New Year falling on different days in different European countries and with the English not adopting the "new style" Gregorian calendar until 1753, well after the French. In contrast to this calendrical cacophony in the Indian Ocean, the regularity of the seasonal monsoon winds, weather patterns, and oceanic currents were commonly observed by all, even though these meteorological and oceanographical seasonal phenomena were known by different names, whether one calls the waters Al Bahr al Hindi, Nanyang, or the Indian Ocean.

Notes

1. Martha Chaiklin, personal communication regarding weather patterns in Japan from the VOC Dagregister Nagasaki, February 14, 1745, 97.

2. "1745." *Wikipedia.* http://en.wikipedia.org/wiki/1745. Accessed November 10, 2010.

References

Andaya, Barbara. 1979. *Perak, the Abode of Grace: A Study of an Eighteenth Century Malay State.* Kuala Lumpur: Oxford University Press.

———. 1983. "Melaka under the Dutch, 1641–1795." In *Melaka: The Transformation of a Malay Capital c. 1400–1980.* Vol. 1, ed. Kernial Singh Sandhu and Paul Wheatley, 195–241. Kuala Lumpur: Oxford University Press.

Atsushi, Ota. 2010. "Imagined Link, Domesticated Religion: The State and the Outside Islamic Network in Banten, West Java, c. 1520–1813." In *Large and Broad: The Dutch Impact on Early Modern Asia: Essays in Honor of Leonard Blussé,* ed. Yoko Nagazumi and Leonard Blussé , 5–25. Tokyo: The Toyo Bunko.

Azra, Azyumardi. 2004. *The Origins of Islamic Reformism in Southeast Asia: Networks of Malay-Indonesian and Middle Eastern Ulama in the Seventeenth and Eighteenth Centuries.* Honolulu: University of Hawaii Press.

Barendse, R. J. 2009. *The Arabian Seas 1700–1763: The Western Indian Ocean in the Eighteenth Century.* 4 vols. Leiden: Brill.

Barnard, Timothy. 2009. "The Hajj, Islam, and Power among the Bugis in Early Colonial Riau." In *Southeast Asia and the Middle East: Islam, Movement and the Longue Durée,* ed. Eric Tagliacozzo, 65–82. Singapore: Singapore University Press.

Bose, Sugata. 2006. *A Hundred Horizons: The Indian Ocean in the Age of Global Empire.* Cambridge, MA: Harvard University Press.

Boxer, Charles. 1948. *Fidalgos in the Far East 1550–1770: Fact and Fancy in the History of Macao.* The Hague: Martinus Nijhoff.

Braginsky, Vladimir. 2004. *The Heritage of Traditional Malay Literature: A Historical Survey of Genres, Writings, and Literary Views.* Leiden: KITLV Press.

Bruijn, Iris. 2009. *Ship's Surgeons of the Dutch East India Company: Commerce and the Progress of Medicine in the Eighteenth Century.* Leiden: Leiden University Press.

Bruijn, J. R., F. S. Gaastra, and I. Schöffer, eds. 1979, 1987, 1989. *Dutch Asiatic Shipping in the 17th and 18th Centuries.* 3 vols. The Hague: Martinus Nijhoff.

Charney, Michael, 1999. "Where Jambudipa and Islamdom Converged: Religious Change and the Emergence of Buddhist Communalism in Early Modern Arakan (Fifteenth to Nineteenth Centuries)." Ph.D. thesis, University of Michigan.

———. 2004. *Southeast Asian Warfare, 1300–1900.* Leiden: Brill.

Coates, Austin. 2009. *Macao and the British, 1637–1842: Prelude to Hong Kong.* Hong Kong: Hong Kong University Press.

Das Gupta, Ashin. 1998. "Trade and Politics in Eighteenth Century India." In *The Mughal State, 1526–1750,* ed. Muzaffar Alam and Sanjay Subrahmanyam, 361–397. Delhi: Oxford University Press.

Furber, Holden. 1976. *Rival Empires of Trade in the Orient, 1600–1800.* Minneapolis: University of Minnesota Press.

Goodman, Grant. 2000. *Japan and the Dutch 1600–1853.* Richmond: Curzon Press.

Hanna, Willard A., and Des Alwi. 1990. *Turbulent Times Past in Ternate and Tidore.* Banda Naira: Pustakar Sinar Harapan.

Ho, Engseng. 2006. *The Graves of Tarim: Genealogy and Mobility across the Indian Ocean.* Berkeley: University of California Press.

Hockly, T. W. 1935. *The Two Thousand Isles: A Short Account of the People, History and Customs of the Maldive Archipelago.* London: H. F. & G. Witherby.

Hogensdorn, Jan, and Marion Johnson. 1986. *The Shell Money of the Slave Trade.* Cambridge: Cambridge University Press.

Larson, Pier. 2000. *History and Memory in the Age of Enslavement: Becoming Merina in Highland Madagascar.* Oxford: James Currey.

Li Tana. 2004. "The Water Frontier: An Introduction." In *Water Frontier: Commerce and the Chinese in the Lower Mekong Region, 1750–1880,* ed. Li Tana and Nola Cooke, 1–17. Singapore: Singapore University Press.

Li Tana and Nola Cooke. 2004. "Preface." In *Water Frontier: Commerce and the Chinese in the Lower Mekong Region, 1750–1880,* ed. Li Tana and Nola Cooke, xi–xiii. Singapore: Singapore University Press.

Nagtegaal, Luc. 1996. *Riding the Dutch Tiger: The Dutch East India Company and the Northeast Coast of Java, 1680–1743.* Leiden: KITLV Press.

Pearson, Michael. 2003. *The Indian Ocean.* London: Routledge.

Pillai, Ananda Ranga. 1985. *The Private Diary of Ananda Ranga Pillai, Durbash to Joseph François Dupleix, Governor of Pondicherry. A Record of Matters Political, Historical, Social and Personal from 1736–1761 (in 12 volumes).* Trans. from the Tamil by order of the Government of Madras. Edited by Rev J. Frederick Price and K. Rangachari. Vol 1. New Delhi: Asian Educational Services.

Poivre, Pierre.1993. "Description of Cochinchina 1749–1750," trans. Kristine Ailunas-Rodgers. In *Southern Vietnam under the Nguyen: Documents on the Economic History of Cochinchina (Dang Trong) 1602–1777,* ed. Li Tana and Anthony Reid. Singapore: ISEAS and the Economic History of Southeast Asia Project.

Ramen, Bhavani. 2007. "Document Raj: Scribes and Writing Under Early Colonial Rule in Madras." Ph.D. thesis, University of Michigan.

Remmelink, Willem. 1994. *The Chinese War and the Collapse of the Javanese State 1725–1743.* Leiden: KITLV Press.

Ricklefs, Merle. 1993. *A History of Modern Indonesia since c1300.* Stanford, CA: Stanford University Press.

———. 1998. *The Seen and Unseen Worlds in Java, 1726–1749: History, Literature, and Islam at the Court of Pakukuwana II.* Honolulu: Allen & Unwin and the University of Hawaii Press.

Salleh, Muhammad Haji. 2006. "A Malay Knight Speaks the White Man's Tongue: Notes on Translating the Hikayat Hang Tuah." *Indonesia and the Malay World* 34 (100): 395–405.

Tran, TonNu Quynh. 2003. "The French Presence in Hoi An." In National Committee for the International Symposium on the Ancient Town of Hoi Ann. *Ancient Town of Hoi An*. Hà Nôi: The Goi Publishers.

Vaughan, Megan. 2005. *Creating the Creole Island: Slavery in Eighteenth Century Mauritius*. Durham, NC: Duke University Press.

Vink, Markus. 2007. "Indian Ocean Studies and the 'New Thalassology'." *Journal of Global History* 2 (1): 41–62.

Voll, John. 1987. "Linking Groups in the Networks of Eighteenth Century Revivalist Scholars." In *Eighteenth Century Renewal in Islam*, ed. Nehemia Levtzion and John O. Voll, 69–92. Syracuse, NY: Syracuse University Press.

Ward, Kerry. 2009. *Networks of Empire: Forced Migration in the Dutch East India Company*. New York: Cambridge University Press.

Wills, John E. 2001. *1688: A Global History*. New York: W.W. Norton.

Winius, George, and Marcus Vink. 1991. *The Merchant-Warrior Pacified: The VOC (The Dutch East India Company) and Its Changing Political Economy in India*. Delhi: Oxford University Press.

7

1874

Tea and Japan's New Trading Regime

ROBERT HELLYER

A historian of Japan can easily identify numerous seminal years in the rough decade between the Meiji Restoration of 1868, Japan's modern revolution, and the short but bitter Satsuma Rebellion of 1877, the last serious internal challenge to the grip on national power held by the new central government formed in 1868. The Meiji Restoration began as a palace coup in which men from two prominent, feudal domains, Chōshū and Satsuma, led an alliance that seized control and "restored" the Emperor Meiji to a position of political dominance. The government established by the alliance subsequently swept away the institutions of the vanquished Tokugawa shogunate *(bakufu)* that had dominated Japan during the previous Edo period (1603–1868). From its new capital at Tokyo (formerly Edo), the Meiji regime (named for the Meiji era, 1868–1912) dismantled the feudal hierarchy, with the samurai class at its top, which had defined Japanese society for centuries. In its place, they created a Western-inspired social system of elites and commoners. The leaders instructed the masses to embrace Western "civilization and enlightenment" and by implication cease being feudal subjects and instead become citizens of a new Japanese nation-state. Under the banner of a "rich nation and strong military," they also urged Japanese to strive for economic expansion to allow Japan to "catch-up" with Western nations, as well as to support the creation of national armed forces.

In foreign trade, Meiji Japan also turned to the West, developing silk and tea exports to the United States and Western Europe. Economic historians have shown how silk and tea, as Japan's two most prominent exports, played a crucial, foundational role in a key aspect of "catching up" with the West: industrialization. Sugiyama Shinya has demonstrated that import substitution and the export of products of traditional industries were at once "interdependent but separate aspects of Japan's industrialization" (1988, 9). He shows that exports of silk and tea did not directly lead to the development of modern industries but were particularly significant in obtaining foreign currency. "The foreign currency obtained through these exports brought about conditions suitable to stable economic development, through restraining the outflow of specie while at the same time limiting the potential entry of foreign capital, by keeping the imbalance of international payments to a minimum level. In addition, it produced the conditions essential to industrialization by increasing import capacity and in particular expanding the possible range of imports of production goods, which form the basis of import substitution" (1988, 9).

This chapter focuses on 1874, the year in which tea exports jumped to a new high, beginning an extended surge of shipments to the United States, the most important foreign market for Japanese tea. It affirms the role of tea in the drive toward industrialization and economic parity with Western nations but uses 1874 to reveal multiple "inside-out" dynamics in Japan's economic development and emergence as a nation-state. Specifically, it examines structures, relationships, agendas, and processes that, as with other key years identified in this volume, transcend conventional divisions of land and sea, political regimes, and cultural boundaries. First, although the tea trade involved two Pacific nations, its structure was not encapsulated in a bilateral, trans-Pacific relationship. British merchants played a key role in developing the trade in the 1860s, and into the 1880s, a good portion of Japanese tea flowed to the United States via the Indian and Atlantic Oceans. Throughout most of the Meiji period, Japanese merchants purchased tea from farmers and handled its transport to major ports. British and American firms dominated the subsequent processing at port factories, as well as the shipment to, and sales of, Japanese tea on the US market. Because Japanese companies failed to make major inroads in shipping and sales on the US market, the Meiji government and Japanese merchant groups had to work in conjunction with Western firms, creating an "inside-out" relationship that defined the trade into the early twentieth century.

Chinese experts, who guided the development of the trade and continued to supervise exports as employees of Western firms, represent another "inside-out" relationship within the Japanese-Western cooperative, commercial structure. As they began to export Japanese tea in the 1860s, British merchants utilized existing Western-dominated global transport networks to ship teas to the United States. Nonetheless, they depended heavily upon Chinese technicians to guide the processing and packing of tea for export. Meiji government officials also actively sought Chinese know-how. They brought experienced Chinese tea men to Japan to supervise the construction of tea processing plants, published Chinese guides for cultivation and refining, and dispatched an investigative mission to China to acquire additional information.

A focus on 1874 exposes another "inside-out" dynamic: the independent politico-economic agendas on both sides of the Pacific that converged to create the trade's growth. While certainly chasing the larger goal of "catching up" with Western nations, the oligarchs heading the Meiji government also sought to use an expansion of tea production to create economic opportunities for groups displaced by recent social and economic reforms. For their part, US leaders saw an increase in tea and coffee imports as a means to stimulate a maritime shipping sector languishing in the wake of the US Civil War (1861–1865). In 1872 they therefore repealed tariffs on coffee and tea, a move calculated to also lower prices and make the two "necessary" beverages more affordable for the working class. Japanese producers and Western export firms quickly capitalized, aggressively expanding exports in a push that in 1874 resulted in new highs in the volume and value of tea exports.

1874 also initiated a major shift in the world tea market. Beginning in that year, Japan demonstrated the ability to challenge China's long dominance in supplying tea to the largest Western consumer-nations: Britain and the United States. Soon after, the colonial producer-states of India, Ceylon, and Java ramped up exports and by the 1880s had also acquired significant shares of the world market at the expense of China. 1874 therefore parallels in significance 1726, which in this volume Nancy Um identifies as pivotal in the history of the global coffee trade. As she demonstrates, the commencement of sales of Javanese coffee in Amsterdam in that year began the decline of Yemen's strategic position as a node of intersection between land and sea trade routes.

The more competitive global tea market contributed to a final "inside-out" dynamic: increased debate over the quality of Japanese tea on the US market.

As the trade developed, Japanese producers and Western merchants used adulteration—especially the adding of minerals to color low-grade tea—to improve profit margins but also to match the tastes of US consumers. In the 1880s, Japanese producers and Western traders became more aware that adulteration harmed the reputation of Japanese tea, especially as concerns about food and beverage purity became more prominent in US public discourse. During the next decade, companies marketing India and Ceylon black teas, which began to stream onto the US market, sought to push consumers to see Japanese (and Chinese) teas as adulterated and impure. It was much less desirable, they suggested, than India and Ceylon teas produced on mechanized plantations.

The Beginning of Japan's Tea Export Trade

Soon after taking power, the Meiji leadership pursued a strategy that would have seemed improbable just over a decade before: developing exports tailored not for Chinese but Western consumers and, by implication, creating a trading regime that would challenge China, long the most dominant economy in East Asia. Throughout the Edo period, the shogunate had carefully supervised foreign trade centered on the China market. In the seventeenth and early eighteenth centuries, it oversaw the shipment of Japanese silver in exchange for Chinese silk. In the mid-eighteenth century, Tokugawa leaders ended the silk-for-silver trade and instead directed that copper, camphor, and marine products (sea cucumbers, kelp, and shark fins) be shipped to China in exchange for chiefly medicinal goods. Under Western military pressure, in 1858 the shogunate signed commercial treaties first with the United States and later with Britain and other European nations. Based on these agreements, Westerners gained privileges such as the right of extraterritoriality. The treaties also established fixed tariffs that the shogunate could not unilaterally amend. Western merchants and diplomats soon began to reside and trade in the treaty ports of Hakodate, Nagasaki, and Yokohama. An additional port, Kobe, was opened to Western traders in 1868.

Despite the advantages provided by the treaties, Western merchants initially found limited Japanese interest in Western European and US manufactured wares, notably cotton and wool cloth and clothing. They therefore competed for a share of established Chinese-Japanese trade flows and began to explore the development of tea exports. Kenneth Mackenzie, the first

Nagasaki agent of the prominent British trading firm Jardine, Matheson, & Company (hereafter Jardine) believed Japanese green tea could compensate for predicted shortfalls in Chinese production. On May 9, 1860, he wrote to his superiors in Hong Kong about the expected good crop for that year, which two months later (July 9) he concluded could make up for an anticipated drop in Chinese production due to the Taiping Rebellion (1850–1864). Writing again on October 30, he emphasized that Japanese tea would be ideal for the green-tea-dominated US market (Jardine Matheson In-correspondence).[1]

Mackenzie sent only a few shipments of Japanese tea to Shanghai and Hong Kong during his short tenure in Nagasaki. Thomas Glover, who became Jardine's Nagasaki agent in 1861, made more progress, especially in reducing costs by streamlining the refining process. From Japanese brokers, Western merchants purchased tea that had been steamed soon after picking to stop the oxidation process. This was sufficient to allow the tea to keep for several months for sale on the domestic market. Yet for it to remain fresh during overseas transit, the tea had to be "fired," heated to remove extra moisture before being packed into chests. With no facility available in Nagasaki, Mackenzie had shipped tea to Shanghai for firing, which added not only transportation costs but also increased the amount lost as waste during a voyage.

Using loans from Jardine, Glover oversaw the construction of a tea-firing factory in Nagasaki that opened in 1862 and utilized what was often called the "Chinese method" of pan firing. Workers would eliminate extra moisture by stirring the tea for thirty to forty minutes in large steel pans. A firing factory, such as the one Glover constructed, included hundreds of pans inlaid into brick stands and heated by small braziers. Another method, basket firing, involved placing a tray on top of a sturdy bamboo basket that rested over a charcoal brazier. The basket would conduct heat and steam up to the tray, where a standing worker would periodically stir the tea, often for close to an hour, to remove extra moisture. Pan firing in particular often produced a yellow-colored tea, which was deemed unsuitable for sale on the US market. Drawing upon Chinese techniques and often under the direction of a Chinese overseer, a chemical pigment such as Prussian blue (Ferric ferrocyanide, also known as Berlin blue) was added to make the tea green and palatable for the US consumer.

While the plant was soon up and running, Jardine officials in Hong Kong and Shanghai quickly realized that Glover lacked the knowledge and experience to produce quality teas. Their correspondences with him suggest that for one, Glover too liberally added color to the first shipments. At their urging Glover sought Chinese know-how, not surprising given China's still-dominant position as the world's chief tea producer and exporter. In a March 19, 1862, dispatch to Hong Kong he wrote, "Your remarks concerning the coloring of these teas have our best attention and we shall see that the balance of your teas should not be so highly colored as to depreciate their value. We are daily expecting an experienced tea boy from Shanghai to superintend the firing establishment." Glover stressed that the Chinese specialist would "have the coloring under his direction" (Jardine Matheson In-correspondence). On July 25, 1862, he also lamented being forced to hire additional and more costly Chinese workers already in Nagasaki to not only fire tea but also teach Japanese workers the refining process (Jardine Matheson In- correspondence).

The scope of Chinese influence was also evident in the methods of packing tea for export. Closely imitating established Chinese practices, Jardine and other Western firms placed the fired tea in lead-lined wooden chests, wrapped in rattan for extra support. On the rattan were attached labels, often illustrated with flower motifs mimicking Chinese styles ("Description of the Tea Plant" 1839–1840, 148–149). In subsequent decades, firms still used rattan-wrapped chests adorned with flower labels (Ide 1993, 40–43). This is not surprising, given that Jardine and other Western exporters continued to rely on skilled Chinese workers; an 1874 directory lists Jardine's Yokohama branch as having nine employees, four of them Chinese: Sui-nam, a shroff (a money changer), A. Chew, the godown man, Agip, the tea boy, and Amoy, No. 1 boatman (Japan Gazette 1874, 14).

The US Market and Meiji Government Efforts before 1874

Popular perception relates that the "tea parties" in Boston and other colonial cities in the 1770s became a watershed in US beverage consumption. Patriotic colonials spurned tea, the "British" beverage, in favor of coffee, starting a trend that continued after the United States became an independent nation. So entrenched has been this idea that one of the more thorough scholars of tea in the twentieth century, William Ukers, asserted that "amid the roar of musketry, a great republic was born—one that was soon to become the wealthiest consumer-nation in the world, but with a prenatal disinclination for tea" (1935, 65).

Over the course of the nineteenth century Americans began to drink more coffee overall, but tea did not disappear from the US beverage menu. In the decades after independence from Britain, US merchant ships calling at Canton loaded tea as their chief return cargo, selling it for high profits in New York or Boston, where it entered the US market or was re-exported to Britain. Trade figures show that US tea consumption rose steadily from an annual average of 3.35 million pounds between 1801 and 1812, to 7 million pounds annually between 1821 and 1833. Between 1821 and 1837, 77 percent of the tea consumed in the United States was green tea (Macgregor 1840, 816–817). Although languishing somewhat in the 1840s, in the 1850s imports increased substantially: from just over 18 million pounds in 1849 to 40.2 million in 1856. During that time, imports of green tea continued to outpace those of black tea (Homans and Homans 1858, 303; Hunt 1857, 610).

US and also British consumption grew as the amount of tea on the world market increased following the Opium War (1839–1842) as more Chinese ports besides Canton supplied tea (Gardella 1994, 48–83). In the 1860s, US and British clipper ships, in voyages via the Indian and Atlantic Oceans that spanned up to four months, transported tea from Japanese and Chinese ports to, chiefly, New York. During the 1870s, steamers began to carry most of the tea by the same route, taking advantage of the Suez Canal to bring their cargoes to New York in forty-five to sixty days (Riggs 1883, 295).

While surprising by today's standards, nineteenth-century Americans were quite familiar with additives in their tea and other beverages. An 1825 manual provided specific tests that a consumer could employ to detect Japan earth (*catechu*, a brown dye made from tree bark) added to black tea and green vitriol (sulfate of iron) to green tea imported from China (Beman 1825, 115–117). US consumers also had to be alert for bogus coffee made from rye flour and glucose (Pendergrast 1999, 59).

Soon after assuming power, Meiji leaders, in conjunction with merchants and municipal authorities, moved to develop tea exports into a national industry. In 1869, the Tokyo municipal government directed that tea and mulberry fields (the latter for silk production) be planted in the gardens of the lords' (*daimyo*) official residences, estates that occupied large swathes of the municipality (DNISK).[2] In Kyoto, merchants proposed guidelines to the municipal government for how companies could purchase tea from regional farmers and sell it to Western exporters at nearby Kobe and other treaty ports (DNISK 1869).[3]

Samurai retainers of the deposed Tokugawa house also emerged to play prominent roles in the new government's plans. After suffering military defeats to Chōshū and Satsuma forces in the summer of 1868, the last shogun, Tokugawa Yoshinobu, retired to his family's ancestral estate in Shizuoka, just south of Tokyo. His portfolio of lands greatly reduced, Yoshinobu enjoyed far less income and therefore could no longer provide stipends, annual grants of rice bestowed by a samurai lord, to most of his retainers and their families. In response, some retainers obtained administrative positions in the new Meiji regime, but around 17,000 more, including many who had fought for Yoshinobu, followed their lord to Shizuoka, hoping for new opportunities. These refugees found employment and housing scarce in the urban area around Sunpu castle, which in 1869 came to be known as the city of Shizuoka, the government seat of what later became the prefecture by the same name (Kawaguchi 1989, 37–41).

Many began to disperse into the countryside, seeking new lives as farmers. Makinohara, an area long deemed too rugged and dry to cultivate, became a site for 300 samurai families to begin new lives as tea farmers (Ōishi 1974, 14–16). The move of these samurai to live without assistance from their lord, essentially an abdication of their elite samurai status, predated the Meiji government edicts that disestablished the samurai class and abolished stipends in the 1870s (Sakeda and Akita 1986, 300–301). Although smaller in number, another displaced group, workers in the transport system across the Ōi River in Shizuoka, joined the samurai-cum-farmers in Makinohara. In the seventeenth century the Tokugawa regime, remembering the bitter military battles of the previous century, had restricted bridge construction across the Ōi to maintain it as a barrier against a possible military strike against Edo. Travelers on the Tōkaidō, the thoroughfare linking Edo and central Japan, therefore relied upon a regulated labor pool of men who transported people and goods across the river. In 1870 the Meiji regime abolished the labor pool in anticipation of building a bridge, a move that placed approximately 1,300 men out of work. Following the pleas of a representative of the displaced laborers, the Meiji government offered modest monetary compensation and land in Makinohara, which thirty-three families accepted in 1871 (Teramoto 1999, 65–66). The former samurai and river transport workers, as well as farmers throughout Shizuoka, embraced the opportunity to cultivate tea because of potential financial rewards. Thanks to increasing foreign demand, a cultivator could earn higher profits for tea than established staples, such as rice, on the Shizuoka market (Kawaguchi 1989, 58–59). Production from Makinohara and other parts of the prefecture soon made Shizuoka the largest tea-producing region in Japan, a position it still holds today.

The new cultivators, even farmers with long familial ties to the land, lacked the requisite experience to grow tea and refine it on the large scale required to sustain an export trade. To assist them, guidebooks began to appear; in 1871 the Hikone domain (today's Shiga prefecture), located near Kyoto, published one such manual. Its authors stressed that the volume would present all aspects of tea production in an accessible way for the benefit of individual cultivators and, by implication, the greater imperial nation *(kōkoku)* (Hikone-han [1871] 1971, 202). A similar guide with more detailed information and diagrams of the tools required to pick and process tea was published in 1873 (Masuda [1873] 1971). A few years later, the Home Ministry commissioned the translation and publication of a guide-book penned by Hu Binghsu from the Lingnan region in southern China. In his treatise, Hu offered information about cultivation in different terrains as well as about refining and packaging green and black teas. He also included illustrations of the pan-firing process. In the introduction to the translation, Oda Kanshi, a ministry official, stressed how the text would allow tea growers and by implication, Japan overall to exploit its natural resource of tea as China had done for centuries (Ko and Takezoe 1877, 1–4).

Another displaced group also benefited from the trade: artists who had previously produced woodblock prints, a source of news during the Edo period. Made redundant by the growth of print newspapers, they found work etching the labels placed upon the tea chests shipped to the United States. The artists created labels, many imitating Chinese flower motifs, but also ones with what would become iconic images of Japan, for example, a woman in a kimono serving tea or arranging flowers (Ide 1993, 40–43).

The Import Boom Begins

Underscoring the important place of engagement with Western nations in their agenda, late in 1871 several members of Japan's ruling oligarchy embarked upon a multiyear journey to the United States and Western Europe. Headed by a nobleman, Iwakura Tomomi, the mission became an opportunity for the leaders to study the political institutions and economic structures of Western nations, including their agricultural production. During the mission Kume

Kunitake, a secretary, noted that the failure of attempts to profitably grow tea in the United States had helped Japan gain a share of the US tea market during the previous decade (2002, 325).

Nonetheless, Kume and his superiors were concerned primarily with diplomatic matters. Following instructions received in Tokyo, the mission worked to renegotiate the treaties Japanese leaders signed in the late 1850s, an agenda that took it to Washington, DC, from February to May 1872. During meetings with Secretary of State Hamilton Fish, the Japanese envoys made little headway, largely because they brought few concrete proposals for a new or revised treaty (Swale 1998, 19–24).

As these meetings took place, an independent—and for Japan's tea trade, a more important—series of events unfolded nearby at the US Capitol. There, Congress debated a bill, first proposed three years earlier, to repeal existing tariffs on coffee and tea. As summarized on March 30, 1872, in a Wisconsin newspaper, the tariff garnered an estimated $30 million in annual revenue for the national treasury, but many believed its repeal would allow rich and poor alike to more easily afford both beverages (*Wisconsin State Register* 1872, column A).

Supporters of the repeal apparently presented a more powerful case by asserting how not only consumers but also US shipping interests would benefit from the abolition of the tariffs. In the Senate, Simon Cameron of Pennsylvania offered testimonials from his constituents voicing strong support for an end to the duties. On March 6, he presented a letter from "T. Thompson and others of Juanita county of Pennsylvania." Thompson and his group remonstrated "against a change of the existing tariff laws abating or abolishing duties upon such articles as are produced in the country." Yet they were "praying for the repeal of all duties upon, tea, coffee, and such other articles of necessity as cannot be produced in the United States" (United States et al. 1872, 1448). To support the shipping interests of his state, long a base for maritime trade, Rhode Island's William Sprague offered an amendment on April 24. It stressed that the tariff revision was "appropriated to restore the ocean commerce of the United States" and, as such, coastal craft, foreign-owned ships, and vessels manned by majority foreign crews would still be subject to the duty (United States et al. 1872, 1448). This broad support helped pass the legislation, and on July 1, 1872, tea and coffee imported directly (and not through, for example, Britain) became duty free.

Japan's exports of tea subsequently climbed from 15.7 million pounds, valued at 4.65 million yen, in 1873, to 23.2 million pounds, valued at just over 7.25 million yen, in the year of our focus, 1874. Over the next decade, exports continued to increase, with 1880 proving to be a banner year: just over 40 million pounds (Japan Department of Finance 1901, 43–45). Of that amount, 84 percent was shipped to the United States (Teramoto 1999, 16–17). Japanese tea gained this market share at the expense of China, which in the period between 1866 and 1870 had supplied an annual average of just over 72 percent of all the tea consumed in the United States, with Japan contributing only 19 percent. Over the next decade, Japan's share increased to 27 percent from 1871 to 1875, and to 44 percent from 1876 to 1880. During the latter period, China's share of imports dropped to just over 49 percent (Sugiyama 1988, 148).

As tea exports began to surge in 1874, the Meiji government created an Industrial Promotion Bureau in the Ministry of Home Affairs to help expand tea production and other nascent industries. The preface of its inaugural publication stressed that the bureau would assess the commercial potential of all products in Japan, beginning by developing tests for wild and domesticated flora and fauna. The bureau would compile the results and other appropriate knowledge and disseminate it via regular publications. With due attribution to the "rich country, strong army" slogan, the publication stressed that through cooperation between the government and the people, profits would be increased and losses minimized, thereby assuring the future wealth of the nation (Kangyōryō 1874, i–ii).

The government established a Tea Office within the bureau, tasking it with developing black tea exports to allow Japan to move beyond selling merely green tea to the US market. In pursuit of that goal, the office issued a guidebook and urged prefectural governments to begin exploring black tea production. In April 1875, it hired two Chinese experts on six-month contracts to supervise large-scale cultivation and refining of an indigenous tea plant believed to be well suited to make black teas. Later in the year, the Tea Office instructed several officials to escort home the Chinese experts and thereafter remain in China for several weeks to study tea cultivation and production practices. The group also brought samples of Japanese green and black teas, which it offered to Western and Chinese tea merchants in Shanghai. Because of the negative reception to the black tea samples, the Tea Office decided to dispatch another investigative mission, this time to India to explore cultivation and refining techniques employed there (Teramoto 1999, 68–69; Kawaguchi 1989, 72–88).

Although samples of Japanese black teas later sent to Europe and the United States received some positive reception and efforts were made to enter the Australian market, Japanese producers proved unable to consistently generate large amounts of quality black tea to compete with Chinese, Indian, and Ceylonese varieties on US, Western European, and British colonial markets. As a result, large-scale production of black tea for export was abandoned in the early 1880s (Ohara 1957, 176–178; Sugiyama 1988, 156).

Meanwhile, Japanese-owned firms, for example from Sayama just northwest of Tokyo, attempted to develop direct sales on the US market (Sunaga 1995). These efforts also proved unsuccessful, largely because of lack of capital. In addition, the privileges awarded to Western merchants through treaties signed in 1850s, coupled with the fact that Japan possessed only a small merchant fleet, meant that British and US companies maintained control over processing, transport, and foreign sales of Japanese tea. Therefore, into the 1890s, Japan's export trade retained a status quo in that Western firms played a dominant role, green tea was the chief product, and the United States remained the most important market.

Japanese tea's continued success on the US market also appears to have been a result of declining national prices for tea, as well as tea's competitive price in relation to coffee. On June 5, 1880, the *New York Times* analyzed trade data to consider how the elimination of duties had affected tea and coffee prices. In the three years prior to 1872, the average declared import price of coffee was 10.9 cents per pound, but jumped to 16.5 cents per pound from 1873 to 1875, before declining to 15.5 cents from 1876 to 1879. The average declared import price for tea was 33 cents from 1870 to 1872 and also rose slightly to an average of 36.6 cents in the period from 1873 to 1875. Between 1876 and 1879, however, the price declined sharply to 26.5 cents. Although stressing the difficulty in determining average retail prices for the decade, the *Times* concluded "we may say that the consumer of tea appears to have derived some benefit from the abolition of duty, but that no decline in price is visible in coffee, the more important article of the two." Here the newspaper was evidently referring to the greater volume of coffee imported; for example in 1879, 363 million pounds of coffee entered the United States, compared to only 59 million pounds of tea (figures rounded to the nearest million) (*New York Times* 1880, 4).

As for Japanese tea specifically, US consumers apparently paid top dollar for fresh teas: pickings of the tender, new shoots of the tea plant, harvested in late April or May and exported first. Frederick Cornes, a British merchant selling Japanese tea on the US market, wrote on April 3, 1874 (to William Henry Taylor) that teas delivered the previous year on the "first steamer fetched 80 cents—2nd 70 cents, 3rd 54 c. [cents] and so on" (Cornes and Davies 2008, Book 14 CD-ROM).[4] If a consumer wanted a pound of low- or middle-grade tea, he or she could purchase it for around the same price as a pound of coffee. A price list of the Oceanic Tea Company (Jersey City, New Jersey, probably from 1880s) includes six grades of Japanese pan-fired and basket-fired tea selling for 20 to 44 cents per pound. "Rio" was the least expensive coffee offered, selling for 19 cents per pound, while "Mocha" and "Plantation Ceylon" both sold for 33 cents per pound (Tea, Warshaw Collection). In 1881, the Union Pacific Tea Company maintained higher prices, selling a low grade of Japanese tea for 50 cents retail and better grades from 70 to 80 cents. The choicest grade, which probably was the first tea of the season, sold for one dollar per pound. The company sold "Mocha" coffee for 30 cents and "Java" from 33 to 35 cents per pound (*New York Times* 1881, 2). Even with its higher per pound price, consumers would choose tea because, as traders of the day noted, it could take up to four times the amount of coffee grounds as tea leaves to brew the same amount of beverage (McDonald and Topik 2008, 117).

The Boom Stalls

Writing in 1904, Ōtani Kahei, president of Japan Central Tea Association, celebrated the tea export boom, stressing that it began in 1874. Nonetheless, he lamented a downside of the rush to expand production: increased adulteration (1904, 421–422).[5] To supply what seemed an ever-growing US market, many farmers took shortcuts such as selling low-grade tea made from older and coarser leaves. Even before the boom began, Shizuoka prefectural officials realized the importance of quality, in September 1873 issuing a decree imploring producers to avoid underhanded practices. The decree stressed that many had worked earnestly in recent years to develop tea production but that some unscrupulous producers added coloring agents in an effort to mask poor-quality leaves. Merchants who unwittingly purchased such spurious tea suffered financial losses. Appealing to a sense of cooperation, the edict cautioned that such dishonest practices would make moot the hard work—the clearing of land and planting of tea—recently contributed by so many in the prefecture (quoted in Hoshida [1888] 1971, 5–7).

Yet Japanese producers were not solely responsible for adulteration; as we have seen, Western export firms also liberally used Prussian blue in line with established Chinese practices. While a desire to profit by selling even poor-quality leaves was certainly one factor, the firms also made green their yellowish, pan-fired teas to meet the tastes of US consumers. In an 1883 presentation (published two years later) Henry Gribble, who had conducted a lengthy study of tea production in Shizuoka and the export trade, defended the use of coloring agents, arguing that

> The use of colouring matter has lately given rise to considerable discussion, and there can be no doubt that, as far as it goes, it is a species of adulteration—just as much adulteration as the use of colours to make some sugar plums white, others pink, or others salmon colour. Certain tastes for colour are developed in the consumers of tea as in the consumers of sugared almonds, and it becomes the necessity of the manufacturer to meet the requirements of his consumer. The American dealers have called for more or less coloured teas, and their demand has been met here by those who prepare it. (1885, 12–13)

Yet even before Gribble's study was published, Japanese tea merchants had realized how adulteration contributed to a rising degree of distrust in the United States concerning Japanese tea. In 1882, Thomas Van Buren, the American consul-general in Yokohama, included in a report to Washington a translation of "Advice to Tea Producers" issued by the Association of Yokohama Tea Merchants that same year. In the document, the association also traced concerns about adulteration to 1874 and stressed that such practices had hurt the reputation of, and therefore prices for, Japanese green tea sold to export firms; from 1873 to 1874 the average price was $33 for 100 *kin* (approximately 132 pounds) but that had dropped to $20 per 100 kin in the period from 1878 to 1881 (US Department of State 1882, 435–436).

As had been the case with the surge of exports that began in 1874, specific trends within the United States helped to fuel a growing distrust of Japanese tea that grew acute in the 1880s. Lorine Swainston Goodwin asserts that increased industrialization after the Civil War prompted many Americans to move from the countryside to obtain work in burgeoning cities. Instead of growing their own food and purchasing locally produced beverages and health remedies, a rising percentage of Americans now consumed packaged foods, beverages, and drugs, transported over long distances by the growing national rail network. Goodwin concludes that women became particularly alarmed by the declining quality of food, beverages, and drugs and therefore became crusaders for stronger government regulation (1999, 47–48). What is more, health advocates began to make pointed attacks on tea as well as coffee in any form. In 1881, John Harvey Kellogg, one of the more forceful and colorful campaigners for healthy diets and living, cautioned that tea and coffee should be avoided, as they "directly excite the animal passions through their influence upon the nerve centers controlling the sexual organs" (1881, 292).

With these concerns in the background, the US federal government implemented "an act to prevent the importation of adulterated and spurious tea," which took effect in March 1883. The act gave the Department of the Treasury the power to hold imported teas in bonded warehouses until it was determined, by testing samples, that a shipment was free of adulteration (Heyl 1883, 136–137). In response, Japan's tea merchants organized a meeting in late 1883 to develop strategies to assure that better-quality teas would be exported. Over the next five years, the Meiji government imposed regulations and shepherded the establishment of merchant organizations. In 1888, the Japan Central Tea Association was formed. In conjunction with partner prefectural associations, it worked to develop strict, self-enforcement measures that would elevate quality standards overall (Otani 1904, 422; Sugiyama 1988, 157–158). On the US market, firms began to increasingly tout Japanese tea as "unadulterated," "pure," or "uncolored" in an effort to assure consumers of its quality. For example in 1888, Corbin, May, and Company, a Chicago wholesaler, advertised its "Tycoon Brand of Strictly Uncolored Japan Tea" (*Lakeside Annual Directory of the City of Chicago* 1888, 2239).

In the United States, the last decade of the nineteenth century witnessed the merging of continued concerns about food and beverage quality with the growth of advertising. Most notably, C. W. Post successfully played upon health concerns about coffee and pioneered the use of saturated advertising to boost sales of Postum, his "healthy" alternative beverage (Pendergrast 1999, 95–103).[6] Representatives of companies selling India and especially Ceylon teas appropriated Post's tactics, attacking the purity of Japanese and Chinese teas in an effort to boost sales of their product. For example, on January 18, 1895, the *Milwaukee Sentinel* ran an interview with a visiting representative of the island's tea industry who cautioned that Japanese teas were still treated with gypsum or Prussian blue, whereas Ceylon tea was pure, composed only of tender leaves from the first picking of the year (*Milwaukee Sentinel* 1895, 5). Advertisements in other daily newspapers repeated such claims, for example asserting on April 13 that the

Blue Cross brand of Ceylon tea is "free from the injurious coloring matter often found in China and Japan teas" (*Morning Oregonian* 1895, 8, col. G). Others appealed to racial prejudice, such as an April 15 advertisement asserting that the Blue Cross brand of "Ceylon tea is carefully prepared under white supervision—China and Japan teas are not" (*Morning Oregonian* 1895, 3, col. G).

The Ceylon and India tea lobbies employed strategies similar to those used against Chinese green tea in Britain earlier in the century, cultivating a perception of green tea as a dangerous product. Erika Rappaport has illustrated how, from the 1820s until the 1870s, merchants, scientists, journalists, and politicians warned British consumers that Chinese manufacturing techniques were dirty and fraudulent. They leveled particularly harsh attacks against Chinese green tea, which was deemed dangerous because of coloring added to it. Rappaport demonstrates the ways in which these criticisms allowed companies selling India and Ceylon black teas to present their products, produced on plantations under British supervision, as more modern and thus healthier alternatives (2006, 126–46). In her chapter in this volume, Nancy Um also reveals the impact of perception on a commodity market, explaining how, in the eighteenth century, individual merchants in Cairo used to their advantage the European presence in Yemen's coffee market. They adroitly overestimated the amount of European demand for Yemeni coffee while simultaneously underestimating their supplies, thereby allowing them to create a perception that prices for Yemeni coffee on the Egyptian market should rise.

No doubt partly as a result of perceptions created by aggressive marketing techniques, in 1897 imports of India and Ceylon teas into the United States reached a new high of 3,781 tons. Although imports of Japanese teas dwarfed that number at 20,623 tons, competition thereafter remained intense, with India and Ceylon teas steadily gaining market share at the expense of Japanese teas. In 1920, for the first time, the import volume of India and Ceylon teas surpassed that of Japanese teas. Thereafter the volume of India and Ceylon teas entering the United States continued to rise, in contrast to declining import volumes for Japanese teas (Teramoto 1999, 150–151).

Conclusion

In 1900 a prominent statesman, Ōkuma Shigenobu, outlined Japan's economic progress since the Meiji Restoration. Not surprising for a former prime minister, he highlighted the central government's role, arguing that in the decade after 1868 Meiji leaders had sagely promoted the export of "natural products and raw materials" to balance often disproportionate imports of Western manufactured goods (Ōkuma 1900, 682).[7] Ōkuma stressed that the government had thereby lain "the foundation for the development of the national resources and industry, the effect of which became gradually apparent in the subsequent ten years [1878–1888]" (Ōkuma 1900, 682–683). Citing as his chief example the match industry now exporting to other parts of East Asia, he opined that Japan was on the cusp of following a path blazed by the United States: moving away from an export trade heavy in agricultural commodities to one based upon manufactured goods (Ōkuma 1900, 683–684). In other words, Japan's agricultural exports like tea had served as a key building block in Japan's quest to "catch-up" with the United States and other prominent Western nations.

By focusing on 1874 we see alternative and distinctly transnational processes in the development of Japan's new trading regime. The Meiji leaders, although key players, were only partially responsible for the growth of the trade. Rather, in cooperation with Japanese tea merchants, they built upon the initiative of British traders and later, by necessity, worked with Western export firms that controlled the flow of Japanese tea on the all-important US market. The transnational nature of the tea export trade is further illustrated by the vital role of Chinese knowledge and expertise before and after the Meiji Restoration. The story of tea trade thus echoes Hamashita Takeshi's conclusions concerning Japan's cotton cloth trade in the 1880s. Hamashita stresses that in order to develop a viable export trade, Japanese merchants imitated their more skilled and market-savvy Chinese competitors. Only with Chinese know-how could Japan begin to compete with China and India in the global market of cotton textiles (Hamashita 1997, 130).

Moreover, by using the lens of 1874 we see that political agendas, combined with socio-economic goals in both Japan and the United States, were pivotal in the trade's development. The 1874 surge was largely contingent upon the decision of US leaders to eliminate tariffs on tea and coffee to help US maritime trade and to display concern for the pocketbooks of working-class Americans. For their part, Japanese leaders sought to create opportunities to help assuage the dissatisfaction that many displaced groups felt with recent reforms and simultaneously push those groups to become invested as citizens in the emerging nation-state. The tea trade presented a means to fulfill both agendas, providing employment for a cross-section of society—ex-samurai, displaced transport workers, and even artists—in what was consistently touted as a cooperative, national enterprise. Finally, the primary challenge to Japan's market share beginning in the 1890s emerged not from US firms marketing other nonalcoholic beverages like Postum, but from those selling British India and especially Ceylon teas, another "inside-out" dynamic that would define Japan's tea export trade in subsequent decades.

Notes

1. Jardine, Matheson, and Company Archives, Cambridge University. I thank Matheson & Company for permission to research the archive and to cite this and other documents from it.

2. Detailed in "Tokyo-fū reisho" [Edicts of the Tokyo Municipality] 8/1869, ME 164–0702 (reel number).

3. Detailed in "Chashōsha kisoku mikomi-sho" [Prospective Guidelines for Tea Trading Companies] 1869/11/9, ME 174–0569 (reel number).

4. Peter Davies includes transcribed copies of Cornes's business letters and records in a CD-ROM companion to his volume.

5. In this text, Ōtani's given name is spelled Kabi but I use the more standard romanization, Kahei.

6. While seeing all stimulants as unhealthy, in the realm of non-alcoholic beverages, Post reserved most of his attacks for coffee. For example he often criticizes the consumption of coffee but does not mention tea in his treatise, *The Modern Practice of Natural Suggestion* (1895).

7. Ōkuma served as prime minister from June to November 1898 and again from April 1914 to October 1916. In the article, he is referred to as Count Okuma.

References

Beman, David. 1825. *The Mysteries of Trade, or the Great Source of Wealth: Containing Receipts and Patents in Chemistry and Manufacturing; with Practical Observations on the Useful Arts, Original and Compiled. Boston: Printed for the Author, by Wm. Bellamy.* Boston: Author.

Cornes, Frederick, and Peter Davies. 2008. *The Business, Life and Letters of Frederick Cornes: Aspects of the Evolution of Commerce in Modern Japan, 1861–1910.* Folkestone: Global Oriental (includes CD-ROM).

"Description of the Tea Plant; Its Name; Cultivation; Mode of Curing the Leaves; Transportation to Canton; Sale and Foreign Consumption; Endeavors to Raise the Shrub in Other Countries." 1839–1840. *Chinese Repository* 8: 132–164.

DNISK (Dai Nihon ishin shiryō kōhon) [Manuscript of Historical Records Related to the Meiji Restoration of Japan]. 1846–1873. Unpublished manuscript collection, Historigraphical Institute, University of Tokyo.

Gardella, Robert. 1994. *Harvesting Mountains: Fujian and the China Tea Trade, 1757–1937.* Berkeley: University of California Press.

Goodwin, Lorine Swainston. 1999. *The Pure Food, Drink, and Drug Crusaders, 1879–1914.* Jefferson, NC: McFarland.

Gribble, Henry. 1885. "The Preparation of Tea (Illustrated)." *Transactions of the Asiatic Society of Japan* 12 (1): 12–13.

Hamashita Takeshi. 1997. "The Intra-Regional System in East Asia in Modern Times." In *Network Power: Japan and Asia,* ed. Peter J. Katzenstein and Takashi Shiraishi, 113–135. Ithaca, NY: Cornell University Press.

Heyl, Lewis. 1883. *United States Duties on Imports, 1883: Revised, Corrected and Supplemented.* Vol. 2. Washington, D.: W. H. Morrison.

Hikone-han. [1871] 1971. *Seicha zukai* [A Guide to Tea Manufacturing]. In *Meiji zenki sangyō hattatsushi shiryō bessatsu* [Documents Related to the Development of Industry in the Early Meiji Period, Supplemental Volumes] 107 (2), ed. Meiji Bunken Shiryō Kankōkai. Tokyo: Meiji Bunken Shiryō Kankōkai.

Homans, Issac Smith, and Issac Smith Homans, Jr. 1858. *A Cyclopedia of Commerce and Commercial Navigation.* New York: Harper.

Hoshida Shigemoto. [1888] 1971. *Chagyō zensho* [The Complete Books of the Tea Industry]. In *Meiji zenki sangyō hattatsushi shiryō bessatsu* [Documents Related to the Development of Industry in the Early Meiji Period, Supplemental Volumes] 107 (2), ed. Meiji Bunken Shiryō Kankōkai. Tokyo: Meiji Bunken Shiryō Kankōkai.

Hunt, Freeman. 1857. *Hunt's Merchants' Magazine.* New York: Freeman Hunt.

Ide, Nobuko. 1993. *Ranji: The Roots of Modern Japanese Commercial Graphic Design.* Tokyo: Dentsū.

Japan Department of Finance. 1901. *Returns of the Foreign Trade of the Empire of Japan for the Thirty-two Years from 1868 to 1899 Inclusive.* Tokyo: Hōyōdō.

Japan Gazette. 1874. *"Japan Gazette:" Hong List and Directory for 1874.* Yokohama: Office of the Japan Gazette.

Jardine Matheson In-correspondence. "Business Letters: Nagasaki, 1859–1886," B10–4. Jardine, Matheson & Company Archives, University Library, Cambridge University.

Kangyōryō [Industrial Promotion Bureau]. 1874. *Kangyō hōkoku* [Report on Industrial Promotion], December 1.

Kawaguchi Kuniaki. 1989. *Chagyō kaika: Meiji hattenshi to Tada Motokichi* [The Creation of the Tea Industry: Tada Motokichi and The History of Meiji Era Expansion] Tokyo: Zenbō-sha.

Kellogg, J. H. 1881. *Plain Facts for Old and Young.* Burlington, IA: Segner and Condit.

Ko Heisū [Hu Bingshu] and Shinichirō Takezoe. 1877. *Chamu sensai* [A Comprehensive Guide to Tea Production]. Tokyo: Naimushō Kannōkyoku.

Kume Kunitake. 2002. *The Iwakura Embassy, 1871–1873: A True Account of the Ambassador Extraordinary & Plenipotentiary's Journey of Observation through the United States of American and Europe.* Vol. 1, *The United States of America.* Trans. Martin Collcutt. Matsudo: The Japan Documents.

Lakeside Annual Directory of the City of Chicago. 1888. Chicago: Chicago Directory Company.

Macgregor, John. 1840. *Commercial Statistics of America: a Digest of Her Productive Resources, Commercial Legislation, Customs, Tariffs, Shipping, Imports and Exports, Monies, Weights and Measures.* London: Whittaker and Co.

Masuda Mitsunari, ed. [1873] 1971. *Seicha shinsetsu* [New Methods of Tea Production]. In *Meiji zenki sangyō hattatsushi shiryō bessatsu* [Documents Related to the Development of Industry in the Early Meiji Period, Supplemental Volumes] 107 (2), ed. Meiji Bunken Shiryō Kankōkai. Tokyo: Meiji Bunken Shiryō Kankōkai.

McDonald, Michelle Craig, and Steven Topik. 2008. "Americanizing Coffee: The Refashioning of a Consumer Culture." In *Food and Globalization: Consumption, Markets and Politics in the Modern World,* ed. Alexander Nuetzenadel and Frank Trentmann, 109–128. New York: Berg.

Milwaukee Sentinel. 1895. Milwaukee, WI. January 18.

Morning Oregonian. 1895. Portland, OR. April 13, 15.

New York Times. 1880. "Free Tea and Coffee." June 5.

———. 1881. "The Cost and Price of Teas, From the *Providence Journal,* March 1." March 2.

Ohara Keiji. 1957. *Japanese Trade and Industry in the Meiji-Taisho Era.* Tokyo: Ōbunsha.

Ōishi Sadao. 1974. *Meiji ishin to chagyō: Makinohara kaitaku shi kō* [The Tea Industry and the Meiji Restoration: A History of the Development of Makinohara]. Shizuoka: Shizuoka-ken Chagyō Kaigi-sho.

Ōkuma Shigenobu (Count Okuma). 1900. "The Industrial Revolution in Japan." *North American Review* 171 (528): 677–691.

Otani, Kabi [Kahei] 1904. "Tea." In *Japan by the Japanese: A Survey by Its Highest Authorities,* ed. Alfred Stead, 421–425. London: William Heinemann.

Pendergrast, Mark. 1999. *Uncommon Grounds: The History of Coffee and How It Transformed Our World.* New York: Basic Books.

Post, C. W. 1895. *The Modern Practice of Natural Suggestion: Or [Scientia vitae].* Battle Creek, MI: La Vita Inn Co.

Rappaport, Erika. 2006. "Packaging China: Foreign Articles and Dangerous Tastes in the Mid-Victorian Tea Party." In *The Making of the Consumer: Knowledge, Power and Identity in the Modern World,* ed. Frank Trentmann, 125–146. New York: Berg.

Riggs, Oscar W. 1883. "The Tea Commerce of New York." *Frank Leslie's Popular Monthly* 16 (3): 295.

Sakeda Masatoshi and George Akita. 1986. "The Samurai Disestablished: Abei Iwane and His Stipend." *Monumenta Nipponica* 41 (3): 299–330.

Sugiyama, Shinya. 1988. *Japan's Industrialization in the World Economy, 1859–1899: Export Trade and Overseas Competition.* London: Athlone Press.

Sunaga Noritake. 1995. "Meiji zenki no seicha yushutsu to Sayama kaisha no katsudō" [The Efforts of the Sayama Company to Export Tea during the Early Meiji Period]. *Saitama-ken shi kenkyū* 30: 2–34.

Swale, Alastair. 1998. "America: 15 January-6 August 1872." In *The Iwakura Mission in America and Europe: A New Assessment,* ed. Ian Nish, 7–23. Surrey, UK: Japan Library.

Tea, ca. 1816–1963. Warshaw Collection of Business Americana, Archives Center, National Museum of American History, Smithsonian Institution, Washington, DC.

Teramoto Yasuhide. 1999. *Senzenki Nihon chagyō-shi kenkyū* [A Study of Japan's Tea Industry in the Prewar Period]. Tokyo: Yūhikaku.

Ukers, William H. 1935. *All about Tea.* Vol. 1. New York: The Tea and Coffee Trade Journal Company.

United States and Francis Preston Blair, John C. Rives, Franklin Rives, and George A. Bailey. 1872. *The Congressional Globe, Senate, 42nd Congress,* March–April. Washington: Blair & Rives.

United States Department of State. 1882. *Commercial Relations of the United States: Cotton and Woolen Mills of Europe, Reports from the Consuls of the United States on the Cotton and Woolen Industries of Europe, In Answer to a Circular from the Department of State.* September 23. Washington: Government Printing Office.

Wisconsin State Register. 1872. Portage, WI. March 30.

8

China and India Are One

A Subaltern's Vision of "Hindu China" during the Boxer Expedition of 1900–1901

ANAND A. YANG

In 1900, an Indian man traveled to China, to Beijing specifically, accompanied by a large contingent of his fellow countrymen. His journey there was unusual, in part because few Indians went to or resided in China at the turn of the twentieth century[1] and in part because virtually no one from India or anywhere else abroad sought out Beijing as a destination, as he and his fellow travelers did that summer, at a time when its foreign residents were under the siege of an insurgent group known as the Boxers. They were moving against the tide because they were members of a large military contingent of almost 20,000 foreigners representing eight nations whose "relief force" was organized into an International Expedition and charged with lifting the siege of the foreign legations and defeating the ruling Qing dynasty, which, by then, openly sided with the Boxer Uprising and its antiforeign and anti-Christian movement.[2]

This chapter tells the story of Thakur Gadadhar Singh, one of the Indian soldiers who constituted the bulk of the British force of 3,000 men (Vaughan [1902] 2000, 47), and the vision of "Chin aur Hind" or China and India, and the rest of Asia that he forged from his experiences in and around Beijing. As a member of the 7th Rajputs, a regiment also known as the 7th Duke of Connaught's Own Bengal Infantry,[3] which had been mobilized in India to

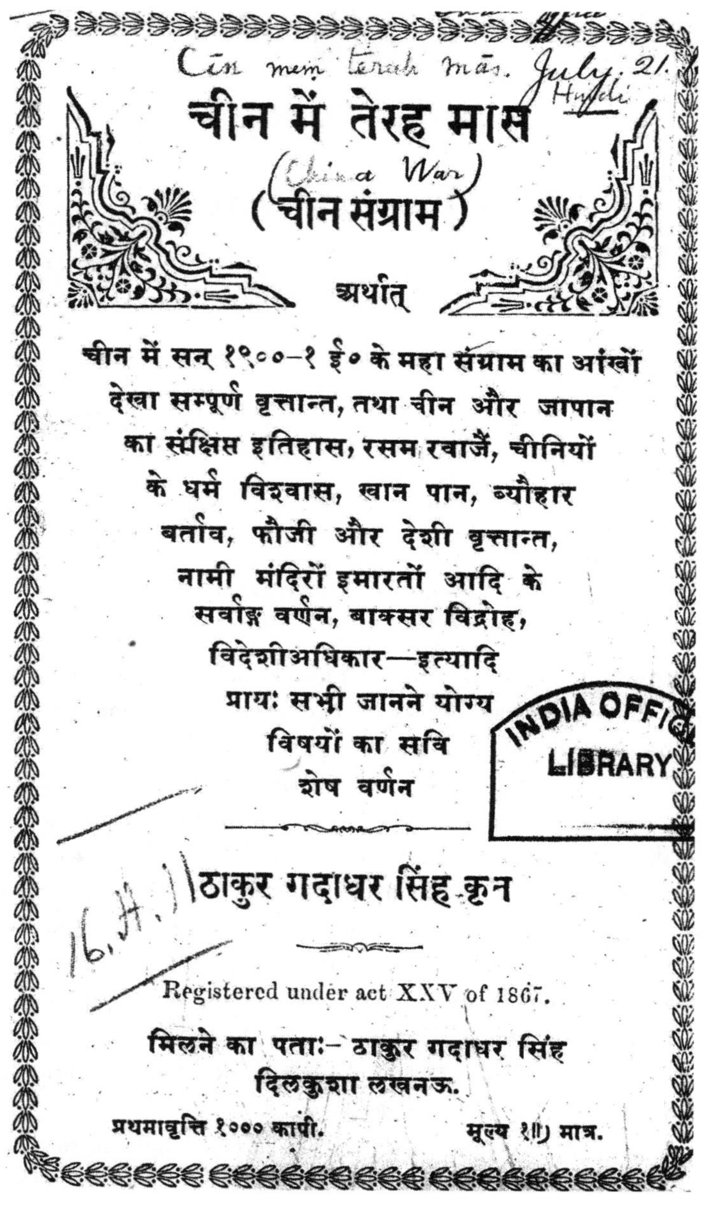

चीन में तेरह मास

(चीन संग्राम)

अर्थात्

चीन में सन् १९००–१ ई० के महा संग्राम का आंखों
देखा सम्पूर्ण वृत्तान्त, तथा चीन और जापान
का संक्षिप्त इतिहास, रसम रवाजें, चीनियों
के धर्म विश्वास, खान पान, ब्यौहार
बर्ताव, फौजी और देशी वृत्तान्त,
नामी मंदिरों इमारतों आदि के
सर्वाङ्ग वर्णन, बाक्सर विद्रोह,
विदेशीअधिकार—इत्यादि
प्रायः सभी जानने योग्य
विषयों का सवि
शेष वर्णन

ठाकुर गदाधर सिंह कृत

Registered under act XXV of 1867.

मिलने का पताः– ठाकुर गदाधर सिंह
दिलकुशा लखनऊ.

प्रथमावृत्ति १००० कापी. मूल्य १।) मात्र.

Cover page of *Thirteen Months in China: (The China) War* by Thakur Gadadhar Singh. (British Library) fight on behalf of the British, he developed a remarkable perspective on the tumultuous events of the Boxer Uprising of 1900–1901. And he lived to tell the tale of this International Expedition in a Hindi text of 319 pages entitled *Chin meh Terah Mas* (Thirteen Months in China) that he self-published (Singh 1902).

Parenthetically subtitled *Chin Sangram* (The China War), this book, as its cover page (see figure on facing page) announces, offers readers "a full eyewitness account of the great war in China in 1900–1901 A.D., and a brief history of China and Japan, customs and practices, Chinese religious beliefs, cuisine, professional conduct, information regarding military and state, and a complete description of famous temples, buildings etc., Boxer uprising, foreign occupation—so on and so forth, generally characteristic descriptions of all knowable and suitable subjects" (Singh 1902).

I will delve into this "eyewitness account" and "brief history" to take a measure of the extraordinary subaltern view of China and the rest of the world that Gadadhar Singh formulated from his thirteenth months campaigning against the Boxers. The sympathetic portrait of the country he had been dispatched to wage war on and in is all the more startling given the prevailing negative attitudes about China and the Boxers across the Allied countries, especially Britain. Contrast, for instance, the narrative he composed with the one compiled by his superior officer, Lieutenant Colonel H. B. Vaughan, who signals his stance on the conflict by designating his account *St. George and the Chinese Dragon*—in short, as a struggle between Christian good and pagan Chinese evil (Vaughan [1902] 2000). Based on his diary and published in 1902, as was Singh's book, the two works could not be more dissimilar, even though they focused on the same sequence of events.

Singh's work is also unusual because the author consulted some of the well-known English language writings on Asia of his day to dilate on "knowable and suitable subjects" without absorbing their Eurocentric biases. Instructive in this regard—although not developed here—is his selective use of these texts, particularly in describing those aspects of the history of China, Japan, and the Boxer Uprising that he did not himself witness personally or experience firsthand.

Singh's reflections on the world he encountered in China also deserve attention because they verge on pan-Asian notions that have generally been associated with elites in China, India, and especially Japan but never with the rank and file. No less striking is the fact that he imagined these ideas at about the same time as the first generation of intellectuals in Asia began to envision their lives and countries in transnational terms.[4] Indeed, his account of China and the Boxers is more in accord with some of the sentiments expressed by the Indian intelligentsia in English and vernacular newspapers of the day who blamed aggressive Western missionaries for the "patriotic" actions of the Boxers (Bayly 2007, 149–150).

Singh's text also stands out because he approaches China through India, specifically from the perspective of an Indian subaltern keenly interested in religion whose tour of duty brought him into direct contact with another part of Asia. His East-East reflections stand in sharp contrast with much of contemporary writings about Asia that were largely inflected by the dominant Western discourse of Orientalism (Said 1978). There were, as yet, few public voices—the Bengali poet Rabindranath Tagore (1861–1941) and the Japanese art critic Okakura Tenshin (1862–1913) were among them—who distinctly broached the possibility of approaching Asia via an "inter-Asian" trajectory.[5] Although the pronouncements of these two men in the early years of the twentieth century, mostly in the form of meditations and exchanges with one another on their own countries and the rest of Asia, principally China, frequently employed the familiar binaries of Eastern and Western civilization and East and West, they also envisioned a cultural and religious unity across Asia that represented a radical departure from earlier modes of thinking. Okakura famously summed up this new construct by opening his 1903 book on *The Ideals of the East* with a dramatic declaration: "Asia is one" (Bharucha 2006, 10–50; Hay 1970, 37–51). Premised on a notion of a shared geography and history within Asia, and also increasingly a unified opposition to the growing power and threat of Western imperialism, such sentiments would give rise to Pan-Asianism as an ideology and movement (Saaler and Szpilman 2011, 1–38).

Singh's consciousness, intensely nationalistic but at times also transnational, as his text reveals, was shaped by his experiences as a member of the Allied forces that fought its way into Beijing and subsequently occupied it. Elsewhere, I have characterized his experiences in China and the many different peoples and situations encountered there as occurring in a "contact zone," to use Mary Louise Pratt's term for "a space in which peoples geographically and historically separated come into contact with each other and establish ongoing relations, usually involving conditions of coercion, radical inequality, and intractable conflict"; in short, a social space "where disparate cultures meet, clash, and grapple with each other, often in highly asymmetrical relations of domination and subordination" (Pratt 1992, 4, 6; see Yang 2007).

In an earlier study, I drew on Singh's rich personal narrative to discuss what he, as a colonized subject fighting in the name of his colonizers, had to say about the Boxer Uprising and the looting of China, and the sense of self-identity and comparisons between China and India, and both of them in relation to Japan and Europe,[6] that he developed as a result of his thirteen months in the country. The rest of this chapter will elaborate on the last of these points to highlight the connections he made between China and India through his newly acquired understanding of the similarities and differences between them and the possibilities he envisioned for a new era in Asia emerging out of the changing situation in China and the rest of the world.

First, a few words about Gadadhar Singh and the China he encountered in 1900 when it was a "semicolony"—and he seemingly construed it as such—a country under "multiple colonialism," to use Paul Cohen's term, in which the multiple colonial effect stemmed from its "partial domination not by one but by a plurality of foreign nations" and thus had a "'layered' or 'spliced' character" to it (1983, 144). The formidable presence of this "plurality" was embodied in the multinational character of the so-called Beijing relief force of eight nations. As a member of this force, Singh recounts many occasions when he fought or participated in activities alongside men of other nations. At times, he came into direct contact with Americans, Japanese, and Russians, as well as the local Chinese populace, and he has observations to make about all of them. In some cases, he recalls conversations with specific individuals, whom he generally identifies by nationality and occupation but not by name. Often, he casts these interlocutors in roles that involve them in making telling statements about China and India, pronouncements that he seemingly could not utter as a loyal soldier of the *Angrezi sarkar,* to use his designation for the British government in India. These others surface periodically in his text, often as his mouthpiece, playing parts whose function was to render judgments that he himself seemingly could not advocate or embrace publically. Not that there are not occasions in the text when he steps up to fire critical salvos at his British masters.

As a native of colonial India recruited to fight on behalf of his British masters, Singh had firsthand experience of the workings of colonialism—at home and abroad. Unusual, too, was his involvement in the International Expedition, because it thrust him, a colonial subject, in the role of advancing the semicolonial project of the foreign powers in China. The Expedition, moreover, represented a new stage in cooperation among the imperial powers—and, increasingly Japan—at the dawn of a new century that brought to a close two decades of intense competition among them for Africa, Southeast Asia, and the Pacific islands. It followed on the heels of the Spanish-American War and occurred even as the British were in the throes of Second Boer War, the latter of which he alludes to by invoking the Battle of Ladysmith of October 1899.

Throughout his text, Singh shows himself to be keenly aware of defining himself in relation to the coalition that had assembled in China to confront the Boxers and the Qing state and ever-conscious of his multiple notions of self and others—really an ensemble of others, because he differentiates among the different Europeans yet lumps them together in relation to the Japanese, notwithstanding the Euro-American-Japanese collective role in the International Expedition. (Americans are also featured in a number of different sections.) About Japan and the Japanese he has much to say: the country and its people for all they had achieved in the face of Western threats and its military for its courage under fire during the Boxer Expedition. Conspicuously absent is any mention of the French troops whose contingent was small (500 in all) but whose numbers included many from Indochina, namely, Vietnam.

Singh's subaltern outlook was undoubtedly also colored by his Hindu reformist beliefs. Although he does not spell out in his 1902 text whether he was formally affiliated with the Arya Samaj, the Hindu reform organization that sought a return to a "purified" Hinduism, he employs language and concerns in portraying China—and in comparing China to India—that suggest an Arya Samaj orientation. He consistently harks back to the Vedas as the sole repository of knowledge and he often identifies his country as "Aryavarta" and his countrymen as "Aryas" (and not Hindus), appellations that Swami Dayananda Saraswati (1824–1883), the founder of that movement, and his successors favored, in order to claim it as the land that Aryas had inhabited from the very beginning of time. Singh also pays considerable attention to such prominent Arya Samaj issues as idolatry, child marriage, and the status of women. Nor would it have been unusual for a sepoy to be an Arya Samajist. Although some elements of this social reform movement opposed Indian involvement in the colonial military, others were known to proselytize sepoys. A decade later, Singh was openly identified as the author of several religious tracts, including *Karuna Kahani,* translated in English as "The Tale of Compassion: An Arya Samajist Narrative" (Singh 1916).

Singh's subaltern account is also striking because it manifests familiarity with contemporary publications on China and Asia in English, including some issued in the aftermath of the Boxer Uprising, and the sensation that had been created around the world by the siege of the foreign legations in Beijing in the summer of 1900. One set of writings that he specifically references is the work of—to use his words—a "respected Englishman," Robert Hart, the former British consular official who had a long and distinguished career as the Inspector General of the Chinese Imperial Maritime Customs Service. Hart's slim volume on *The Peking Legations: A National Uprising and International Episode,* which first appeared in the *Fortnightly Review* in November 1900, was reprinted as a book published in Shanghai that same year and later included in a book of essays compiled as *"These from the Land of Sinim": Essays on the Chinese Question* (Hart 1901). Critics took issue with Hart's analysis for its seemingly sympathetic portrait of the Boxers and its apparent attempt to convey "a Chinese point of view."[7] In Singh's estimation, as he noted in citing Hart's stance on intrigues in the Imperial Court, the Englishman was an "unbiased person" (Singh 1902, 109).

Singh also consulted at least two other sources, both popular books: Neville P. Edwards's illustrated *The Story of China with a Description of the Events Relating to the Present Struggle* (1900), which was rushed into print to explain why "the sick man of Asia" was suddenly challenging the "white nations" or the "world," as its author put it; and journalist Henry Norman's *The People and Politics of the Far East. Travels and Studies in the British, French, Spanish and Portuguese Colonies, Siberia, China, Japan, Korea, Siam and Malaya,* first published in 1895 and reissued several times, which was based on four years of first-hand experiences of an "attentive traveler."

Almost from the opening lines of his book, Singh expresses an affinity for China. The first time it surfaces in the text—by design, I believe—is when he describes the initial approach of his ship to Chinese soil, at Dagu (Tanggu district), the entry point into Tianjin and Beijing. He remembers this moment as an occasion when he surveyed the nearby landscape and detected many deserted and destroyed villages. On some broken buildings he saw French, Russian, and Japanese flags aflutter, and in some villages he espied a few people alive, skeleton-like old people standing upright with the help of their walking sticks (Singh 1902, 17). The foreign powers stood tall, in other words, while China and its people were battered and broken.

Singh wears his sympathy for China on his sleeve. "Even hearts of stone," the author remarks as his ship approached Dagu, "would have melted and felt compassion." "[I]t was not necessary for my heart to be moved by pity," he adds, "because I had come to fight against the Chinese. But . . . I felt an emotion that was born not out of duty but in the mind." In attempting to fathom why he felt that way, he mentions that he realized that the "Chinese are Buddhists. (At that time I did not know about Confucianism.) They share this religion with the people of Hindustan. As neighbors and fellow residents of Asia, they are also of the same 'country.' There are not many differences in [presumably he means skin] color and customs. Why did God inflict times of trouble on them! Did God not want to help them?" (Singh 1902, 17). Thus, he makes a case for a special relationship based on religion and geographical contiguity—China and India were neighbors and shared Buddhism in common.[8]

This compassionate outlook frames his "eyewitness" account. In fact, much of the first third of the book, which consists largely of the author's recollection of his regiment's march into Beijing and the subsequent takeover of the capital by the International Expedition, depicts the Chinese sympathetically, as victims of foreign aggression and brutality. The Allied forces in China, to cite his evocative metaphor, were engaged in *shikar,* in "hunting," a word that also means "prey" or "victim." In graphic detail, he recalls occasions when Allied troops treated Chinese bodies and possessions as game to be hunted down—killed, raped, or plundered, depending on what their prey was. He documents many instances of the Allied soldiers indulging in *shikar,* in brutalizing the local population. He also reports that everyone, even his fellow Indians, participated in the looting of Beijing (Yang 2007, 52–57).

Perhaps because the author envisions himself as giving voice to China and the Chinese people throughout his account, there are few vignettes involving him in conversation with local inhabitants. One notable exception to this rule is his account of a lively discussion he had with a Chinese physician, a *hakim* or native doctor as he terms this person. In this instance, he portrays himself as defending the British in the face of the latter's insistence that none of the foreign forces could be exculpated for the excesses they had committed on Chinese soil. No doubt, his verbal exchanges with Chinese people were few and far between because language divided them (Yang 2007, 56).

Again and again, Singh's text reveals how differently different his views of China were. One incident that dramatically sums up this difference occurred when he and his men were landing in Dagu. He follows up his first impressions of China with an account of a conversation he had with a "Bluejacket," that is, with a member of the naval force who greeted him in a tugboat that came to unload the troops from the ship in order to transport them to the shore. That he alludes to this encounter right after he articulates sympathy for the Chinese is no coincidence. On the contrary, this passage, which closes out his account of the ocean voyage, appears intended to remind himself—and his reading public—that he harbored no seditious sentiments, even as he manifested strongly positive feelings towards those he had come to fight against. Striking as well is the fact that the "ship soldier" with whom he had the verbal exchange was an Irish soldier whose interest in him stemmed from his ability to speak English. But he then quickly adds that there were other Indian soldiers who spoke English and there were other Bluejackets present who did not seek him out.

The Irishman, according to the Indian subaltern, informed him about the battles that had taken place earlier in Dagu and Tianjin—presumably involving the failed June attempt of some 2,000 troops to break the siege of the Beijing Legation quarter—and dispensed helpful advice based on the former's war experiences. Their discussion then veered off in a different direction. Singh remembers the Irish soldier telling him that he, too, was not English—he was Irish—that he also had come to wage war on behalf of the British government, and that he considered his actions appropriate because of the "mutual sympathy" he felt, by which he obviously meant his support for the British. Furthermore, in his estimation, the Chinese were "*jangli*"—to use Singh's term for what the Irishman told him, that is, the Chinese were not civilized, they were of the jungle or wild (Singh 1902, 17–18).

That the European featured in Singh's account of extending a hand of friendship is an Irishman is fitting. Ireland's dual and contradictory role as a colony and as a colonial power—its people served on behalf of the British Empire—was well known in India. Indeed, nationalist leaders and the press in India were familiar with Ireland's struggles for Home Rule in the late nineteenth century and often debated the value of their lessons for India (Silvestri 2000).

Appreciative though Singh was of the Irishman's efforts to befriend him, as he candidly states in his account, he took issue with the latter's portrayal of China as uncivilized. For unlike his new "friend," Singh's "mutual sympathy" extended to China and its people. In fact, for him, China and India were comparable and compatible because they were the two most ancient civilizations of the world; the latter, moreover, he credits (erroneously) with having produced the oldest book in the world, the Vedas. However, in modern times these longstanding civilizations had declined considerably; both countries in his day, as he acknowledged, were mired in poverty and lagged far behind Europe economically (Singh 1902, 17–18).

Singh evidently did not agree with the widely held view among the conquering forces in China that they were there on a civilizing mission. This had been the message drilled into the Indian troops from the moment they set out from India. Singh recalls his commanding officer sending off his regiment at Fort William in Calcutta on June 29, 1900, on the eve of their departure, with a speech informing the men that they were being entrusted with a special mission "because the *Hind sarkar* [Indian government] has faith in you . . . In China the representatives of 'world powers' [Singh's term is *sansar shaktiyon*] are suffering because of the actions of the followers of a new order or community *(sampradaya)* called Boxers. You should carry out the orders of the government, and quickly. Your force has previously gone on an expedition to China in 1858–59. So this is not a new trip *(yatra)* for you. We hope that you will be successful" (Singh 1902, 1). The 7th Rajputs, in other words, were charged with representing the world or civilized powers against the Boxers, a movement widely perceived as dabbling in magic and superstition and fiercely opposed to Christianity and Western technology. As Singh repeatedly heard from the men of the Allied force, they were fighting against China and its wild *(jangli)* and barbarous society and culture. He did not accept this characterization, nor did he approve of the *shikar* that many of his comrades were embarked on, a victimization that he was not willing to justify in the name of civilization and the civilized powers of the world.

In Singh's eyes, civilization did not hang in the balance in China at the turn of the twentieth century. In this respect, he countered many of the accounts of China in his day, including some of the texts he relied on, such as Edwards's *Story of China,* which portrayed the country as "hampered and cramped to an extraordinary degree by their rock-fixed customs, superstitions, and prejudices" (Edwards 1900, 8). Moreover, as Singh's remarks on foreign looting and other incidents of maltreatment of the Chinese suggest, he questioned whether the world powers had any claim to the mantle of civilization because they were the hunters and aggressors, indiscriminate and savage in their *shikar* of innocent Chinese men, women and children (Yang 2007, 56–57).

For Singh, China was indubitably civilized, as was India, an equation that he insistently makes in his text, at times by recounting conversations with foreigners. His recollection of a chance meeting with an American postal officer is especially revealing in this regard, as it divulges some of the provocative thoughts he entertained that were not befitting a soldier of the Raj.

In an episode that he characterizes as "An American's Criticism *(Ek Amerikan ki Alochna),*" Singh (1902, 297–301) recounts an incident that occurred on March 6, 1901, when he and his fellow Rajputs were raucously celebrating the spring festival of Holi. An American, dressed in civilian garb, who was touring Beijing, chanced upon their revelry and was initially taken back by their racket. Concerned that their visitor might consider them *jangli*—that word again—because they were drumming, singing, and jumping up and down, Singh says, he decided to draw him into a conversation.

What is fascinating about this encounter, as remembered by the author, is how their conversation, initially about singing and playing music, segues into a discussion of independence and, ultimately, a critique of Singh and his fellow Hindustanis; in short, of India. Apparently what led to this turn in their conversation were the correlations and conclusions that the American made about music and caste.

As in other encounters with foreigners presented in the text, the meeting with an American seems purposeful—even deliberate—for it is left to the latter to make an interjection about independence and to recount how the United States had broken away and gained independence from England. That Singh chooses not to repeat the particulars of this part of their dialogue is intriguing as well, as is his unlikely explanation that he decided not to do so because his readers did not need to hear an American history lesson that they already knew.

The "mutual sympathy" with the American is evident from their frank and friendly conversation. So is the use to which Singh puts this encounter, and all the others that *Thirteen Months* features. They are staging grounds for declarations better left unsaid by a soldier of the Raj: they represent moments when the author can step outside his prescribed and safe role as a colonized mimic man to assume the garb of a subaltern, albeit through ventriloquism, and at less risk than he would incur had he "outed" himself completely. Here and elsewhere, his interlocutors do the talking—they say outright what he dares to think but cannot speak.

As Singh tells it, the American wondered whether the tradition of excellence in singing and playing musical instruments in Hindustan had been kept up and developed in their time, as new forms of music and musical instruments were emerging. And if that were the case, he wanted to know why the soldiers did not sing and play proficiently. In response, Singh told him that his men were not musically accomplished but were capable of singing and performing well in their own way, and that singing and music were still performed beautifully in his country. His interlocutor cut him off at that point and said that he was aware that there were some people whose profession by caste was to sing, play music, and dance. What the American was apparently suggesting was that music was not widely known and developed in India, which is why the troops and many others in Indian society did not have much musical ability.

Thereafter, their conversation veered off in a completely different direction. "Then he said why is that you people think of your subjugation positively? Do you like your dependence on others for your entertainment?" This statement is less of a non sequitur than it appears to be because Singh's book makes clear that the American is implying that the people of Hindustan tend to depend on others, whether it is a social and cultural dependency shaped by caste or political subordination because of foreign rule. This last point, however, is not broached until several lines later. And, in case there is any confusion here for the reader, Singh follows up this exchange with an interjection about why their discussion had shifted course so abruptly. These questions arose, he writes, because they were discussing music being the professional occupation of a particular caste whose participation was essential to the celebration of festivals such as Holi. Apparently the point of this conversation was that the American was advocating self-reliance and independence for the people of India to make them better off, as they would be if they attended to their musical needs themselves, as did their counterparts in Europe, rather than depend on others, as per the caste system. Everybody in Europe, soldiers and civilians alike, he claimed, were familiar with theater, opera, dance, and singing. As Singh tells it, he fell silent upon hearing this comment because he knew that his new friend had spoken the truth.

Next they talked about the military. According to Singh, the American told him that the Indian troops in China had distinguished themselves by their bravery and had demonstrated that they were on par with and, in some respects, even superior to their European counterparts. They had shown their mettle by their hard work and willingness to carry out orders effectively. He then followed up these observations by bringing up the subject of caste. He apparently did so because he had heard that people in Hindustan maintained strict rules about not sharing cooked food with one another, a practice he had not seen Indian soldiers uphold in China where they were living and eating communally. Singh obviously approved of this situation because he remarks that people need to interact with one another if they wish to see their religion fulfilled. He adds that he became reflective then and heard an inner voice say: "Liberation comes from breaking free of one's bonds."

His "visitor friend," the author tells us, had other criticisms—but also praise. The American noted that if India continued to make the kind of progress it had to date in breaking free of caste restrictions, acquiring Western knowledge, and learning about new civilizations from its people going abroad, then it was just a matter of time before it became an independent power. His choice of words, as reported by Singh, seems carefully calibrated: he utilizes power or *shakti* (or force), a locution that he makes sure his readers—and presumably the censors—notice by adding the English word power in parenthesis next to the Hindi word *shakti*. Conspicuously absent in this context is the term *desh* or country, which would have been the more logical term to use, especially because the author employs it extensively throughout his text. Presumably, he avoids that word because it would have underlined the idea of India as an independent state more overtly than he was willing to do, even though he was evidently repeating what the American had said. Furthermore, as if to allay any concerns, he follows up with a statement clearly intended to exonerate him of having any incendiary designs: "I said that noble or liberal Hindustanis do not even dream of such a possibility. Hindustan today is very happy and considers its continuing contentment to be of paramount importance. It wants British rule to remain stable in Hindustan forever" (Singh 1902, 300).

The American was not done yet. Once again, as Singh's account details, he interrupted, this time by stating that however true the latter's declaration may have been about his own country, it did not accord well with the natural tendency in people everywhere to seek self-rule. People accepted foreign rule only if they did not know how to take care of themselves. But if they had the knowledge and ability to do so, it was not appropriate to give somebody else authority over them. (Note also that the American has just praised the military ability of the Indian troops.) Thus, as Singh's new friend put it—and this was the bombshell he dropped that Singh presumably wanted his readers to hear—when Hindustan is ready for self-rule, the British would be compelled to turn over Hindustan to Hindustanis, whether or not the people wanted independence. It is at this juncture in the narrative that the author has the American relating a "full story" of the war between the United States and England that led to the former's independence (Singh 1902, 299–300).

This episode ends with Singh mentioning that he decided not to reprise the American story of independence. Nor did he feel the need to repeat the "full story," he writes, because his visitor's political criticisms were not applicable. He then concludes by stating, in what is the final line of the "Criticism" section, that he cares only about his religion and his story and not what an American, who had independence on his brain, had to say (Singh 1902, 301).

Singh was evidently not prepared or willing to align himself with the pro-independence camp. Had he done so, he would have been one of the early voices calling for *swaraj* or self-rule, and perhaps one of, if not the first, in uniform to openly make that demand. The thought of independence had clearly crossed his mind though, not only because it had come up in conversation during his thirteen months, but also because its future in China was seemingly in jeopardy and he was an eyewitness on the scene.

Nor was he the only one who believed that he was beholding the possible end of China's long run as an autonomous country, an earthshaking change that his country had experienced a century earlier, as he was wont to point out in his observations. As the Bengali weekly *Hitavadi,* associated with Tagore, lamented in 1900: "The last of the Asiatic empires is going to disappear. Is that not a matter for sorrow to the people of Asia" (cited in Hay 1970, 34). No doubt, for Singh, such sentiments came easily because of his "mutual sympathy," an outlook that made him acutely aware of the parallels between the two countries he characterized as inextricably bound together by geography and religion.

The final section of Singh's book, entitled "Chin aur Hind," or "China and India," not coincidentally, follows on the heels of a nine-page account of the "Loot and Atrocities" perpetrated by the world powers who were in China ostensibly to rescue and restore civilization from the throes of Boxer-led savagery. He provides "eyewitness" testimony of these excesses, which, to one degree or another, all the foreign forces were guilty of, even his fellow Indian soldiers. Yet, as he astutely remarks in the opening lines of this section, in 1894–1895, news reports had condemned the Japanese for the atrocities they had committed in China during the Sino-Japanese War. Moreover, in that earlier war, as he points out, it was widely reported that the civilized races of Europe would never have acted in the brutal manner that the *jangli* Japanese had done (Singh 1902, 301).

Intentionally as well, I believe, this interrogation of Western claims to superiority is preceded by the episode involving the American postal officer who, in effect, advocates India's independence or, at least, outlines the conditions under which it would have the right to stake that claim. American troops, incidentally, in Singh's account and in studies of the Allied occupation, are generally said to have been the most disciplined and orderly in Beijing (Yang 2007, 53–54).

For Singh, an Indian in China who had learnt much from his thirteen months there and from the readings he had done, the two countries were closely interrelated and intertwined. No wonder his discussion of "Chin aur Hind" opens with the following rhetorical flourish: "Who does not know that Hindustan and China are the biggest, most fertile, and oldest of civilizations in Asia" (Singh 1902, 309). Moreover, they were, as noted earlier in his text, neighboring countries that shared an affinity by virtue of being members of the belief community of Buddhists. In addition, he acknowledges having a special attachment to China because it was in "distress," a sentimental connection that obviously stemmed from his concern that China was about to succumb to foreign rule. And in lamenting this future condition of subjection, he was clearly making a point about the past, specifically India's past that had led to its subjugation and its tragic fate as a colonized country.

Curiously, the author makes few personal interjections in this concluding section. Instead he is content to consider the two countries comparatively, first from an economic and then a sociopolitical perspective. The economic discussion underlines their backwardness, especially in relation to England and Europe. But they had not always lagged behind; in fact, as the author comments about China, it had a continuous history dating back 2,500 years. Furthermore, throughout much of its history, it was independent and prosperous. Only recently had its condition weakened and become infirm, so much so that its economic level had fallen far behind, as was also the case with India. The income levels of these two countries at the time of his writing, he states, was on par with what England had attained 400 years earlier. His source for much of this and related information, he tells his readers, was an English missionary who had investigated the comparative conditions of China, India, and England.

Both China and India were mired in poverty because they lacked trade. Trade, he avers, was the basis of a prosperous life. To be successful at it required hard work and good morals. Europe generally and England specifically became affluent by gaining control of the production and distribution of commodities that had once been the economic mainstays of Asia: tea, which China once monopolized, and cloth, whose trade India once dominated.

In Singh's estimation, China also had not progressed because it was slowed down by several impediments. The first was its arrogance of knowledge: it believed it was familiar with everything that was worth knowing, and it did not seek to learn any lessons from others. Therefore, it did not expand its knowledge capacity. Its corrupt officials constituted another obstacle—they stood in the way of economic growth and trade. The country's large population was also a problem, as was its wastefulness, in that people spent excessively on weddings, festivals, and other kinds of rituals. A fifth shortcoming, according to the author, was female illiteracy. Opium smoking was sixth on his list, a drag on the country's development because it drained the wealth of the country and the energy of its people, whose addiction enfeebled them and prevented them from exerting themselves. Aware that the opium trade was completely in the hands of the British, who could stop it if they chose to do so, he simply observes that they did not take action because it was a lucrative enterprise. India's weakness, on the other hand, was not opium but its dependence on other foreign goods, particularly cloth. He adds that India was also not capable of developing economically as long as it did not have a robust trade. The seventh and final obstacle was the Chinese belief in false gods, a failing which he believed characterized the people of Hindustan as well.

Singh ends this discussion and his *Thirteen Months in China* on a religious note. For him, true religion was an engine that had the capacity to propel all its believers forward. (The Boxers, in his estimation, had strong beliefs, but the wrong ones.) The ship of religion, to cite another metaphor he employs, offered its passengers a moral journey that was both agreeable and secure: it could guarantee a voyage to safer shores. In other words, India and now China, which stood on the eve of destruction as an independent country, had sailed into dangerous waters because of their false religious beliefs.

Surprisingly, the book winds down without making much of the economic and sociopolitical comparisons that the author emphasizes had subordinated and impoverished both China and India, making the latter a colonized country and the former seemingly on the verge of becoming divided up among the foreign powers or taken over by a single country. Nor does Singh return to express the "mutual sympathy" he felt for the country and its people. Perhaps he had made his point earlier, when he envisioned a silver lining in the dire straits that China seemed to be in at the beginning of the twentieth century, what with the world powers engaged in its *shikar,* in ravaging and looting it. God, he writes, may have inflicted "these difficult times for the welfare of China. For China, too, will fall into the hands of our all powerful [British colonial] government . . . Then it will became a matter of great happiness . . . Place China, too, in the hands of that great power in which Aryavarta has been placed. By creating a 'Hindu[stan] China' [country] establish a huge state in Asia. So be it" (Singh 1902, 17). In other words, he envisioned the possibility of the two countries becoming conjoined, almost a Chindia, to use today's parlance. Hope for China in its hour of greatest need—and India, which had already endured over a century of colonial rule—lay in a future that linked their destinies together as one country united by a shared geography and history and fused together by the British empire.

"Who does not know," as Singh states in the first line of his concluding chapter entitled "Chin[a] and Hind[ustan]" that "both of these countries in Asia are very large, fertile and the most ancient of civilizations" (1902, 317). What he did not know in advance but was optimistic about was their future, his hopes seemingly pinned on their solidarity in a new century when Japan was emerging as a major power and unity within Asia providing a counterweight to growing Western imperialism in the region.

Gadadhar Singh, a Hindustani soldier who had been dispatched as a member of the 7th Rajputs to save the world from the Boxer Uprising, entered the contact zone of China in 1900–1901 and emerged as a subaltern who astutely and perceptively sought to interrogate the mantle of civilization that Europe claimed for itself and denied Asia. His tour of duty prompted him to develop a distinct sense of kinship with the country and people he had been commanded to fight against, a sentiment that grew into an incipient pan-Asian view of the world that recognized Asia as one and not Europe. That he imagined and expressed this transnational consciousness at the beginning of the twentieth century in a vernacular account is all the more remarkable because he was among the first men in uniform to have entertained such thoughts and one of the few in a small group of thinkers who was not from the ranks of elite intellectuals. He emphasized the links and bonds between the two countries because China's present reminded him of India's past, and also awakened him to the possibilities of a different and novel future for his own country and region, including a different and shared destiny if the two countries were welded together under the British Empire.

Notes

1. One of the few studies of Indians in China in the colonial period is Thampi 2005. In 1900 most Indians resided in eastern China, especially Guangzhou, Hong Kong, and Shanghai, and were predominantly merchants, traders, soldiers, policemen, and watchmen.

2. A recent treatment of the Boxer Uprising is Bickers and Tiedemann 2007. Two excellent studies of the Boxers are Cohen 1997 and Esherick 1987.

3. The 7th Rajputs numbered 500 in all (Vaughan 1902). The British contingent was the third largest after the Japanese (10,000) and Russians (4,000).

4. See the essay on "Asia Redux: Conceptualizing a Region for Our Times," by Prasenjit Duara and others in *JAS* 69, 4 (2010).

5. Or "Asia Inside Out," as the essays in this volume highlight in documenting intra-Asian and interregional flows of commodities, ideas, and people both before and after 1900.

6. Several of the paragraphs here are derived from Yang 2007.

7. On Hart's motives in writing these essays, see his personal correspondence (Fairbank, Bruner, and Matheson 1975, 1232–1249). See also the special issue of *Modern Asian Studies* 40, 3 (2006), on "Robert Hart and the Chinese Maritime Customs Service," especially the essay by Hans van de Ven.

8. Tagore and Chinese intellectuals such as Liang Qichao (1873–1929) deployed similar arguments to emphasize the longstanding fraternal relationship between China and India (Bharucha 2006, 74–75).

References

Bayly, C. A. 2007. "The Boxer Uprising and India: Globalizing Myths." In *The Boxers, China, and the World,* ed. Robert Bickers and R. G. Tiedemann, 147–155. Lanham, MD: Rowman & Littlefield.

Bharucha, Rustom. 2006. *Another Asia: Rabindranath Tagore and Okakura Tenshin.* Delhi: Oxford University Press.

Bickers, Robert, and R. G. Tiedemann, eds. 2007. *The Boxers, China, and the World.* Lanham, MD: Rowman & Littlefield.

Cohen, Paul A. 1983. *Discovering History in China: American Historical Writing on the Recent Chinese Past.* New York: Columbia University Press.

———. 1997. *History in Three Keys: The Boxers as Event, Experience, and Myth.* New York: Columbia University Press.

Duara, Prasenjit. 2010. "Asia Redux: Conceptualizing a Region for Our Times." *The Journal of Asian Studies* 69 (4): 963–983.

Edwards, Neville P. 1900. *The Story of China with a Description of the Events Relating to the Present Struggle.* London: Hutchinson.

Esherick, Joseph W. 1987. *The Origins of the Boxer Uprising.* Berkeley: University of California Press.

Fairbank, John King, Katherine Frost Bruner, and Elizabeth MacLeod Matheson, eds. 1975. *The I.G. in Peking: Letters of Robert Hart, Chinese Maritime Customs, 1868–1907,* vol. 2. Cambridge, MA: Harvard University Press.

Hart, Robert. 1900. *The Peking Legations: A National Uprising and International Episode.* Shanghai: Kelly and Walsh.

———. 1901. *"These From the Land of Sinim": Essays on the Chinese Question.* London: Chapman & Hall.

Hay, Stephen N. 1970. *Asian Ideas of East and West: Tagore and His Critics in Japan, China, and India.* Cambridge: Harvard University Press.

Norman, Henry. 1895. *The People and Politics of the Far East: Travels and Studies in the British, French, Spanish and Portuguese Colonies, Siberia, China, Japan, Korea, Siam and Malaya.* London: T. Fisher Unwin.

Pratt, Mary Louise. 1992. *Imperial Eyes: Travel Writing and Transculturation.* London: Routledge.

Saaler, Sven, and Christopher W. A. Szpilman. eds. 2011. *Pan Asianism: A Documentary History.* Vol. 1, *1850–1920.* Lanham, MD: Rowman & Littlefield.

Said, Edward W. 1978. *Orientalism.* New York: Pantheon.

Silvestri, Michael. 2000. "'The Sinn Fein of India': Irish Nationalism and the Policing of Revolutionary Terrorism in Bengal." *The Journal of British Studies* 39 (4): 454–486.

Singh, Thakur Gadadhar. 1902. *Chin meh Terah Mas: (Chin Sangram).* Lucknow: Thakur Gadadhar Singh.

———. 1916. *Karuna Kahani.* Ajmer: Prakash Book Depot.

Thampi, Madhavi. 2005. *Indians in China 1800–1949.* New Delhi: Manohar.

Vaughan, Lt. Col. H[enry] B[athurst]. [1902] 2000. *St. George and the Chinese Dragon.* Dartford, Kent: Alexius Press.

Yang, Anand A. 2007. "(A) Subaltern('s) Boxers: An Indian Soldier's Account of China and the World in 1900–1901." In *The Boxers, China, and the World,* ed. Robert Bickers and R. G. Tiedemann, 43–64. Lanham, MD: Rowman & Littlefield.

9

Before the Gangrene Set In

The Dutch East Indies in 1910

ERIC TAGLIACOZZO

Examining a single year in the life cycle of a society is a bit like dendrochronology—it takes the "tree ring approach" to the history of a particular place and the people that populate it. A number of scholars have now begun to do this in different scattered global locales, with one of the classic examples perhaps being the Chinese "Soulstealers" episode of 1768 that Philip Kuhn made famous (Kuhn 1990). Yet there are different ways of walking this same path that can yield interesting historical results. A similar attempt might be tried for the Dutch East Indies (or Indonesia), and to some extent the Malay world surrounding, in the *fin de siècle* period. At the start of the twentieth century, the Indies was a bustling locale, and one that seemed to be on an upward trajectory: Holland was apparently close to the apex of its dominion over the archipelago, and determined anticolonial action in the guise of massive strikes, labor disputes, or (most importantly) antistate political entities had yet to showcase themselves. Yet even at this seeming highpoint of imperial rule, the stage was being set for disasters that were just around the bend.[1] Holland's largest colony was indeed in robust health across a number of indices, a number of which we will scrutinize in this article. There was little by way of concern that the future offered anything different from the past in this respect, and most Dutchmen looked forward to more "success" on the colonial front and felt that the moral right of rule was with them. A number of these same Dutch colonial denizens would have been absolutely astonished to witness the cataclysms that would arrive only three decades later, when the world that had been constructed in the past 300 years by their compatriots came crashing down in the matter of an instant.

My contribution here isolates this moment to the year 1910—with a bit of temporal latitude before and after this date to take into account existing records—and queries how the Dutch Indies appeared at this high-point of colonial glory. It was the moment before the gangrene set in. A feeling of hope was evident in the air of the colony, and most colonials felt that their "civilizing efforts" were bearing fruit, a notion challenged only in awkward silence, at this juncture at least, by the local inhabitants of the colony themselves. Importantly, this feeling of success was very much one projected externally: the Dutch showcased their dominion to other colonial powers as an example of what was possible by the exercise of "enlightened rule." I show this dialectic in its numerous organizational components below, primarily structured on archival data from the National Archives of the Netherlands (and also from London, which brought together vital data on the jointly ruled archipelago of the Malay World), but also from colonial-era journals from that time, as well as contemporary scholarship. The article traces the expansion of colonial state vision in the first third of the essay, militaristic projects to enforce this in the second third of the piece, and attempts at maintaining what has been "won" in the final third of the article. In each part I illustrate how the Dutch accomplished benchmarks of coercion in both actuality (on the ground) and the theater of rule. I also point out, however, the very fragile strength of this emerging control, even though many period Dutchmen were convinced that theirs was a project that would last and last—despite gathering proof to the contrary.

Envisioning the Parameters of the State

Constructing a colonial imperium that mirrored similar processes taking place among other imperial powers elsewhere in the region, not to mention the world, required a number of projects to be set into motion. One of the most crucial among these was exploration: actually knowing the extent of colonial territory. Dutch maps of Sumatra, for example, contained all of the major geographical landmarks by 1910 and had catalogued Sumatra's peoples, as well as their physical environments. What remained were explorations of a different sort, which filled in gaps in existing knowledge or took the process of discovery at a slower, more leisurely pace. The military apothecary W. G. Boorsma, for example, was given permission to set out on a chemical-pharmacological expedition, the special concern of which was to collect new plants that might be useful in the fabrication of medicines. J. T. Cremer set out for the Batak highlands in 1907, but did so this time not with a column of laden-down coolies, but in an automobile, which could barely traverse the recently cut roads.[2] Not to be outdone, other explorers of the late period also ventured to the northern shores of Toba's great lake, but did so by way of petrol-fuelled motorboats. Even the coasts of Sumatra, which had been circumnavigated for years by Dutch traders, adventurers, and military men in various steamships, yielded up small discoveries, such as a waterfall at Mansalar, which could now be used as a navigation aid (Meerwaldt 1911, 63; "Waterval" 1911, 109). All of these voyages enhanced Dutch knowledge of the "periphery," yet there was gradually a discernable slowing of the gathering of data as Batavia's servants in the periphery had fewer and fewer locales left to find and claim.

The surveying of the islands of the lower reaches of the South China Sea had become part of a coherent program of development in the Indies by 1910 as well. Mining interests took the lead in new surveying operations and expeditions, mapping Bangka (for example) in incredible detail and starting work on Belitung, and even the tiny islands off Belitung's coasts, after 1894.[3] The island of Blakang Padang, facing Singapore in the Riau Archipelago, was also extensively surveyed at this time. Though formerly it had been seen as a useless scrap of land with few natural resources and only a marginal population, by the first decade of the twentieth century planners were seeing the island as a complementary port near Singapore, with coal sheds, docking complexes, and a series of interconnected lighthouses. This sort of exploration, indeed, with coherent and definitive development purposes in mind, was among the last stages of discovery along the length of the Indies' frontiers. Even many of the myriad reefs and atolls which made up the maritime boundary of the Netherlands Indies, from Aceh eastward to coastal New Guinea, were explored and chronicled by Dutch oceanographers at this time ("Blakang Padang" 1902; Niermeyer 1911, 877).

Some of this interest was pure science or was fueled by the emerging nationalist impulse to mark the boundaries of the archipelago with Dutch flags. Parts of this may even be attributable to trying to "get there first," before other European powers planted flags in these same landscapes. But a significant part of it was also economic and utilitarian, as exploration was bent to the service of the state to locate new resources and wealth. Yet particularly after the *fin de siècle,* one concern drove exploration forward faster and with more energy than any other factor, and this was the search for natural resources. The case of Borneo can be taken again as an example here, to show how much the creation of the frontier owed to state and private interests racing to find ores throughout the entirety of the island. Applied geology drove empire forward in this sense; the geologist's shovel and the explorer's sextant were tools of equal importance in "opening" up the frontier. On the British side of the Anglo/Dutch divide, this was happening very early: only a few years after the founding of British North Borneo, for example, the governor of that territory was calling weekly "Gold Committee" meetings, which involved state officials and several Chinese prospectors.[4] By the turn of the century in these same dominions, these informal meetings had given way to coded telegraph correspondences about potential diamond districts, as well as oil and mineral rights being leased to various concerns.[5] In Brunei, which became a British Protectorate, such dealings were even earlier, as the Sultan there cut prospecting deals for antimony and tin with English speculators in the mid-nineteenth century.[6] Yet it was in Sarawak where the greatest amounts of minerals and ores were being found, pulling English officials deeper and deeper into the forest in search of raw materials and their profits (Hart-Everett 1878, 30). The Resident of Bintulu, Sarawak, a man named A. Hart-Everett, gives an idea of the kinds of resources being found in 1878: gold, iron, cobalt, and copper were all being discovered, as well as platinum, cats' eyes, and spinelle rubies. Diamonds were also turning up, such as one huge stone of seventy-six carats that was slipped into Sarawak from across the Dutch border (Hart-Everett, 1878: 6).[7] This was one of the largest diamonds ever chronicled in colonial times in the Indies.

Yet actual "out-in-the-field" surveying was not the only tool at the disposal of these modernizing colonial states in 1910. Dutch East Indies cartography had become a much more sophisticated science than in previous decades as well, with its evolution being fueled by a variety of important sources. One of the first of these was popular interest and national pride. Dutch cartographers attended international congresses with their new data on the Indies, and the Dutch press back home picked up on their discoveries as well, fanning the new knowledge out to a wider reading public (Kan 1904–1905, 715; Oort

1909, 363–365). Perhaps more important, however, was the role industry and production was beginning to play, as mining and agricultural concerns mapped out huge tracts of land with potentially colossal profits in mind. This is seen in the detailed maps produced of the mining concession Karang Ringin in Palembang, for example, as well as in the Kahayan mine plots leased out by Batavia deep in Eastern Borneo's interior.[8] The contentious nature of the Anglo/Dutch border itself, however, was perhaps the main phenomenon advancing the mapping of the frontier, as both European powers jockeyed over the laying of the boundary. As British cognizance of this region's topography increased, claims on territory became more specific, forcing the Dutch to catch up cartographically. This happened only slowly, however. An incident in 1909, in which the Dutch envoy to London seemed himself not to know the nature of Dutch claims in Eastern Borneo, acted as an alarm for The Hague to acquaint all of her foreign service personnel with the Indies' "true boundaries."[9] Around this time, therefore, maps started to be produced which sketched the Dutch presence on the ground in hyperaccurate detail, such as one which combined roads, railroad lines, toll offices, and garrisons (not to mention administrative divisions, mineral deposits, industrial centers, and lighthouses) all on one map ("Nieuwe Kaart" 1908, 680). These efforts became the template-maps for later decades in the twentieth century as well.

All of this activity was terrestrial, yet Dutch vision of the intricacies of the frontier had also advanced exponentially on the sea. The archives of the Hydrography Service show increasing numbers of maps being deposited into the central data-files: Riau and Lingga, the mouths of the Asahan River, and various parts of the Eastern Borneo coast were all mapped, sometimes down to extraordinary detail.[10] British maps of the maritime border region in Northeastern Borneo, and Dutch maps completed on the reefs and tiny islands separating Borneo from Sulawesi, opened these states' vision onto the kinds of locales where smugglers and pirates traditionally practiced their activities.[11] The older hydrographic schooners were retired and replaced with steamers that could undertake surveying under nearly any conditions.[12] There were still complaints in the years around 1910 of some areas being under-surveyed, such as the border waters between North Sulawesi and the Southern Philippines, and even certain channels south of Singapore, but these grumblings in both the British and Dutch colonies' presses were now few and far between.[13] Instead, a picture emerges of the waters of the Anglo-Dutch frontier being almost entirely charted after 1910, when a useful map was

Dutch exploration photo of a Lhokseumawe grave, 1910. (Courtesy of KITLV/Royal Netherlands Institute of Southeast Asian and Caribbean Studies)

published showing the dates of area surveys in the *Tijdschrift voor de Aardrijkskundige Genootschap.*[14] The enormous length and porosity of the frontier, which seemed endless and unmappable in the mid-nineteenth century, had become a fairly known quantity by the early twentieth century. Batavia and Singapore had committed these spaces to the archives now, where they could be examined and archived in compliance with the coercive programs of both of these colonial regimes.

With respect to agreements and accords with autochthonous princes in the Malay world, European relations with local lords in the periphery had been whittled down to more of an exact science by 1910 as well. Formal contracts, known as the *korte-verklaringen* and the *lange politieke contract* in Dutch ("short declaration" and "long political contract"), were standardized to regulate Batavia's pull on states along the frontier. The system of reportage between Singapore and Batavia began to function on more regular lines as well, with the two colonial powers sharing news of their relations with local states in a more timely and precise fashion. Advances in mapping and exploration helped this process along, as there were fewer unknown areas around the turn of the century, and contracts were spelled out in considerably more detail.[15] Nevertheless, complications remained with the semi-independent local lords of the periphery, even until after the turn of the century. Compensation payments to rulers were repeatedly withheld to modulate behavior, while in some locales the government reserved the right to appoint its own civil functionaries, including port authorities and police in Riau.[16] In one revealing incident in 1907, the Sultan of Sambas (in West Borneo) was admonished by Batavia for offering to the King of England edible birds' nests as a gift. The action and Dutch response to this offer show how sensitive relations with these polities still were: a gift along these lines could be construed as form of vassalage, something Batavia would do anything to avoid.[17] The incident also illustrates however how closely the Dutch watched their subject-peoples, as their own reach into the "wild spaces" of the Indies grew at this time. All indigenous potentates were very much required to heel to Batavia's will and to make sure that their words and actions backed up the notion of Dutch rule in these remote parts of the archipelago.

Constructing an Imperium

Understanding the parameters and dimensions of one's imperium was only part of the requirements, however. Holland's colonial armed forces, or the

KNIL, were not always up to the military adventurism required by an aggressive colonial regime for much of the nineteenth century. After the turn of the twentieth century, however, the KNIL gradually was becoming a more effective organization, both in Java and in the Outer Islands along the Anglo-Dutch frontier. Elsbeth Locher-Scholten has shown how relationships based on trade between the Dutch and indigenous polities eventually could become based on coercion as well. This was often a decades-long process and one that took Byzantine twists and turns as each side tried to outmaneuver the other in the realm of politics. Locher-Scholten's window in examining these processes has been a Sumatran one, and particularly one based on Jambi, in the southern part of that huge island (Locher-Scholten 2003). Yet with the Dutch in the Indies over the course of the nineteenth century, politics often gave way to force, and this was not just the case in the more populated, Straits of Malacca locales in the Indies.

Advances in the medical and sanitary regimes around the colonial armed forces was one very important reason why this was so. The Dutch military avidly read English and French medical journals, keeping up with the latest advances in tropical knowledge from places as far away as Madagascar and French Guyana. The Dutch also had started to build up a reservoir of practical knowledge themselves, having to do with clothing, food supplies, drinking water, and seasonal precautions. It was around this time that water-resistant clothing began to be studied in field tests in the Indies, as well as other kinds of fabrics that would be suitable for long expeditions in the border residencies (Van Haeften 1895, 80; Vink 1899, 676; "Waterdichte Kleedingstuken" 1897, 224; van de Water 1902, 1: 230, 2: 212). Studies on boots also were commissioned, in trying to find the right kind of shoe for traction and insulation during monsoon campaigns.[18] Funds were set up to promote exercise and gymnastics among the troops, while detailed instructions were also handed out on how to keep water fresh during prolonged periods in the bush.[19] By 1896 a whole range of conserved foods were available to be able to sustain government troops far from any supply lines: Australian meats that had been cooked over 100 degrees Centigrade in chloro-calcium baths, dried fish, dried vegetables, and sardines were among these preserves ("Verduurzaamde Levensmiddelen" 1896, 482). Even drunkenness and beri-beri were down, rendering the KNIL a more fit policing force by the early twentieth century.[20] With many less men in recovery-rooms of one sort or another, more were fit to fight.

Yet there were also other explanations for why the broad spaces of the "Outer Islands" were more easily penetrated by colonial militaries in the early twentieth century. Some of these were organizational. In Sarawak, the Brookes built a network of forts up-country in order to establish a permanent presence in rural areas; these instillations could be found at Bentong, Kabong, Muka, Bintulu, and up the Baram and Trusan Rivers (Harfield 1900, 622–639). For the Dutch, a complex, accordion-like system whereby the military and civil governments of the Outer Islands cooperated in "trouble" districts allowed for flexibility in watching over potentially rebellious populations. When circumstances were peaceful, many of the army units in these far-flung residencies were reduced in size and reassigned to other areas. This happened in parts of Aceh and Southeastern Borneo, two notorious flashpoints, right at the turn of the century.[21] In other districts, however, such as the Upper Dusun and Upper Kapuas regions of Western Borneo, authority was maintained under a military umbrella at the expense of the civil administration. This often caused problems between the two branches of Dutch authority, as the latter saw their jurisdiction disappearing into the coercive powers of the military. From the standpoint of Batavia, however, concessions of this nature were almost always preferable to the opposite possibility, which was lack of control over local populations, especially in the border residencies. Batavia was only too happy, most of the time, to skimp on local administrative efficiency (having civil servants in charge who knew the local customs and had long-standing ties with local peoples) if the military could ensure order in these newly conquered places.[22] This was simply a question of priorities.

These occurrences evolved in the terrestrial sphere, yet they are also apparent in the sources that tell us about changes by sea. Technological advances in naval capabilities were the spark that lit the fire in Dutch policy circles around this time. Just before the turn of the twentieth century, urgent circulars were being sent out to Dutch envoys in many major capitals to find out how much the various powers were spending on their respective naval forces. These instructions went out to Dutch plenipotentiaries in London, Paris, Berlin, and Washington, but they also were sent to less exalted powers (such as Sweden, Norway, and especially the minor colonial nations such as Portugal and Spain), to see how similarly small states were integrating the new changes into their navies.[23] From the Dutch envoy in Paris, Batavia learned that French fleet expansion was imminent, with improvement of colonial ports (such as Saigon), funds for colonial cable laying, and a colonial defense fund all on the table. From the Dutch representative in Berlin, further information was received about German naval capabilities in the Pacific,

Dutch colonial military forces in Aceh at the turn of the twentieth century. (Courtesy of KITLV/Royal Netherlands Institute of Southeast Asian and Caribbean Studies)

which was important to Batavia because of Berlin's interests in telegraphs and shipping in the area, not to mention its territorial expansion in certain island chains in this vast ocean.[24] Yet it was the obvious obsolescence of the Indies' marine in comparison to British naval strength in the Straits that really gave Batavia cause for alarm. Clippings from *The Times* (of London) showed that English armor-plate experiments, steam trials, and shallow draught construction were making Dutch ships obsolete in the archipelago, a situation which was tolerable while amity existed between the two powers, but which was not deemed as desirable for the long term.[25] The news in 1910 that Japan was planning to build ships of even greater technological advancement than Britain's deepened this anxiety further, as the Dutch realized that their naval presence in the region was inadequate compared with its neighbors.[26] This was true vis-à-vis both the British and Japanese.

This was a concern, but for internal policy issues, however, such as the surveillance and interdiction of smugglers, the Indies' marine around 1910 was now a much more effective force than it had been in the nineteenth century. The evidence of this improvement is nearly everywhere apparent. In Sumatra, more and more steamers were assigned now specifically for upriver patrols, traveling to formerly unreachable spaces where political resistance and "illegal" commerce had functioned almost at will.[27] Off the coast of Eastern Borneo, a long stretch of shoreline that was seen as troublesome for decades (housing pirates, smugglers, and a variety of other people antithetical to Batavia's state-making project), improvements were also made, as ships were slotted into grids to patrol the entirety of the shoreline.[28] Centralized control over many areas of the Outer Islands had improved so much that certain patrolling stations were actually relieved of ships.[29] This is not to say that the Indies' marine was now unassailable, or that it did not continue to have some major problems, which certainly affected abilities to patrol effectively against smugglers along the borders. Sanitation on board these ships, for instance, continued to be dismal, spawning disease and sickness among crews that often limited these vessels' practical effectiveness (van Rossum 1907, 2: 274, 3: 287)). Yet the tide had turned against many structural problems that had curtailed Batavia's state-making abilities in the periphery. By 1910, smugglers making their entrance into the Indies by sea, for example, had to evince considerably more ingenuity in doing so than at any time in the previous several decades. This was true nearly everywhere on the elongated, 3,000-mile frontier.

The setting up of state-of-the-art colonial regimes in the Malay world also owed much to policing. Yet even by 1910, several aspects of policing along the lands and seas of this frontier still allowed for a porous distribution of goods, away from the eyes of the state and against its explicit instructions. Policemen were regularly censured for graft and illegal practices, such as one member of the force in Singapore who was jailed for freeing an incarcerated suspect without any instructions to do so.[30] The police forces of large, difficult-to-govern residencies, such as Dutch West Borneo, may have increased in size, but not necessarily in professionalism, if the reports of border administrators are to be believed.[31] When military units were withdrawn from the *Buitenbezittingen* (or "Outer Islands") upon pacification, these units were often replaced by an exactly corresponding number of police officers, showing that a similar level of coercion was needed in the area, even if its composition or tactics had changed.[32] These kinds of signals reveal that pacification and policing along the frontier was still highly problematic, even into the early twentieth century. A total of 1,535 Indies policemen for all of the Outer Islands in 1896 was still a very small number; the extra 700 men who had joined this force by 1905 made hardly a dent in this problem (Ruitenbach 1905, 1009). By 1912, instructions were being promulgated to police about what commands they should shout in Malay to quell riots.[33] With a huge, mobile, and multiracial population straddling both sides of the frontier, the police of both colonial powers were not in a position to fully command the border at any time. This was the case both before and after the turn of the twentieth century.

Such advances in policing were concretized by concomitant legal advances. A formal agreement on extradition between British North Borneo and the Netherlands Indies did not take place until 1910. The establishment of coal mines on the frontier, with the attending problems of runaway coolie labor, finally helped this "gentleman's agreement" into law.[34] Yet the informal channels that often characterized diplomacy in the region functioned well enough, for long enough, to convince many administrators on both sides of the frontier that existing agreements were sufficient as they stood. This time of "gentlemen's agreements" was fast drawing to a close, however. The rise of industry and capital-intensive enterprises in Borneo forced new legal structures into existence, especially as they related to movement across the frontier. British North Borneo eventually put into effect extradition ordinances for Labuan (1890), Sarawak (1891), and Hong Kong (1896), all at least partially as a result of these processes.[35] The agreement with Hong Kong, in fact, was predicated on the establishment of direct steam service between the two colonies. Laborers presently had an easy escape hatch, if they could get on returning ships, to leave their contracts and try to get back to villages in South China with their cash advances in hand.[36] Discussions on extradition with the Sultanate of Brunei also were eventually ratified into law, as Brunei had become a favorite place for counterfeiters (as well as slave- and coolie-traffickers) to flee to, away from British North Borneo.[37] The construction of an interior legal architecture and the fabrication of legal bindings between area states were manners in which to solidify coercion, therefore, though it is clear that these measures were still works in progress around this time.

Keeping What Has Been Won

It was one thing for knowledge-projects to exist, and another for them to be enforced; maintaining this evolving tableaux of territories and state-powers upon them was still another. Railroads are a good example here vis-à-vis statecraft: rail construction was going on all along local frontiers, in different guises but with unified effect. In Johor, the numbers of people using the expanding British railway jumped from 159,317 in 1912 to 418,047 just four years later, with the net revenues for Federated Malay States railroads the equivalent of over a million dollars just after the turn of the century.[38] In Aceh, the Dutch military built the first stages of a steam-tram in 1876, one that eventually was expanded and taken over by the state in 1916. The goal of this line was to help with the pacification process, an aim that was met, but only after several decades of trying.[39] In South Sumatra, rail construction was tied to the idea of opening these fertile lands to Javanese transmigrants, who would come from overpopulated Java and make new lives there. This project was also only partially successful, expanding the state's presence in Lampung and elsewhere, but never quite helping as many settlers as had been hoped.[40] In Borneo, some of the most dramatic plans of all for expansion were anticipated, with one expert drawing up schemes for Borneo to be criss-crossed with rail lines in the space of only six years (Eekhout 1891, 955). On the Dutch side of the Borneo border, this never really happened. Yet the British did indeed expand their rail net in Borneo (mostly on the coasts), though this was met almost everywhere with huge problems, such as floods, construction-site collapses, and massive landslides.[41] Empire-building via railroad technology, even around 1910, was still a very uncertain process in this part of the world. This did not stop either colonial state from setting down the groundwork for later decades, however.

If this was so for railroads overland, then it was also true for steamships in the maritime realm. By 1910, the sea-based expansion of the state in local waters had evolved into a broad, interconnected grid. Although steam shipping outweighed sail in Singapore statistics shortly after the Suez Canal opened in 1869, it would not be until the years around the *fin de siècle* that steam lines connected the vast breadth of the archipelago (Bogaars 1955, 99–143). In Palembang, steam-shipping figures were up, as well as Batavia's abilities to keep track of such movements; in Jambi this was also true, especially with clearance work (on sandbars, projecting jungle, and shifting shoals) proceeding on heavily trafficked rivers.[42] Makassar was budgeted huge new sums of money to make port improvements for steam facilities, and services in Borneo were expanded as well, both in the Western and Southeastern residencies of the island.[43] As perhaps the most signal indication of the expansion of these facilities, aims, and resources, however, part of Aceh was turned into a giant refueling station, based on the offshore island of Weh. By 1900, an immense dry-dock had been installed on the island, complete with coal sheds, wharfing facilities, and a Chinese work camp for repairs.[44]

In this place, the formerly wildest of the "Wild West" corners of the archipelago, a kind of maritime infrastructure and control had been established that formerly would have been impossible. *Koninklijke Paketvaart Maatschappij* (KPM) stations now stretched from Sabang (the name of the Weh docking station) to Merauke in New Guinea, on the opposite side of the Indies.[45] Batavia and Singapore were instructing themselves on how to rule the sea as part and parcel of their larger state-making efforts in the archipelago.

Such programs of self-improvement on the state level also were pursued through economic policies as well. Export duties were levied on a wide range of forest products which easily exited the Indies' so-called Outer Islands, including bees' wax, benzoin, damar, rhino horn, and certain kinds of wood (Review of the Netherlands Indian Tariff Law, 1921). Tax revenues on trade items such as these brought in larger and larger sums every year to Batavia.[46] When there were problems, such as downturns in the market for the abovementioned forest products, Dutch civil servants wrote voluminously on how revenues might be raised, showing how important these taxation schemes had become to the central government.[47] Yet other actors also sought to make money from the taxation of such goods. Local chiefs, such as several in Riau in 1897, also tried to take advantage of the upturn in general trade, taxing the transit of forest products from their own dominions, only without the permission of the state. This was not allowed, and such entrepreneurs were swiftly punished.[48] The important thing for Batavia was that greater peace in the Outer Islands brought greater means for enforcing taxation, as fewer regions still held the ability to evade state designs. Only a few places, like Makassar, were periodically made into tax-free ports like Singapore. By 1910, therefore, duties were levied on an entire range of new items: radium bromide and menthol eucalyptus throat drops, as well as steel shipping-masts, playing cards, and heavy gravel-breaking equipment.[49] Both regimes found that they could push their taxation regimes along the boundary separating them much more rigorously than they had ever been able to previously.

Yet the taxation of customs goods was not the only way to enforce the coercive desires of regimes along the frontier. Blockades and shipping regulations *(scheepvaartregelingen)* were also tools used to strengthen colonial borders and make money for the state at the same time. Since the early part of the nineteenth century, Batavia had been imposing rules on who could, and could not, trade between ports in the outstretched waters of the Indies archipelago. Foreign shipping had been forbidden to participate in the so-called

Koninklijke Paketvaart Maatschappij (KPM) ship in Makassar Harbor, early twentieth century. (Courtesy of KITLV/Royal Netherlands Institute of Southeast Asian and Caribbean Studies)

coasting trade, or internal commerce between ports in the Indies, since 1825. This in itself was a form of border strengthening, as it gave Dutch vessels a huge advantage in local trade (Tractaat 1912). A phalanx of interests eventually came together to dispute this privilege, however, including Straits Settlements traders, who were shut out from the coasting trade, and large Dutch agricultural concerns, which wanted free competition to lower transport costs ("Voorstel" 1887, 938–942). Only in 1912 was this form of boundary-construction abandoned in Indies waters and foreign competition let into the Dutch archipelago to compete in the trade between the various Indies harbors themselves.

Human agents, and not just policies, were also utilized to enforce the controlling programs of these regimes. By 1910, ethnographers were spending more and more time on the Indies' frontiers and learned local circumstances and customs—including local laws, the start of the so-called adat studies movement—far better than previously. This was also state-building of a kind. Vague, generalized accounts of large culture areas started to be replaced with much more in-depth studies, which chronicled local life to a degree never seen before. The details of real cultural values inside various local communities began to be much more seriously explored. Instead of thumb-nail sketches of local groups, such as "The Punan," "The Melenau," "The Kelabit," or "The Bataks," articles appeared now on "The Tobacco Pipes of the Boven Musi Kubu" (Snelleman 1906), "Indigenous Pharmacoepia of the Padang Lowlands" (Kreemer 1907), and "Treatment of the Sick Among the Central Bornean Dayaks" ("Ziekenbehandeling" 1908). Certainly there was a high degree of scientific autonomy in these studies. Yet ethnography, self-consciously or not, was being used more and more by the state to identify aspects of material culture important to local peoples. Especially in the border residencies, these commodities might also be important enough to be traded across political boundaries. The Dutch collected these articles and indexed them in a central filing system called the *Zakelijke Aantekeningen,* located in The Hague. The *Zakelijke Aantekeningen* became a kind of centralized database for knowledge-collection in the Indies, an archive of periodical literature numbering in the thousands of entries by the twentieth century. When observers in the field noted that Dayaks in Central Borneo (straddling the Anglo/Dutch frontier), for example, would "do anything for glazed corals," Batavia noted this in files ("Ruilhandel" 1909–1910, 185). Bugis, Chinese, and Malay traders (not to mention Europeans) made upriver journeys to trade in these items, selling them as ornaments. If such things were so valuable to interior populations, what might they give up for them? Birds' nests? Camphor crystals? Sheets of gutta percha? Such forest products were supposed to be taxed, and all the more so because of the high prices they all fetched at market.

There were now larger and larger numbers of state agents in the periphery to enforce the dictates of the modernizing colonial state. Old problems, such as dismal chances for promotion and even more dismal pay-schemes for Outer Islands administrators, were being revamped. Batavia was trying to remove two of the primary causes of complaint that often led to bad government, including graft and smuggling in the periphery.[50] There were also attempts made to redraw the political contracts with self-governing polities in the border residencies, which gave local rulers a little more room to earn a decent living, rather than having to resort to smuggling and other illegal activities to maintain their status.[51] Yet problems persisted, which were often serious enough to impair government functioning in the outstretched borderlands where the state needed this presence most. Controleurs were still badly overworked and responsible for a huge variety of tasks: education, infrastructure, harbor control, and governance were among these duties. These burdens often overtaxed their effectiveness ("Controleur" 1910, 2). Authority in the self-governing areas remained broken and diffuse, with a variety of interests—sultans, their children, strongmen, and *orang kaya* (or rich merchants)—all holding sway over different territories.[52] Some of Batavia's Dutch civil servants, such as one notorious womanizer in Manado, also exercised their authority in ways objectionable to the local populace, lowering the government's prestige in local eyes.[53] These events were occurring simultaneously and all along the emerging boundaries in this part of the world. The fact that they did happen all at the same time seems to show us how diffuse colonial power was on the frontier at this junction, both from Batavia and its neighbors' perspective.

Conclusion

In the years around the *fin de siècle*, the Netherlands Indies possessed a somewhat unreal air. Fighting for territory in this part of the world was now almost finished: Batavia's authority was almost unquestioned by now, and Dutch troops could be found from Sabang to Merauke, from the far west all the way east across the archipelago. The evidence of Batavia's authority was just about everywhere as well, as steamships, telegraphs, and railroads were clear symbols that "civilization" was being spread, at least to the taste of those who viewed the changing of the land from such concrete angles (Mrazek 2002). If Holland was almost finished with its militarism and was now more engaged in construction rather than destruction, then both of these processes were signals to the world that the colony was an inalienable component of the Dutch presences across the globe and that the Indies was a locale unquestionably under Batavia's thumb and integral to the evolving political economy. In Marieke Bloembergen's clever phrasing (2006), the "colonial spectacles" at hand were at once actual and metaphorical: the shadow-play of statecraft was performed around the clock by the authorities in a conspicuous manner, but these same "spectacles" may have been opaque in that serious difficulty was not far away, though Batavia did not seem to envision this state of affairs with any lasting precision.

There was an enormous price for this opacity of vision in the 1940s, when the Japanese and the Republican Indonesian movement after them finally dislodged the Dutch from the Indies, one after another, and with great violence in both cases. This story has been told by other scholars, but here I have tried to illuminate how the Indies may have appeared prior to these things occurring—in a time of colonial optimism, not when things had spiraled out of colonial control. In the *fin de siècle* period, the feeling imparted by the Indies was diametrically opposite to the crushing war and instability that was utterly normative in the 1940s. This earlier time of stability over conflagration likely felt as if it would have lasted forever. There are almost no surviving clues that tell us that anyone in the colony, on either side of the colonial divide, thought that the current state of affairs would end anytime soon. The Malay-language media were on the whole quite pliant, and the emergence of the first anticolonial political parties was still a year or two away, while Indonesian socialism did not appear until the following decade. Holland's mechanics of coercion seemed to have little to fear. Yet Dutch abilities across a number of indices of rule were beginning to fester from the inside and would end up not standing the test of time that so many Dutchmen thought they would. Though strong and solid when viewed externally, they were gangrenous on the inside, and capabilities of rule decayed from inside the body politic itself. The Dutch regime ultimately disintegrated in the middle of the twentieth century, and what had taken more than three centuries to build ultimately unraveled in the space of just three months.

Notes

1. Three sources can help us here; see, for example, Cribb 1994; Locher-Scholten 1994; and Shiraishi 1990. Cribb's authors show the strength but also the fragility, in some areas, of advancing Dutch dominion. Locher-Scholten puts forth an argument of how and why the Dutch imperium expanded in the Indies. Shiraishi then shows how this imperium was eaten from within by the colony's nascent impendence movements. Nota bene: Some ideas expressed here have appeared in my essay in the Dutch journal *Bijdragen tot de Taal-, Land-, en Volkenkunde*, 166, 2/3, 2010: 270–292.

2. Algemeen Rijksarchief, the Hague, Netherlands (hereafter, ARA), 1897, Mailrapport (hereafter, MR) #611; Cremer 1907, 245.

3. The extensive surveying of Bangka began even earlier, in the 1870s. See ARA, 1894, MR #535; and Zondervan 1900, 519.

4. "Memorandum on Gold in North Borneo, 30 May 1934" in Colonial Office (hereafter, CO) 874/996. This document gives a short history of gold prospecting in North Borneo's territory from the earlier period.

5. British Borneo Exploration Company, London, to R. W. Clarke, Telegraph, 29 Oct 1908, in CO 874/350; see also the list of consignees in "Oil and Mineral Rights Agreements, 1905–1920," in CO 874/349.

6. "Sultan Omer Allie Sapprodin to Capt. Mason," 6 Dec. 1847; also "Sultan Omer Allie Sapprodin to William Glidden," 7 Dec 1847, in CO 144/2.

7. Such diamonds were very, very rare in this part of the world

8. ARA, Bijzondere Voorwaarden der Mijnconcessie Karang Ringin (Afdeeling Moesi Ilir, Resident Palembang) under Besluit #30, 7 Feb. 1902, in 1902, MR #149; Bijzondere Voorwaarden der Mijnconcessie Kahajan (Dayaklanden, Borneo Z.O.) under Besluit #44, 27 Feb. 1902, in 1902, MR #204.

9. The Dutch ambassador in London, Baron Gericke, was confused as to the nature and extent of Dutch claims in East Borneo when a piratical act there necessitated Anglo/Dutch cooperation in 1909. In private correspondence between the Dutch Ministers for the Colonies and Foreign Affairs after this, both stressed the importance of having Dutch envoys familiar with the outlines of Dutch territory in the Indies. Atlases and maps were sent shortly thereafter to Dutch representatives in Berlin, London, Tokyo, Peking, Paris, Constantinople, Stockholm, St. Petersburg, Washington, and Bangkok. See ARA, Ministerie van Kolonien (hereafter MvK) to Ministerie van Buitenlandse Zaken (hereafter, MvBZ), 15 July 1909, #I/14735; MvK 26 Nov 1909, #I/23629, all in (MvBZ/A/277/A.134).

10. See ARA, Archief van de Dienst der Hydrografie (Ministerie van Marine), Box 9: Brievenboek #9, 1891–95: 35, 245, 285.

11. See the English map of Northeastern Borneo, completed in the early twentieth century, which can be found in CO 531/20. Also see the Dutch map "Straat Makassar," reproduced in "Noordooskust Borneo" (1907) 1 May, #6. The penetration of state vision into the maritime periphery becomes more and more apparent in these maps as time passed.

12. See the photos in "Hydrographische Opname in Oost-Indië" 1907, 756–757. The surveying sailing craft *Bloemendaal* is in the foreground of a photograph in this article, beached and now removed from service. The survey steam vessel *Van Gogh*, meanwhile, continues to ply the seas in the background. The symbols the photographer is playing with are obvious: progress steams on, while the old science is left on the beach.

13. See Public Records Office (hereafter, PRO)/Ministry of Trade 10/Harbour Department/#1031/File H/12434 "Alleged Uncharted Reef in the Middle Channel of the Singapore Straits, 1906"; Hickson 1889, 188–189; and Coops 1904, 129.

14. The shaded areas are those that have already been surveyed by the time of publication. The dates indicate the precise years in which the area was mapped. See Craandyk 1910, 75–76.

15. See PRO, Dutch Consul, London to Foreign Office (hereafter, FO), 20 Aug 1909, and FO to British Consul, Hague, 26 Aug, 1909, both in FO/Netherlands Files, "Treaties Concluded Between Holland and Native Princes of the Eastern Archipelago" (#31583). This was true not only between the British and Dutch in Southeast Asia, but also between British Malaya and Siam, for example. For the case of Perak and the Siamese dependencies of Kedah, Kelantan, and Trengganu, see *Perak Gov't Gazette,* 1900: "Agreements Between Her Britannic Majesty and His Siamese Majesty, 29 Nov 1899," 350.

16. ARA, Kommissoriaal, Raad van NI, Advies van de Raad, 10 Jan 1902, in 1902, MR #124a; and in 1902, MR #7; see also "Overeenkomsten met Inlandsche Vorsten: Lingga/Riouw," (1907), 235.

17. "Aantword Namens de Soeltan van Sambas" 1907, 2. It may also have been the case that the Dutch feared advancing British influence here, or a compact between London and Sambas.

18. "Voor de Practijk" 1906, 669. For an account of the rigors of guerrilla warfare in the border residencies, see Gayo 1983, 217–235.

19. ARA, Rapport 29 March 1899, in 1899, MR #292; Cayaux "Voorschriften voor de Watervoorziening," (1906), 80.

20. ARA, Aantal Lijders aan Beri-Beri, Die op Ultimo November 1898 Onder Behandeling Zijn Gebleven, in 1899, MR #67; Koster 1902, 21.

21. ARA, 1899, MR #706; ARA, Commander, NEI Army to GGNEI, 10 Nov 1888, #1022, in 1899, MR #94; ARA, 1899, MR #709.

22. Memorie van Overgave, Borneo Zuid-Oost, 1906, (MMK #270), 1; van den Doel 1994a, 60–67.

23. ARA, MvBZ Circulaire to the Dutch Envoys in London, Paris, Berlin, and Washington, 1 Feb 1895, #1097; MvBZ Circulaire to Dutch Envoys in Austro-Hungary, Sweden, Norway, and Russia, 2 Nov 1896, #11265; Dutch Consul, Lisbon to MvBZ, 18 April 1895, #59/38; Dutch Consul Madrid to MvBZ, 1 Feb 1901, #36/10, all in (MvBZ/A/421/A.182).

24. ARA, Dutch Consul, Paris, to MvBZ, 14 Feb 1900, #125/60, in (MvBZ/A/421/A.182); ARA, Dutch Consul, Berlin to MvBZ, 3 Aug 1904; 22 May 1903; 5 April 1902; 6 July 1899; 17 June 1898; 13 July 1897, and 30 Nov 1896, all in (MvBZ/A/421/A.182).

25. "The Navy Estimates" in *The Times* (of London), 3 March 1897, enclosed in ARA, Dutch Consul, London, to MvBZ, 5 March 1897, #113, in (MvBZ/A/421/A.182).

26. "The Destroyer Yamakaze" in *The Japan Times,* 4 June 1910, enclosed under ARA, Dutch Consul, Tokyo, to MvBZ, 13 June 1910, #560/159, in (MvBZ/A/421/A.182).

27. ARA, 1902, MR #25, 48, 92, 132.

28. ARA, Memorie van Overgave, Borneo Zuid-Oost, 1906, (MMK #270), 24.

29. ARA, 1899, MR #36.

30. *Utusan Malayu,* 30 Jan 1909, 1. The best secondary source on policing in the Indies is Bloembergen 2009.

31. Memorie van Overgave, West Borneo (MMK, 1912, #260), 43–4.

32. M. W. Sibelhoff "Gewapende Politiedienaran," (1907), 864–865; Memorie van Overgave, Billiton (MMK, 1907, #250), 32.

33. ARA, Police Commissioner's Instructions, enclosure inside Asst Resident, Batavia, to Resident, Batavia, 26 Feb 1912, #50, in MvBZ/A/40/A.29bisOK.

34. Gov. British North Borneo (hereafter, BNB) to BNB Co. Directorship, 21 Jan 1908 in CO 531/1; FO Jacket, 25 Feb 1910, in CO 531/2.

35. *BNB Official Gazette* #2, Vol 17, 1 Feb 1906, in CO 874/800.

36. CO Jacket, 8 Dec. 1894, in CO 144/69.

37. "Draft Agreement Between Brunei and North Borneo for the Surrender of Fugitive Criminals," 19 March 1908, in CO 531/1.

38. See *Johore Annual Report,* 1916, 23; *Perak Gov't Gazette,* 1902, 6; and *FMS Annual Report for 1901.*

39. De Krijthe, *"Bergkoningin,"* (1983); "Spoor- en Tramwegen" 1921, 69, passim; ARA, 1902, MR #117, 526; ARA, Extract Uit het Register der Besluiten van de GGNEI, 13 Dec 1901, #272, 35, in 1902, MR #38; "Spoorweg-Aanleg op Noord-Sumatra" 1899, 817.

40. Memorie van Overgave, Palembang 1906 (MMK #206), 4; Memorie van Overgave, Lampongs 1913 (MMK #216), p. 110; ARA, 1902, MR #153; Van der Waerden 1904, 175.

41. British Consul, Borneo to FO, 5 March, 1904, in CO 144/78; BNB Co. HQ to CO, 19 Oct 1910 Confidential in CO 531/2.

42. Memorie van Overgave, Palembang, 1906, (MMK #206), 4; ARA, 1902, MR #93; Memorie van Overgave, Jambi, 1908 (MMK #216), 47.

43. ARA, Directeur Burgerlijke Openbare Werken to GGNEI, 31 May 1902, #8564/A, in 1902/MR #542.

44. "Sabang-Baai" 1903, 237–238; Heldring 1900, 630. For a useful analysis of the expansion of harbors generally in North Sumatra during this time, see Airress 1995.

45. ARA, 1902, MR #402. The best modern history of the KPM is a Campo 1992.

46. ARA, Directeur van Financien to GGENI, "Rapport van 5 Jan 1894, #15" in 1894, MR #32; Memorie van Overgave, Borneo Z.O, 1906 (MMK #270), 14.

47. Memorie van Overgave, Jambi, 1908 (MMK #216), 46.

48. ARA, 1897, MR #281; ARA, 1897, MR #527.

49. Of course, this opened up smuggling opportunities on a whole range of new items as well.

50. ARA, Directeur Binnenlandsch Bestuur to GGNEI, 9 Feb 1892, #834, in 1892, MR #634; "Het Corps Ambtenaren," (1887/1888), 286; "Kontroleurs op de Bezittingen Buiten Java" 1884, 14–15.

51. Memorie van Overgave, Sumatra Oostkust, 1910 (MMK #182), 7, 24.

52. Memorie van Overgave, Riouw, 1908 (MMK #236), 1–2; 8. For a good overview, see van den Doel 1994b.

53. ARA, Process Verbaal 4 April 1893, in 1893, MR #608.

References

Airriess, Christopher. 1995. "Port-Centered Transport Development in Colonial North Sumatra." *Indonesia* 59: 65–92.

"Antwoord Namens de Soeltan van Sambas aan de Heer J. L. Swart." 1907. *Koloniaal Weekblad,* no. 20 (16 Mei): 2–4.

"Blakang Padang, Een Concurrent van Singapore." 1902. *Indische Gids* 2: 1295.

Bloembergen, Marijke. 2006. *Colonial Spectacles: The Netherlands and the Dutch East Indies at the World Exhibitions, 1880–1931.* Singapore: Singapore University Press.

———. 2009. *De Geschiedenis van de Politie in Nederlands-Indie.* Leiden: KITLV Press.

Bogaars, G. 1955. "The Effect of the Opening of the Suez Canal on the Trade and Development of Singapore." *Journal of the Malayan Branch of the Royal Asiatic Society* 28 (1): 99–143.

Campo, J. N. F. M. a. 1992. *Koninklijke Paketvaart Maatschappij: Stoomvaart en Staatsvoorming in de Indonesische Archipel, 1888–1914.* Hilversum: Publikaties van de Fakulteit der Historische en Kunstwetenschappen.

Cayaux, H. B. 1908. "Gerechtelijk-Scheikundige Onderzoekingen in Nederlandsch-Indië." *Het Recht in NI* 90: 1–26.

"Controleur op de Buitenbezittingen." 1910. *Koloniaal Weekblad* (19 Mei): 2–3.

Coops, P. C. 1904. "Nederlandsch-Indische Zeekaarten." *Het Nederlandsche Zeewezen* 3: 129–130.

Craandijk, C. 1910. "Het Werk Onzer Opnemingsvaartuigen in den Nederlandsch-Indischen Archipel." *Tijdschrift voor Aardrijkskundige Genootschap* 27: 75–76.

Cremer, J. T. 1907. "Per Automobiel naar de Battakvlakte." *Eigen Haard* 16: 245–253.

Cribb, Robert, ed. 1994a. *The Late Colonial State in Indonesia: Political and Economic Foundations of the Netherlands Indies, 1880–1942.* Leiden: KITLV Press.

Doel, H. W. van den. 1994a. "Military Rule in the Netherlands Indies." In *The Late Colonial State in Indonesia: Political and Economic Foundations of the Netherlands Indies 1880–1942,* ed. Robert Cribb, 60–67. Leiden: KITLV.

———. 1994b. *De Stille Macht: Het Europese Binnenlands Bestuur op Java en Madoera, 1808–1942.* Amsterdam: Bert Bakker.

Eekhout, R. A. 1891. "Aanleg van Staatsspoorwegen in Nederlandsch Borneo en Zuid-Sumatra." *Tijdschrift voor Aardrijkskundige Genootschap,* 2nd ser., 8: 955–983.

Gayo, M. H. 1983. *Perang Gayo Alas Melawan Kolonialis Belanda.* Jakarta: PN Balai Pustaka.

Haeften, J. van. 1895. "Voorkomen van Darmziekten Bij het Leger te Velde." *Indisch Militair Tijdschrift* 2: 80.

Harfield, Alan. 1984. *British and Indian Armies in the East Indies, 1685–1935*. Chippenham: Picton Publishing.

Hart-Everett, A. 1878. "Notes on the Distribution of the Useful Minerals in Sarawak." *Journal of the Straits Branch of the Royal Asiatic Society* 1: 13–30.

Heldring, E. 1900. "Poeloe Weh. Zijne Topographische Beschrijving en Eenige Opmerkingen met Betrekking tot de Beteekenis van het Eiland." *Tijdschrift voor Aardrijkskundige Genootschap*, 2nd ser., 17: 622–639.

Hickson, S. 1889. *A Naturalist in North Celebes*. London: John Murray.

"Hydrographische Opname in Oost-Indië." 1907. *Eigen Haard* 48: 756–759.

Kan, C. M. 1905–1906. "Geographical Progress in the Dutch East Indies 1883–1903." *Report of the Eighth International Geographic Congress. Held in the United States 1904–1905*, 715–723. Washington, DC: Government Printing Office.

"Kontroleurs op de Bezittingen Buiten Java en Madura." 1884. *Indische Gids* 1: 14–20.

Koster, J. L. 1902. "Een Stem over de Drankquestie in het Nederlandsch-Indisch Leger." *Tijdschrift voor Nederlandsch Indie* 21–41.

Kreemer, J. J. 1908. "Bijdrage tot de Volksgeneeskunde bij de Maleiers der Padangsche Benedenlanden." *Bijdragen tot de Indische Taal-, Land-, en Volkenkunde* 60: 438–487.

Kuhn, Philip. 1990. *Soulstealers: The Chinese Sorcery Scare of 1768*. Cambridge, MA: Harvard University Press.

Locher-Scholten, Elsbeth. 1994 . "Dutch Expansion in the Indonesian Archipelago Around 1900 and the Imperialism Debate." *Journal of Southeast Asian Studies* 25 (1): 91–111.

———. 2003. *Sumatran Sultanate and Colonial State: Jambi and the Rise of Dutch Imperialism, 1830–1907*. Ithaca, NY: Cornell University Southeast Asia Program.

Meerwaldt, J. H. 1911. "Per Motorboot 'Tole' het Tobameer Rond." *Rijnsche Zending* 63–69, 83–87, 113–116.

Mrazek, Rudolf. 2002. *Engineers of Happy Land: Technology and Nationalism in a Colony*. Princeton, NJ: Princeton University Press.

Niermeyer, J. F. 1911. "Barrière—Riffen en Atollen in de Oost Indiese Archipel." *Tijdschrift voor Aardrijkskundige Genootschap* 877–894.

"Nieuwe Kaart van Sumatra." 1908. *Indische Mercuur* 31 (38): 680–681.

Oort, W. B. 1909. "Hoe een Groote Kaart tot Stand Komt." *Onze Eeuw* 9 (4): 363–385.

Review of the Netherlands Indian Tariff Law: Tariffs of Import and Export Duties Up to 1 July 1921 (Government Edition). 1921. The Hague: Official Printing Office.

Rossum, J. P. van. 1907. "Bezuiniging bij de Zeemacht Tevens Verbetering." *De Gids* 2: 47–66, 474–491; 3: 287–305.

"Ruilhandel bij de Bahau's van Midden-Borneo." 1909/1910. *Katholieke Missiën* 35: 185–186.

Ruitenbach, D.J. 1905 "Eenige Beschowingen in Verband met het Huidige Politie-Vraagstuk" *Indische Gids*, 2: 985–1014.

"Sabang Baai." 1903. *Het Nederlandsche Zeewezen* 2: 236–247.

Shiraishi, Takashi. 1990. *An Age in Motion*. Ithaca, NY: Cornell University Press.

Snelleman, J. F. 1906. "Tabakspijpen van de Koeboe's aan de Boven-Moesi-Rivier (Sumatra)." *Aarde en Haar Volken* (12 Mei).

"Spoor-en Tramwegen." 1921. *Encyclopaedie van Nederlandsch Indie* Vol. 4, 68–85.

"Spoorwegaanleg op Noord-Sumatra." 1899. *Tijdschrift voor Nederlandsch Indie* 817–820.

Tractaat van Londen 1824; Tractaat van Sumatra 1872; Bepalingen Inzake Kustvaart Doorschoten, met Aantekeningen in Handschrift. Indische Staatsblad # 477, 479, 1912.

"Verduurzaamde Levensmiddelen." 1896. *Indisch Militair Tijdschrift* 1: 482–490.

Vink, J. A. 1899. "Sprokkelingen Uit den Vreemde op het Gebied der Hygiène voor een Leger in de Tropen." *Indisch Militair Tijdschrift* 2: 676–686.

"Voor de Practijk." 1906. *Indisch Militair Tijdschrift* 2: 669.

"Voorstel tot Opheffing van het Verbod dat de Vreemde Vlag Uitsluit van de Kustvaart in Nederlandsch Indië." 1887. *Indische Gids* 1: 938–942.

Waerden, J. van der. 1904. "Spoorwegaanleg in Zuid-Sumatra." *Indisch Bouwkundig Tijdschrift* 7 (9): 173–182.

Water, J. van de. 1902. "Doelmatige Kleeding. Algemeene Eischen aan Kleeding te stellen." *Indisch Militair Tijdschrift* 1: 230–246; 2: 212–227.

"Waterdichte Kleedingstukken." 1897. *Indisch Militair Tijdschrift* 1: 224–225.

"Waterval van Mansalar." 1911. *Tijdschrift voor Aardrijkskundige Genootschap* 28: 109.

"Ziekenbehandeling onder de Dayaks (Midden Borneo) Door een Missionaris Capucijn." 1908. *Katholieke Missiën* 33: 99–101.

Zondervan, H. 1900. "Bijdrage tot de Kennis der Eilanden Bangka en Blitong." *Tijdschrift voor Aardrijkskundige Genootschap* 17: 519–527.

1956

Bangalore's Cosmopolitan Pasts and Monocultural Futures?

ANDREW WILLFORD

As Bangalore has come to signify "progress" and economic possibility, both within India, and to the outside world, to whom it turns for investment, it—as the capital of the linguistically drawn state of Karnataka—has become increasingly charged by movements to make the city more monocultural and monolinguistic. The very unsettling forces of globalization that produce inward migration, development, and landscape transformations, coupled with the redrawing of political maps within a postcolonial context, now organized along imaginaries of singular linguistic and cultural identification, produce monocultural fantasies that contradict the densely textured forms of pre- and early modern cosmopolitanism that have been inscribed onto the landscape of the Deccan, and in the Bangalore region in particular.

More generally, the processes by which postcolonial technologies of statecraft create modern forms of identification is investigated. Here, the characteristically modern and serial forms of identification that take hold under certain conditions of enumeration and imagination demonstrate alternative possibilities through their suppression. These possibilities, while muted in the violence of serial identification, subsist in the layered cultural practices and idioms that mark what might be called cosmopolitan pasts. The question, then, is to what extent pluralism can survive the onslaught of modernity, allowing for what Ashis Nandy has called an incorporation of the Other's myths as one's own (2002).

This chapter ultimately points to sites of cultural practice that work against the monocultural imaginaries that threaten the older fabrics of cosmopolitanism that have continuously existed within the greater Bangalore region. I argue that it is only in the postcolonial rendering of linguistic states that a linear history has demanded territorial linguistic nationalism and, with it, an impossible disentangling of entangled and complex linguistic and cultural pasts (see too Yang, this volume, on this point in different contexts). While many scholars, including several in this volume, point towards the maritime interconnections that linked specific Asian locales within wider circuits of circulation, I call attention to the historical crossroads that was South Asia's Deccan and suggest that it was a zone of contact between several overlapping empires and a wider world. But with the birth of the modern Indian state, the more fluid and protean identities that emerged within the Deccan became increasingly ossified due to the measurement of language affiliation. That is, there has been, at the level of statecraft and regional politics, a disentangling of more fluid and protean identities. Ironically, these "modern" parochialisms have emerged at the very moment when Bangalore has become, arguably, India's most cosmopolitan and global city.

1956 is the watershed moment, I suggest, in this narrative, as this was the year in which Bangalore became the undivided capital of the linguistic state of Karnataka. Given the "serial" imagination that ensued from this legal designation, a new possibility for imagining differences came into being. As Benedict Anderson (1998) has shown, the processes by which both "bound" (e.g., measurement through census) and "unbound" (imagined communities through newspapers, novels, films) seriality in identities are imagined can produce the phantasm of types, or the silencing of the fractal and porous or fluid nature of identities. These differences, I suggest, have become the basis for institutionalizing political divisions.

But the impossibility of these identities to exist without a suppression of a more complex multiplicity raises a question of rationalization. While it could be argued that a cynical and tactical implementation of new forms of identification can be worn like a coat, it is more plausible, I would suggest, to say that the positive investment in an identity claim occurs following its violent first iteration. That is, as arbitrary identities are created and sustained by statecraft and adjudicated by law, people, in a more imperceptible way, invest in the enactment of identities. But they can never fully occupy these identities, given the fluid pasts these identities attempt to efface.

Bangalore in History

Bangalore lies on the cool Deccan plateau directly between Madras and the tropical Malabar coast. Though the history of the city begins in the sixteenth century CE, the region—comprising of many ancient villages, forts, and pilgrimage sites—has been at the crossroads of South Indian history since the seventh century CE. During the last 2,000 years, the region has been ruled by various southern empires, resulting in the spread of religious ideas, the migrations and mixing of linguistically diverse populations, and the emergence of synthetic local traditions.

Between the sixth and eighth centuries CE, the Chalukya Empire ruled much of the central Deccan from their capital cities of Vatapi and Aihole, in present-day northern Karnataka. At the southeastern border of their empire were tensions with the other great southern empire of this period, the Pallavas. The Pallavas ruled from Kanchipuram and Mahabalipuram (near present-day Madras). The Bangalore region was to fall under both Chalukya and Pallava rule and cultural influence during this period (Thapar 1966; Sastri 1975). The distinctive Tamil school of Hinduism known as Saiva Siddhanta developed in the Pallava- and Pandyan-controlled areas (Pandya was a kingdom in the deep south). This form of Hindu practice, and the development of Tamil poetry and hagiography that emerged from it, spread to the Deccan, where Kannadigas (Kannada speakers) and Telugus also developed this branch of Saivism (Thapar 1966; Ramasamy 1997).

The next empire to exert cultural influence upon the Bangalore region was that of the Cholas. As the Pallavas and Chalukyas declined in power,[1] the Cholas attained dominance over much of the Deccan and Tamil-speaking areas in the tenth and eleventh centuries. The Cholas ruled from Thanjavur, in present-day Tamil Nadu. Their rule was a golden age for Tamil literature, the arts, and the development of a classical Dravidian style of temple architecture. By 1024 CE, the Bangalore region was under Chola rule and was called Nikarilacholamandala (Gangrams 1994; Annaswamy 2003).

By the twelfth century, the Hoysalas gained ascendancy over the Chola territories near today's Bangalore. The Hoysala Empire assumed much of the territory formerly under the Chalukyas and was patron of Kannada. But whereas Saivism flourished among Tamils, Vaishnavism took root within the Hoysala realm.Vaishnavism was popularized in Karnataka in the eleventh and twelfth centuries by Ramanuja, a Tamil Brahmin who became famous throughout India due to the development of a school of Vedanta known as Visishtadvaita, which reconciled personal devotion with Vedanta philosophy.

The last great empire to rise in the South was that of Vijayanagara. This empire, which arose in the mid-fourteenth century, came to dominate much of South India for over 300 years. Though based in northern Karnataka, it extended deep into Tamil- and Telugu-speaking areas as well. Vijayanagara allowed a degree of local autonomy within Tamil (Chola) territories, operating as a confederation with loyalty to one Hindu-preserving emperor (Sastri 1975; Stein 1994).

The city of Bangalore was founded by a Vijayanagara chieftain named Kempegowda I in 1527.[2] Both Kempegowda I and his son, Kempegowda II utilized Vijayanagara revenues to build a fort, clear roads, build temples, and erect watchtowers in the city. The Vijayanagara king Krishnadevaraya granted control of the land south of Bangalore (present-day southern Karnataka) to a Tamil Brahman (Iyengar) named Govindaraja. As in earlier times, the region was linguistically cosmopolitan under Vijayanagara rule.

The seventeenth and eighteenth centuries were politically turbulent after the fall of Vijayanagara. In 1638, Bangalore was captured by the Sultan of Bijapur. The city was then sold to Chikkadevaraja Wodeyar, the Raja of Mysore, in 1687. Eventually, however, the city was surrendered to Hyder Ali, a general in the Mysore army, in 1759. Hyder Ali and his son Tippu had gradually supplanted the Wodeyars as monarchs in the kingdom after a series of decisive battles against the Magadi kingdom to the north. Under Hyder Ali and Tippu Sultan, Bangalore grew as an important satellite to Srirangapatna, from where the Sultan ruled from (Nair 2011).

The British captured Bangalore in 1791 and returned rule to the Wodeyar Rajas from Mysore. But the British also built the largest cantonment in South India adjacent to the old city in 1809. The "Cantonment" also became the principal British administrative center for the region. Railway links between Madras and the Cantonment allowed for increased trade between the two cities; more importantly, the Cantonment section of Bangalore became an administrative and military extension of the Madras Presidency. The Cantonment attracted a large population of immigrants to Bangalore in order to serve the needs of the growing British population. Civil servants, traders, contractors, artisans, laborers, and servants were recruited to the Cantonment. Most were Tamil speakers (Srinivas 1994; Nair 2005).

In effect, the Cantonment and the old city became two entities. One result of this division was the dramatic growth of the city. Additionally, Bangalore, though always at the crossroads of various empires in the South, became a border town between the Tamil- and Kannada-speaking states. After independence, the Cantonment section of Bangalore remained part of the Madras Presidency until 1956, when state boundaries in India were redrawn along linguistic lines.

With the creation of Karnataka in 1956 and the redrawing of state boundaries, the Tamils in Bangalore found themselves a minority within the capital of a Kannada-speaking state. But the multilinguistic legacy of the city made English the lingua franca for government and law. Most Bangaloreans grew up speaking many languages, including Kannada, Telugu, Hindu-Urdu, and Tamil and were thus able to communicate freely with each other.

Postindependence Bangalore has become one of the most developed and prosperous cities in all of India. Its favorable climate has also attracted many expatriates and multinational corporations. Yet, in spite of these developments, the city has witnessed increased linguistic tensions. I now turn to the Tamil-Kannadiga tensions that erupted in Bangalore in response to a dispute over the kidnapping of a Kannada film icon by a Tamil bandit and would-be political rebel. I suggest, in turn, that this incident, while related to an annual conflict over the sharing of Cauvery River water between Karnataka and Tamil Nadu, is really symptomatic of the provocation caused by serial forms of identification.

Rajkumar's Abduction

On July 30, 2000, the Kannada film hero Rajkumar was kidnapped by a notorious Tamil bandit and smuggler named Veerapan. Rajkumar was not just any film icon, he was the Kannada equivalent of Tamil Nadu's actor-turned politician, MGR. Rajkumar, a star since the 1960s, had long been a champion of Kannadiga identity and rights in Karnataka.[3] His abduction led to small riots across the city of Bangalore, as bands of Rajkumar fan club members and Kannada associations threw stones at businesses with glass facades, universities, and other establishments associated with the elite. Public transport was halted in solidarity with the hero, and people were also forced to abandon private vehicles and walk home. Random attacks against Tamils occurred, particularly directed against the poor, mostly migrant laborers to the city.

These attacks recurred after the death of Rajkumar of natural causes a few years later. As one Tamil professional told me,

> After the death of Rajkumar, random attacks against the poor Tamils became a problem again. The middle-class don't bother about these things. It is a lower middle-class phenomena. Cauvery [water] is an issue once a year, and leads to protests and violence. After the death, people were throwing stones at glass windows of auto dealerships and into the IISc [Indian Institute of Science] compound. There were all sorts of atrocities for two days while they decided what to do with the body. On the TV, no Tamil stations were allowed for two months—they were blocked, even the satellite ones. Tamil shops and taxi drivers put Rajkumar photos up to survive. There was even a moratorium on Tamil movies for 60 days after their release in order to support Kannada films.[4]

This individual's comment, which was echoed by several other professionals I met, both amongst Tamils and Kannadigas, is significant as it locates the source of violence as emanating from the lower middle-class, and not the poor. Moreover, the poor, particularly the migrant laboring poor, were on the receiving end of this violence. This parallels what Hansen (2001) has observed for the Shiv Sena-led violence against minorities in Mumbai and speaks to the creation of a political constituency forged on communal affiliation, as explicitly linked to perceived economic threats.

Back to the earlier kidnapping: for 108 days, Rajkumar was held hostage by Veerapan. Throughout his ordeal, rallies, *bandhs* (strikes), and prayer meetings were held throughout the city, organized by his fans and family members (Nair 2005, 235). When he was finally released after successful negotiations between Tamil business and cultural leaders and Veerapan, the city erupted in a "carnival of joy" (Nair 2005, 235). Tamil-owned businesses survived the ordeal by placing photos of the film hero in their shop fronts.

A prominent Tamil businessmen explained to me that the consequences of the kidnapping were high, and thus the stakes for his release were consequential to all Tamils in Karnataka. Though Veerapan engaged in this criminal act ostensibly on behalf of the plight of Tamils in Karnataka,[5] his actions were believed to endanger Tamil interests and to embolden hard-line Kannadigas.

Veerapan had, as a result of this kidnapping, become a Robin Hood for some Tamils, but many were quick to distance themselves from him, particularly those in public positions. R. S. Maran, then-President of the Tamil Sangam of Bangalore, expressed frustration with the government's eagerness to negotiate with Veerapan, having ignored the Sangam's nonviolent petitions for years. This was, as Janaki Nair argues, not just about a film hero; rather, the "predicament of Rajkumar was in fact the predicament of Kannada itself, held hostage to what was perceived as the more robust nationalism of the Tamils" (Nair 2005, 237).

In order to understand this feeling of being "held hostage," one needs to revisit the colonial boundaries and demographics of a city located between two major states. As discussed earlier, Bangalore was, in fact, bifurcated between the Madras Presidency and the Mysore State at the administrative and geographic level. The Cantonment fell under British control and was demographically dominated by Tamils. The Kannadiga parts of town were largely in the old city, away from the Cantonment. Drawing linguistic states in 1956 and, in particular, making Bangalore Karnataka's capital city generated the impetus to homogeneity out of pluralism. In short, enumeration, serialization, and statecraft created the conditions of insecurity, as identities became fixed out of greater multiplicity.

As Nair argues, the very "cosmopolitanism" of Bangalore—both its historic pluralism and its modern IT economy, which brings people from all over India and the world to the metropolis—is its condition of lack, as far as the aggrieved Kannadiga community experience it. Demography is hard to pin down in such a context. According to a 1991 census, 35 percent of the city's residents considered Kannada their mother tongue, as compared to 25 percent for Tamil. More recently, I had been told that Telugus outnumber both Kannadigas and Tamils. Kannada activists considered themselves increasingly a minority within their capital city, and feared "losing Bangalore to outsiders." Suggestions for Kannadiga in-migration from other parts of Karnataka have been made, and pro-Kannada legislation in education, public spaces, and administrative use have not assuaged this sense of insecurity. Indeed, prior to much of the pro-Kannada agitation, many Tamils did, in fact, describe their lives within the Cantonment areas as unaffected by Kannada language and politics. As R. S. Maran, former President of the Tamil Sangam, [6]told me, "we thought we were living in Tamil Nadu." He was referring to the "Tamil" nature of certain parts of the city and, as well, to the understanding that many older Tamils felt they had been living under the jurisdiction of the Madras Presidency, prior to the creation of Karnataka.

In order to understand recent sentiments surrounding the kidnapping of Rajkumar, it is important to look at one watershed event in the relations between Tamils and Kannadigas in Bangalore: the Cauvery riots of 1991 and their aftermath. Understanding the impact of this event upon the relations between communities, in turn, helps us understand the hardening of divisions between what was once a more integrated Bangalore. Following this, I turn to the rise of the Kannada movement, suggesting that even in a Tamil response to this, the vestiges of an old pluralism undercut the exclusivist claims by one community or another. In short, a historicity that confounds seriality is still part of a "landscape of urban memory" (Srinivas 2000).

The Cauvery Riots

The Cauvery River flowed quietly on the morning of December 13, 1991, oblivious to the battle over her waters that was waging between Tamil Nadu and Karnataka. This struggle had become a war of wits between the Chief Ministers of both states: J. Jayalalitha and S. Bangarappa respectively. Two days earlier, the Central Government, under then Prime Minister P. V. Narasimha Rao, had instructed the Cauvery tribunal to award Tamil Nadu 205 million cubic feet of water from Karnataka. It was widely reported in the national news media as a major victory for Jayalalitha over Bangarappa. This was a blow to Bangarappa's status (and perhaps to his ego as well) as a favored "son of the soil" among the farmers in Karnataka. For months, he had promised that not "one drop" of Cauvery water would be given to Tamil Nadu. Now he faced the humiliation of the Central Government's decision.

On December 12, the Rajkumar Fans Association staged a large procession in order to protest the Central Government's decision. This procession indulged in stone throwing and the chanting of anti-Tamil slogans. It was reported later by witnesses that the police did nothing to stop marchers who were getting out of hand. To the contrary, Bangarappa had ordered a "state *bandh*" (general strike) to protest the award. The *bandh*—aside from being unconstitutional—provided an opportunity for various "*goondas*" (thugs) to incite or engage in rioting against Tamils in Karnataka.

Riots were initially instigated by a rumor spread in the press and by word of mouth throughout Bangalore and Mysore that a Kannadiga woman had been molested and assaulted in the Nilgiri Mountains in Tamil Nadu. Angered Kannadigas in Mysore and Bangalore attacked Tamils and their properties. Soon violence escalated against Tamils in Bangalore. Eyewitness reports to the violence even implicated the police. There were accusations that the police, acting under the orders of certain "chauvinist politicians," had aided the rioters. The angry mobs focused their hostility against the poorest of all people in Bangalore, the migrant labor force living in squatter settlements and slums in and around the city (Nair 2005). The established and wealthier Tamil neighborhoods in Bangalore were spared the worst, as poor farmers and construction laborers bore the brunt of the violence. According to an independent tribunal investigating the riots, a number of incidents occurred which suggested police involvement, or at best, indifference to the victims (IPHRC 1992).[7]

The Tamil working-class and migrant-laborer area of Srirampuram in Bangalore was the site of a major disturbance. Reports by victims suggested police involvement (IPHRC 1992, 9). In M. G. Nagar, a slum area, there were reports of violence perpetrated by Rajkumar fan clubs against Tamil migrants. One witness said that a mob of about 1,500 had attacked Tamils while shouting "*Rajkumar ki Jai*" ("Victory to Rajkumar"). Another reported that the mobs were carrying Rajkumar photos when they attacked (IPHRC 1992, 13–15). The invocation of Rajkumar was due in part to the actor's pro-Kannada activism, but it was also in response to the allegiance that Tamils showed to their film and political hero, MGR. It was not uncommon to see MGR flags and pictures prominently displayed in migrant labor slums. In this sense, we see the emergence of an "unbound serial" identity in Anderson's sense (1998), which had taken root among Tamils through the film industry, being mimicked by that of another. That is, Rajkumar became the Kannada mirror of MGR's ubiquitous image. Thus the slogans and pictures were aimed at insulting the symbolic champion for the Tamils.

It was estimated that over 100,000 Tamils had fled from Karnataka into neighboring Tamil Nadu. The estimated cost in damages exceeded 100,000,000 rupees. Also, over 290 people were injured and 12 were reported to have died as a result of the riots in and around Bangalore (IPHRC 1992).

Many Tamils, including influential members of the Bangalore Tamil Sangam, accused Bangarappa of inciting the riots by calling for the *bandh*. It was believed by many that he had used the Cauvery dispute as a pretext to deflect criticisms of corruption against his government.[8] Many Tamil farmers had resided in Karnataka for decades and thus had as much to lose as Kannadigas if water was given to Tamil Nadu. Therefore, these Tamils were "perplexed" by the turn of events which had led to the attacks (Saritha Roy, 1992).

Bangarappa's critics suggested that he had utilized the Cauvery pretext in order to clear slums for economic and political gain. They argued that he was targeting the recent large influx of migrant workers who—it was being argued by certain Kannadiga politicians—were taking jobs away from Kannadigas (*India Today,* January, 1992). Others suggested that Tamils were being driven off their land and properties as a political reward for the *goondas* and Kannadiga landlords who were loyal to the Chief Minister. In the rural outlying districts of Bangalore, it was suggested that Tamil tenant farmers, being outside of the village's moral economy and having no *panchayat* (village council) representation, were easy targets in riots aimed at clearing them from the lands they had helped make fertile (IPHRC 1992, 24). In fact, during the riots in and around Bangalore, local police encouraged Tamils to go to Tamil Nadu for "their own safety": "The evidence shows that at Bangalore and surrounding towns people were put in the trains and they were sent to Tamil Nadu. In the district places the government itself arranged government State Transport buses to Tamil Nadu" (IPHRC 1992, 53). As a result of this action, tens of thousands of Tamils left Karnataka. The eagerness with which the Tamils were deported suggested government involvement to critics: "The police were keen to see that the Tamilians were sent to Tamil Nadu . . . it was a planned and systematically executed conspiracy to loot the Tamilians and to drive them away" (IPHRC 1992, 31; *India Today,* January, 1992). Most incriminating was the evidence that certain powerful politicians had instructed the police to "go soft" on the rioters (*Deccan Herald,* November 29, 1992; *The Hindu,* November 27, 1992).

Kannada organizations also presented evidence that Kannadigas had also been affected by the disturbances. But whereas the Tamil cases mostly concerned violence or property damage, the Kannadiga groups seemed to justify their discontent by arguing that Tamils had become too influential in Karnataka through the help of the DMK and the AIADMK (the prominent political parties in Tamil Nadu).[9] Kannada Shakti Kendre (a pro-Kannada organization) president and Professor of Kannada, Dr. M. Chidananda Murthy, argued before the tribunal that Kannada should be made the sole administrative language in Karnataka in an attempt to thwart the growing influence of the DMK and AIADMK in Bangalore. He argued that Kannada was endangered through the increasing political power of Tamils in Bangalore. He also criticized the State Government for not issuing an "executive order" preventing people from conducting political and legal transactions in languages other than Kannada or English (*The Hindu,* January 16, 1992).

Aside from the physical costs of the riots, there was an additional loss of trust between the Tamil community and the State Government. Tamils began to question their security in the state (*India Today,* January 31, 1991). Businesses that had been vandalized for having Tamil signboards replaced them with Kannadiga ones.

The incident produced a heightened consciousness of Tamil identity. Some Tamils, it was reported in the *Deccan Herald,* wanted Central Government rule for Bangalore as a result of the riots. This position angered Kannadiga politicians and the Deputy Commissioner of Police in Bangalore. Deputy Commissioner Kempaiah reported to the Cauvery Tribunal that it had come to his attention as early as 1984 that some Tamils felt discriminated against and had requested that Bangalore come under the Central Administration's control. He said that the Rajkumar Fans Association and other organizations had taken "strong exception" to this request. Kempaiah went on to explain that the Tamil Sangam and local DMK and AIADMK branches were the only major organizations in Bangalore which did not support the December 13 *bandh.* This, he argued, resulted in tensions between Tamils and the Kannadigas. Furthermore, Kempaiah pointed out, the Tamil Sangam in Bangalore had been an active supporter of the cause of the LTTE (Liberation Tigers of Tamil Ealam in Sri Lanka) prior to Rajiv Gandhi's assassination (*Deccan Herald,* November 1, 1992). Also, he argued that Tamil groups have "lacked loyalty to Karnataka" through their continuing allegiance to the Tamil language and reported that even after Rajiv's death, there were members of the Tamil Sangam who were willing to help the LTTE (*Deccan Herald,* November 1, 1992). He also criticized the Tamil Sangam for unveiling a large Sri Thiruvallavur statue in front of the organization's premises.[10] He said that many pro-Kannada organizations were against the unveiling of this statue, as there were not any statues in the city honoring Kannada poets and saints.[11]

Kempaiah had utilized a media platform to make a case against the Tamils. He chronicled many stereotypical grievances against Tamils and, by extension, rationalized the behavior of the Rajkumar Fans Association and other groups. Also, by invoking the Rajiv Gandhi assassination—still an open sore at this time—he indirectly accused Tamils of antinationalist sentiments and activities. Raising the bogey of Tamil radicalism and hinting at anti-Karnataka activities and sentiments, in turn, reinforced Tamil suspicions that the police were instructed by the State Government to not interfere with the rioting. Such public anti-Tamil sentiment only heightened a sense of Tamil identity and solidarity.

Arguably, the violence at the heart of the Law was revealed to the Tamil community through these acts and their rationalizations. That is, the arbitrary foundations of linguistic statehood were made clear by the police and the Chief Minister's collusion with the violent acts, even if only through its post-facto rationalization. As Agamben (2005) has argued, a "state of exception" to legal rights shores up an "anomie" at the heart of the Law. In this case, the law's conjoining to an identity claim born of the serial imagination, in Anderson's sense, over and against the more plural and porous identities that existed prior to 1956, opened a hole in the whole of the Law, whilst also providing the grist for its critique or deconstruction. As Derrida (2002) argues, building on Benjamin and Schmitt, the interpretability of a legal decision is always retroactive in the sense that it becomes grounded in subsequent decisions. These subsequent decisions serve as the supplement of the "arche-violence" of an original (and arbitrary) decision. In the context of an ethno-nationalist claim, the supplementary logic comes in the form of an archive of difference that is often retroactively constructed in the form of rationalizations for some form of originary violence inscribed into the law. In this case, the retroactive "case" against Tamils became the archive for the police and state to justify their exceptionality. Reciprocally, an emergent victim's narrative takes nurturance in the perceived lack in the Other's claim, equally generative of an archive to establish its counterclaim.

While living in Bangalore just six months after the Cauvery disturbances, and during the media coverage of the inquiry proceedings, I found that Tamil-Kannadiga tensions ran high. When I mentioned to Kannadigas that I was studying Tamil language and culture, I was often told that Bangalore was "a Kannada area," and some suggested that I "go to Madras to learn about Tamils." I was told that the Tamils in Bangalore did not want to interact with Kannadigas. The Tamils, as I was told, kept to themselves, spoke their language with each other, refused to learn Kannada, and patronized businesses in their own communities. One Kannadiga told me that Telugus and Malayalees were more "integrated" with the Kannadigas than the Tamils were. The impression I received from Kannadigas was that the Tamils were "insular" and "kept to themselves." Another Kannadiga said that the Tamils were successful because "they worked hard" and had good business sensibilities. Kannadigas, on the other hand, she said, were "lazy and apathetic." Tamils would sometimes say that they were resented because of their "hard work" and success. There was a common sentiment among Kannadigas that because they were "so easy-going and tolerant," they were slow to react to the increased Tamil presence in the state. The Tamils were perceived to be an industrious community that had become wealthy and politically influential.

Most Tamils I met spoke proudly of their cultural heritage. I was told numerous times that Tamil was the "oldest continuously used language in the world" and that Dravidian culture stems from the genius of the "Tamil civilization." But I was rarely told by any Tamils that they felt loyal to Tamil Nadu over Karnataka. To the contrary, loyalty to Karnataka was displayed in all Tamil-speaking areas. In fact, I could not find a signboard in Tamil on any businesses—even in Tamil enclaves. But I was told that this was due to threats to burn down or vandalize shops with signs in Tamil.[12] One Bangalore-based DMK activist that I spoke with explained: "I used to have the signs in front of my bookstore in Tamil, but now, for the last ten years—especially after Cauvery—almost all of the Tamil signs had to be taken down . . . It is because of the politicians." Another Tamil activist said that "Kannadigas and Mewaris [Rajasthani merchants] support one another in attempting to hurt the businesses of Tamils." The same activist suggested that the ethnic stereotypes really served the economic interests of these non-Tamil businesses. Threats against businesses having Tamil signboards sometimes made news in the local papers, prompting more Tamil businesses to remove their Tamil lettering.

Most Tamils I met celebrated Rajyotsatva Day (Karnataka Statehood Day) and spoke proudly about the prosperity, cleanliness, and orderliness of Karnataka as compared to Tamil Nadu. On the other hand, Tamils were aware of negative Kannadiga perceptions of them; they resented the stereotypes that were expressed in the newspapers. Some even suggested that the Kannadigas were "jealous" of the Tamils because of their work ethic. One elderly Tamil woman from a middle-class background told me that she had gone into a shop in the Cantonment she had patronized for years and spoke in Tamil as she always had done. A policeman who happened to be in the store told her to speak in Kannada because she was "not in Tamil Nadu." She said that this frightened her and made her self-conscious about her Tamil identity for the first time. The implication for her and others was that one could no longer take one's neighborhood or mother tongue for granted. Rather, there were now precautions to take, whether it be removing Tamil signboards or watching out for Kannadiga police (or Rajkumar fans) before speaking Tamil (even in so-called Tamil speaking areas).

The awakening of ethnic and linguistic sentiment in Bangalore cannot be understood in terms of the Cauvery dispute in and of itself—though this provided a catalyst to mobilize chauvinistic forces.[13] A look at the pro-Kannada movement and the subsequent awakening of Tamil consciousness in Bangalore highlights the historical antecedents to the riots.

The Kannada Movement

The Kannada movement seeks to awaken the Kannadigas to the "plight of the Kannada language" and to apply political pressure to ensure that the State Government commits to funding and legislation designed to promote the Kannada language and its literary tradition, while also making it the sole administrative language of education, business, and government.[14]

The president of the Kannada Shakti Kendra (Center for Kannada Power), Dr. Chidananda Murthy, has been one of the most outspoken proponents of the Kannada movement. He has argued that Tamils are fast growing in population and influence in Bangalore; but, he maintains, they do not assimilate or attempt to learn the Kannada language. Furthermore, he felt that Tamil migrants had taken jobs away from Kannadigas. Arguing before the Cauvery inquiry, he said:

> Many Tamils maintain their separate identities and do not mix with the locals. This had given rise to an apprehension in the minds of Kannadigas that Tamils may claim Bangalore city in the course of time. (*Deccan Herald,* January 14, 1993)

He suggested that Tamil organizations should bear the responsibility costs for offering Kannada courses to Tamils. Saying that the State Government should not have to bear the cost of educating Tamil migrants, he added that those who come to Karnataka should take it upon themselves to learn Kannada (*Deccan Herald,* January 16, 1993). The Kannada Sahitya Parishat President, Go. Channabasappa, called upon the State Government to regulate the influx of immigrants and to show the political will necessary to "insure the primacy of Kannada in the State" (*Deccan Herald,* October 20, 1992).

Various pro-Kannada groups applied pressure to the State Government in response to a perceived threat to their language. The growing Kannada movement helped Bangarappa get elected as Chief Minister, as he had campaigned on a pro-Kannada platform. In the year following the riots, in September 1992, the Kannada Development Authority (a State-sponsored organization) announced that 1993 would be "Kannada Awareness Year." The State Government promised to act on the recommendations of the Kannada Development Authority. The Authority asked for assistance implementing extensive Kannada education in border areas with Tamil Nadu, and they requested 5,000 Kannada typewriters be made available. Also, the Authority argued that although the State was supposed to have conducted all administrative affairs in Kannada since 1963, in 1992 only 5 percent of administrative work was conducted in Kannada (English was used primarily)—this, in spite of the fact that 90 percent of all Government employees were Kannadigas.

In addition to these pro-Kannada political pressures, there were more moderate and intellectual forces within the Kannada Movement. Most prominent among these was U. R. Ananthamurthy, the award-winning author of the Kannada and English bestseller, *Samskara: Rites for a Dead Man.* On the occasion of Rajyotsatva Day (Karnataka Statehood Day), Ananthamurthy argued:

> [T]he absurdity (in India) . . . the more literate you are, the less languages you know. There are two issues which need to be addressed—mobility and selfhood. We need to be mobile within the country even while we retain our selfhood. (*Deccan Herald,* October 30, 1992)

Ananthamurthy suggested, like many Tamil activists, that the Cauvery violence was state-sponsored and "shameful." But at the same time, he requested that the State Government help "reconstruct" Kannada by deemphasizing the importance of English and Hindi. Following this sentiment and moving it towards a general critique of the "Westernization" that the opening of markets to foreign investors in India is creating, Dr. R. Nagaraj argued:

> The movement can be used effectively as a weapon against the onslaught of the so-called universal market culture which seeks to destroy local cultures and traditions. It can be a very genuine protest against the cultural invasion of the commercial West. But unfortunately, I don't find such a larger understanding of issues in today's Kannada movement. (*Deccan Herald,* October 30, 1992)

While providing a cultural and intellectual justification for the Kannada Movement, both Ananthamurthy and Nagaraj were also unhappy with recent settlers who, in the words of Nagaraj, "are yet to integrate themselves with Kannada culture and Karnataka" (*Deccan Herald*, October 30, 1992). At the same time, they cast the struggle as one between the central government and Kannada rather than focusing their criticism on Tamils or other recent settlers. Rather, they suggested that the recent ethnic strife was a symptom of market forces.

While there is apparently room for debate and disagreement within the Kannada Movement, I was told that the climate had changed dramatically for Tamils in Bangalore. A local Tamil academic explained how he had to show public sympathy for the Kannada Movement, as he was one of only five Tamil-speaking faculty at his college. Also, Kannadiga colleagues, while privately sympathetic to Tamils, would not speak in support of the Tamil plight publicly. He spoke of the passions over language that guide the "historical consciousness" of Tamils and Kannadigas, noting that such sentiments are easily manipulated by political leaders. Quoting Chidananda Murthy, the pro-Kannada activist who said of the riots, "they are about history, not about water," he described the use of Vijayanagar motifs used as decorations throughout Bangalore during Rajyosatva Day. He added that the "Cholas and Pallavas are part of the average Tamil's consciousness." Criticism was also leveled against leaders of the Tamil movement: "most Tamil academics are 'fundamentalists' with little or no respect for Kannada." His criticism also took a more negative turn:

> There is a fundamental flaw in the Tamil mind and culture. One can look at a Tamil today and see 1,000 years of thought guiding him. The emphasis on subjectivity is such that the dissenting or questioning mind is not present. Why else would people kill themselves for a man who did nothing for them.[15] It is this emphasis on the "One," and surrendering to the "One" that leads to the despotic leaders' ability to rule over others. The gurus don't want you to question them intellectually—they want absolute control and surrender on the devotees' part. Those like Vivekananda and Radhakrishnan who interpreted Indian thought as being skeptical and democratic were influenced by English thought. They were at least 50 percent Western. Thus their message was completely misunderstood.[16]

The "One" he speaks of is whatever ideology motivates people towards emotionalism over reason. Thus he was equally critical of religious, ethnic, or linguistic fanaticisms—all of which, he maintained, were tearing at the fabric of India and Bangalore.

But he seemed to also imply that linguistic and religious tensions in Bangalore were ultimately underscored by economic concerns. He cited the rise in Hindu fundamentalism that corresponded, he maintained, with the increasing corruption of the State Government. That is, he suggested that those most vulnerable to corruption charges (the business and political elite) were pouring money into various Hindu movements. At the same time, those unhappy with the perceived corruption within Bangarappa's administration were turning towards Hindu right-wing parties and organizations as the "clean alternative." About the Tamil situation in Bangalore, he said:

> Tamils are accused of not mixing with the Kannadigas because they like to live in places like Ulsoor and Sivagi Nagar and patronize their fellow Tamil businesses. Lots of Tamils work in Hosur [about 40kms from Bangalore] in Tamil Nadu in some industry, but they live in Bangalore to reap the benefits of the climate and amenities. They are resented because they work in Tamil Nadu and pay taxes to that state. Tamils are always thought to be loyal to Tamil Nadu.

He is suggesting here that Tamil professionals or wealthy industrialists (laborers working in Hosur would live there, as Bangalore rents are far costlier) are buying up properties in Bangalore and, as others pointed out earlier, turning it into a "Tamil city." Ultimately, the pro-Kannada movements' efforts to homogenize the city's cultural identity are linked to insecurity that a growing Tamil bourgeoisie is laying claim to the city. The discourse of Tamil exclusivity and fanaticism being suggested by pro-Kannada leaders—while drawing upon certain Tamil extremist sentiments—is tied to economic concerns.

Rajyotsatva Day

The annual Rajyotsatva Day (literally, "Karnataka Re-unification Day," but sometimes also called "Karnataka Statehood Day") celebrations on November 1 have grown in size and potential volatility in Bangalore. The day commemorates the redrawing of states in 1956, which resulted in the creation of Tamil Nadu and Karnataka out of the Mysore State and Madras Presidency.[17] The celebrations have often turned into anti-Tamil parades. For example, I was told about an altercation between the Rajkumar Fans Association and a line of moviegoers waiting to see a MGR film. This, I was told by Tamils, had turned into a mini-riot. This day also features a Rajkumar film festival. Rajkumar made dozens of films in which he played heroes and kings from the Vijayanagar period. His films romanticize the greatness of the Kannadiga-dominated Empire and has served as a potent symbol of Karnataka identity. The "re-unification" day recalls past glories and makes explicit the primordial link between the old empire and the modern state of Karnataka. That is, the creation of the state in 1956 was imagined as the "re-unification" of Vijayanagara. As Tamil cinemas are often "stoned" on this day, I was warned to avoid being near one. This was especially true, I was told, if a Kannadiga film had a scene in which Vijayanagara citizens are defeated in a battle by Tamils.

The focus of attention for many Kannadigas in Bangalore on Rajyotsatva Day was a temporary fairground that was erected near the Central Market and Kempegowda Circle, in the heart of the city. Spectacular wooden arches and pillars are propped up and decorated with paint and thousands of lights. The festive atmosphere is the principal occasion for speeches and special events. Famous Kannadigas like Rajkumar, Chidananda Murthy, and Bangarappa often gave anti-Tamil speeches in the public square. A local professor in Bangalore informed me that, in addition to anti-Tamil speeches, the decorations, that is, the arches, pillars, and banners, were charged with meaning to Kannadigas and Tamils. The arches utilized motifs from the Vijayanagar era—a golden age of Kannadiga political and cultural hegemony over most of South India.[18] Minor incidents, I was told, often broke out when processions from this site passed through Tamil-speaking areas. The Tamils, for their part, would sometimes carry a Chola-style arch in reaction. For the most part, however, Tamils made it a point to celebrate Rajyosatva Day. Decorations were highly visible in Tamil sections of town. Cardboard Vijayanagar arches acted as facades in front of many Tamil-owned shops. In the neighborhood where I lived, in the heart of the former Cantonment, was a vigorous display of loyalty to Karnataka. Along the business district of the neighborhood were decorative lights, streamers, and music. A Tamil-Muslim merchant indicated to me that Tamils were mostly responsible for the colorful display, and in the same breath asked me: "Do you know of our language problems?" He then suggested that the ostentatious display of loyalty was born out of fear of vandalism by gangs of young Kannadigas. After singling out the Rajkumar fans as particularly "against us," he spoke of the "sweetness of MGR's face" in comparison with Rajkumar's apparent harshness of character. As we spoke in his shop, auto-rickshaws buzzed by us with the Karnataka's state flag prominently displayed. In fact, for the entire month of November, all transport vehicles (buses, taxis, rickshaws, and lorries) displayed, at the minimum, the Karnataka flag.

Perhaps most striking about the "performance" of ethnicity that this celebration presented was the trend to seek historical antecedents to make sense of existing sentiments. The imagining of golden ages serves to "naturalize" differences. That is to say, revivalisms of various kinds often require "inventions of tradition" (Hobsbawm and Ranger 1983) to mobilize sentiments around the historical consciousness of a particular group. In short, contemporary battles are imagined—such as the competition for jobs, privileges, and water—as contested origin myths. These are boundary-making devices for defining the moral community. Evocative symbols seem to generate primordial ethnic attachments. For some, however, when battles come to concern ancient empires, or even regional film stars, rather than issues of substance, there is little hope for productive dialogue. Indeed, many Tamils and Kannadigas viewed the whole exercise as propaganda for the Chief Minister.[19] But seen in a less cynical light, imagined pasts serve, as Derrida (1995) argues, as the necessary supplement to the Law. The claim of 1956 was of a linguistic state organized around a language's purported territorial hegemony. In Bangalore, as both a border zone between states and a particularly pluralistic city over time, these claims are perceived as lacking. Thus, the necessity, whether consciously or not, of supplementary justification comes in the form of historical myth-making. In this sense, the futural aspirations of imagined communities are necessarily anchored in revisioning the past.

An interesting factor in the imagining of the primordial seems to be the mass media—and especially the impact of film images. The emergence of separate Tamil and Kannadiga film industries has played a significant role in the creation of linguistic nationalism. This example illustrates Anderson's (1998) notion of how "unbound serialism" takes hold of the imagination. Invention is the mother of necessity. In this case, the arche-violence of naming (or bound serialism, in Anderson's terms) opens up a breach, or an impossibility in what it purports to separate—in this case distinct ethnic and linguistic groupings. This performative act requires its supplement, in Derrida's terms, in order to foreclose or suture the impossibility of the breach. But as this is temporary, and inherently deconstructible, the engine of supplementation, an "archive fever" (Derrida 1995), is never exhausted.

In sum, the Kannada Movement produced a climate which contributed to the election of Bangarappa, which in turn led to his handling of the Cauvery dispute in an apparently reckless manner. Even before Bangarappa was Chief Minister, the project of awakening Kannadiga cultural identity had been fueled by the rapid economic growth in the city and the subsequent arrival of more immigrants to an already multilinguistic city. Underlying the linguistic and cultural pride of Kannadiga nationalism, however, is a pragmatic concern as well: without pro-Kannada legislation, what is to be the economic fate of the capital city, and who will protect the economic privileges of the Kannadiga bourgeoisie? *Bumiputraism* is one solution to this problem.[20] That is, the elites and bourgeoisie legitimize their economic agendas through politically charged ethnic crusades. These, in turn, require invented traditions or supplementary forms of evidence/violence; and much transmission of these images seems to rely upon "unbound seriality" created by the mass media. These projects, of course, also produce resistances. Thus, there has been a heightening of Tamil cultural identity in response to the Kannada Movement.

Tamilism

There has been a revival of religious ritualism among Tamils within Bangalore during the last twenty or so years, primarily after the riots discussed above.[21] While Tamils no longer have enclaves where they are free to put signboards up in their native tongue, they can express their Tamil identity through ritual performances. In Ulsoor, a predominantly Tamil area, a Murugan Temple is the sight for a very dramatic display of Saivite religious practices. Though the details of this revival are not addressed here, it has been suggested to me by some Tamils that this is an expression of ethnic identity and solidarity in the only way possible. I was told by one that the *kavadi* ritual,[22] in particular, allowed a "psychological freedom to chant and sing aloud in Tamil," and that this will "not be tolerated by Kannadigas during non-festival days." By this he suggested that open expressions of Tamilness are confined to the spectacle of the religious ritual, where, one could argue, its potential political significance was defused. Those who participate in the *kavadi* rituals are generally from working-class backgrounds. I was told that one reason for the increasing popularity of these folk traditions stemmed from an increasing demand for migrant labor in the construction industry. A high percentage of these migrants are poor Tamils from the border region. The increasing numbers reflect a growing population of poor Tamils from rural areas; at the same time, their poverty, and political insecurity resulting from anti-Tamil rhetoric and riots, leads them to seek divine intervention through vow-taking.

Drawing an ethnic distinction between Tamils and Kannadigas is often ambiguous—and as I have suggested, requires great historical imagination. Making this demarcation also requires stereotypes. The revival of Tamil folk traditions that are considered unorthodox by brahminical Hinduism serve to identify the "backward" Tamil laborer as an "alien" in modern Bangalore. This, however, is complicated by working-class Kannadiga interest in the same rituals.

Kumaraswami Festival

The Kumaraswami Koyil (temple) in Hanumanth Nagar, an old and bustling neighborhood in Bangalore, sits perched upon a hill, an auspicious location for a temple dedicated to this deity. Kumaraswami—also known as Murugan, Subramaniam, Karthikeya, or Skanda—is most popular among Tamils. During the temple's annual festival for the god, thousands of devotees gather to offer their devotions. Many of them travel from various parts of Bangalore, as this temple has come to have great significance among Murugan worshippers in the area. The growing popularity of this temple and its festival is also due to the increasing emotional and symbolic significance that Tamils attach to this place. This sentiment is growing in the shadow of the Kannadiga movement and its more strident anti-Tamil populism.

I observed celebrations in August 2009. At the base of the temple, devotees gathered in preparation for their pilgrimage up the steps of the shrine on the hill. Between the houses, on the street outside the temple compound, a carnival atmosphere prevailed. One could see the bright colors of sanctified food consisting of puffed rice and fried snacks *(prasadam),* pinwheels for children, toys, and brightly decorated *kavadis* (arched poles decorated with peacock feathers). Devotees dressed in red and yellow prepared for their offerings, which included, among other things, milk, fruit, and other auspicious items. Chanting of the Lord's name could be heard throughout the festival grounds. The rhythmic chanting of *"Aro-hara, vetri vel Murugan, Aro-Hara Veera Vel"* ("hail the Lord, Victory to Murugan's Lance, hail the Lord's heroic lance").

Devotees ascend to main shrine dedicated to Kumaraswami in Hanumanth Nagar, Bangalore. (Photo by Andrew Willford)

A fairly heavy police presence was felt at the celebration as devotees were escorted in procession up the right side of the stairs to the shrine, whilst family members ascended on the left side of the stairs.

The police presence may have been related to the fact that just that week the Thiruvalluvar (the Tamil saint) statue had finally been publicly unveiled, much to the protests of Kannadiga activist groups. Demonstrations against the statue and against Tamil interests had been threatened, but nothing significant had materialized. At this particular festival, it was estimated by devotees that I asked that the composition of the crowd was mixed. Though predominantly Tamil, I was told that at least 15 percent of the devotees were, in fact, Kannadigas. The Kannadiga presence was felt in other ways, as well. Though most of the *pusaris* (priests) were Tamils, the signs within the temple were all in Kannada, which was an obvious political concession in response to the pro-Kannada movement. Though the crowd was harmonious and multilingual, thus indicating a fabric of urban *bhakti* (devotion) within the landscape that cross-cuts language, differences were manifest. For example, one man whom I interviewed together with his family came to this festival each year. He, a middle-aged Tamil man, had his head shaved at the temple during the festival, as this is considered a meritorious act and sacrifice. He said he comes, in part, because this is the "Tamil god." Moreover, this is one of the few temples where acts of possession and self-mortification, more common among Tamils, he claimed, were enacted. While I witnessed some *kavadi*-bearers who appeared entranced and had *Vels* (lances) piercing their tongues and cheeks, he said that if I were to come in the evening, then the crowd of devotees would be exclusively Tamil. Also, at night, the acts of self-mortification were more ubiquitous, he claimed.

This man, who came with his wife and two young daughters, said he would continue to bring his family for the festival, as this temple "is for the Tamil people because it is a Tamil God and is on the hill." And, he claimed, there was reason to celebrate, given the long-awaited unveiling of the Thiruvalluvar statue in Bangalore. He was extremely happy about the statue, which had been covered up in legal limbo for over twenty years. Now the two sides had come together *(raandu pakkum)* and he felt only happiness *(santosham maddum)*. But here, and with other Tamils I spoke to, the victory was one for the Tamils, in particular. Though he was glad that Kannadigas had not acted violently in protest, he continued to assert with pride that this is a Tamil temple and a Tamil-oriented festival. The truth of Kumaraswami worship, however, is that, although it is very popular among Tamils, it is not unpopular amongst Kannadigas. Thus, what we witness in this festival is a shared religiosity and a porous boundary between communities. There

Devotees offering kavadi to Kumaraswami. (Photo by Andrew Willford)

are many such shrines and traditions within the fabric of life in Bangalore (Srinivas 2000; Nair 2005).

Another devotee, a young Tamil man aged twenty-five, explained his special relationship with the temple. He told me that he must carry *kavadi* at the temple for the rest of his life, in order to fulfill a vow he had made. He also performed the same vow at the most important Murugan shrine in Tamil Nadu, in Palani. This devotee explained that he had a problem with a stammer in his speech. This had caused him great anguish during his school years. But after carrying *kavadi,* and specifically, after carrying the *Vel* through his cheeks and tongue in a state of possession, his speech "became clear." In preparation for his offering, for forty days he would eat vegetarian food and practice abstinence. His diet consisted mainly of milk and fruit. The *kavadi* pole itself would be washed in cow urine first so as "to avoid mistakes, and as it gives strength." He would then bathe in cold water. Sometimes he, or his siblings, would also offer milk, curds, or cheese sprinkled with rose water to the deity. When asked who carries *kavadis,* he said, emphatically, that it was "just Tamils" *(Tamil maddum).* But then he modulated his response to say that Kannadigas increasingly come for the festival, and some might even carry the *kavadi*. He then said that Telugus also carry the *kavadi* sometimes.

What became clear to me after witnessing the festival and speaking with devotees was that, while Tamils still outnumbered non-Tamils at this event, there was an increasingly plural character that transcended mother tongue. Signs were visible in Kannada, as was literature about the temple. Priests spoke both languages fluently, if not many more (Telugu, Malayalam, etc.). Though it was clear that many Tamils perceive this deity and this shrine as signifying a Tamil space within the symbolic landscape of the city, it is impossible to mark it as exclusive. Moreover, although, on the one hand, Tamil ritualism might be reviving in response to the perceived assertiveness of the more strident aspects of the Kannada movement, this revivalism takes shape within shared idioms and devotional templates that resonate across the artificial and arbitrary boundaries of identities crafted through the magic of boundaries and censuses. Thus, the weight and traces of history can affect, and indeed deconstruct, projects of historical revisionism as wedded to modern ethno-nationalist projects.

Conclusion

How can we understand the sharpening linguistic divides in Bangalore, and with it, the imagining of communities somehow separate and unique, serially bound, as neat as a census and map would have us imagine (Anderson 1998)? As Ashis Nandy has observed for Cochin, an old "cosmopolitanism" or pluralism still exists within the city grounded in what he calls "tacit memories." These are found, he argues, in "an identifiable, communicable, 'unconscious'" (2002, 170). How are these tacit memories produced? Nandy suggests that certain myths resonate in the public imagination of Cochinites as a result of a shared civic culture. This involves, among other things, the capacity to incorporate the Other's myths as one's own as part of a public historical repertoire. This repertoire, while public and communicable, is also "tacit," or located in patterns of practice and belief that resist conscious imposition. A serialization of identities, in Benedict Anderson's sense, as fostered by mass media and census taking, has not occurred there. Bangalore is, perhaps, somewhere in between the modern communal realities of South Asia (and, as we learn from Tagliacozzo, Siu, and others in this volume, parts of Southeast and East Asia, as well) that grew out of the enumeration of communities through censuses and mapping and the ancient cosmopolitan pluralism of Cochin. On the one hand, the Deccan's crossroads continues to bear the marks of a shared repertoire of culture, religiosity, and multilingualism. Polylingual Vaishnavism,[23] Saivism, urban *bhatki* across linguistic lines, iconographic forms, and a common film culture are just some of the expressive idioms that are shared across communities (Srinivas 2000; Nair 2005; 2011). There are many others (music, poetry, arts, drama, and film).

But at the same time, 1956 did create the conditions of linguistic insecurity for today's Kannada speakers in Bangalore. The creation of a linguistic state with a linguistic capital along the tristate border of Tamil Nadu, Karnataka, and Andhra Pradesh was bound for complications, given the demographic complexity of the region. The city itself was redrawn by statemaking. 1956 brought Bangalore into the state of Karnataka. Prior to this, it was bifurcated between the Madras Presidency and Mysore State. Thus, for much of its recent history, it was not regarded a specifically "Kannadiga" city, but rather, a multilinguistic city lying at the crossroads of empires, states, and borderlands, interconnected to other parts of South Asia and the wider region. In this sense, this case parallels many other examples whereby plurality and complex identifications were simplified through the technologies of colonial and post-colonial statecraft.

Theoretically, how might we understand the productive demand for ethnic and linguistic singularity? As I have argued in the context of Malaysia (2006), the demand can be understood in instrumental terms. That is, a political claim obviously produces and is produced out of differentials of power. But what of the feverish and irrational compulsion to difference that often marks the politics of difference in postcolonial spaces? What accounts for this passion? Paradoxically, I believe that differences take hold in the imagination precisely in the face of an impossible demand (Hansen 2004). What I mean is that the arche-violence of the law, or the arbitrary demand, is partially perceived by subjects as arbitrary, not as natural. The retroactive work of naturalization is the product of an ethnographic "archive fever" (Derrida 1995). The originary lack inherent in the violence of the Law is supplemented through the archive of an ethnographic state (Dirks 2002). Grounding itself in conventions provides an aura retroactive historicity to the violence of the Law and state. The ethnographic archive—an archive of difference—supplements and grounds what is partially perceived to be an untenable ideology. Indeed, the excess of identification that often occurs where ideology appears most absurd and untenable suggests that the tenacious hold of ethnic and religious boundaries is contingent upon both the violence of the state and Law and of its supplement in the form of the archiving of difference. The Law, however, is ultimately deconstructible, as the archive which sustains its legitimacy becomes more spectral as it grows in authority and ubiquity.

Put in the terms of this chapter, the emergence of a linguistic and ethnic identification provides for an impossible demand upon the plurality of life in Bangalore. Genealogy and memory are contradicted by the demands of the state. But an ethnographic and historic archive reworks the historiography of the region, as conjoined to a political imperative. Kannadiga chauvinism becomes plausible only in the face of its untenable narrative, given the pluralism of Bangalore. The pluralism is generative of the chauvinism; and concomitantly, the chauvinism takes hold in the impossibility of its claim, as conjoined to the Law it is generative of. But for every claim for singularity and sovereignty, as buffeted by ethnographic and historiographic claims (the feverish archive of past empires, etc.), a counter is conjured. Moreover, in conjuring the quintessential archival memorialization of the one, the other is also somehow made to appear, even as a specter. Thus, there is a deconstructability in the heart of the Law, as Derrida argues, that undercuts claims to exclusivity. This theoretical claim is illustrated by my ethnographic experience in Bangalore. The Murugan temple discussed above could never be simply an exclusively Tamil shrine, however much aggrieved Tamils imagine it to be so. For every example, the incorporation of the Other is also possible. In this sense, Nandy's thesis of incorporation and multiplicity, rather than communal identification, thankfully rings partially true for Bangalore, as well, despite the sometimes polarizing trends in recent years. In viewing the city and region through the *longue durée*, a modality of cultural flow, both radiating outward and inward to and from the Bangalore region, has and continues to mitigate against the totalizing serialization of identities.

Notes

1. There were many other smaller kingdoms vying for supremacy in the Bangalore region. The Kadambas and Gangas (both in the central and northern Deccan) were also of great importance (Thapar 1966).

2. Legend has it that the city was originally a village named Bengaluru—the "town of boiled beans"—after a Hoysala king was offered boiled beans by an old

woman when he visited her village while on a hunting exhibition. It is believed that Kempegowda founded the city upon the site of that village (Venkatarayappa 1957).

3. Rajkumar is a leader in the Kannada revival movement. He has presided over rallies demanding that Kannada be made the compulsory language for all administrative jobs in Karnataka. His roles in movies often cast him as a Hoysala or Vijayanagara hero—potent symbols of Karnataka nationalism and pride. In this sense, he is the Kannada counterpart to MGR (M. G. Ramachandran), the Tamil film-star-turned-politician, who often portrayed Chola or Pandyan heroes.

4. Personal communication, January, 2008.

5. Specifically, he called for a permanent solution to the Cauvery water dispute, compensation for all Tamil riot victims from the Cauvery-related violence of 1991, the inclusion of Tamil as an administrative language in Karnataka, the installation of the Thiruvallavur (a Tamil saint) statue in Bangalore, and investigations into atrocities committed by the Special Task Force in the forest against so-called smugglers, such as himself and his followers (Nair 2005, 236).

6. The Sangam is the leading Tamil organization in Bangalore dedicated to promoting its language, literature, and fine arts. The Sangam has become increasingly politicized in response to the various pro-Kannada movements' anti-Tamil sentiments.

7. The Indian People's Human Rights Commission (IPHRC) was formed in 1987, consisting of human rights activists, academics, and lawyers from different parts of India. The IPHRC organized the Indian People's Human Rights Tribunal, which consisted of ex-judges of the Supreme and High Courts of India. Both were based in Bombay/Mumbai. The Commission took up cases in which there is suspected significant violations of human rights by the State. They gathered evidence and published reports on such cases.

8. For example, there were reports in the media that Bangarappa had granted lucrative liquor licenses to political supporters while simultaneously preaching temperance to Kannadigas. Also, he was accused of living opulently at the expense of state taxpayers.

9. The Dravida Munnetra Kazhagam (Progressive Dravidian Federation) and All-India-Anna Dravida Munnetra Kazhagam, respectively. Both parties claim to carry on the legacy of the Tamil movement. The two parties have alternated rule in Tamil Nadu for the last forty-plus years.

10. The author of the *Tirrukural*, a classic Tamil religious and moral text.

11. There are, however, numerous statues of Wodeyar Rajas—the patrons of Kannada arts and culture in the Mysore State since 1399 CE.

12. In subsequent years, I did occasionally notice Tamil signboards in Tamil-dominated areas such as Ulsoor, suggesting that some of the anti-Tamil rhetoric had dissipated. But there were occasional flare ups of anti-Tamil violence and rhetoric, particularly when the distribution of Cauvery water across state lines became politicized on an annual basis.

13. I develop these themes more fully in a book manuscript tentatively titled *Bangalore's Cosmopolitan Pasts and Monocultural Futures (?): A Study of Civility and Difference.*

14. It is sometimes referred to as the "Gokok Agitation"—after a report issued by a minister by that name suggested that Christian Kannadigas were discriminated against in churches dominated by Tamils. Gokak argued that Kannada should replace Tamil as the language of worship. This "report" stirred other Kannadigas to make more general observations about the status of Kannada in public spheres in Bangalore.

15. He is referring to the suicides that followed the death of MGR in 1987.

16. Personal communication, December 1992.

17. Andhra Pradesh and parts of Kerala were also part of the Madras Presidency prior to the creation of linguistic states.

18. This is an imagined age in the sense that the Vijayanagara Empire, though vast, was more linguistically and ethnically complex than the Kannada movement would have it. The same holds true for the Cholas (Sastri 1975).

19. Bangarappa's pro-Kannada posturing could not save him in the end, as scandals and a perception of widespread corruption eventually led to his resignation in December 1992. Congress I party leaders (his party) asked him to step down for the "best interests of the State and Party."

20. Some Kannadigas in Bangalore use this term to refer to their community as the legitimate "sons of the soil" in Karnataka.

21. This is the perception of many Tamils and Kannadigas I spoke with in Bangalore. But there is no statistical data that I know of to validate this perception. Nevertheless, this perception that this is the case is socially relevant, and a major theme I develop in the longer book manuscript.

22. A traditional dance associated with devotions to Lord Murugan involving a pole and arch suspended upon the shoulders. *Kavadi* dancers often fall into trance or enter a state of divine grace *(arul).*

23. In this chapter, I did not have space to devote to the interesting history of the spread of Vaishnavism in the Deccan, nor of the case of the bilingual Iyengars (Vaishnava Brahmins) of Karnataka. (See Lal, 1986; Bayer 1986; Nair 2011).

References

Agamban, Giorgio. 2005. *State of Exception.* Trans. David Attel. Chicago: University of Chicago Press.

Anderson, Benedict. 1998. "Nationalism, Identity, and the Logic of Seriality." In *The Spectre of Comparisons.* London: Verso.

Annaswamy, T. V. 2003. *Bengalaru to Bangalore: Urban History of Bangalore from the Prehistoric Period to the End of the 18th Century.* Bangalore: Vengadam Publications.

Bayer, Jennifer. 1986. *Dynamics of Language Maintenance among Linguistic Minorities: A Case Study of the Tamil Community in Bangalore.* Mysore: Central Institute of Indian Languages.

Derrida, Jacques. 1995. *Archive Fever: A Freudian Impression.* Trans. Eric Prenowitz. Chicago: University of Chicago Press.

———. 2002. *Acts of Religion.* London: Routledge.

Dirks, Nicholas. 2002. "Annals of the Archive: Ethnographic Notes of the Sources of History." In *From the Margins: Historical Anthropology and its Futures,* ed. Brian Axel, 47–65. Durham, NC: Duke University Press.

Gangarams. 1994. *Bangalore: Scenes from an Indian City.* Bangalore: Gangarams Publications.

Hansen, Thomas. 2004. *The Wages of Violence.* Princeton, NJ: Princeton University Press.

Hobsbawm, Eric, and Terence Ranger, eds. 1983. *The Invention of Tradition.* Cambridge: Cambridge University Press.

Indian People's Human Rights Commission (IPHRC). 1992. *Cauvery: What Language Does She Speak . . . ?* Bombay: IPHRC Publication.

Irschick, Eugene F. 1969. *Politics and Social Conflict in South India: The Non-Brahman Movement and Tamil Separatism, 1916–1929.* Berkeley: University of California Press.

Lal, Sam Mohan. 1986. *Convergence and Language Shift in a Linguistic Minority: A Sociolinguistic study of Tamils in Bangalore City.* Mysore: Central Institute of Indian Languages.

Nair, Janaki. 2005. *The Promise of the Metropolis: Bangalore's Twentieth Century.* Delhi: Oxford University Press.

———. 2011. *Mysore Modern: Rethinking the Region under Princely Rule.* Minneapolis: University of Minnesota Press.

Nandy, Ashis. 2002. "Time Travel to a Possible Self." In *Time Warps.* Newark: Rutgers University Press.

Rai, Saritha, 1992. "Suicidal Indifferance: Slammed for instigating anti-Tamil violence, Karnataka CM's Bangarappa's fate hangs in balance". *India Today,* Jan. 15, 1992.

Ramanujam, A. K. 1973. *Speaking of Siva.* Baltimore: Penguin Books.

———. 1993. *Hymns for the Drowning: Poems for Visnu by Nammalvar.* New Delhi: Penguin Books.

Ramaswamy, Sumathi. 1997. *Passions of the Tongue: Language Devotion in Tamil India, 1891–1970.* Berkeley: University of California Press.

Sastri, Nilakanta. 1975. *A History of South India.* Madras: Oxford University Press.

Srinivas, M. N. 1994. "Reminiscences of a Bangalorean." In *Bangalore: Scenes from an Indian City,* 6–27. Bangalore: Gangarams Publications.

Srinivas, Smriti. 2000. *Landscapes of Urban Memory:* Minneapolis: University of Minnesota Press.

Stein, Burton. 1994. *Vijayanagara.* New Delhi: Cambridge University Press.

Thapar, Romila. 1966. *A History of India: Volume One.* New Delhi: Penguin Books.

Venkatarayappa, K. N. 1957. *Bangalore: A Socio-Ecological Study.* Bombay: University of Bombay.

Willford, Andrew. 2006. *Cage of Freedom: Tamil Identity and the Ethnic Fetish in Malaysia,* Ann Arbor: University of Michigan Press.

Newspapers and Magazines

Deccan Herald
Frontline
The Hindu
India Today

2008

"Open City" and a New Wave of Filipino Migration to the Middle East

NAOMI HOSODA

In October 2008, shocking news arrived in the Philippines from the Middle East. A report announced that more than 6,000 Filipinos were stranded in Oman and Iran because of changes made to the visa regulations in the United Arab Emirates (UAE). The media discovered that these individuals had become stranded in a number of border towns in the UAE while they made what is popularly referred to as a "visa run." The visa renewal process that previously took a few days now lasted weeks or months. Some of the stranded Filipinos were no longer able to feed themselves. They asked for help from the Philippine embassies in their respective countries for humanitarian reasons. This news surprised people in the Philippines. It revealed the fact that most workers who had believed they had travelled to the "promised land of Dubai" were actually "illegal" workers. Their only remaining options were petitions for rescue by the Philippine government or survival in Oman or Iran without official status to stay and work.[1]

Dubai has recently attracted world attention because of its many innovative, large-scale construction projects and sporting events. Even before the world news media began to report on the spectacular growth of the city, during my visits to the Philippines I became intrigued with events in Dubai, one of the seven emirates of the UAE. In 2006, I spent time with my friend

Marlene, whom I have known for a decade and who resides in Dubai, during her month-long vacation in Manila. Marlene suggested, "Let's go to Dubai! There are plenty of jobs and the city is so clean and beautiful. You should come and see it yourself." I recalled that she had previously disliked the idea of Middle Eastern travel. Therefore, I asked her whether she no longer minded travel to the Middle East. She responded, "It's different. It's an open city." Following our meeting in Manila, she flew back to Dubai. Shortly after, another friend sent me an email to inform me that he had also begun to work in Dubai. Several months later, I happened to visit Dubai for the first time. Upon arrival, I discovered male and female Filipino people in every corner of the city. They worked, strolled along the streets, visited malls, ate, and participated in chats on their personal computers in Starbucks. In addition, it did not take long to discover that Filipinos in Dubai are employed in a wide range of professions. These ranged from domestic work and semiskilled work at construction sites and shops and restaurants, to professional fields such as accounting, engineering, and sales management.

A number of recent studies conducted on the Filipino global migration have closely investigated structural constraints imposed on migrants. Other studies have investigated aspects of human agency that migrants have demonstrated as they carved out their own space. Several studies have examined migrants' sense of belonging in the host country, in the Philippines, or both (e.g., Faier 2009; Lan 2006; Constable 1997). Researchers have also studied how Filipina migrants have been "transgressing . . . the nation-state" on a global scale (Parreñas 2001, 1). However, these studies do not address contemporary Filipino workers' situations in the Middle East. First, many studies have focused on the lives of women who work in female-centered professions such as domestic work, entertainment, and nursing. Yet, in major Middle Eastern cities, one can see that both male and female Filipino workers are represented in many sectors of the society (Johnson 2010). Second, these studies have relied on field research conducted in a number of locations around the world. For decades, employers in the Middle East have hired the largest number of Filipino contract workers. Yet this area remains relatively unexplored, particularly on empirical bases. Just recently, several ethnographic studies were published that focused on Filipina domestic workers in the Middle East (de Regt 2008 in Yemen; Liebelt 2011 in Israel) and on Filipino professionals (Nagy 2008 in Bahrain; Johnson 2010 in Saudi Arabia). In the UAE, Christ (2012) investigated how Filipina migrants in Dubai shared everyday knowledge with compatriots to cope with their status as temporary workers in a multiethnic society. However, despite the publication of these recent works and, in part, owing to the representation of the Middle East in mass media and in everyday discourse, the image of the Middle East remains depressing.

In spite of this portrayal of the Middle East, the Filipino population in the UAE showed phenomenal growth: it increased from 170,000 in 2001 to almost 600,000 in 2009. One can assume that this was a rational response to rapid economic growth in the global city of Dubai during this period. However, I was intrigued to find that Dubai as described in migrants' narratives had become differentiated from other areas in the Middle East, with special focus on the social marker, "open city." Therefore, this essay hopes to examine the process Filipinos have undergone over the last decade as they searched for luck in Dubai. I will explore a variety of different encounters Filipinos have had with Dubai. I hope to elucidate the complex nature of the phenomenon involved. Rather than relying on terminology related to the grand theory of globalization, I based my research on the concept of "global engagements" popularized by Anna Tsing (2000). This concept suggests that researchers should investigate practices that impact the ways that people and places become connected and transformed. It also illustrates how particular channels facilitate, organize, and constrain movements.

As part of my discussion of relationships between Filipinos and Dubai, I must note that, in this essay, I consider that both Filipinos and the Dubai that has been constructed in Filipinos' imaginations are fluid entities. The ways that we perceive place/space and its relationship to a particular group of people is a concept that has generated significant debate among ethnologists over the past few decades (Gupta and Ferguson 1997; Olwig and Hastrup 1996). Corsin-Jimenez argued that if we point at cases in which a geographical place might mean nothing to people who live there because of their lack of social relationships associated with that place, then space is not, after all "a category of fixed and given ontological attributes" (2003, 140). He stressed that, unless we regard space as a carrier of value and meaning to ourselves, we cannot make sense of the "spatiality of non-places" and the existence of places that lack any attachment (Corsin-Jimenez 2003, 150). Perhaps the work of Retsikas (2007) is more relevant to this essay. Retsikas examined the changing character of a frontier area located in East Java. He observed the relationship that exists between the area and the people who stop, settle, and move again. Based on an argument presented in Corsin-Jimenez's research, this study demonstrated a process similar to the process by which people transform themselves. Places also transform themselves "through people's engagements—material as well as discursive—in, through, and with them" (Retsikas 2007, 971).

I base my argument on narratives collected from interviews I conducted with fifty-nine Filipino workers (thirty-nine females and twenty males) in the UAE in 2009 and 2010.[2] In addition, I collected supplementary information from interviews with Philippine government officials, representatives from international organizations, journalists, UAE travel agents, recruiters in the Philippines, production staff for movies and TV programs in Manila, employers and colleagues of Filipino workers in Dubai who originated from other nations, and Filipino community leaders in the UAE. In keeping with professional practices in the discipline, I use pseudonyms to protect the identity of project participants.

Filipinos and the UAE

Labor relations between the Philippines and Dubai began during the oil boom that occurred in the Middle East in the 1970s. Up until that time, the mainstream flow of Filipino migrants was directed towards the United States. These migrants included doctors, nurses, and teachers. Groups headed towards the Middle East were composed of workers required for the construction of buildings and infrastructure. Thus, the emergence of Middle Eastern labor mobility was cynically termed "from brain drain to brawn drain." This statement implies the never-ending commodification of Filipinos as workers for the world. In addition, during these oil boom years, the dominant form of outmigration shifted from permanent emigration to contract-based temporary migration.

Although real economic development in the Philippines had not occurred as expected, the remittances that workers sent home became a pillar of the country's economy. The spread of overseas migration was facilitated by the institutionalization of both public and private sectors. The Philippine government seeks out employment opportunities worldwide. It regulates the operations of more than 1,000 recruitment agencies. It also tries to oversee the rights of its migrant workers. The Philippines was the first of several countries in Asia that Sent Out workers to craft a law that aims to protect its overseas workers. Further, the Philippine government's effort to create "Great Filipino Workers" for the globalizing labor market is noteworthy. This term was devised by the former president of the Philippines, Gloria Macapagal-Arroyo. The government, orchestrated with overseas employment agencies, and some of the workers themselves have been marketing *Filipinos* as highly competent workers who possess educational achievements, English-language fluency, and "tender loving care" (Guevarra 2010, 2–3).

The country sends all kinds of skilled and low-skilled workers throughout the world. As of December 2008, an estimated 8.2 million Filipinos—an amount that is equivalent of 10 percent of the country's population—were working and/or living in over 170 countries around the world (CFO 2008; POEA 2009). The Middle East has remained the leading attracting point for *temporary* Filipino workers. It received 2.2 million out of a total amount of 3.2 million temporary workers in 2008. In the Middle East, the Gulf States (Bahrain, Kuwait, Oman, Qatar, Saudi Arabia, and UAE) are the most popular destinations for temporary work among Filipinos. By far, Saudi Arabia has been the most popular destination for Filipino contract workers for decades (i.e., more than a million Filipinos reside there). The UAE, Qatar, and Kuwait were the next most popular destinations in 2008 (CFO 2008).

In the Gulf region, as stated earlier, Filipino population growth in the UAE in recent years has been outstanding. Growth was especially spectacular between 2004 and 2007. Population figures increased 2.5 times, from 200,000 to 530,000 during this three-year period (CFO 2008).[3] What triggered this rapid Filipino population growth in the UAE? To begin with, it was Dubai's economic boom over the last decade, which also encouraged individuals from diverse regions of the world to seek employment opportunities there. Following the formation of the UAE in 1972, the emirate of Dubai pursued a rather different route for development from the others because it was faced with limited oil reserves. The government's decision to diversify from an oil-reliant economy to an economy that focuses more attention on manufacturing, commerce, and tourism has become a development model in the Gulf. In fact, UAE's GDP growth rate in real terms between 2004 and 2008 remained as high as 6 to 10 percent (IMF 2009).

The UAE's foreign population multiplied during these economic boom years in Dubai. By 2008 it reached 5.9 million, a figure that represents 87 percent of the total population of the country. Although all of the Gulf States host a considerable number of foreign nationals, only the UAE and Qatar have populations in which the ratio of foreigners to locals exceeds 80 percent (Janardhan 2011, 94–96). Of the different nationalities that reside in Dubai, Filipinos currently constitute the fourth-largest population, exceeded only by migrants from South Asian nations, i.e., India (1.5 million), Pakistan (850,000), and Bangladesh (800,000) (Horinuki 2010). In contrast to South Asian workers, who are primarily male, both male and female Filipino workers are employed in various industries. They are particularly noticeable in the service industry, and more women are found than men in the UAE in 2000s (POEA 2009).

Emergence of an "Open City"

Brian is a civil engineer who was born and raised on Samar Island in the Visayas. He is currently the leader of a Filipino community association located in Dubai. Brian migrated to the UAE in 1995. He presently lives with his wife and two children in an apartment house in Deira, a downtown area of Dubai. Brian relates how he came to Dubai in this way:

> I had no prior knowledge of this country. I didn't care because I was going abroad to support my family. I could have gone elsewhere, to Saudi, Kuwait, Singapore, Indonesia, wherever I could find a good job. I came [to Dubai] because my sister invited me here because she knew I was looking for a good job. Then my wife followed. She seemed disappointed because Dubai was such a small town—no skyscrapers, shopping malls, or transportation system existed at that time. "Manila was better!" she grumbled.[4]

Based on my interviews in Dubai, I learned that, in particular, Filipinos who arrived in the UAE up until the early 2000s had no specific concept of Dubai or the UAE unless they had prior experiences working in the Gulf region. In other words, the term "Dubai" served as an indicator of a place that had no social significance of its own to the majority of Filipinos. People did not talk about it with any specificity. It was simply a place where overseas jobs were available. The important factors included numerical information related to employment conditions such as salary, placement fees, and benefits. However, in general, the Middle East is not a favorite destination among Filipinos who aspire to go abroad.[5]

The emergence of Dubai as an "open city" (a vernacular, colloquial expression in the Filipino language) occurred in this context. Angeline, a former travel agent in the Deira district, decided to risk (*nakipagsapalaran,* see, also, below) a trip to Dubai on a visit visa in 2006, because:

> I spent five years working very hard in a factory in Taiwan. I knew there was an age limit on how long I could continue in Taiwan. So I returned to the Philippines before I became 30 years old. I began to look for another opportunity. Then, I heard that Dubai is an "open city." I saw Dubai on TV. It was beautiful; it had skyscrapers and glittering shopping malls. Actually, I did not understand, until I came here, that, in Dubai, people observe Muslim practices. TV reporters [who appear on Filipino TV channels] wore the same type of clothing we wear in the Philippines and that are shown in fashionable stores.[6]

Angeline's comment and Marlene's previous description of Dubai, in conjunction with other Filipinos' narratives, reveal that Dubai has become increasingly differentiated from other Middle Eastern cities. It has gained a distinct name that is accompanied with a particular set of images. These are summarized by the term, "open city." No record exists of when the use of the expression "open city," in this context, was popularized. However, we can presume that, by the 1990s, a few major international destination cities were referred to as "open cities." After that, the image of Dubai as an "open city" spread widely throughout Philippine society during the 2000s. My informants cited Hong Kong as another typical "open city." A similar expression, "open country," has a slightly different connotation from the term "open city," because "open country" typically refers to English-speaking immigrant destination countries such as the United States, Canada, Australia, and New Zealand.

If we make a judgment based on the ways that the "open city" has been described by interlocutors, we can assume that the word implies at least two aspects of the city's characteristics: it has a modern and cosmopolitan atmosphere and it has easy entry. The first aspect has been publicized in both personal communications and in reports by the media. Marlene, for instance, made distinctions among different cities with respect to economic and social conditions. Filipinos who currently reside or have resided in the region make similar distinctions. In these discussions, Dubai and Saudi Arabia are frequently placed at opposite ends of the spectrum. First and foremost, Dubai represents modernity; it emphasizes hyperconsumerism and current technology. Second, the city has developed increasingly liberal attitudes towards different religious and cultural activities. It allows male and female foreign residents the freedom to talk to one another and move about in public places. As a result, foreign residents can more easily socialize among themselves than foreign residents are allowed to in neighboring emirates and countries. Nine out of ten people in Dubai are foreign residents. Thus, exposure to different cultures and peoples can also be counted as an "open city" feature. In addition to personal communication by letter and telephone, Internet communication technologies and, in particular, Facebook, YouTube, Skype, and so on, have helped spread images of life in Dubai among Filipinos who reside outside the Middle Eastern region. Although these representations of life abroad that are presented in photos and videos may be less-than-accurate presentations of everyday life, they may act as strong forces to attract individuals who hope to find better opportunities abroad.

During the 2000s, Filipino mass-media representations of Dubai exerted a strong impact. They made Dubai appear to be a distinct destination for temporary employment. As Angeline noted, Filipino TV variety programs began to feature Dubai as a glamorous tourist spot and as a location where a large Filipino community thrived. However, in all respects, the blockbuster Filipino movie *Dubai*, which was released in 2005, set the image of Dubai as a dream location for travel. In the movie, popular Filipino actors and actresses portray semiskilled workers, yet they live in a spacious apartment house and enjoy a middle-class life style. This portrayal changed Filipinos' perceptions of migration to a Middle Eastern city. Moreover, the movie was one of several films in the OFW film series produced by Star Cinema Company. This company chooses specific major world cities that contain high concentrations of Filipinos as shooting locations. The production of this movie in Dubai portrayed the city, in the minds of viewers, as being on a par with other industrialized and fashion centers such as San Francisco, Hong Kong, and Milan.[7]

My informants stated that, following the movie's release, an unprecedented number of Filipinos migrated to Dubai. They hoped to discover a good life in the city. Brian recalled that a number of people who claimed to be somewhat related to his family in the Philippines came to his house to introduce themselves.

> This movie definitely positioned Dubai in the mind of Filipinos. Yet, they didn't know that this is the same place where Sarah Balabagan was convicted of murder by self-defense and was about to be executed? Too bad

they only realized after landing here that a delivery boy can afford to rent space only for a bed, not a condominium.[8]

In May 2006, the media reported that the number of Filipino job seekers who entered the UAE on visit visas on a daily basis had increased from about 400 during the whole previous year to about 600 per day.[9]

Visit Visa Entry

The other reason why Dubai is often referred to as an "open city" is because migrants can easily enter the city on visit visas. Entry to the UAE on visit visas was presumably the most common way for Filipino job seekers to migrate between 2005 and 2008 (Hosoda 2009). According to a local news report in Dubai, as early as May 2006, the Philippine Consulate in Dubai, the Philippine Labor Office, and the Filipino community began to notice that an alarming number of Filipino job seekers were entering the UAE on visit visas, rather than on employment visas. These organizations then formed a fact-finding committee to devise a strategy to stop this flow of illegal migrants.[10]

The use of visit visas spread, until the visa rule was changed in 2008. Prior to that time, the UAE government did not require official proof of family relationships (kinship) from visa applicants and their respective sponsors. Therefore, a self-claimed "relative" of a foreign visitor could easily serve as the official sponsor of that visitor. Marlene designated her former office-mate as a "relative." Angeline found that an unknown person's name appeared as her sponsor on an application document.

Visit visas were considered convenient for employers and employees: employers could hire workers without having to go through red tape. They could hire workers at lower costs. Workers could immediately find employment without having to go through red tape. In addition, visit visas offered flexibility. If either party had trouble, they could cease employment relationships immediately. Workers could begin to search for other opportunities and employers could begin to search for new employees.

No statistical records on these foreign residents were publicly available by country of origin or by visa status. However, staff of travel agencies and journalists in Dubai recalled that visit visas were used by migrants of many nationalities (cf. Osella and Osella 2012, 118). They stated, however, that visit visas were especially popular among Filipinos. Some travel agent staffers and journalists further related this phenomenon to Filipino national character, stating that Filipinos are more optimistic than other nationalities.

Contrary to such generalized assumptions, a close examination of interlocutors' narratives and a review of their biographies revealed to me that visit visa holders tended to be the ones who were likely to have difficulties if they attempted to go abroad as documented contract workers. In general, most overseas jobs advertised in the Philippines are designed for younger people who possessed college degrees and/or skilled work experience, with the exception of domestic workers, who are largely considered unskilled. The demographic backgrounds of interlocutors who entered the UAE and sought employment with visit visas varied, yet I could point out that the majority of them were in their thirties or forties, without a college diploma or long-time work experience. A considerable number of women in this category were single mothers or former overseas contract workers in their thirties and over. If we consider "the ethos of (overseas) labor migration" that operates in contemporary Philippine society, in which overseas migration is largely imagined to be the best way to solve economic or personal problems and/or fulfill one's aspirations (Guevarra 2010, 4), then we might presume that the channel to Dubai based on visit visas has allowed individuals who were in a disadvantageous position to meet the requirements of official channels to become overseas workers.

Ana's Story

Ana was born in 1976. She was raised in a small town near Tacloban, Leyte, in the Visayas. She is the third of four children of parents who grow coconuts and rice in their own field. Similar to her siblings, she pursued her studies at a college in Tacloban. However, in her third year, she dropped out because she became pregnant. She separated from her husband after five years of marriage and became a single mother of two children. To support her family, she worked in small stores and eateries in Tacloban. Yet it was difficult to make ends meet. When Ana's friends informed her of an opportunity to look for a job in Dubai where an individual could earn a monthly salary of 30,000 pesos (US$630) as a restaurant waitress, she decided to take it. She borrowed 80,000 pesos from her relatives, paid that amount to a travel agent in Cebu, and left the Philippines in March 2007.

Anna recalled, after her arrival in Dubai: "Things are so expensive here! I had heard this, but I did not realize it until I left the Philippines. I was terrified." After she met a woman whom the travel agent said was her contact, the woman explained to Ana that the job that Ana had expected to fill had already been filled by another applicant. Ana was then brought to a residential building, where she shared a room with nine other Filipinos. Each woman rented a single bed in a double-decker bed structure for AED 600 (US$160) per month.

Ana began to search for jobs. She learned employment tips from *kabayans* ("compatriot," in Filipino language). The first approach required that she "visit any shops, stores, and offices, and leave the CV. This is called 'door-to-door' approach. The person who does it is 'a Johnny Walker,' because you keep on walking and walking." Ana recalled, "I never did this type of thing in the Philippines. But, here, there is no choice. I must do anything possible." She also checked personal advertisement sections of newspapers and inquired about job openings with her new friends and acquaintances. Several shops returned her calls and they negotiated terms of employment. First, she worked at an Indian jewelry shop. However, she quit one week later because she feared sexual harassment by her boss. Since that time, she has changed employers several times because, at that time, it was relatively easy to find job openings, provided she was not choosy. She needed to maximize her income so that she could send money home to her children.

In addition, Ana had to remember to keep her visit visa current. This meant going on "visa runs" to nearby countries on a bimonthly basis. "Every time I exited, I felt scared and prayed to God because I knew that there were Filipinos who had been stranded at 'exit points' for a variety of reasons. Friends or travel agencies didn't keep their promises to process their visas. If that happens, it is the end!" Despite the risk, she did not change her visa status for more than a year. "It can be a big decision to choose when to change your visa status, because you never know if a better offer will arrive later," she explained. "It is like a game, because, each time, you keep on asking yourself, 'Now, do I take it or not?'"

Ana changed her visa status from visit visa to employment visa, which means that she could no longer quit and start working for another employer at her will, because she learned that the UAE government had tightened the law on visit visas in mid-2008. Her employer is an Indian who runs a small shoe store located in the Karama District, an area filled with shops that cater to Filipinos and other Asian migrants. She receives AED 1,700 (US$460) per month. She is given one day off per week. However, she never takes a day off because her employer adds an extra AED 500 to her salary if she works seven days a week. "Life here is simply a matter of luck *(suwerte-suwerte lang).* I am a loser *(bigo)* because I couldn't get luck *(suwerte).* How can I go back to my family empty-handed? I don't have savings and my debt is waiting for me." She feels pleasure only when she visits nightclubs where she can dance and forget her difficulties.[11]

Taking Chances

A Tagalog (or Filipino) word, *pakikipagsapalaran,* can be broadly translated to mean "taking a chance or risk." This term is closely associated with the image of an individual who migrates from his or her familiar territory to an unknown place to pursue *suwerte* (luck or fortune).[12] Reports have revealed that other ethnic groups who reside in insular Southeast Asia, such as Bugis, Minangkabau, and Iban, possess similar cultural notions as part of their way of life, that are related to high geographical mobility among these ethnic groups (Hosoda 2008, 314).

Ana was not the only interlocutor who employed the metaphor of a game to describe life in Dubai. In contrast to life in her hometown, Ana faces risks and chances on a daily basis in Dubai. Based on data collected from the narratives and practices of these interlocutors, debt appears to be the key that describes visa holders' endeavors. Because migration to another location where no family members or relatives reside is considered a kind of risky game, a bet must initially be placed. The game's outcome will be determined if the individual wins more than the bet they placed. If not, that individual is referred to as a *bigo* (failure). This is a highly shameful experience for the migrant, as well as for his or her family. Although this may not represent the typical bondage-labor case in which family members are sold to illegal recruiters and forced to work without any freedoms, the cultural and "emotional economy" of migration continues to bind migrants' behaviors (Lindquist 2009, 8). At times, it may hamper them from returning home, even at the risk of their safety.

Attempts to cross the border of legality have received significant scholarly and public attention (Battistella and Asis 2003; van Schendel and Abraham 2005). From the point of view of interlocutors, even if migrants entered Dubai on visit visas rather than employment visas, they might not have difficulties because of one simple reason: a rumor has spread that no one who enters the country on a visit visa has ever been caught for working illegally. Moreover, attempts to cross the border of legality in small ways, and here or there, is considered a part of the package of risks involved in migrants' pursuit of luck because no *pakikipagsapalaran* can occur without risk.

As Ana's case reveals, visit visa holders encounter a variety of challenges upon arrival at Dubai International Airport. They must decide how to continue their pursuit of luck based on their limited budgets and on their personal social capital. Many migrants who used the names of unknown individuals as their sponsors felt cheated in one way or another because of over-pricing or broken promises.

Skyrocketing housing prices in Dubai were the first and most serious problems that affected the millions of foreigners who lived in Dubai until 2008. At that time, Dubai was one of the most expensive cities in the world. This phenomenon left most foreign workers few opportunities for housing. They could reside in workers' camps provided by their employers or in apartment rooms packed with eight or more country-mates. Each resident occupied a "bed-space" (Christ 2012, 690). To survive in the city and manage their budgets, they also were required to learn where to buy groceries and to use Internet communications, how to use public transportation and to apply for jobs, and how not to violate certain laws of the UAE, which can result in immediate deportation.

The "visa run" is a key aspect of life in Dubai. It was also casually referred to as a "tax" in Dubai among interlocutors. Although the UAE is a well-known tax-free country, Filipinos who resided on visit visas soon realized (until July 2008) that fees were systematically imposed every two months when they exited the country to attempt visa renewals. A number of travel agencies in Dubai offer visa renewal (or change) package tours to UAE's bordering visa-free towns (commonly termed "exit points") that include airplane tickets, overnight hotel accommodations, and visa processing fees that include renewed sponsorship, for around AED 1,500 (US$410) per person.

The Dubai Labor Market and Migrants' Network

After a short stay in Dubai, similar to a stay just about anywhere in the world, an individual begins to reflect on differences and similarities between his or her home country and the host country. Workers in Dubai are situated in the midst of globalized labor competition. Therefore, they cannot help but compare themselves with other nationalities or ethnic groups that are also in search of new opportunities.

Some Filipino interlocutors came to realize the incongruity that exists between the view of Filipinos as highly competent workers and unfair social practices that exist in the homeland. Leo, who works as an office clerk for a construction company, believes Filipinos are popular workers in Dubai because "people know we are clean, we know how to take care of ourselves, and we also adjust easily to the workplace environment."[13] Linda, a teacher in a public school for special children, considers the Philippine higher education system to be high in quality and closer to the "global standard," in comparison with education systems in other countries in Asia that send migrants.[14] Workers' high self-esteem stands in high contrast to Philippine society, where corruption, low wages, and high criminal rates are highly visible. Unlike the Philippines, the UAE appears to have requirements that are more stringent in the area of legal enforcement. Workers' sentiments about these issues, with the exception of wage differences, may lead to or enhance individuals' unwillingness to return to the Philippines and encourage their willingness to remain outside the country.

However, even in these individuals' opinions, the UAE is not necessarily considered an ideal place to remain indefinitely. This may be a result of the UAE's no-immigrant policy and racial and ethnic discrimination. In the Gulf States, foreign workers are not considered "immigrant workers," but rather, they are considered "temporary contractual workers" (Janardhan 2011, 105). This means that they have almost no chance to acquire citizenship regardless of the length of time they have worked in the country. In addition, social stratification based on race and ethnicities ranks Western and Arab expatriates higher than other expatriates. This has affected foreign workers' salary and benefits standards. It has also affected everyday personal relationships in and out of workplaces (Kapiszewski 2001, ch. 8). During my interviews, Filipinos stated that they considered themselves ranked somewhat in the middle of the ladder because Filipino workers were rarely seen in either of the extremes (as business elites and or as lowest paid workers) in the Dubai job market.

My interlocutors made differentiations among Asian workers. They stated that South Asians, and, in particular, Indians, would overwhelm other Asians because of their population volume, firm economic presence, and extensive social networks in Dubai. The interlocutors hinted that Indians have a longer history of migration and stronger connections with the Emirati elite than Filipinos in Dubai.

Ethnographic studies have also emphasized Indian business leaders' influence on Dubai's economic development (Vora 2011). Indians have historically developed informal networks of Indians, especially Indians from Kerala (Osella and Osella 2012). Osella and Osella's study illustrated how the web of informal networks that exist among Indians who migrated from Kerala allowed them to help newcomers. This includes assistance to workers who arrive with visit visas as they reestablish their lives in Dubai or other Gulf cities. These are not just predetermined person-to-person relationships. They are also "friend of a friend of a friend of a friend" referral systems that attempt to find solutions among Indian migrant communities.

Although Filipinos who work on visit visas also make frequent use of similar informal networks when they need local information for survival, some differences exist in the ways that Filipinos tend to interact with *any* Filipinos they meet on the street and may expect to receive assistance. Indeed, the phrase "Filipinos know well how to help others" was occasionally quoted by some of my interlocutors when they were asked to describe their ethnic advantages over other ethnic groups. It may be helpful to consider the so-called Filipino cultural trait that values reciprocal communication (Christ 2012, 690–691) to explain this phenomenon. In my opinion, two other issues may have caused Filipinos' provision of mutual assistance to extend beyond their kin and circles of friends. First, Filipino Migrant workers have forged Filipinos' diasporic identity in the homeland and abroad. This identity was partially created by the national government's projects that developed the "Great Filipino Workers" image. In addition, commercial and media enterprises now connect Filipinos who are scattered around the globe. Local NGOs have highlighted Overseas Filipino Worker (OFW) issues as national political issues.[15] As a result, some have argued that the OFWs' sense of belonging does not rest in the home country or in the host country. Rather, it rests in the transnational space (see, e.g., Parreñas 2001).

Second, the pattern of the flow of migrants to Dubai using visit visas that occurred during the mid-2000s may have encouraged the strong growth of *kabayan* street communities' mutual assistance (see Hosoda 2013 for details). Many migrants arrived without knowing a single relative or friend. Therefore, thousands of Filipinos went out onto the streets and into public spaces to personally search for better opportunities that might be found in the quickly changing urban environment. Although law enforcement is strictly maintained in this "open city," interpersonal relations in public spaces are largely uncensored and open to all people. These conditions appear to have engendered an atmosphere in which Filipino citizens of varied backgrounds, and without previous acquaintance, can share a variety of information. It should be noted that class divisions exist to a certain degree, and also that all individuals must carefully avoid others who might attempt to take advantage of compatriots.

The so-called chain migration, or a series of migration within a family, relatives, or townmates, was once a feature that characterized Filipino overseas migration, with the exception of migration patterns of professional workers (e.g., Lindquist 1993). Currently, however, it appears that the chain migrations no longer serve as important requirements. This is the case even among lower-class workers who seek opportunities in emerging cities by movement and by way of unofficial channels, as long as their destination has a large Filipino transnational community and is located within an "open city."

The 2008 Crisis and After

In 2008, the arena of the *pakikipagsapalaran* project changed drastically. First, in July 2008, the UAE government took a stand against foreigners who entered on visit visas and were assumed to be engaged in economic activities. The government announced the Ministerial Decision No. 322 of 2008,[16] which changed the rules for visit visas. The processing fee was increased. In addition, migrants were mandated to exit the UAE for more than one month prior to application for a new visa. Migrants were required to submit proof of family relationship to someone already resident. This decision came as a huge blow to visit visa holders, as well as to travel agencies. The incident that caused thousands of Filipinos to become stranded in Iran and Oman, described at the beginning of this essay, occurred because of this change to the law. Further, the new rule stipulated that people who were discovered working on visit visas would be banned for life from the UAE. Their employer would have to pay fines of AED 50,000. Thus, the government sent a clear message that foreigners' chaotic border-crossings and economic activities within the country based on visit visas had reached an abrasive level. Second, beginning in November 2008, Dubai's property market experienced a major deterioration because the global economic crisis took a heavy toll on property values. A series of employment cuts occurred in the construction and tourism industries. This caused a mass deportation of workers. The Philippine government sent a rescue team to safeguard and assist 3,000 workers who were at risk for job loss between January and February 2009.[17]

Following imposition of the new visit visa rule, coupled with the Dubai crisis effect, the number of Filipinos entering with visit visas was believed to have diminished. The number of individuals who made "visa runs" also declined. In early 2010, I visited travel agencies in the Karama district and learned that travel agents had already either stopped or downsized visa renewal services. Yet the flow of migrants has not completely stopped. Filipino travel agents cited the image of Dubai as the Promised Land that remains in the minds of Filipinos who are desperate for shortcuts to overseas employment. According to these travel agents, the majority of visit visa holders who were unable to change their visa status to employment within the days they were allowed to stay in the UAE would return to the Philippines. Those who decided not to return to the homeland after their visit visa expired would survive for one month in hotels located at "exit points" in Iran or Oman. The latter would carry big travel bags filled with emergency food, clothing, kitchenware, and entertainment DVDs.

The 2008 changes to the legal and labor market exerted different effects on visit visa holders. Jun, a 31-year-old freelance programmer from Samar Island, did not appear to be greatly affected by the crisis. He came to Dubai on a visit visa because he felt that his hometown and work were not challenging. Jun believed that he found better luck in Dubai. He earns AED 5,000 (US$1,350) per month as the manager of a bearing company. He studies architecture and enjoys Dubai's glittering nightlife. However, he admitted that racism and life in a crammed bed-space continues to make him feel depressed. He plans to move to the UK or Canada, where his aunt and cousins reside.[18]

There are many similar cases to Jun. These Filipinos who ventured out to Dubai with visit visas achieved, more or less, what they had hoped to achieve. However, I believe that the majority of migrants remain at the crossroads. They must constantly wonder whether to stay or do something else. Some migrants, like Ana, have settled for jobs much below their expected level for the sake of safety. Others have a "bought visa," which refers to getting an employment visa by making an UAE resident a "dummy" sponsor for a fee, and attempted to start their own business. These include driving services, Internet job search consultancies, and room rentals. Some other migrants have moved to different countries, including countries officially banned by the Philippine government (e.g., Afghanistan and Iraq).[19] Angeline found a

Pakistani boyfriend who provides lodgings. She cares for other boarders to earn income. She resigned from her job in 2009. She has been contemplating whether she should marry her boyfriend and move to Pakistan.

At times, newspaper reports and rumors on Dubai streets broadcast tragic endings to *pakikipagsapalaran* projects. News reports announced that a remarkable number of Filipinas were forced to become prostitutes to survive in the UAE. These reports led to calls for the Philippine government to crack down on travel agencies that advertise employment opportunities in Dubai and other areas in the UAE.[20] Other migrants have chosen to overstay their visas. They await the day when the UAE government will announce amnesty or, alternatively, when they will have to surrender to authorities. The official estimate of the number of Filipino undocumented workers (i.e., those who overstay) was 35,000 in 2008 (CFO 2008). However, many of my informants assumed that this number was an underestimation.

A permanent return home was not an option available to the majority of interlocutors. Although they maintained no emotional attachment to the UAE, for many, their experiences in the country provided a sense of confidence in the globalizing labor market. Although their experiences included a series of hardships, they found, at the very least, that there are ways to survive. They also acknowledged that the UAE has some valuable aspects, such as a clean environment, less corruption, more safety, and an absence of poverty that the present-day Philippines cannot offer. Permanent reintegration into the Philippines may be difficult for interlocutors until they approach retirement age.

Conclusion

From the mid-2000s, the UAE, for the first time, rapidly emerged as the second most popular destination for temporary Filipino workers. This essay examined the relationship between Filipinos and Dubai based on narratives provided by Filipino individuals who live in the city. These narratives were recorded and analyzed to elucidate the complex process by which both Filipino employment seekers and the city of Dubai were transformed because of mutual engagement.

The term "Dubai" signifies different meanings to different groups of people, based on the period and their experiences. It was once considered a "nowhere" for most Filipinos. It was simply a country located somewhere abroad that possessed no value, other than the fact that it could provide authorized migrant workers with income they could remit. By the 2000s, Dubai had been unofficially named an "open city" in which job seekers could envision themselves as explorers who might find opportunities beyond their imaginations. Dubai differed from other overseas locations because it allowed a wider range of Filipinos to enter the city without having to engage in a great number of time-consuming authorization processes imposed by the Philippine government. It also allowed them to stay as visitors (exploring chances), rather than (contract-bound) workers. The city came to be known as a place where workers could participate in a game that involved a search for luck, rather than simply working on a job that was predetermined by a job contract. If a worker was lucky, he or she might become someone different: a winner. Put differently, Dubai transformed itself into a place where overseas-worker aspirants could take a different route towards self-realization. Upon arrival in Dubai, nevertheless, most of those workers who chose this different route soon realized that their pursuit might be open-ended. They faced higher risks or bets than they expected.

This Dubai boom among Filipinos reveals a number of developments that involve contemporary Philippine society and migration. First, the creation of Dubai demonstrates that a large pool of OFW aspirants still exist in the Philippines who have not yet qualified as "Great Filipino Workers." Some have stated, "where there is authorized migration flow, there is also unauthorized migration flow," because unauthorized migrants do not differ from authorized migrants with respect to motivation (Battistella and Asis 2003, 13–14). The difference lies in their access to legal or illegal migration channels. For some overseas-worker aspirants, the visit-visa route appeared to short-circuit the regulated predeparture process by leaving all the risks to the individuals involved. The government attempted to promote and produce "Great Filipino Workers," in part, as a measure to protect its own citizens. The harder the government promoted this idea, the greater possibilities it produced. Ironically, it also produced increased flows of unauthorized migrants.

Second, Dubai's unique position in current Filipino migration trends allows us to make a paradoxical inference that a limited space boundary for Filipino workers exists in the global economy. Visit visa holders remained in their *pakikipagsapalaran* projects despite high costs and elevated risks because some *kabayan* found middle-class occupations that paid satisfactory salaries and provided benefits. In other parts of the world, such as Japan, Hong Kong,

Taiwan, and Italy, Filipino workers have been confined to the lower strata of the service industry (e.g., household and care services, factories, or agriculture). However, in this part of the Middle East, they can be employed in a variety of professions. Indeed many have become a part of the core of workers in the society, although hierarchical ethnic boundaries still exist. This social situation, which combined higher standards for salaries and social environment with possible upward social mobility, must have exerted an encouraging influence on workers who wanted to try their luck at something new. They hoped they would also experience significant advancements one day in the future.

Both the Philippine and the UAE governments continue to stop the entry of illegal Filipino workers into the UAE. Yet, the flow of Filipinos who rely on visit visas to the UAE to find better luck has not stopped, although the changes that occurred in 2008 greatly reduced the volume of the flow. The legend of Dubai lives on among Filipinos who are desperate to leave the country. It will, perhaps, continue to live on until another attractive "open city" is discovered.

Notes

1. Reports acquired from the *Philippine Daily Inquirer* (September 27, 2008; October 25, 2008), Arabian Business.com (September 28, 2008), and other sources.

2. These fieldwork projects in the UAE and the Philippines were supported by the Japan Society for the Promotion of Science (JSPS) for academic years 2008–2010 (Kakenhi Kiban B: Grant Number 20401007), and for academic years 2007–2010 (Kakenhi Kiban A: Grant Number 19251005), respectively.

3. This estimate equals the sum of temporary, permanent, and undocumented Filipinos.

4. Interview conducted with Brian in Karama, Dubai, on March 1, 2010.

5. For example, the survey I conducted among 152 nursing students in Metro Manila and on a Visayan island in 2009 revealed that the Middle East was their least favorite place to work. The main reasons cited by respondents were low wages, safety concerns (war), and wide religious and cultural gaps.

6. Interview conducted with Angeline in Deira, Dubai, on February 8, 2009.

7. Interview conducted with Ms. Rory Quintos, director of the film *Dubai*, in Cavite, Philippines, on March 23, 2011.

8. Interview conducted with Brian in Deira, Dubai, on February 15, 2009. Sara Balabagan was employed as a domestic worker in the UAE. She was sentenced to death because she stabbed her employer, who had attempted to rape her. Her case

caused a significant amount of controversy in the Philippines. It was made into a film following her release in 1996. Her case is one of the two best-known incidents of crimes inflicted on overseas Filipina workers. The other case concerned Flor Contemplacion, who was executed in Singapore in 1995.

9. *Gulf News*, April 8, 2006, "Movie Cited as Factor in Increasing Visit Visa Violations."

10. *Gulf News*, May 22, 2006, "Illegal Filipino Workers 'Open to Abuse'."

11. Interview conducted with Ana in Karama, Dubai, on February 1, 2009.

12. I have discussed the concepts of *pakikipagsapalaran* and *suwerte* in the sociocultural context of Samarons' internal migration to Manila in other publications. See, e.g., Hosoda (2008) for details. Aguilar (1999) also contextualized Filipino international migration as a form of gambling in which the individual seeks his or her *suwerte*.

13. Interview conducted with Leo in Deira, Dubai, on February 13, 2009.

14. Interview conducted with Linda in Karama, Dubai, on February 19, 2011.

15. See also Rodriguez (2010).

16. See the details of the Ministerial Decision of 2008 available on the UAE government portal at http://www.government.ae/html/print/preview.jsp?art_id=29428&lngId=en_US.

17. Interview conducted with Jocelyn Hapal, Philippine Overseas Workers Welfare Administration officer and a member of the rescue team for the Philippine Consulate, Dubai, on February 7, 2009.

18. Interview conducted with Jun in Satwa, Dubai, on February 10, 2009.

19. See also Davidson (2007, 193, 285). Also, see a special report entitled "OFWs Defy Ban for High Pay in Afghanistan," *Philippine Daily Inquirer* (August 23, 2009).

20. "Travel Agencies Blamed for Stranded OFWs outside UAE," *Philippine Daily Inquirer* (September 27, 2008). In 2010, the Philippine government responded to these types of calls by requiring Filipinos who hope to visit relatives in the UAE to present attested guarantee letters written by sponsoring relatives to immigration authorities at Philippine airports. Many OFWs (overseas Filipino workers), however, see this new requirement as another form of costly red tape. They believe the entire scheme will not eliminate the vulnerability of visit visa job seekers.

References

Aguilar, Filomeno Jr. 1999. "Ritual Passage and the Reconstruction of Selfhood in International Labour Migration." *Sojourn* 14 (1): 98–139.

Battistella, Graziano, and Maruja M. B. Asis. 2003. "Southeast Asia and the Specter of Unauthorized Migration." In *Unauthorized Migration in Southeast Asia*, eds. Graziano Battistella and Maruja M. B. Asis, 1–34. Quezon City: Scalabrini Migration Center.

Christ, Simone. 2012. "Agency and Everyday Knowledge of Filipina Migrants in Dubai, United Arab Emirates." *International Handbook of Migration, Minorities and Education*, ed. Zvi Bekerman and Thomas Geisen, 677–694. New York: Springer.

Commission on Filipinos Overseas (CFO). 2008. Stock Estimate of Overseas Filipinos as of Dec. 2008. http://www.cfo.gov.ph/pdf/statistics/Stock%202008.pdf (accessed June 1, 2010).

Constable, Nicole. 1997. *Maid to Order in Hong Kong: Stories of Filipina Workers.* Ithaca, NY: Cornell University Press.

Corsin-Jimenez, Alberto. 2003. "On Space as Capacity." *Journal of Royal Anthropological Institute* (n.s.) 9: 137–153.

Davidson, Christopher M. 2007. *Dubai: The Vulnerability of Success.* New York: Columbia University Press.

De Regt, Marina. 2008. "High in the Hierarchy, Rich in Diversity: Asian Domestic Workers, Their Networks and Employers' Preferences in Yemen." *Critical Asian Studies* 40 (4): 587–608.

Faier, Lieba. 2009. *Intimate Encounters: Filipina Women and the Remaking of Rural Japan.* Berkeley: University of California Press.

Guevarra, Anna Romina. 2010. *Marketing Dreams, Manufacturing Heroes: The Transnational Labor Brokering of Filipino Workers.* New Brunswick, NJ: Rutgers University Press.

Gupta, Akhil, and James Ferguson, eds. 1997. *Culture, Power, Place: Explorations in Critical Anthropology.* Durham, NC: Duke University Press.

Horinuki, Koji. 2010. "The Dynamics of Human Flow, Control, and Problems in the UAE: The Relationship between Labour-Sending and Receiving Countries in 2000s." Paper presented at Gulf Studies Conference, Exeter University, June 30–July 3.

Hosoda, Naomi. 2008. "Connected through 'Luck': Samarnon Migrants in Metro Manila and the Home Village." *Philippine Studies* 56 (3): 313–344.

———. 2009. "Dobai Zaiju no Firipin-jin no Seizon Senryaku (Survival Strategies of Filipinos in Dubai)." *UAE* 46: 25–28.

———. 2013. "*Kababayan* Solidarity? Filipino Communities and Class Relations in United Arab Emirates Cities." *Journal of Arabian Studies: Arabia, the Gulf, and the Red Sea* 3 (1): 18–35.

International Monetary Fund (IMF). 2009. IMF Country Report No. 9/124. http://www.imf.org/external/pubs/ft/scr/2009/cr09120.pdf (accessed June 1, 2010).

Janardhan, N. 2011. *Boom Amid Gloom: The Spirit of Possibility in the 21st Century Gulf.* Reading, UK: Ithaca Press.

Johnson, Mark. 2010. "Diasporic Dreams, Middle Class Moralities and Migrant Domestic Workers among Muslim Filipinos in Saudi Arabia." *The Asia Pacific Journal of Anthropology* 11 (3–4): 428–448.

Kapiszewski, Andrzej. 2001. *Nationals and Expatriates: Population and Labour Dilemmas of the Gulf Cooperation Council States.* London: Ithaca Press.

Lan, Pei-chia. 2006. *Global Cinderellas: Migrant Domestics and Newly Rich Employers in Taiwan.* Durham, NC: Duke University Press.

Liebelt, Claudia. 2011. *Caring for the 'Holy Land': Filipina Domestic Workers in Israel.* Oxford: Berghahn Books.

Lindquist, Bruce. 1993. "Migration Networks: a Case Study in the Philippines." *Asian and Pacific Migration Journal* 2 (1): 75–104.

Lindquist, Johan. 2009. *The Anxieties of Mobilities: Migration and Tourism in the Indonesian Borderlands.* Honolulu: University of Hawaii Press.

Nagy, Sharon. 2008. "The Search of Miss Philippines Bahrain—Possibilities for Representation in Expatriate Communities." *City and Society* 20 (1): 79–104.

Olwig, Karen Fog, and Kirsten Hastrup, ed. 1996. *Siting Culture: The Shifting Anthropological Object.* London: Routledge.

Osella, Caroline, and Filippo Osella. 2012. "Migration, Networks, and Connectedness across the Indian Ocean." In *Migrant Labor in the Persian Gulf,* ed. Mehran Kamrava and Zahra Babar, 105–136. London: Hurst.

Parreñas, Rhacel Salazar. 2001." Transgressing the Nation-State: The Partial Citizenship and 'Imagined (Global) Community' of Migrant Filipina Domestic Workers." *Signs* 26 (4): 1129–1154.

Philippine Overseas Employment Administration (POEA). 2009. 2009 Overseas Employment Statistics. http://www.poea.gov.ph/stats/2009_OFW%20Statistics.pdf (accessed June 1, 2010).

Retsikas, Konstantinos. 2007. "Being and Place: Movement, Ancestors, and Personhood in East Java, Indonesia." *Journal of the Royal Anthropological Institute* (n.s.) 13: 969–986.

Rodriguez, Robyn. 2010. *Migrants for Export: How the Philippine State Brokers Labor to the World.* Minneapolis: University of Minnesota Press.

Tsing, Anna. 2000. "The Global Situation." *Cultural Anthropology* 15 (3): 327–360.

Van Schendel, Willem, and Itty Abraham, eds. 2005. *Illicit Flows and Criminal Things: States, Borders, and the Other Side of Globalization.* Bloomington: Indiana University Press.

Vora, Neha. 2011. "From Golden Frontier to Global City: The Shifting Forms of Belonging Among Indian Businessmen in Dubai." *American Anthropologist* 113 (2): 306–318.

Contributors

Acknowledgments

Index

Contributors

Robert Hellyer is Associate Professor of History, Wake Forest University. A historian of early modern and modern Japan, he served on the faculty of the University of Tokyo, taught at Allegheny College, and was a postdoctoral fellow at Harvard's Reischauer Institute of Japanese Studies before coming to Wake Forest in 2005. His monograph *Defining Engagement: Japan and Global Contexts, 1640–1868* was published by the Harvard University Asia Center in 2009. He is working on a transnational project, "An Everyday Cup of Green Tea: Japanese Producers and American Consumers in a Trans-Pacific Trade, 1850–1950," for which he received Smithsonian, Japan Foundation, and NEH fellowships to support research in Japan and the United States.

Naomi Hosoda is Assistant Professor at International Office, Kagawa University, Japan. She obtained her PhD in Southeast Asian area studies from Kyoto University. Her main research interest is the anthropology of Filipino migrants, with a focus on cultural normality, family, and transnational community. Her works in English include: "The Sense of *Pamilya* among Samarnons in the Philippines," in Yoko Hayami et al., eds., *The Family in Flux in Southeast Asia: Institution, Ideology, Practice* (Kyoto University Press, 2012); "Connected through 'Luck': Samarnon Migrants in Metro Manila and the Home Village," *Philippine Studies* 56 (2008);

and "The Social Process of Internal Migration in the Philippines: A Case of Visayan Migrants in Manila," *Afrasia Working Paper Series* (2007).

Victor Lieberman is the Raoul Wallenberg Distinguished University Professor of History and Professor of Asian and Comparative History at the University of Michigan. His books include *Burmese Administrative Cycles: Anarchy and Conquest, c. 1580–1760* (Princeton University Press, 1984), which won the Harry J. Benda Prize from the Association for Asian Studies; *Strange Parallels: Southeast Asia in Global Context, c. 800–1830, Volume 1: Integration on the Mainland* (Cambridge University Press, 2003), which won the World History Association Book Prize; and *Strange Parallels: Southeast Asia in Global Context, c. 800–1830, Volume 2: Mainland Mirrors: Europe, Japan, China, South Asia, and the Islands* (Cambridge University Press, 2009), which was described in the *American Historical Review* as "the most important work of history produced so far this century" and was the subject of a special edition of the *Journal of Asian Studies.* His next book, *Why Was Nationalism European? Political Ethnicity in Southeast Asia and Europe, c. 1400–1850,* will be published by Harvard University Press.

Peter C. Perdue is Professor of History at Yale University. He has taught courses on East Asian history and civilization, Chinese social and economic history, the Silk Road, and historical methodology. His first book, *Exhausting the Earth: State and Peasant in Hunan, 1500–1850 A.D.* (Harvard University Press, 1987), examined long-term agricultural change in one Chinese province. His second book, *China Marches West: The Qing Conquest of Central Eurasia* (Harvard University Press, 2005), discusses environmental change, ethnicity, long-term economic change, and military conquest in an integrated account of the Chinese, Mongolian, and Russian contention over Siberia and Central Eurasia during the seventeenth and eighteenth centuries. He is a coeditor of two books on empires: *Imperial Formations* (SAR Press, 2007) and *Shared Histories of Modernity* (Routledge, 2008), and he has contributed to a world history textbook, *Global Connections,* forthcoming from Cambridge University Press. He is now beginning a new project of comparative research on Chinese frontiers.

Helen F. Siu is Professor of Anthropology at Yale University. Since the 1970s, she has conducted fieldwork in South China, exploring the nature of the socialist state and the refashioning of identities through rituals, festivals, and commerce. Lately, she explores the rural-urban divide in China, cross-border dynamics in Hong Kong, and historical and contemporary Asian connections. In 2001, she established the Hong Kong Institute for the Humanities and Social Sciences at the University of Hong Kong with an interdisciplinary and interregional research agenda (www.hkihss.hku.hk). Her monograph and coedited volumes include *Mao's Harvest:*

Voices of China's New Generation (Oxford University Press, 1983, coeditor Zelda Stern); *Furrows: Peasants, Intellectuals, and the State* (Stanford University Press, 1990); *Down to Earth: The Territorial Bond in South China* (Stanford University Press, 1995, coeditor David Faure); *Agents and Victims in South China: Accomplices in Rural Revolution* (Yale University Press, 1989); *Empire at the Margins: Culture, Ethnicity, and Frontier in Early Modern China* (University of California Press, 2006, coeditors Pamela K. Crossley and Donald S. Sutton); *SARS: Reception and Interpretation in Three Chinese Cities* (Routledge, 2007, coeditor Deborah Davis); *Hong Kong Mobile: Making a Global Population* (Hong Kong University Press, 2008, coeditor Agnes Ku); and *Merchants' Daughters: Women, Commerce and Regional Culture in South China* (Hong Kong University Press, 2010).

Eric Tagliacozzo is Professor of History at Cornell University, where he primarily teaches Southeast Asian Studies. He is the author of *Secret Trades, Porous Borders: Smuggling and States along a Southeast Asian Frontier, 1865–1915* (Yale University Press, 2005), which won the Harry J. Benda Prize from the Association of Asian Studies (AAS) in 2007. His second monograph, *The Longest Journey: Southeast Asians and the Pilgrimage to Mecca,* was published by Oxford University Press in 2013. Tagliacozzo is also the editor or coeditor of four books: *Southeast Asia and the Middle East: Islam, Movement, and the Longue Durée* (Stanford University Press, 2009); *Clio/Anthropos: Exploring the Boundaries between History and Anthropology* (Stanford University Press, 2009); *The Indonesia Reader: History, Culture, Politics* (Duke University Press, 2009); and *Chinese Circulations: Capital, Commodities, and Networks in Southeast Asia* (Duke University Press, 2011). He is the Director of the Comparative Muslim Societies Program at Cornell, the Director of the Cornell Modern Indonesia Project, and the editor of the journal *INDONESIA.*

Nancy Um is Associate Professor in the Department of Art History at Binghamton University. Her research explores the Islamic world from the perspective of the coast, with a focus on material, visual, and built culture on the Arabian Peninsula and around the rims of the Red Sea and Indian Ocean. Her book *The Merchant Houses of Mocha: Trade and Architecture in an Indian Ocean Port* (University of Washington Press, 2009) relies upon a cross-section of visual, architectural, and textual sources to present the early modern coastal city of Mocha as a space that was nested within wider world networks, structured to communicate with far-flung ports and cities across a vast matrix of exchange. Her current book project explores the materially oriented social practices and rites that undergirded the overseas trade in Yemen in the early eighteenth century. She has received research fellowships from the Fulbright program, the National Endowment for the Humanities, the Getty Foundation, and the American Institute for Yemeni Studies.

Heidi A. Walcher is a historian of modern Iran. She was at the School of Oriental and African Studies and currently teaches at the Institute of Near and Middle Eastern Studies at the University of Munich. She has worked extensively on the political and social history of nineteenth-century Isfahan. Her research further focused on patterns of change and transformations through imperialism and "modernity," the Constitutional Revolution, the Jews of Isfahan, the Church Missionary Society, African slave trade during the Qajar period, various figures of the Qajar family, and aspects of urban, diplomatic and global history. Her publications include *In the Shadow of the King: Zill al-Sultan and Isfahan under the Qajars* (I. B. Tauris, 2008); "Between Paradise and Political Capital: The Semeiotics of Safavid Isfahan," in *Transformations of Middle Eastern Natural Environments* (1998); "Face of the Seven Spheres: Urban Morphology and Architecture of Isfahan in the Nineteenth Century," *Iranian Studies* (part 1, 2000; part 2, 2001); "Isfahan—Qajar period" in *Encyclopaedia Iranica* (2006/07); and "Aqa Najafi" in *Encyclopedia of Islam.*

Kerry Ward is Associate Professor of World History at Rice University, where she is also Director of African Studies and Associate Director of the Chao Center for Asian Studies. She is the author of *Networks of Empire: Forced Migration in the Dutch East India Company* (Cambridge University Press, 2009). Ward has published in the fields of world history, Indian Ocean history, South African and Indonesian colonial history, slavery and forced migration, and historical memory and public history. She is Secretary of the World History Association.

Charles J. Wheeler researches early modern Vietnam, maritime China, and the South China Sea. He obtained his PhD in History from Yale University. His publications address the role of the sea in Vietnamese history; Sino-Vietnamese merchant elites; littoral society, political ecology, and piracy in the South China Sea; ethnohistory and political identity in Vietnam's Cham regions; and the role of Buddhism in the Chinese merchant diaspora.

Andrew Willford is Associate Professor of Anthropology and Asian studies at Cornell University. His previous research focused upon Tamil displacement, revivalism, and identity politics in Malaysia. A forthcoming book, *Tamils and the Haunting of Justice: History and Recognition in Malaysia Plantations* (University of Hawai'i Press, 2014) examines how Tamil plantation communities face the uncertainties of retrenchment and relocation in Malaysia. His current research focuses upon mental health and neurological care in North America and India. Recent publications include *Cage of Freedom: Tamil Identity and the Ethnic Fetish in Malaysia* (University of Michigan Press, 2006); *Spirited Politics: Religion and Public Life in Contemporary Southeast Asia* (Southeast Asia Program Publications, Cornell University,

2005, ed. with Kenneth George), and *Clio/Anthropos: Exploring the Boundaries between History and Anthropology* (Stanford University Press, 2009, ed. with Eric Tagliacozzo).

Anand A. Yang is the Job and Gertrud Tamaki Endowed Professor of International Studies and History; Director, South Asian Center; and Co-Director, Global Asia Institute at the University of Washington, Seattle. He is the author of *The Limited Raj: Agrarian Relations in Colonial India* (University of California Press, 1989) and *Bazaar India: Markets, Society, and the Colonial State in Gangetic Bihar* (University of California Press, 1998); edited the volumes *Crime and Criminality in British India* (University of Arizona Press, 1985) and *Interactions: Transregional Perspectives on World History* (University of Hawai'i Press, 2005); and has published numerous articles in journals in Asian studies, history, and the social sciences. His forthcoming book is entitled *Empire of Convicts.*

Acknowledgments

Asia Inside Out is a three-year project put together by Eric Tagliacozzo, Helen F. Siu, and Peter C. Perdue. It has been supported by the Hong Kong Institute for the Humanities and Social Sciences (HKIHSS) of the University of Hong Kong, and the Inter-Asia Initiative of Yale University. The Yale Council on East Asian Studies and the Department of Anthropology hosted a brainstorming workshop in December 2009 where we sought intellectual synergy from colleagues in various disciplines (authors of this volume plus Sumathi Ramaswamy, Adam McKeown, K. Sivaramakrishnan, William Kelly, Erik Harms, and Narges Erami). We held a follow-up workshop highlighting the theme "Critical Times" in Hong Kong in December 2010. A group of authors traveled to southwest India to explore a regional construct that had been shaped by significant historical moments in the global political economy. We thank the HKIHSS for generous funding and its staff (Emily Ip and Kwok-leung Yu in particular) for their remarkable administrative support.

We have enjoyed the intellectual companionship of a growing community of colleagues in sharpening the themes of the Asia Inside Out project and in preparing the book. Many share our enthusiasm for rethinking Asian connections across time and space, and they have offered critical comments. We thank among others Deborah Davis, James Scott, Tim Harper, David Ludden, Alan Mikhail, Angela Leung, Prasenjit Duara, Seteney Sharmi, Takeshi Hamashita, and James Chin. We thank Eric Chan Chun Ho and Siow Boon Chia for their creative efforts in drafting early versions of a map for the volume. Credit goes to Isabelle Lewis for competently accommodating our ideas of mapping Asian connections. We also thank Kwok-leung Yu, Venus Lee, Joan Cheng, and Yvonne Chan of HKIHSS, and Andrew Kinney of Harvard University Press, for their tireless editorial and technical attention.

We are most grateful to our editor, Kathleen McDermott, for maintaining faith in the project. From the moment we sought her out to explore our ideas, she has been a patient listener. She made us sharpen our thoughts and skillfully navigated us through the publishing process. Getting us all to the finish line must have been like herding cats, but it is an effort much appreciated.

Index